Global Challenges to Democracy

Following democracy's global advance in the late twentieth century, recent patterns of democratic erosion or "backsliding" have generated extensive scholarly debate. Backsliding toward autocracy is often the work of elected leaders operating within democratic institutions, challenging conventional thinking about the logic of democratic consolidation, the enforcement of institutional checks and balances, and the development and reproduction of democratic norms. This volume tackles these challenges head-on, drawing theoretical insights from classic literature on democratic transitions and consolidation to help explain contemporary challenges to democracy. It offers a comparative perspective on the dynamics of democratic backsliding, the changing character of authoritarian threats, and the sources of democratic resiliency around the world. It also integrates the institutional, civil society, and international dimensions of contemporary challenges to democracy, while providing coverage of Western and Eastern Europe, South and Southeast Asia, Africa, Latin America, and the United States.

Valerie J. Bunce is the Aaron Binenkorb Professor of International Studies Emerita in the Department of Government at Cornell University. She studies democracy, authoritarianism, and regime change with a specialization in Russia and Eastern Europe. She is the author of *Subversive Institutions: The Design and the Destruction of Socialism and the State* (1999), co-author of *Defeating Authoritarian Rulers in Postcommunist Countries* (2011), and co-editor of *Citizens and the State in Authoritarian Regimes: Comparing China and Russia* (2022). She was elected to the American Academy of Arts and Sciences in 2010.

Thomas B. Pepinsky is the Walter F. LaFeber Professor of Government and Public Policy at Cornell University, and a nonresident senior fellow at the Brookings Institution. He studies comparative politics and political economy with a primary specialization in Southeast Asia. His most recent book is *Pandemic Politics: The Deadly Toll of Partisanship in the Age of COVID* (2022), with Shana Kushner Gadarian and Sara Wallace Goodman.

Rachel Beatty Riedl is Peggy J. Koenig '78 Director of the Center on Global Democracy at Cornell University, and a professor in the Department of Government and the Brooks School of Public Policy. Her current research examines the politics of democratic opposition to executive-led backsliding in Africa and beyond. She is a member of the Council on Foreign Relations, and the author of *Authoritarian Origins of Democratic Party Systems in Africa* (2014) and co-author of *From Pews to Politics: Religious Sermons and Political Participation in Africa* (2019).

Kenneth M. Roberts is the Richard J. Schwartz Professor of Government at Cornell University. His research interests lie at the intersection of political parties, social movements, populism, and crises of democratic representation in Latin America and beyond. He is the author of *Changing Course in Latin America: Party Systems in the Neoliberal Era* (2014) and a co-editor of *Democratic Resilience: Can the United States Withstand Rising Polarization?* (2021).

Global Challenges to Democracy

Comparative Perspectives on Backsliding, Autocracy, and Resilience

Edited by

VALERIE J. BUNCE
Cornell University

THOMAS B. PEPINSKY
Cornell University

RACHEL BEATTY RIEDL
Cornell University

KENNETH M. ROBERTS
Cornell University

CAMBRIDGE
UNIVERSITY PRESS

CAMBRIDGE
UNIVERSITY PRESS

Shaftesbury Road, Cambridge CB2 8EA, United Kingdom

One Liberty Plaza, 20th Floor, New York, NY 10006, USA

477 Williamstown Road, Port Melbourne, VIC 3207, Australia

314–321, 3rd Floor, Plot 3, Splendor Forum, Jasola District Centre, New Delhi – 110025, India

103 Penang Road, #05–06/07, Visioncrest Commercial, Singapore 238467

Cambridge University Press is part of Cambridge University Press & Assessment, a department of the University of Cambridge.

We share the University's mission to contribute to society through the pursuit of education, learning and research at the highest international levels of excellence.

www.cambridge.org
Information on this title: www.cambridge.org/9781009602600

DOI: 10.1017/9781009602570

First published 2025

A catalogue record for this publication is available from the British Library

Library of Congress Cataloging-in-Publication Data
NAMES: Bunce, Valerie, 1949– editor. | Pepinsky, Thomas B., 1979– editor. | Riedl, Rachel Beatty, editor. | Roberts, Kenneth M., 1958– editor.
TITLE: Global challenges to democracy : comparative perspectives on backsliding, autocracy, and resilience / edited by Valerie J. Bunce, Cornell University, New York, Thomas B. Pepinsky, Cornell University, New York, Rachel Beatty Riedl, Cornell University, New York, Kenneth M. Roberts, Cornell University, New York.
DESCRIPTION: Cambridge ; New York, NY : Cambridge University Press, 2025. | Includes bibliographical references.
IDENTIFIERS: LCCN 2024055292 | ISBN 9781009602600 (hardback) | ISBN 9781009602563 (paperback) | ISBN 9781009602570 (ebook)
SUBJECTS: LCSH: Democracy – Case studies. | Comparative government – Case studies.
CLASSIFICATION: LCC JC423 .G584 2025 | DDC 320.3–dc23/eng/20250228
LC record available at https://lccn.loc.gov/2024055292

ISBN 978-1-009-60260-0 Hardback
ISBN 978-1-009-60256-3 Paperback

Contents

Figures

Tables

Acknowledgements

The editors of this volume and many of its contributors spent decades studying the spread of liberal democracy across the world in the late twentieth century. Rarely did we think we would ever find ourselves collaborating to try to understand why that democratization wave stalled, and then shifted into reverse. With specializations in different world regions where democratic gains were in jeopardy, however, the editors became increasingly engaged in conversations about democracy's shared struggles and common concerns. This book grew out of those conversations, and it was greatly enriched by the volume's contributors as they joined our discussions.

A distinctive feature of this book is its cross-regional, global perspective on modern democracy and its discontents, along with its focus on both institutional and societal dimensions of contemporary challenges to democracy. Given our formative intellectual experiences, we have made explicit efforts to draw insights from the study of democratic transitions and consolidation to help understand contemporary processes of democratic erosion or backsliding.

Like any collaborative project, this book has been in the works for quite some time. Our first steps were taken pre-Covid 19, and the ensuing pandemic put several of our initial meetings on hold while we waited for better times. We wish we could say that the challenges to global democracy that motivated our efforts have receded in the years since our project began, but alas, we believe the questions addressed in this volume have only become more urgent over time. While we cannot claim to have discovered ready-made solutions to the travails of modern democracy, we hope this volume contributes to our understanding of the nature of the challenges, and how best to safeguard and revitalize democracy in the years to come.

In producing this volume, we have incurred many debts to people and programs around Cornell University and beyond who helped bring the project to fruition. We are especially grateful to Cornell's Mario Einaudi Center for International Studies, which provided the bulk of the funding for this project and substantial administrative support. Three of the Einaudi Center's areas studies programs—the Latin American and Caribbean Studies Program, the Southeast Asia Program, and the Institute for European Studies—helped launch the initiative and organize several virtual and in-person workshops. The Einaudi Center's Democratic Threats and Resilience Initiative, Cornell's Government Department, and the American Democracy Collaborative led by our colleague Suzanne Mettler also played a supportive role. Ken Roberts would also like to thank the Institute for Advanced Study's School of Social Science in Princeton, NJ for providing a stimulating environment for research and writing.

We are also grateful for the input we have received from many scholars who participated in our workshop discussions, provided feedback on seminar presentations, or read all or parts of the manuscript. We especially thank Ronald Herring, Suzanne Mettler, Sidney Tarrow, Brian Taylor, David Ost, Chip Gagnon, Sharon Werning Rivera, Karrie Koesel, Tsveta Petrova, Elizabeth Plantan, Aleksandar Mitovski, Jana Grittersova, Milan Svolik, Milada Vachudova, Manfred Elstrom, Elton Skendaj, Igor Logvinenko, Lucan Way, Santiago Anria, Jill Frank, Deborah Yashar, Wendy Brown, Didier Fassin, David Samuels, and James Loxton for providing feedback that has helped us clarify our arguments and integrate the multiple contributions to this volume.

None of this would have been possible without the assistance of a remarkably efficient team of administrators at Cornell, including William Phelan, Leah Marx, Dinnie Sloman, and Jerrica Brown. We are also deeply appreciative for the encouragement and support of Editor Rachel Blaifeder at Cambridge University Press, who took interest in this project from the very beginning and waited patiently as the manuscript developed. Rachel's editorial team of Jadyn Fauconier-Herry, Chloe Quinn, and Dhanraj Subbiah worked tirelessly to manage the production process, while Eric Anderson provided expert assistance on the indexing.

We close on a more poignant personal note, as our esteemed friend, colleague, and volume contributor Nicolas van de Walle very sadly passed away while this book was in production at Cambridge. A titan in the study of African politics, democracy, and development, Nic left his mark on the field in innumerable ways, both as a scholar and as a teacher and mentor to a generation of students who cherished his wit, wisdom, and compassion. Nic touched many of our lives in ways that will never be forgotten, and we were honored to serve as his colleagues and call him a friend. It is to his memory that we dedicate this volume, in gratitude for his lifetime contributions to the cause of democracy, in Africa and beyond.

Valerie Bunce
Thomas Pepinsky
Rachel Beatty Riedl
Ken Roberts

Department of Government
Cornell University

Introduction

1.1 PART I INSTITUTIONAL DIMENSIONS OF DEMOCRATIC BACKSLIDING AND RESILIENCE

As explained in Chapter 1, state institutions are inevitably transformed into sites of regime contestation between democratic and autocratic forces when democratic backsliding is threatened or underway. That is especially the case in social and political contexts where exclusionary forms of majoritarian rule or ethnonationalism contest liberal and pluralist civil societies. The challenge for scholars is to identify the conditions under which key institutional sites serve as bastions of democratic accountability and resilience, and how and when these sites can be neutralized or even transformed into weapons of autocratization. Often referred to as "referee institutions" (such as constitutional courts and electoral commissions) and tools of horizontal accountability for checking executive aggrandizement (including ombudsman, investigative bureaus, and information commissions), key state agencies must be sufficiently capacious and nonpartisan to serve as guardrails in times of democratic contestation and regime uncertainty.

In his analysis of democratic erosion in India, Milan Vaishnav explains how patterns of institutional deference, neglect, and interference have undermined the capacity of the Supreme Court, the Electoral Commission, and other federal agencies to enforce checks and balances on an executive branch and a ruling party inclined toward exclusionary Hindu nationalism. Paradoxically, he suggests that horizontal institutional accountability has been least effective when it is most urgently needed to check the power of a dominant party. Meredith L. Weiss and Allen Hicken then examine the challenges of consolidating democratic regimes in Southeast Asis in contexts where diverse institutional and civic actors have highly fluid and contingent commitments to the democratic process. They argue that political polarization and the failure of democratic regimes to deliver on their promises have routinely provided openings for parties and leaders to seek short-term competitive advantages by flaunting democratic rules or norms, at considerable expense to the stability and quality of democracy itself.

As these chapters show, democratic institutions can be purposefully weakened in order to serve as instruments of autocratization. From political parties to the legislature, the courts and the bureaucracy, incumbent efforts to reduce the scope, power, independence, and professionalism of democratic institutions may allow them to be captured by autocratic forces. Once captured, they can tilt the balance of power toward an ethnonationalist, religious nationalist, or dominant party state – one which presumes the alignment of the state with a particular sociocultural and/or political identity. Such alignments make institutional capacity a target of regime contestation, by opposition forces seeking to buttress the independence of institutions in order to level the playing field, as well as by autocratic incumbents seeking to shed institutional constraints.

In their chapter on democracy in Africa's low-income states, Jaimie Bleck and Nicolas van de Walle explain how weak state institutions can have differential effects on horizontal (institutional) and vertical (electoral) accountability. Institutional weakness tends to insulate incumbent executives from horizontal checks and balances, making abuses of power more likely, but vertical accountability to voters and civil society may still exist even in contexts of limited state capacity. State institutions are also a centerpiece of Frances Cayton and Bryn Rosenfeld's chapter on democratic backsliding in Eastern Europe and beyond. They demonstrate that a politicized bureaucracy can strengthen electoral support for autocratic incumbents by doling out patronage jobs and diverting civil servants to functions that provide electoral advantages. This vicious cycle further reduces the power of horizontal checks and balances on executive authority, while potentially strengthening the role of the bureaucracy and illiberal political economies as assets for autocratic survival.

Finally, the chapter by David A. Bateman, Robert C. Lieberman, and Aaron Childree shifts attention to electoral administration in the US and its relationship to democratic erosion. Efforts to alter election and voting laws and electoral administration, they argue, have often been associated with restricted access to the ballot, and even with potential electoral malfeasance. Manipulation of electoral administration can thus weaken vertical accountability channels and the power of the electorate to remove incumbents or register voter preferences.

Taken together, these chapters illustrate the myriad ways in which the "winner's dilemma" can be associated with the erosion of both vertical and horizontal accountability mechanisms. This section problematizes democratic institutions and state capacity by asking toward what ends they are used, recognizing that incumbent prerogatives and political opportunism may compromise the long-term ability of state and guardrail institutions to perform their intended roles. What regimes deliver and to whom is ultimately a question not only of state capacity, but also of the balance between public service and partisan interest. So also is the provision of public order, which is closely related to public support for democracy as a regime type.

I.2 PART II CIVIL SOCIETY, SOCIAL MEDIA, AND POLITICAL MESSAGING

If democratic institutions are, at least potentially, arenas of regime contestation, the same is true of civil society – the myriad forms of voluntary, self-constituted civic and community associations organized around diverse group interests, preferences, values, and cultural identities or practices. The notion that strong, independent civil societies are the bedrock of political pluralism and liberal democracy has a long and distinguished intellectual lineage (De Tocqueville 2002; Putnam 1994). In accordance with that lineage, civil society networks and social movements have often been at the forefront of resistance to authoritarian regimes and autocratization processes in recent times (Bunce and Wolchik 2011; Brancati 2016; Meyer and Tarrow 2018). They often defend democratic spaces by monitoring and publicly exposing incumbent corruption or abuses of power, observing election campaigns and balloting, providing alternative sources of information, and protesting against antidemocratic behavior.

Nevertheless, the historical record should guard against facile assumptions that there is a universal or unidirectional prodemocratic tilt to civil society. As Berman (1997: 402) demonstrated, in the absence of strong and responsive political institutions, Germany's vibrant civic associational life not only fragmented society and undermined the Weimar Republic, but also provided "a critical training ground for eventual Nazi cadres" and a social base for Hitler's assault on state power. Illiberal civil society networks are especially likely to emerge in response to cultural and political contestation over the "boundary question" introduced in Chapter 1 – that is, contestation over who is a member of the political community and the identities and rights associated with such membership. Given the flexibility of ideological scripts and sociocultural identities, aspiring autocrats routinely seek to politicize context-specific cultural anxieties and connect them to antiestablishment sentiments. In particular, they use exclusionary identity politics and ethno-nationalist or religious-nationalist scripts to mobilize support, fuel illiberal civil society, divide democratic forces, and exploit the institutional levers at hand for antidemocratic purposes.

Civil society, therefore, is often a battlefield where the countervailing forces of democratic and autocratic actors collide, as described in Chapter 1. In response to the challenges posed by independent civil society actors and social protest movements, ruling autocrats may try to organize and control civil society "from above," impose burdensome registration and regulatory requirements on independent civic groups, or resort to outright repression and banishment.

The chapters in this section provide ample evidence of the dialectical interplay between democratic and authoritarian currents within civil society, as well as the patterns of interaction between state and societal actors that either foster or restrain democratic backsliding. Lindsay Mayka examines the rise of illiberal civil society actors in Latin America that seek to restrict the citizenship rights of marginalized groups deemed to be threatening to the social order. These marginalized groups typically include feminists, the LGBTQ+ community, and low-income youth from racialized minority groups that are often blamed for rising crime levels. Focusing on the Hungarian case, Béla Greskovits analyzes the civil society networks nurtured by an autocratic national-populist right-wing party, shedding new light on the social bases of authoritarian political mobilization within democratic institutions.

Michael Bernhard shifts the focus to prodemocratic forces within civil society, exploring civic opposition to autocratic leaders in post-Communist Europe. Bernhard treats civil society resistance as a form of social accountability that complements vertical (i.e., electoral) and horizontal (institutional) forms of accountability and may in fact serve as the ultimate, if imperfect, "last defense" of democracy against autocratic populist challenges. Mark R. Beissinger follows by adopting a broad comparative perspective on this civil society resistance to identify the conditions under which it is more or less likely to be effective. In particular, he highlights the critical role of the timing of civic resistance vis-à-vis the erosion of institutional and electoral checks on autocratic executive power.

Focusing more on political communications, Alexandra Cirone assesses the impact of social media and deliberate disinformation campaigns on political polarization and distrust in democratic institutions, such as elections. Her chapter examines the democratic consequences of political contestation over communication channels and the validity of alternative sources of information. Finally, M. Steven Fish argues that conventional democratic and liberal modes of political messaging are unlikely to be effective against an autocratic challenger, given the latter's political style and messaging. To defend democracy and defeat autocrats in the electoral arena, Fish suggests that conflict-embracing "dominance" messaging may be needed to win over voters unresponsive to simple policy cues. Together, these chapters bring the societal dimensions of democratic backsliding into play, and examine how they intersect with electoral and regime institutions.

1.3 PART III INTERNATIONAL DIMENSIONS OF THE STRUGGLE BETWEEN DEMOCRACY AND AUTOCRACY

Democratic backsliding necessarily entails changes in the form and/or function of domestic political institutions, but it is not a strictly domestic affair. Domestic political contention between democratic and autocratic forces can be heavily conditioned by international influences on both sides of the ledger. These influences may come in a variety of forms, including ideological diffusion, transnational political linkages, and material support for favored political or civic actors. In their influential work on the end of the Cold War and the spread of competitive authoritarianism, Levitsky and Way (2010) stressed the importance of close ties to the West – or the lack thereof – in shaping the prospects for full democratic transitions during the third wave. More recent work has highlighted the international linkages and political outreach of powerful autocratic states – including Russia, China, Iran, and Saudi Arabia – in supporting allied forces and countering Western democracy promotion efforts, especially within their regional spheres of influence (Koesel and Bunce 2013; Kästner 2019). The literature on international diffusion and counter-diffusion helps to explain how autocratic forces may learn from the rhetoric, transnational networks, and models of political mobilization found elsewhere around the globe to buttress their domestic political projects.

The international dimensions of democratic backsliding, however, go well beyond the direct support offered by Western democracies or autocratic powers to their political allies in other states. Processes of globalization and regional political and economic integration can have important domestic political ramifications, placing new issues on the political agenda and generating new cleavages in domestic political affairs. They may realign domestic political actors in support or opposition to international trends and leverage, while shifting the balance of power among these actors. Since national states inevitably mediate their society's exposure to transnational forces they cannot control, they routinely become focal points of contestation over alternative responses to regional and global trends.

The chapters in this final section examine how autocratic parties and movements in domestic political arenas are shaped, often in unexpected ways, by larger regional and global forces. Mabel Berezin analyzes the electoral growth and political "normalization" of the autocratic nationalist right as it moved from the margins to center stage in European party politics in the early decades of the twenty-first century. Berezin explains how the failure of the European Union to respond effectively to the regional challenges of austerity, migration, and terrorism eroded the security regimes that democratic nation states had offered their citizens, creating antagonisms between the local and the global that nourished the rise of the nationalist right on a regional scale. In post-Communist Europe, Dorothee Bohle and Aida A. Hozić examine how the rise of the authoritarian right and democratic backsliding were enabled – not tamed – by the internationalization strategies of German and West European Christian Democratic parties, and by the ideological reorientation of European Christian Democracy in response to the post-1968 hegemonic challenge of the cultural and political left. Finally, Stefano Palestini and Cristóbal Rovira Kaltwasser analyze the role of Spain's far-right VOX party and its transnational network *Foro Madrid* in the diffusion of Europe's populist radical right script to Latin America. This diffusion played on a range of cultural tensions and sociopolitical identities, many of them politicized by the conservative backlash against the rise of new leftist social and political forces. Paradoxically, the diffusion of this populist radical right script has sometimes resulted in the adoption of language and tactics that claim citizenship rights for exclusionary purposes.

REFERENCES

Berman, Sheri. 1997. "Civil Society and the Collapse of the Weimar Republic," *World Politics* 49, 3: 401–429.
Brancati, Dawn. 2016. *Democracy Protests: Origins, Features, and Significance.* New York: Cambridge University Press.
Bunce, Valerie J. and Sharon L. Wolchik. 2011. *Defeating Authoritarian Leaders in Postcommunist Countries.* New York: Cambridge University Press.
De Tocqueville, Alex. 2002. *Democracy in America.* Translated by Harvey C. Mansfield and Delba Winthrop. Chicago: University of Chicago Press.
Kästner, Antje. 2019. "Autocracy Promotion," in Wolfgang Merkel, Raj Kollmorgen, and Hans-Jürgen Wagener, eds. *The Handbook of Political, Social, and Economic Transformation.* Oxford: Oxford University Press, pp. 411–415.
Koesel, Karrie J. and Valerie J. Bunce. 2013. "Diffusion-Proofing: Russian and Chinese Responses to Waves of Popular Mobilizations against Authoritarian Rulers," *Perspectives on Politics* 11, 3: 753–768.
Levitsky, Steven and Lucan A. Way. 2010. *Competitive Authoritarianism: Hybrid Regimes after the Cold War.* New York: Cambridge University Press.
Meyer, David S. and Sidney Tarrow. 2018. *The Resistance: The Dawn of the Anti-Trump Opposition Movement.* New York: Oxford University Press.
Putnam, Robert D. 1994. *Making Democracy Work: Civic Traditions in Modern Italy.* With Robert Leonardi and Raffaella Y. Nanetti. Princeton, NJ: Princeton University Press.

Global Challenges to Democracy: Backsliding, Resiliency, and Democratic Theory

Kenneth M. Roberts, Valerie J. Bunce, Thomas B. Pepinsky, and Rachel Beatty Riedl

Democracy's retreat on the global stage since the first decade of the twenty-first century is a sobering reminder that history does not follow any predefined script. The new century commenced on a democratic high note, riding the crest of what Huntington (1991) labeled the "third wave" of democratization – the broadest and deepest expansion of democratic governance the world has ever seen. Over sixty countries transitioned from authoritarian rule to some form of democracy between the mid 1970s and early 2000s (Mechkova, Lührmann, and Lindberg 2017: 163), leading prominent voices to hail the global triumph of liberal democracy at the post-Cold War "end of history" (Fukuyama 1989). A more somber tone set in, however, by the second decade of the twenty-first century in response to a series of high-profile cases of democratic erosion or "backsliding" toward autocracy (Diamond 2015; Bermeo 2016; Snyder 2017; Waldner and Lust 2018; Przeworski 2019; Diamond 2020). Although scholars disagree on whether democracy's forward momentum has shifted into reverse (Lührmann and Lindberg 2019) or merely leveled off (Little and Meng 2024), there is little doubt that democratic regimes are on the defensive in much of the world, facing novel challenges and uncertainties.

The annual reports of global research and tracking agencies like V-Dem (Varieties of Democracy Institute) and Freedom House have sounded alarm bells, as their ratings of democratic practices and political and civil liberties, respectively, show a steady erosion of democratic standards on a global scale in the early twenty-first century. Freedom House (2024: 2) has recorded eighteen consecutive years of declines in its global index of political rights and civil liberties, with more countries restricting than expanding freedoms every year since 2006. V-Dem's comprehensive dataset based on expert surveys shows the number of countries meeting the minimum threshold for democracy peaking at 100 in 2011 (Mechkova, Lührmann, and Lindberg 2017: 163), then falling gradually to 91 countries by 2023 (Nord et al. 2024: 11). In 2023, V-Dem identified forty-two countries moving in an autocratic direction, and only eighteen countries expanding democratic practices, a striking reversal of the trend lines found at the beginning of the century. Cross-national patterns of autocratization helped bring V-Dem's 2023 average country score on its core Liberal Democracy Index back down to the level of 1998, while its global population-weighted average – heavily influenced by India's democratic decline – fell back to the level of 1985 (Nord et al. 2024: 7, 9–10).

Dire warnings of a global democratic retreat, however, have been countered by scholars who question the generalizability of the trend, the reliability of backsliding measures, and the inflated impact of the Indian case on global measures weighted by population. Little and Meng (2024) have challenged V-Dem's reliance on subjective expert assessments of democratic practices rather than objective empirical indicators, suggesting that the former may be susceptible to shifting coder standards that produce time-varying coder bias (see also the symposium "Comment and Controversy," 2024). Studies by Miao and Brownlee (2022), Levitsky and Way (2023), and Treisman (2023) have emphasized the continued resilience of democracy in affluent societies, suggesting that democratic breakdowns are largely confined to countries at lower levels of economic development.

This vigorous debate over the measurement, extent, and scope conditions of democratic backsliding is much welcomed. Indeed, the debate attests to the significance of the subject matter, and to the urgency of understanding the underlying causal processes and political dynamics associated with democratic backsliding. Only then is it possible to identify the factors that make societies more or less susceptible – or resistant – to backsliding pressures, and to assess the effectiveness of different strategies to contain and reverse democratic decline. As Little and Meng (2024: 2) suggest, "Although a correct accounting of global trends is a key first step, it is arguably more important to understand where backsliding is happening, how it happens, and when it leads to democratic breakdown."

This volume addresses these questions from a cross-regional comparative perspective, recognizing that contemporary patterns of democratic backsliding have defied political expectations along multiple fronts. They have challenged assumptions that new democracies were destined to progressively, if fitfully, stabilize or "consolidate" over time. Recent democratic setbacks, moreover, have not been limited to the more institutionally fragile cases of third-wave democracies; significant democratic erosion has also occurred in countries once thought of as regional leaders or showcases of democracy, such as Hungary and Poland in Eastern Europe, Venezuela and Brazil in Latin America, India in South Asia, Benin in Africa, and Turkey and Tunisia in the Middle East and North Africa. Arguably, that list should be extended to include the liberal hegemon itself, the US (Mettler and Lieberman 2020; International Idea 2021). This short list includes the country long considered to be the world's largest and most diverse democracy (India), as well as the world's oldest and most economically powerful democracy (the US). In short, democratic erosion has afflicted countries at relatively advanced levels of economic development (Riedl et al. 2023), as well as those with long-standing democratic traditions. Although democratic breakdowns are a rarity (to date) in affluent societies, a troubling number of them are struggling to contain the growing presence and political weight of actors with illiberal or manifestly autocratic tendencies. Such patterns cast doubt on the scholarly conventional wisdom that prosperity immunizes countries against the threat of democratic breakdown (Przeworski et al. 2000; Przeworski 2005), or that "stability breeds stability" (Linz 1978: 8).

Adding to the puzzle, in many countries the principal challenges to democracy did not arise from actors *outside* the democratic order – that is, from militaries or insurgent groups seeking to topple a democratic regime through a coup or revolution. Instead, the challenges emerged endogenously from *within* democratic regimes themselves, as leaders and parties competing in the democratic arena exploited regime institutions to concentrate powers, marginalize opponents, and neutralize or dismantle essential checks and balances (Bermeo 2016; Levitsky and Ziblatt 2018; Mounk 2018; Haggard and Kaufman 2021). Svolik (2019b: 20) aptly characterizes such endogenous backsliding as "the subversion of democracy by democratically elected incumbents" – paradoxically, identifying a democratic counterpart to earlier scholarly work which suggested that communist governing institutions were, over the long term, subversive and self-negating of their own political logic (Bunce 1999). Explaining when and why democratic institutions become subversive and self-negating – rather than a self-enforcing equilibrium (Weingast 1997; Przeworski 2005; Svolik 2019a) – has emerged as a pressing concern, and an analytical centerpiece in this volume. Whether democratic backsliding is attributable to political polarization, cultural rifts, performance crises, institutional defects, or tensions arising from social and economic inequalities, its causal logic and dynamic properties cry out for scholarly attention.

Needless to say, this democratic path to autocracy is far from universal, and (fortunately) it is rarely, if ever, uncontested. Rival parties, government and judicial officials, voters, civil society networks, the media, and social movements invariably push back against ascendant autocrats, albeit with varying degrees of success. In many countries, the US included, societal actors in resistance to aspiring autocrats do not simply aim to preserve historic democratic gains, but to advance toward new democratic breakthroughs that could make existing representative institutions more inclusive, equitable, or participatory (Meyer and Tarrow 2018). The outcomes of these struggles are often unpredictable, as they rest heavily on the balance of institutional leverage, societal support, and the mobilizational capacity of autocratizing and democratizing forces. Even in the midst of democracy's recent global "recession" (Diamond 2015), countertrend cases moving in a prodemocratic direction can be found (Carothers and Feldman 2023), albeit predominantly in smaller countries with less weight on the international stage, as V-Dem notes (Alizada et al. 2021: 7).

Such contradictory processes and countervailing pressures do not lend themselves to easy conceptualization and theorization. Indeed, they clash with some of the dominant ways of thinking about democracy – heavily conditioned by Cold War-era conflicts – that informed much of our leading scholarship during the heyday of the third wave. As Carothers (2002) aptly forewarned, recent political events pose formidable challenges to modes of theorizing about democracy that rely on linear or teleological assumptions about democratic endpoints; static notions of democratic consolidation; the self-enacting resiliency of institutional checks and balances; and endogenous processes of democratic norm construction and behavioral conformism (see the sections below). They have also forced scholars to reassess the nature and sources of the threats to democracy, recognizing that the central challenge is not always to induce the compliance of those who *lose* elections (Przeworski 1991: 15), but rather those who emerge victorious and try to turn the transitory institutional leverage of incumbency into a source of permanent competitive advantage (Singer 2018). There is, then, both a "loser's dilemma" and a "winner's dilemma" embedded in the study of democratic resiliency. If the third wave of democratization in the late twentieth century demonstrated the fallacy of believing that democracy has rigid structural or cultural preconditions – such as particular levels of economic development, class configurations, or civic cultures (Schmitter and Karl 1991) – recent patterns of backsliding have revealed the contingent and potentially contested underpinnings of democratic institutions in *any* political order, given the presence (whether latent or active) of markedly authoritarian political and cultural currents.

In short, contemporary political conflicts call for a reassessment of the analytical cornerstones for the study of democratic resiliency and backsliding. Building on foundational works in the study of democratization and democratic theory, we argue that these cornerstones should include: (1) the contingency of the political pacts or compromises, the behavioral norms, and the competitive equilibria that undergird democratic regimes; (2) the countervailing roles of individual and collective actors who challenge or defend the institutional arrangements of any established democratic order, typically by seeking to expand or restrict democratic inclusion and contestation; and (3) the dynamic processes that make democracy a perpetual work in progress. As Tilly (2007: xi) recognized, "democratization is a dynamic process that always remains incomplete and perpetually runs the risk of reversal."

So conceived, this volume suggests that democracy is best understood not as a standardized regime template or a static endpoint of political development, but rather as a dialectical frontier that advances – and sometimes recedes – by fits and starts, according to the dynamic interplay of these countervailing forces. To be sure, the relative strength of pro- and antidemocratic forces – and, therefore, the levels of democratic contingency and resiliency – varies considerably across cases. But so also does it vary over time within any given country, as the metaphor of a dialectical frontier suggests. The resiliency of the political bargains that undergird any democratic order rests heavily on the iterative character of the open competition for public office that secures the adherence of rival political actors. It is precisely this iterative process of democratic contestation that backsliding undermines.

1.1 CONSTRUCTING AND DECONSTRUCTING DEMOCRATIC ORDERS

Drawing from his extensive statistical analysis of democratic transitions and breakdowns around the world historically, one of the most eminent scholars of comparative politics, Adam Przeworski, calculated the odds of democracy breaking down in the US as 1 in 1.8 million country years, given the country's advanced level of economic development (and not even factoring in the long-standing duration of its democratic regime; see Przeworski 2019: 133). Although President Donald Trump did not beat those astronomical odds in his first term, it was not for lack of trying; comparativists readily recognized Trump's efforts to overturn the November 2020 election results as what is known in Latin America as an *autogolpe*, or executive "self-coup," whereby an incumbent president seeks to break with the constitutional order to concentrate powers or avoid leaving office (Tufekci 2020; Cameron 2021).[1] More troubling, perhaps, Trump's ill-fated power grab, which culminated in a violent mob assault on the national legislature, could not be shrugged off as the desperate gambit of a rogue president or sore loser. His Republican co-partisans in Congress largely supported or tolerated his efforts to overturn the official election results, and the bulk of the party closed ranks behind Trump to block his removal from office via impeachment, opted out of congressional investigations of the assault on the national capitol, and adopted a series of restrictive voting laws in the states they controlled. Indeed, the GOP (Grand Old Party) sought to remove subnational election officials charged with certifying the vote and install party loyalists. Trump's hold over the Republican Party base positioned him to be the frontrunner for the party's presidential nomination in 2024 while he was facing four criminal indictments involving eighty-eight felony charges ("Tracking the Trump Criminal Cases" 2024) – and threatening to unleash the Justice Department on his political adversaries if he returned to presidential office. Ultimately, neither Congress, the Supreme Court, the Republican Party, nor the electorate deemed Trump's efforts to block democratic alternation in office by electoral means to be disqualifying for subsequent participation in the democratic process, and voters opted to return him to the White House in the November 2024 elections. The kind of

---

[1] The model of an *autogolpe* is certainly not without historical precedents; see, for example, Karl Marx's classic account of Louis Bonaparte's self-coup in *The Eighteenth Brumaire of Louis Bonaparte* (New York: International Publishers, 1963).

breakdown that Przeworski (2019: 133) dismissed as "out of the realm of the imaginable," based on historical precedents, apparently no longer is.

Przeworski (2019: 18–19) himself questioned whether "history is a reliable guide to the future" – a query worth bearing in mind when statistical projections from the historical record offer reassurance that democracy is impregnable in affluent societies. Much greater attention should be paid to the historical structural and institutional conditions that helped stabilize Western democracies in the postwar era; do their causal mechanisms remain operative in the contemporary period of globalized financial capitalism, diminished state sovereignty, transnational population flows, uprooted party systems, increasingly concentrated wealth, and rising economic precarity? If they do not – if contemporary democracies face a different problem set than their twentieth-century predecessors – mechanistic projections of historical regularities to the present and future are unconvincing and potentially misleading.

Political science offers no ready-made formulas for sustaining democracy in a two-party system like that of the US where one of the major parties has become an insurgent actor, or a political vessel for those who are. Indeed, in his classic study of democratic breakdowns, Juan Linz (1978: 24) declared that a two-party system subject to "maximal ideological distance" and "centrifugal competition" is destined for either self-destruction or civil war.[2] Political scientists are hard-pressed to explain how a long-established – and supposedly "consolidated" – democracy could not only give rise to the kinds of autocratic forces seen in the US today, but also entrench them in governing institutions where they can subvert democracy from within. The US case thus poses in stark relief some of the limitations of conventional theorizing about democracy and democratization. If democracy is understood to be consolidated when it becomes, metaphorically, "the only game in town" (Przeworski 1991: 26; Linz and Stepan 1996: 5; Schedler 1998: 91), what causes other, nondemocratic "games" to emerge on an established democratic playing field, "deconsolidating" democracy? What induces parties and politicians embedded and socialized within a democratic order to violate its norms and begin playing by a different set of rules, or no rules at all? Why do large numbers of citizens vote for such actors rather than punish or eschew them, and how do democratic institutions – such as parties, legislatures, elections, and courts – get repurposed or "weaponized" to perform autocratic political functions quite different from those they were set up to perform?

Leading studies of democracy and democratization have long been cognizant of the regime's limited reach and contingent character. O'Donnell and Schmitter

---

[2] Writing during the early stages of rising partisan polarization in the US, Linz (1990: 53) also suggested that American democracy had avoided the destabilizing "perils of presidentialism" precisely *because* of "the uniquely diffuse character" of its moderate, two-party system with centripetal competitive dynamics in the postwar era.

(1986) emphasized the tentative, uncertain, and indeterminate course of democratic transitions; Linz and Stepan (1996: 6) recognized the potential for democratic deconsolidation; Levitsky and Way (2010) explained why regime transitions often culminate in hybrid forms of competitive authoritarianism rather than liberal democracy; and Carothers (2002), Tilly (2007), Bermeo and Yashar (2016), Ziblatt (2017), and Berman (2019) highlighted the trial-and-error logic, and the zigzagging course, of historical processes of democratization. Such caveats, however, were easy to overlook as the third wave of democratization spread across the globe at the end of the Cold War – a time when the major ideological rivals to liberal democracy weakened or collapsed internationally, and Western democracies were seemingly uncontested in their national settings. Scholars aptly characterized the third wave as "the greatest period of democratic ferment in the history of modern civilization," and they lauded its "snowballing" effects as it diffused across countries and regions (Diamond and Plattner 1993: ix). As stated by Plattner (1993: 28), the demise of communism left liberal democracy as the "dominant principle of political legitimacy," providing it with "unchallenged preeminence" in a world with "no serious geopolitical or ideological rivals" (Plattner 1993: 28).

More recent processes of democratic backsliding have shattered this optimism, and made it imperative to reassess our understanding of democracy's cornerstones, institutional resiliency, and potential frailties. A useful starting point is Przeworski's (1991: 10) pithy definition of democracy as "a system in which parties lose elections." By stripping democracy to its bare essentials – competitive elections where somebody wins, and others must lose – this definition offers a window on two central challenges in the study of democratic resiliency, what might be labeled the "loser's dilemma" and the "winner's dilemma." The loser's dilemma is centered on the challenge of inducing democratic participation and compliance with democratic outcomes among those who lose elections or have little expectation of prevailing in the electoral arena (see Anderson et al. 2005; Wong and Friedman 2008). Przeworski (1991: 15) flagged this challenge as *the* central question "concerning the durability of democracy." Given the uncertainty surrounding democratic outcomes and the inevitability of electoral defeats, political actors with little chance of winning elections – in particular, elite actors who are, by definition, few in number – may forego the democratic process and invest in military, economic, or other power resources that can secure their dominance through authoritarian means (Gibson 1996; Ziblatt 2017).

Although Przeworski paid less attention to the winner's dilemma, he clearly recognized it. "The central difficulty of political power," he asserted, "is that it gives rise to increasing returns to scale" (Przeworski 1991: 25). The dilemma, then, consists of the possibility that the victors in any round of democratic contestation will try to capitalize on their success by tilting the playing field and locking in competitive advantages. The threat to democracy comes not from those who fear losing and refuse to subject their vital interests to the uncertainties of electoral contestation, opting instead for authoritarian alternatives; rather, the threat arises from those who win elections and exploit the advantages of incumbency to concentrate powers and erode institutional checks and balances. The latter is the primary logic of subverting democracy by endogenous means.

1.1.1   The Third Wave and the Loser's Dilemma

Given its focus on democratic transitions and consolidation, scholarship on the third wave of democratization naturally gave priority to resolving the loser's dilemma. This dilemma crystallized as the third wave spread from Southern Europe in the mid-1970s to Latin America in the 1980s and much of Eastern Europe, East and Southeast Asia, and Africa in the late 1980s and 1990s. These were regions of the world notably lacking some or all of the historical, structural, and cultural conditions long presumed to have been vital to the gestation of liberal democracy in its North Atlantic bastions (Bermeo and Yashar 2016), such as industrialization and economic development, vibrant civil societies, and liberal or tolerant civic cultures (see, for example, Lipset 1959; Almond and Verba 1963; Moore 1966; Rueschemeyer, Stephens, and Stephens 1992; Ansell and Samuels 2014). Although broad-based civic movements for democratization were a driving force in many regime transitions, especially in Eastern Europe (Bunce 2003), important actors with authoritarian pasts nearly always remained on the political stage as democratic regimes were being constructed (Grzymala-Busse 2002; Riedl 2014; Albertus and Menaldo 2018; Loxton 2021).

Scholarship on democratic transitions, therefore, centered on the challenge of constructing democratic regimes in "unlikely places" – that is, in countries and regions that lacked many of the putative preconditions for liberal democracy. Indeed, it often endeavored to explain how to build "democracy without democrats," in the absence of strong democratic civic cultures, and in the presence of political actors who were antidemocratic (perceiving electoral contestation to be an existential threat to their interests) or, at best, contingent democrats. The latter included actors willing to cooperate with or provide cover for antidemocratic forces in pursuit of their political goals (the "semi-loyalists," in Linz's [1978: 32] terminology), as well as those who might only accept democratic contestation when it produced outcomes to their liking. An overriding concern of "transitologists," therefore, was to induce participation and compliance with democratic processes among those who expected to lose elections and lacked principled commitments to the regime form.

The loser's dilemma elicited three basic responses in the study of third-wave democracies: political pacts, strategic equilibria, and endogenous norm construction. All three responses were informed by a prescient article by Dankwart Rustow (1970) that anticipated and influenced a generation of scholarship on regime transitions. Rustow offered a compelling account of how democracy could be established in unlikely places, among distrustful political antagonists, in the absence of favorable preconditions beyond a shared understanding of the boundaries and composition of the national political community. In this account, polarized conflict and gridlock – what Rustow (1970: 355) characterized as a "hot family feud" – were the logical precursors to democratization, rather than a prior normative consensus or a social contract. Democracy was forged by institutional compromises between elite political adversaries who could not impose their preferred – often nondemocratic – order on rivals. It was, then, a "second-best" choice for the major actors, a set of institutions designed to process, regulate, and bound political contestation that otherwise threatened to spiral out of control with mutually destructive consequences.

Securing mutual adherence to the terms of a democracy's institutional compromise was the obvious catch, given the uncertainties of democratic contestation and the inevitability that some actors would lose competitive elections. For O'Donnell and Schmitter (1986: 37–47), the answer to this dilemma lay in the negotiation of explicit political pacts between rival elites that reduced uncertainties and offered mutual guarantees for vital interests. This could be done, for example, by bounding competition, narrowing the issue domain, and/or sharing power. To induce elite compliance, especially where authoritarian regimes had relied on the support of conservative military and economic establishments, transitional pacts often required that mass-based parties exercise self-restraint in their mobilization of electoral support or social demands in the democratic arena. As O'Donnell and Schmitter (1986: 38) readily acknowledged, such pacts were "undemocratic" means of constructing democracy, even if they were instrumental to the participation of recalcitrant elites. Pacts also created the risk that short-term constraints on democratic participation or contestation adopted to facilitate a regime transition might become institutionalized over time, creating fault lines in the new democratic order that generate iterative forms of social and political conflict (Karl 1987). We will return to this point in Section 1.2.

Przeworski (1991; 2005) offered a second response to the loser's dilemma, arguing that it was possible to achieve mutual compliance as a strategic equilibrium in the absence of either explicit pacts or consensual democratic norms. Formulating Rostow's argument in game theoretic terms, Przeworski (1991: 12) conceptualized democracy "as a system of processing conflicts" by subjecting rival actors and their interests to institutionalized competition. This system, he argued, could be established – and consolidated – as a self-enforcing strategic equilibrium between rival, self-interested actors when iterative cycles of the democratic "game" lengthen actors' time horizons and lower the stakes of losing in any particular electoral contest (see also Weingast 1997 and Svolik 2019a). Rival actors, therefore, comply with the rules of competition, tolerate a measure of uncertainty, and consent to losing so long as they get to play the game again in future iterations (Przeworski 1991: 26–34) – and, critically, so long as incumbents do not try to rig the game by turning transitory victories into permanent competitive advantages.

This conceptualization of democracy's genesis had widespread appeal, as it did not restrict the regime type to countries endowed with a favorable set of preconditions by historical experiences or cultural endowments. Neither did it require that bitter rivals negotiate and settle on the terms of a foundational pact. Democracy could emerge virtually anywhere as a mode of conflict regulation and generalized "contingent consent" to iterative and institutionalized political contestation (Schmitter and Karl 1991: 82–83).

Nevertheless, many scholars remained skeptical of the resiliency of democratic regimes that rested solely on a decentralized strategic equilibrium. Przeworski himself recognized structural or material constraints on the prospects for sustaining such a self-enforcing equilibrium, arguing that poor countries have a much narrower bound of actor distributional incentives to comply with it, making democratic regimes inherently fragile. By contrast, in wealthy countries loss aversion – the risk of losing what has been gained – makes democracy so "impregnable" that it "lasts forever" once established (Przeworski 2005: 253). Focusing on ideational rather than material foundations, Mainwaring and Pérez-Liñán (2013: 53) claimed that "democracy without democrats" may be possible, "but it is likely to be a very fragile equilibrium." To buttress that equilibrium and move toward a more durable consolidation of democracy, normative underpinnings might be needed to provide an ideational protective belt that restrains self-interested actors and safeguards institutional practices.

As Linz and Stepan (1996) argued, democratic consolidation has behavioral and attitudinal as well as institutional dimensions. It exists when "no significant political groups seriously attempt to overthrow the democratic regime or secede from the state"; when "the overwhelming majority of the people believe that any further political change must emerge from within the parameters of democratic formulas"; and when "all the actors in the polity become habituated to the fact that political conflict will be resolved according to established norms and that violations of these norms are likely to be both ineffective and costly." Consolidation signifies, therefore, that democracy has become "routinized and deeply internalized in social, institutional, and even psychological life, as well as in political calculations for achieving success" (Linz and Stepan 1996: 5). Such internalization requires "serious thought and action concerning the development of a normatively positive appreciation of those core institutions of a democratic political society" (Linz and Stepan 1996: 8).

Developing this normative appreciation among self-interested rivals is no easy matter when democratic competition produces losers as well as winners. It is surely not an automatic process where democracy has emerged instrumentally as an institutional compromise to process and regulate political conflict. Nevertheless, Rustow (1970) offered a third response to the loser's dilemma –

a framework for understanding how democratic norms could develop endogenously through the very logic of democratic competition itself, even where these norms were in embryonic form at the outset of a democratization process. Rather than being a precondition or a proximate cause of democratic rule, Rustow believed, democratic civic cultures could be a fortuitous byproduct of the institutional arrangements that incentivize democratic practices. The practice of resolving political conflicts by institutionalized means could generate norms endogenously through processes of joint political learning, confidence building, and democratic habituation. Through positive feedback loops, these norms could then reinforce and reproduce democratic behavior over time. "Both politicians and citizens," Rustow argued, can "learn from the successful resolution of some issues to place their faith in the new rules and to apply them to new issues." Such political learning could even generate a "double process of Darwinian selectivity in favor of convinced democrats: one among parties in general elections and the other among politicians vying for leadership within these parties" (Rustow 1970: 358–360).

This type of endogenous process allows political actors to be transformed over time as they adapt their leadership, organization, ideology, and strategic behavior to a new set of incentives shaped by contingent consent and institutionalized modes of contestation. Levitsky and Ziblatt trace the development of the essential democratic norm of mutual tolerance to just such an endogenous process in early US political history. "It was only gradually," they argue, "over the course of decades, that America's opposing parties came to the hard-fought recognition that they could be rivals rather than enemies, circulating in power rather than destroying each other" (Levitsky and Ziblatt 2018: 103). Likewise, the norm of forbearance, or self-restraint in the exercise of institutional prerogatives, was a learned and habituated code of conduct, often relying on unwritten rules that "serve as the soft guardrails of democracy, preventing day-to-day political competition from devolving into a no-holds-barred conflict" (Levitsky and Ziblatt 2018: 101). More recently, Lindberg (2006: 149) has argued for a similar process of endogenous norm development in Africa during the third wave of democratization, suggesting that "the incentives structures of electoral institutions tend to pull elites together rather than divide or disperse them." Actors "learn the rules through experience," Lindberg argues, "and their calculations change once they realize that the process is continuous." Political learning thus makes elections "self-reinforcing and self-improving," and causes "democratic qualities in society to expand and deepen" (Lindberg 2006: 108, 157).

Crucially, under such processes of endogenous norm construction, democratic compliance does not rest solely on political goodwill or collegiality. Once established, democratic norms alter actors' calculations of their self-interests and the expected utility of alternative courses of action. Violators can expect to be punished or ostracized by other actors (see Weingast 1997), and as Rustow's double Darwinian metaphor suggests, they may be placed at a competitive disadvantage in both intraparty and inter-party selection processes. Norm compliance, in other words, is rewarded by voters and other political actors, rather than exploited by rivals.

These various responses to the loser's dilemma provided grounds for cautious optimism as democratic transitions unfolded during the third wave and – in some countries, at least – appeared to be progressing toward consolidation (Lindberg 2006; Mainwaring and Pérez-Liñán 2013). Nevertheless, contemporary processes of democratic backsliding suggest that different "solutions" to the loser's dilemma may ultimately be vulnerable to the winner's dilemma. This vulnerability raises questions about the analytic utility of "consolidation" conceived as a static endpoint of political development. It also raises the disturbing possibility that Rustow's endogenous process of norm construction, with its double Darwinian selection mechanisms, could actually shift gears and reverse course, generating endogenous patterns of democratic erosion or backsliding. It is to these challenges that we now turn.

1.1.2   The Winners' Dilemma and Democratic Backsliding

As Grief and Laitin (2004: 634) argue, institutional equilibria are stable and self-enforcing under a greater or lesser range of conditions, but they can become "self-undermining" when "the behaviors that they entail ... cultivate the seeds of their own demise." Such is the logic of endogenous institutional subversion, as depicted in Bunce's (1999) analysis of the demise of communist single-party rule. It is also the logic of Svolik's account of backsliding as "a vulnerability ... inherent to democratic politics" (Svolik 2019b: 23), driven by the competitive interaction of players within democratic institutions. This logic recognizes that the mutual compliance associated with democracy's strategic equilibrium is vulnerable to a number of basic shifts in competitive dynamics – for example, major shifts in the power balance between rival actors, the ideological differences that demarcate and align their respective social blocs, their capacity to impose costs on – or reap rewards from – noncompliance, or the political mobilization of previously excluded or subaltern groups (and the counter-mobilization of those resistant to sharing the democratic stage). Any of these shifts can alter political actors' strategic calculations of the expected utility of alternative courses of action, whether compliant or noncompliant with democratic rules. In so doing, they may also reveal the boundaries and contingencies of the political bargains, whether tacit or explicit, that undergird any historically contextualized democratic equilibrium, and of the normative scaffolding that surrounds it.

The winner's dilemma is centered on the understanding that political power is susceptible to increasing returns to scale (Przeworski 1991: 25), whereby the victor in any given cycle of democratic contestation transforms the transitory institutional prerogatives of incumbency into sources of cumulative and potentially permanent competitive advantage. Examples are legion, but they include efforts to stack the courts, assert partisan control over electoral commissions and oversight agencies, politicize the bureaucracy to capture and distribute partisan rents, gerrymander districts, restrict voting eligibility or procedures, purge electoral lists, alter party registration rules or seat allocation formulas, and impose financial or regulatory constraints on independent media and civil society organizations. Paradoxically, attempts to secure increasing returns flip Przeworski's intertemporal solution to the loser's dilemma on its head; whereas iterative cycles of democratic contestation provide incentives for losers to remain in the democratic game, they create inducements for winners to *rig* the game by tilting the democratic playing field for future iterations. Efforts to secure increasing returns, or mere suspicions that rival actors harbor such intentions, are clearly highly polarizing, as they raise the stakes of any cycle of democratic contestation and shorten actors' time horizons. Indeed, they can transform free and fair electoral contestation into a single-shot, winner-takes-all exercise. As such, they destabilize the competitive equilibrium and political stalemate that Rustow (1970) saw as the genetic foundations for democratic institutions.

Under Rustow's formulation, the endogenous development and internalization of democratic norms – in particular, the norm that Levitsky and Ziblatt labeled forebearance, or self-restraint – would provide an antidote to the winner's dilemma, or incumbency-induced efforts to secure increasing returns. Actors who refused to comply with such norms would be selected out of leadership roles by placing themselves at a competitive disadvantage in both intra- and inter-party contests. Przeworski, on the other hand, believed democracy's strategic equilibrium was self-enforcing, and therefore not dependent on leaders' normative commitments; increasing returns could be contained by institutional designs to disperse power, and by civic opposition (Przeworski 1991: 25–26).

Indeed, the winners' dilemma has a time-honored institutional antidote – namely, the separation of powers and institutional checks and balances on political authority. This antidote is deeply rooted in the liberal tradition of Montesquieu and Madison, with its distrust of popular majorities and concentrated power. In this tradition, the primary safeguard against increasing returns or abuses of power is the dispersion of political authority across multiple and independent institutional sites. A constitutional framework for limited government and the rule of law, along with strong legislative bodies, an independent judiciary, and federal institutions, are all designed to fragment or disperse authority, lower the stakes of competition, and place institutional constraints on the prerogatives of incumbency.

Madison (1787) was famously wary of parties or "factions" in pursuit of narrow interests or passions, and he placed his confidence in a plurality of societal interests and the separation of powers to preclude the emergence of any dominant political faction. The rise of modern parties, however, can change the equation, as they allow aspiring autocrats with broad popular appeal to capture, concentrate power, and coordinate across multiple institutional sites – from executive offices to legislative bodies, the courts, watchdog agencies, and electoral commissions. A disciplined and opportunistic party with autocratic leanings can thus undermine the separation of powers and progressively neutralize the checks and balances that are essential for horizontal accountability. Indeed, parties can become instruments of Przeworski's increasing returns to political power; no institutional design guarantees that a majoritarian party or movement will not employ the institutional prerogatives it enjoys to gain control over the courts and electoral institutions, rewrite or reinterpret laws and constitutions, chip away at opposition political rights and the independence of the media, and tilt the democratic playing field in ways that lock in competitive advantages.

In short, institutional checks and balances are neither automatic nor self-enacting. Institutional sites are occupied by political actors with varying degrees of commitment to their parchment functions or original intent, and checks only become operative when their occupants choose to exercise them. Rather than safeguarding democracy, they may be transformed into shields that insulate incumbents from democratic oversight and accountability, or even repurposed into instruments of partisan advantage. Such institutional polymorphism lies at the heart of endogenous processes of democratic subversion, and it illustrates the inherent limitations of more essentialist conceptions of regime checks and balances. Efforts to repurpose and weaponize institutions inevitably politicize them, transforming routine political contests into highly polarizing, existential battles where victors enjoy increasing returns, and transitory losses carry the risk of permanent subjugation. Such high-stakes battles undermine the iterative character of democratic competition and the intertemporal perspectives that are essential for reproducing actors' contingent consent (Przeworski 1991: 29).

Rustow's endogenous model of democratic consolidation, through its "double process of Darwinian selectivity," assumes that parties and voters will punish, or at least weed out, autocrats who attempt to weaponize institutions to achieve increasing returns. Endogenous processes of democratic backsliding, however, demonstrate that competitive dynamics do not always favor committed democrats in either intraparty or inter-party contests. Survey experiments conducted by Krishnarajan (2023) across 23 countries discovered a consistent pattern of perceptual bias and political rationalization, whereby citizens' policy preferences conditioned their perceptions of democratic and antidemocratic behavior. Albertus and Grossman (2021) found that although most citizens in Brazil, Argentina, Mexico, and the US recognized and disapproved of transgressions against democracy, a sizeable minority of citizens in each country supported them; partisans of the incumbent were more willing to support transgressions, while substantial majorities opposed punishments like impeachment outside the ballot box.

As Svolik argues in his analysis of democratic subversion in Turkey, Hungary, and Venezuela, endogenous backsliding does not require that citizens fail to recognize leaders' autocratic tendencies or prefer autocracy over democracy. It only requires a context of acute social and/or political polarization that "presents aspiring authoritarians with a structural opportunity." In such contexts, "even voters who value democracy will be willing to sacrifice fair democratic competition for the sake of electing politicians who champion their interests. When punishing a leader's authoritarian tendencies requires voting for a platform, party, or person that his supporters detest, many will find this too high a price to pay" (Svolik 2019b: 24). Democratic subversion, therefore, does not require a mass party of committed authoritarians.

Svolik's (2019b: 24) trade-off between democratic principles and partisan interests can exist within party organizations as well as the general public. Clever autocrats – like Hungary's Viktor Orbán – find ways to progressively dismantle democracy without openly breaking the law, using every democratically accessed institutional site to reconfigure the playing field. They are accompanied and enabled not only by coteries of ideologically hardened fellow travelers and sycophants, but by extensive circles of contingent but opportunistic democrats whose career or policy interests are advanced by towing the party line. The latter may balk at blatantly stolen elections or violent assaults on government institutions, but they are likely to tolerate myriad forms of democratic enfeeblement, incrementally enacted, when they serve other interests (see Singer 2018). These co-partisans do not think of themselves, nor recognize their party, to be authoritarian – but they may allow democracy to be progressively subverted, as Przeworski (2019: 176–183) put it, by stealth, with no clear line in the sand to demarcate when a political order has ceased to be democratic.

1.1.3 Backsliding and the Boundaries of National Political Communities

The process of democratic backsliding can take many forms, and as the preceding section suggests, it frequently takes place within the established (formal) rules of the game for democratic contestation. The institutional forms of political competition do not necessarily change, nor do most of the rules for electoral competition. Rather, the informal practices of democratic politics tend to erode first – that is, the practices that govern how people participate in politics, and determine whose voices are heard in the democratic arena. Left unchecked, backsliding may progress slowly and gradually until electoral competition itself is severely compromised, and both vertical (electoral) and horizontal (institutional) mechanisms of accountability are seriously impaired (O'Donnell 1994).

Given its multiple dimensions in both civic and institutional arenas, we see a narrow focus on electoral competition as missing a key dynamic in democratic backsliding over the past twenty years. Much as Schmitter and Karl (1991) identified a "fallacy of electoralism" in identifying what constitutes democracy, we see a fallacy of electoralism in locating the sources of democratic backsliding. We turn instead to the work of democratic theorists like Robert Dahl (1971) and Dankwart Rustow (1970), who emphasized the importance of inclusive citizenship within the accepted bounds of a political community as a key prerequisite – or for Rustow, *the* key prerequisite – for sustainable democracy. In our analysis, democratic backsliding in the modern world often starts with the unwinding of a consensus about who is a "true" citizen and whose voice should legitimately be heard in democratic politics.

In this analysis, the rise of exclusionary forms of populism (Mudde and Rovira Kaltwasser 2013) in the US, Europe, Latin America, and elsewhere often has an organic link with democratic backsliding. Populists mobilize their supporters by identifying a pure people who can be arrayed against a corrupt elite, as well as against supposed outsiders or "impure" people whose behavior or identity is incompatible with the will of the true people. In the US, for example, the long-standing argument that immigration is an existential threat to American democracy – a view most closely identified with the Republican Party of Donald Trump – capitalizes on the idea of a "real" American people under threat from outsiders entering the country. In analogous ways, beliefs about a "replacement" of white Americans by an anonymous "other" – people of color, religious minorities, progressives who seek radical political change – portray white Americans as the true Americans, and others as a nonbelonging and undeserving "something else" whose participation in democratic politics creates an existential threat to democracy itself (Parker and Barreto 2013; Hochschild 2018).

Processes of defining the national body politic in ways that exclude imagined others can be found in many other national contexts. Anti-immigrant and anti-minority views have long been common among populist radical right parties in Europe, and those like the Party for Freedom (PVV) in the Netherlands and the Freedom Party of Austria (FPÖ) propose that these outsiders comprise a threat to the national body politic that justifies an exclusionary response (see Goodman 2019). Democratic backsliding under the Modi government in India has been abetted by the mobilization of exclusionary Hindu nationalist identities that challenge the citizenship rights of Muslims, as Milan Vaishnav explains in this volume (Chapter 2). In Thailand, phrases like "Thai-style democracy," usually associated with the Crown and the bureaucracy, imply that there is a form of politics which is essentially Thai in character (see Hewison and Kitiriangiarp 2010 for a discussion). As a consequence, those Thai citizens whose vision of democratic politics demands thorough going reform to the country's conservative establishment institutions are demonstrating themselves to be *not Thai*, and hence not deserving of a voice in democratic politics. In the Philippines, Duterte's murderous war against drug dealers and drug users configures vice crimes as threats to the country's political order, and those who commit them as enemies of the Philippine people (see Pepinsky 2017; 2020). In Indonesia, followers of unrecognized religious traditions – such as Ahmadis and Shia – face state discrimination for having violated the country's normative understanding of what religions Indonesians may profess, and hence lying outside of the country's normal democratic political order. In Latin America, as

Lindsay Mayka explains in Chapter 7 of this volume, conservative populist figures like Brazil's Jair Bolsonaro exploit widespread fear of crime and violence to challenge the citizenship rights of poor and often racialized youth, questioning their belonging to the national political community.

What these diverse examples share is a common logic of political exclusion: holders of particular views or people holding particular identities fall outside of the boundaries of the national political community by writ of their views and identities themselves. Just as Rustow and others argued that the sole precondition for democracy is agreement on the bounds of the political community, sowing discord about where those boundaries lie is the first step in undermining that consensus which forms the bedrock for democratic political competition. Efforts by those who face exclusion to claim their legitimate place *within* the democratic system, in turn, may precipitate efforts by antidemocratic forces to restrict political participation – using tools in Schedler's (2002) "menu of manipulation" but drawing, as many electoral authoritarian regimes do, on legal principles to control political competition. This logic of exclusion and democratic erosion is best understood as running Rustow's process-based account of democratization in reverse: rather than an emerging consensus on the boundaries of the political community preceding democratization, the politicization of the boundaries of the political community undermines the agreement necessary for democratic competition to resolve political differences.

1.2 DEMOCRACY'S DIALECTIC

When incumbents are determined to narrow the boundaries of the political community and/or repurpose institutions to allow increasing returns to power, the resiliency of democratic rule hinges on the strength of civic and political actors in resistance, and on their ability to maintain access to, and the independence of, key institutional sites. The dialectical interplay between these countervailing forces is qualitatively different from that which occurs under "routine" – that is, institutionally "consolidated" and normatively bounded – democratic competition between partisan rivals. The interplay is not merely programmatic or policy-based, but constitutive in character, as it politicizes the very composition, functions, and operative rules of essential regime institutions. Its stakes, therefore, are orders of magnitude higher; when incumbents commit to eviscerating checks and balances, social and political actors in resistance are likely to seek major overhauls of regime institutions that harbored or enabled the rise of antidemocratic forces. Contemporary political conflict in the US provides ample evidence of such constitutive and dialectical interplay, as the rules surrounding the composition of the Supreme Court, electoral institutions, legislative filibusters, and statehood itself (or the lack thereof) are increasingly being questioned, in large part because of the ways they can skew representation and disempower popular majorities (see Levitsky and Ziblatt 2023).

The static notion of democratic consolidation does not readily capture such constitutive and dialectical forms of contestation – that is, the countervailing forces at work in any democratic order that alternately seek to restrict or expand democratic inclusion and contestation and, if necessary, alter their very ground rules (see Yashar 1999). Neither does it capture the contingent character of existing institutional arrangements and the political settlements that undergird them. Scholarship on third-wave transitions and their foundational "pacts" (O'Donnell and Schmitter 1986; Karl 1987), along with more recent research on the authoritarian origins of many democratic regimes (Rield 2014; Albertus and Menaldo 2018), make it abundantly clear that democratic regimes are often constructed around a series of tacit or explicit political compromises that internalize reserve domains of power and privilege – along with their derivative patterns of inequality or exclusion – as the price that is paid to bring recalcitrant actors on board. Recent work on American political development forcefully underscores the point; as Mettler and Lieberman (2020: 192) demonstrate, during times of crisis historically, a "deeply disturbing pattern" emerged whereby "political leaders effectively preserved American democracy by restricting it." Such restrictions – such as federal tolerance of black disenfranchisement and single-party subnational authoritarianism in the post-Reconstruction US South (Mickey 2015), or, in contemporary Chile, a "democratic" constitution bequeathed by a military dictator – often create the fault lines for future iterations of regime contestation, as disadvantaged groups mobilize to challenge institutional constraints on their representation.

Societal pressures to expand or "deepen" democracy are ubiquitous, since no democracy is ever complete, in the sense of achieving full political equality and inclusion. But new democratic breakthroughs to incorporate or empower subordinate constituencies are invariably countered by those who occupy privileged positions in the established order. If, as Stenner (2005) suggests, authoritarianism is rooted in an intolerance of difference – whether that be defined in terms of race, ethnicity, religion, social status, partisanship, or political ideology – a dialectical approach helps to show how efforts to empower previously excluded or subaltern groups can trigger a counter-mobilization of authoritarian currents among guardians of the traditional order. The long-term patterns of social mobilization and counter-mobilization that realigned US politics following the civil rights movement and desegregation in the 1960s offer a paradigmatic example (Parker and Baretto 2013; McAdam and Kloos 2014; Blum 2020). This realignment transformed centripetal competition between two moderate, catch-all parties into a highly polarized regime cleavage between partisan adversaries, one advocating multiracial democracy, and the other dominated by exclusionary ethno-nationalist and religious-nationalist currents with markedly authoritarian tendencies. Some version of the latter currents can be found in virtually every society, whether they are active and visible, or latent and subterranean; a dialectical approach is well suited to identify the political settlements under which they lie dormant, the social struggles that trigger their activation, and the constitutive conflicts inevitably spawned by their mobilization.

A dialectical approach can also shed light on the process by which many autocratic challenges to democracy assume populist forms, with a binary division of the political field between established elites and a party or leader who claims to embody the popular will of an aggrieved "people." Populist movements may challenge liberal democratic regimes and the professional politicians who control them, but they do so in the name of democracy itself, alternately conceived as an unbridled assertion of popular sovereignty. Populism crystallizes the inherent (though not necessarily irreconcilable) tensions between liberal and majoritarian strands of democratic theory, or between Dahl's (1971: 4–7) two primary axes of polyarchy: a liberal axis of public contestation, reflecting a conception of democracy as a form of institutionalized pluralism, and a majoritarian axis of participation and inclusion, where popular sovereignty lies. Populist challenges typically capitalize on failures or crises of political representation under established democratic rulers, promising "the people" a more just and authentic mode of governance – though not always one that is tolerant of minority political rights, or of institutional checks on the party or leader who claims the people's mandate.

The populist dialectic helps to explain why leaders with autocratic tendencies sometimes obtain significant support in public opinion and sectors of civil society, even when they provoke vigorous resistance on the part of other societal actors. In diverse national settings, autocrats of varied ideological persuasions – from Viktor Orbán to Narendra Modi or Hugo Chávez – have demonstrated not only that they can compete and win in electoral contests, but that they do not have to conceal their autocratic ambitions to do so. Indeed, many have dared to flaunt them, politicizing latent societal prejudices or animosities between different social, cultural, or identity groups, stoking fear and intolerance of out-groups or adversaries, and publicly flouting democratic norms and procedures that restrain their freedom of action or protect their political rivals. When citizens reward rather than punish such behavior in the voting booth, there can be little doubt that politicians are tapping into reservoirs of support for authoritarian alternatives – and, paradoxically, employing democratic instruments to advance them. Such is the endogeneity of democratic backsliding.

Although many activist groups will push back against democratic backsliding, civil society is hardly a homogeneous lot, much less a uniformly liberal one. Successful autocrats do not necessarily concentrate their support among the disorganized or atomized masses; many tap into the group identities forged by organized civic networks around churches, ethnic communities, nationalist or "patriotic" orders, gun clubs, and police or military forces. Civil society, therefore – like state institutions – is an arena where the dialectical interplay between democracy's countervailing forces unfolds. Civil society networks can be force multipliers that provide mobilizing resources for both democratic and autocratic political projects – that is, for democratic backsliding as well as democratic resilience and "deepening" (see Berman 1997). An understanding of contemporary challenges to democracy requires an examination of this dialectical interplay to explain the social bases – in public opinion, the voting booth, and civil society networks – of both authoritarian and democratic alternatives.

1.3 OUTLINE OF THE VOLUME

The efforts of democratic actors in civil society and diverse institutional arenas to defend or, in many cases, expand democratic practices place a premium on scholarly efforts to theorize democratic resiliency, alongside democratic backsliding. Such theorization should start with an understanding of democracy as perpetually contested terrain – a dialectical frontier, so to speak, rather than a predefined endpoint of political development, a standardized procedural minimum, or a static complex of "consolidated" institutions. The contributions to this volume provide explorations of that frontier across a wide range of national and regional contexts.

The volume is organized into three thematic sections. Part I examines institutional dimensions of democratic backsliding and resilience. Starting with democracies in the Global South, it includes chapters on the erosion of democracy's institutional guardrails in India by Milan Vaishnav, and the sources of democratic institutional fragility in Southeast Asia by Meredith L. Weiss and Allen Hicken. The complex relationship between state capacity and democratic accountability in sub-Saharan Africa is then examined by Jaimie Bleck and Nicolas van de Walle. Shifting attention to institutional challenges in the Global North, Frances Cayton and Bryn Rosenfeld explain how the politicization of the public sector can be a source of autocratic support in Eastern Europe and beyond. David A. Bateman, Robert Lieberman and Aaron Childree conclude the section with an analysis of the political manipulation of electoral administration in the US.

Part II examines democratic struggles in different social spheres, including civil society, social media, and political messaging. Starting with Latin America, Lindsay Mayka analyzes the politicization of crime and gender hierarchies and the narrowing of citizenship rights. Shifting the focus to Eastern Europe, the section includes a chapter by Béla Greskovits on civil society networks and authoritarian political mobilization in Hungary, as well as a chapter by Michael Bernhard on civil societies and democratic "social accountability" in post-Communist Europe. Mark R. Beissinger then explores the institutional conditions and political timing that influence the effectiveness of civil society resistance to backsliding in Eastern Europe. Alexandra Cirone analyzes social media and the corrosive effects of disinformation on democracy. M. Steven Fish concludes the section by exploring the impact of political messaging and "dominance" strategies on the effectiveness of campaigns against autocratic figures.

Finally, Part III examines regional and international dimensions of the rise of the populist radical right and the challenges it poses to democracy in Europe and beyond. It starts with a chapter by Mabel Berezin on transnationalism, the erosion of citizen security, and the "normalization" of the nationalist right in Europe. Next, Dorothee Bohle and Aida A. Hozić analyze the transnational alliances between mainstream parties and the radical right that have undermined the capacity of European institutions to defend democracy in Eastern Europe. Stefano Palestini and Cristóbal Rovira Kaltwasser then explore the cross-regional political linkages fostered by the *Foro Madrid*, which connects the populist radical right in Spain and Europe to their affiliates in Latin America. Valerie J. Bunce concludes with an agenda-setting essay on the lessons learned and how they should influence our understanding of democracy, its political fragilities, and diverse efforts to defend and sustain it.

Taken together, these chapters shed new light on the nature of the challenges confronted by democracies in contemporary global politics. They dissect the sources and limitations of popular support for democratic and autocratic alternatives, the institutional sites they struggle to control, and the civic spheres over which they contend. Understanding these challenges, we believe, is not only essential for safeguarding existing democracies, but also for reinforcing their capacity to point the way toward better, and more expansive, democratic futures.

REFERENCES

Albertus, Michael and Guy Grossman. 2021. "The Americas: When Do Voters Support Power Grabs?" *Journal of Democracy* 32, 2: 116–131.
Albertus, Michael and Victor Menaldo. 2018. *Authoritarianism and the Elite Origins of Democracy*. New York: Cambridge University Press.
Alizada, Nazifa, Rowan Cole, Lisa Gastaldi, Sandra Grahn, Sebastian Hellmeier, Palina Kolvani, Jean Lachapelle, Anna Lührmann, Seraphine F. Maerz, Shreeya Pillai, and Staffan I. Lindberg. 2021. *Autocratization Turns Viral. Democracy Report 2021*. University of Gothenburg: V-Dem Institute.
Almond, Gabriel A. and Sidney Verba. 1963. *The Civic Culture: Political Attitudes and Democracy in Five Nations*. Princeton: Princeton University Press.
Anderson, Christopher J., André Blais, Shaun Bowler, Todd Donavon, and Ola Listhaug. 2005. *Losers' Consent: Elections and Democratic Legitimacy*. Oxford: Oxford University Press.
Ansell, Ben W. and David J. Samuels. 2014. *Inequality and Democratization: An Elite-Competition Approach*. New York: Cambridge University Press.
Berman, Sheri. 1997. "Civil Society and the Collapse of the Weimar Republic," *World Politics* 49, 3: 401–429.
Berman, Sheri. 2019. *Democracy and Dictatorship in Europe: From the Ancien Régime to the Present Day*. Oxford: Oxford University Press.

Bermeo, Nancy. 2016. "On Democratic Backsliding," *Journal of Democracy* 27, 1: 5–19.

Bermeo, Nancy and Deborah J. Yashar, eds. 2016. *Parties, Movements, and Democracy in the Developing World*. New York: Cambridge University Press.

Blum, Rachel. 2020. *How the Tea Party Captured the GOP: Insurgent Factions in American Politics*. Chicago: University of Chicago Press.

Bunce, Valerie J. 1999. *Subversive Institutions: The Design and the Destruction of Socialism and the State*. New York: Cambridge University Press.

Bunce, Valerie J. 2003. "Rethinking Democratization: Lessons from the Postcommunist Experience," *World Politics* 55, 2 (January): 167–192.

Cameron, Max. 2021. "The US Capitol Raid Was a Failed Self-Coup Previously Seen in Dying Regimes," *The Conversation*, Jan. 10 (https://tinyurl.com/2s36dax7).

Carothers, Thomas. 2002. "The End of the Transitions Paradigm," *Journal of Democracy* 13, 1: 5–21.

Carothers, Thomas and Benjamin Feldman. 2023. *Understanding and Supporting Democratic Bright Spots*. Washington, DC: Carnegie Endowment for International Peace (https://tinyurl.com/4xkf2jns).

"Comment and Controversy: Special Issue on Democratic Backsliding." 2024. *PS: Political Science and Politics* 57, 2.

Dahl, Robert. 1971. *Polyarchy: Participation and Opposition*. New Haven: Yale University Press.

Diamond, Larry. 2015. "Facing Up to the Democratic Recession," *Journal of Democracy* 26, 1: 141–155.

Diamond, Larry. 2020. *Ill Winds: Saving Democracy from Russian Rage, Chinese Ambition, and American Complacency*. New York: Penguin Books.

Diamond, Larry and Marc F. Plattner. 1993. "Introduction," in Larry Diamond and Marc F. Plattner, eds. *The Global Resurgence of Democracy*. Baltimore: Johns Hopkins University Press, pp. ix–xxvi.

Freedom House. 2024. *Freedom in the World 2024: The Mounting Damage of Flawed Elections and Armed Conflict*. Freedom House: Washington, DC (Freedom House. 2024 annual report.pdf).

Fukuyama, Francis. 1989. "The End of History?" *The National Interest* 16 (Summer): 3–18.

Gibson, Edward L. 1996. *Class and Conservative Parties: Argentina in Comparative Perspective*. Baltimore: Johns Hopkins University Press.

Goodman, Sara Wallace. 2019. "Liberal Democracy, National Identity Boundaries, and Populist Entry Points," *Critical Review*, 31: 3–4, 377–388.

Grief, Avner and David D. Laitin. 2004. "A Theory of Endogenous Institutional Change," *American Political Science Review* 98, 4 (November): 633–652.

Grzymala-Busse, Anna. 2002. *Redeeming the Communist Past: The Regeneration of Communist Parties in East Central Europe*. New York: Cambridge University Press.

Haggard, Stephan and Robert Kaufman. 2021. *Backsliding: Democratic Regress in the Contemporary World*. New York: Cambridge University Press.

Hewison, Kevin, and Kengkij Kitirianglarp. 2010. "'Thai-Style Democracy': A Conservative Struggle for Thailand's Politics," in Lotte Isager and Soren Ivarsson, eds. *Saying the Unsayable: Monarchy and Democracy in Thailand*. Copenhagen: NIAS Press.

Hochschild, Arlie Russell. 2018. *Strangers in Their Own Land: Anger and Mourning on the American Right.* New York: New Press.

Huntington, Samuel P. 1991. *The Third Wave: Democratization in the Late 20th Century.* Norman: University of Oklahoma Press.

International Idea. 2021. *The Global State of Democracy 2021: Building Resilience in a Pandemic Era.* Stockholm: International Institute for Democracy and Electoral Assistance (https://tinyurl.com/3e68zsxd).

Karl, Terry Lynn. 1987. "Petroleum and Political Pacts: The Transition to Democracy in Venezuela," *Latin American Research Review* 22: 63–94.

Krishnarajan, Suthan. 2023. "Rationalizing Democracy: The Perceptual Bias and (Un)Democratic Behavior," *American Political Science Review* 117, 2: 474–496.

Levitsky, Steven and Lucan A. Way. 2010. *Competitive Authoritarianism: Hybrid Regimes after the Cold War.* New York: Cambridge University Press.

Levitsky, Steven and Lucan A. Way. 2023. "Democracy's Surprising Resilience," *Journal of Democracy* 34, 4: 5–20.

Levitsky, Steven and Daniel Ziblatt. 2018. *How Democracies Die.* New York: Crown Publishing.

Levitsky, Steven and Daniel Ziblatt. 2023. *Tyranny of the Minority: How American Democracy Reached the Breaking Point.* New York: Crown Publishing.

Lindberg, Staffan I. 2006. *Democracy and Elections in Africa.* Baltimore: Johns Hopkins University Press.

Linz, Juan J. 1978. *The Breakdown of Democratic Regimes: Crisis, Breakdown, and Reequilibration.* Baltimore: Johns Hopkins University Press.

Linz, Juan J. 1990. "The Perils of Presidentialism," *Journal of Democracy* 1, 1: 51–69.

Linz, Juan J. and Alfred C. Stepan. 1996. *Problems of Democratic Transition and Consolidation.* Baltimore: Johns Hopkins University Press.

Lipset, Seymour Martin. 1959. "Some Social Requisites of Democracy: Economic Development and Political Legitimacy," *American Political Science Review* 53, 1: 69–105.

Little, Andrew T. and Anne Meng. 2024. "Measuring Democratic Backsliding," *PS: Political Science and Politics* 57, 2: 149–161.

Loxton, James. 2021. *Conservative Party-Building in Latin America: Authoritarian Inheritance and Counter-Revolutionary Struggle.* Oxford: Oxford University Press.

Lührmann, Anna and Staffan I. Lindberg. 2019. "A Third Wave of Autocratization Is Here: What Is New About It?" *Democratization* 26, 7: 1095–1113.

Madison, James. 1787. *Federalist Papers* #10.

Mainwawring, Scott and Aníbal Pérez-Liñán. 2013. *Democracies and Dictatorships in Latin America: Emergence, Survival, and Fall.* New York: Cambridge University Press.

McAdam, Doug and Karina Kloos. 2014. *Deeply Divided: Racial Politics and Social Movements in Postwar America.* Oxford: Oxford University Press.

Mechkova, Valeriya, Anna Lührmann, and Staffan I. Lindberg. 2017. "How Much Democratic Backsliding?" *Journal of Democracy* 28, 4: 162–169.

Mettler, Suzanne and Robert C. Lieberman. 2020. *Four Threats: The Recurring Crises of American Democracy.* New York: St. Martin's Griffin.

Meyer, David S. and Sidney Tarrow, eds. 2018. *The Resistance: The Dawn of the Anti-Trump Opposition Movement.* Oxford: Oxford University Press.

Miao, Kenny and Jason Brownlee. 2022. "Debate: Why Democracies Survive," *Journal of Democracy* 33, 4: 133–149.

Mickey, Robert. 2015. *Paths Out of Dixie: The Democratization of Authoritarian Enclaves in America's Deep South, 1944–1972.* Princeton: Princeton University Press.

Moore, Barrington. 1966. *Social Origins of Dictatorship and Democracy: Lord and Peasant in the Making of the Modern World.* Boston: Beacon Press.

Mounk, Yascha. 2018. *The People vs. Democracy: Why Our Freedom Is in Danger and How to Save It.* Cambridge, MA: Harvard University Press.

Mudde, Cas and Cristóbal Rovira Kaltwasser. 2013. "Exclusionary vs. Inclusionary Populism: Comparing the Contemporary Europe and Latin America," *Government and Opposition* 48, 2: 147–174.

Nord, Marina, Martin Lundstedt, David Altman, Fabio Angiolillo, Cecilia Borella, Tiago Fernandes, Lisa Gastaldi, Ana Good God, Natalia Natsika, and Staffan I. Lindberg. 2024. *Democracy Report 2024: Democracy Winning and Losing at the Ballot.* University of Gothenburg: V-Dem Institute.

O'Donnell, Guillermo. 1994. "Delegative Democracy," *Journal of Democracy* 5, 1: 55–69.

O'Donnell, Guillermo and Philippe C. Schmitter. 1986. *Transitions from Authoritarian Rule: Tentative Conclusions about Uncertain Democracies.* Baltimore: Johns Hopkins University Press.

Parker, Christopher S. and Matt A. Barreto. 2013. *Change They Can't Believe In: The Tea Party and Reactionary Politics in America.* Princeton: Princeton University Press.

Pepinsky, Thomas B. 2020. "Migrants, Minorities, and Populism in Southeast Asia," *Pacific Affairs* 93, 3: 593–610.

Pepinsky, Thomas B. 2017. "Southeast Asia: Voting against Disorder," *Journal of Democracy* 28, 2: 120–31.

Plattner, Marc F. 1993. "The Democratic Moment," in Larry Diamond and Marc F. Plattner, eds. *The Global Resurgence of Democracy.* Baltimore: Johns Hopkins University Press, pp. 26–38.

Przeworski, Adam. 1991. *Democracy and the Market: Political and Economic Reforms in Eastern Europe and Latin America.* New York: Cambridge University Press.

Przeworski, Adam. 2005. "Democracy As an Equilibrium," *Public Choice* 123, 3/4: 253–273.

Przeworski, Adam. 2019. *Crises of Democracy.* New York: Cambridge University Press.

Przeworski, Adam, Michael E. Alvarez, Jose Cheibub, and Fernando Limongi. 2000. *Democracy and Development: Political Institutions and Well-Being in the World, 1950–1990.* New York: Cambridge University Press.

Riedl, Rachel Beatty. 2014. *Authoritarian Origins of Democratic Party Systems.* New York: Cambridge University Press.

Riedl, Rachel Beatty, Paul Friesen, Jennifer McCoy, and Kenneth M. Roberts. 2023. "Democratic Backsliding, Resilience, and Resistance," *World Politics* 75, 5 (Advanced Access: https://muse.jhu.edu/pub/1/article/917802/pdf).

Rueschemeyer, Dietrich, Evelyne Huber Stephens, and John D. Stephens. 1992. *Capitalist Development and Democracy.* Chicago: University of Chicago Press.

Rustow, Dankwart. 1970. "Transition to Democracy: Towards a Dynamic Model," *Comparative Politics* 2 (April): 337–363.

Schedler, Andreas. 1998. "What Is Democratic Consolidation?" *Journal of Democracy* 9, 2: 91–107.

Schedler, Andreas. 2002. "Elections without Democracy: The Menu of Manipulation," *Journal of Democracy*, 13 2: 36–50.

Schmitter, Philippe C. and Terry Lynn Karl. 1991. "What Democracy Is . . . and Is Not," *Journal of Democracy* 2, 3: 75–88.

Singer, Matthew. 2018. "Delegating Away Democracy: How Good Representation and Policy Successes Can Undermine Democratic Legitimacy," *Comparative Political Studies* 51, 13: 1754–1788.

Snyder, Timothy. 2017. *On Tyranny: Twenty Lessons from the Twentieth Century.* New York: Crown Publishers.

Stenner, Karen. 2005. *The Authoritarian Dynamic.* New York: Cambridge University Press.

Svolik, Milan W. 2019a. "Democracy As an Equilibrium: Rational Choice and Formal Political Theory in Democratization Research," *Democratization* 26, 1: 40–60.

Svolik, Milan W. 2019b. "Polarization versus Democracy," *Journal of Democracy* 30, 3: 20–32.

Tilly, Charles. 2007. *Democracy.* New York: Cambridge University Press.

"Tracking the Trump Criminal Cases." 2024. *Politico* (https://tinyurl.com/2b9cs7rp).

Treisman, Daniel. 2023. "How Great Is the Current Danger to Democracy? Assessing the Risk with Historical Data," *Comparative Political Studies* 56, 12: 1924–1952.

Tufekci, Zeynep. 2020. "This Must Be Your First," *The Atlantic*, Dec. 7 (https://tinyurl.com/4vxfzy2y).

Waldner, David and Ellen Lust. 2018. "Unwelcome Change: Coming to Terms with Democratic Backsliding," *Annual Review of Political Science* 21: 93–113.

Weingast, Barry. 1997. "The Political Foundations of Democracy and the Rule of Law," *American Political Science Review* 91, 2: 245–263.

Wong, Joseph and Edward Friedman. 2008. *Political Transitions in Dominant Party Systems: Learning to Lose.* London: Routledge.

Yashar, Deborah J. 1999. "Democracy, Indigenous Movements, and the Postliberal Challenge in Latin America," *World Politics* 52, 1: 76–104.

Ziblatt, Daniel. 2017. *Conservative Parties and the Birth of Democracy.* New York: Cambridge University Press.

PART I

INSTITUTIONAL DIMENSIONS OF DEMOCRATIC
BACKSLIDING AND RESILIENCE

2

Backsliding in India?

The Weakening of Referee Institutions

Milan Vaishnav

2.1 INTRODUCTION

For more than seven and a half decades, India has enjoyed the moniker of "world's largest democracy." In addition to this distinction, the country is the most enduring democracy in the developing world. India adopted universal suffrage in 1947, despite an extremely low per capita income. Since then, the country has sustained its commitment to democratic governance despite poverty, inequality, unprecedented diversity, and sprawling geography (Varshney 2013). This makes India both an important outlier as well as an exemplar for poor, multiethnic democracies the world over (Stepan, Linz, and Yadav 2011).

However, anxieties about global democratic backsliding have not left India untouched. Since 2021, Freedom House has listed India among the ranks of "Partly Free" nations in its annual "Freedom in the World" publication, a demotion from its earlier status as "Free." The V-Dem Institute (2024), which calls India an "electoral autocracy," lists the country as one of the world's ten most significant "autocratizers," based on the magnitude of its decline on the organization's index measure of liberal democracy.

Indeed, India is perhaps the developing world's most potent counterpoint to the conventional understanding in political science that "stability breeds stability," or the notion that democratic longevity provides a veneer of protection against democratic regression. As Roberts, Bunce, Pepinsky, and Beatty Riedl point out in Chapter 1 in this volume, many of the world's

Email: mvaishnav@ceip.org. The author is grateful to Aislinn Familetti, Tara Kavasseri, Caroline Mallory, and Megan Maxwell for editorial and research assistance and to Bilal Baloch, Caroline Duckworth, Ronald Herring, Madhav Khosla, Thomas Pepinsky, Suyash Rai, Kenneth Roberts, participants at the Cornell University Workshop on Global Challenges to Democracy, and an anonymous reviewer for valuable feedback. All errors are the author's own.

showcases of democracy – including India – have given lie to the belief that consolidated democracies are "self-sustaining."

When it comes to India's democratic distress, scholars have articulated three principal lines of concern (Khosla and Vaishnav 2021). First, under the tenure of Prime Minister Narendra Modi and his Hindu nationalist Bharatiya Janata Party (BJP), India appears to have moved decisively in a more majoritarian direction (Varshney and Staggs 2024). The BJP's success has led revisionists to assert that India is, first and foremost, a homeland for Hindus, who comprise roughly 80 percent of the population.

Second, Modi has centralized executive power to an extent not seen since the heyday of former Prime Minister Indira Gandhi, who famously suspended many constitutionally enshrined freedoms during a period of Emergency Rule in the mid-1970s. For his part, Modi has consolidated authority both within his political party and across the governmental machinery (Sircar 2021). Finally, the Modi government has repeatedly demonstrated contempt for dissent and painted vocal critics of the government as "anti-national" (Palshikar 2018). India's legal and constitutional framework has long been characterized by significant constraints on free expression; Modi has assiduously doubled down on those limits.

The objective of this chapter is not to enumerate alleged democratic woes but rather ask whether India is slowly becoming an "elections-only" democracy (Guha 2015). In India, democratic backsliding appears to progress without significant alteration to the established rules of electoral competition. To its credit, India manages to demonstrate an impressive level of electoral vibrancy. More than 8,000 candidates representing 744 parties contested India's 2024 general election. Voter turnout, both in national and regional elections, has risen significantly compared to previous decades. Female voters, whose participation in elections has long been muted, now turn out to vote in greater proportion than their male counterparts.

Unfortunately, vibrant electoral participation belies a variety of liberal deficits (Varshney 2022). Creeping majoritarianism, the expansion of executive power and rising intolerance of dissent have led to doubts about the quality of Indian democracy. Considering these trends, this chapter evaluates the health of institutional guardrails protecting India's democratic commitments by focusing on referee institutions that promote government accountability and ensure a level playing field for incumbents and challengers.

In every functioning democracy, there are "referee institutions" that enforce the rules of the game. Like officials on a football pitch, they ensure that contesting parties adhere to a common set of rules and sanction those who violate them. These institutions are not players on the field, but instead ensure that the match is played fairly (Kapur 2007; Tushnet 2021).

This chapter analyzes the behavior of three such institutions – the Supreme Court, the Election Commission of India (ECI), and a clutch of horizontal federal accountability institutions – and their encounters with a new dominant political entity, the BJP. In the early years of the Indian republic, the scope of these referee institutions was limited (some had not even been established). Executive power was highly concentrated in the dominant Congress Party, which held almost uninterrupted power in Delhi between 1947 and 1989. This dominance left little space for institutions independent of the executive to flourish. It was neither in the interest of the Congress Party to place checks on its power, nor in the interest of referee institutions to confront a popular political executive with demonstrated longevity.

As the Congress' grip on power faltered and coalition governance flourished, the executive branch weakened, and political power fragmented. India's referee institutions now had the political space to exert their authority without fear of confronting a dominant political force. Furthermore, other political parties jockeying for power now had an incentive to support stronger institutions that would ensure a level playing field. As Ahuja and Ostermann (2018) have argued, state-based or regional challengers sought strong, nonpartisan federal bodies to police incumbents. At the same time, new institutions were set up to check government power.

In 2014, the BJP won the first single-party parliamentary majority in three decades. Five years later, it not only repeated that feat, but *grew* its parliamentary tally. In the interim, the BJP steadily expanded its footprint at the state level, constructing a pan-Indian political machine that rivaled the Congress Party of yesteryear. This political shift led some scholars to herald the dawn of a new political era – known as India's "fourth party system" – in which the BJP firmly established itself as the pole around which politics in India revolves (Vaishnav and Hintson 2019). Although the BJP failed to secure a parliamentary majority in the 2024 general election, it still operates as the central gravitational force in Indian politics. The fourth party system has been weakened, but only partially (Vaishnav and Mallory 2024).

As the BJP's dominance has grown, referee institutions have again become subordinate to a powerful executive. Today, there are three discernible patterns of interaction between the executive and India's referee institutions: *deference*, *interference*, and *neglect*. While not all referee institutions have experienced each of these dynamics in equal measure, they have all experienced at least one. This logic suggests an important paradox: institutional checks and balances have functioned most effectively when they are least needed (when the party system is fragmented) and least effectively when needed the most (when a single party is dominant). Indeed, as Weiss and Hicken note in their contribution to this volume (Chapter 3), institutions explicitly designed with a multiparty coalition government in mind are typically ill-suited to check governments run by a dominant party.

The empirical evidence discussed in this chapter points to a reality long overlooked but highlighted in Chapter 1 of this volume by Roberts, Bunce, Pepinsky, and Beatty Riedl: the central challenge of democracy is not necessarily guarding against the subversive actions of actors who *lose* elections but rather protecting against the overreach of those who *win* them. As the India case reveals and the aforementioned scholars note, "a disciplined and opportunistic party can … undermine the separation of powers and progressively neutralize the checks and balances that are essential for horizontal accountability." Therefore, one cannot assume the automatic activation of institutional checks and balances.

The sequence of events described in this chapter raises a further question: Is India under Modi's BJP simply experiencing mean reversion? According to this argument, the quarter century of coalition rule during which independent institutions flourished was simply a historical anomaly. Institutional subjugation, on the other hand, is the norm.

While there is truth to this argument, one key difference separates the Congress' institutional subjugation from that of the BJP: the Congress was often opportunistic in its undermining of referee institutions, while the BJP's machinations are organized around an ideological commitment to *Hindutva* (Hindu nationalism). Criticism of the party and of its ideological project, therefore, is tarred as "anti-national." This term equates support of BJP policies with loyalty to the sovereign Indian nation. The result is institutional atrophy closely intertwined with a new imagination of the Indian "nation."

2.2 EVALUATING INDIA'S REFEREE INSTITUTIONS

In India, many critical referee institutions have existed on paper for decades, but their prominence is only traced back to the late 1980s and early 1990s. The Congress Party dominated politics both at the center and in India's states for the first several decades of India's independence. Its hegemony gradually weakened in the late 1960s and declined precipitously in the second half of the 1980s, ushering in a quarter century of coalition government in New Delhi (Yadav 1999). Between 1989 and 2014, no single national party could successfully exert its dominance; instead, unruly coalitions of more than a dozen political parties constructed tenuous parliamentary majorities.

It was during this era of fragmentation that referee institutions – such as the ECI, the Supreme Court, and other horizontal accountability agencies – were granted the political space to regenerate. Most political parties found it in their enlightened self-interest to support (or at least not actively undermine) a credible umpire who could monitor their rivals – even if that meant greater scrutiny of one's own behavior (Ahuja and Ostermann 2018).

In 2014, Modi and the BJP achieved the first single-party parliamentary majority in three decades. In an era of single-party dominance – as was the case in the era of Congress hegemony – the ruling party is arguably less committed to maintaining referee institutions that might clip its wings. In turn, those institutions – and critical actors within them – are incentivized to gain favor with the ruling party to perpetuate their own standing (Vaishnav 2018).

Referee institutions must now engage with a new political hegemon. Broadly speaking, there are three patterns of interaction between the executive and these institutions: deference, interference, and neglect.

2.2.1 Supreme Court

The role of India's Supreme Court in upholding democracy and the rule of law has varied over time. While the formal powers of the Court are quite broad, two developments triggered a major shift for the apex Court in the 1970s and 1980s (Khosla and Padmanabhan 2017).

The first was the weakening of executive power. As the power and authority of India's legislature and executive waned, the judiciary filled the breach. The Court positioned itself as one institution that could effectively respond to policy issues without succumbing to internecine political battles. In the 1970s, the Court developed what became known as "the basic structure doctrine," whereby it limited Parliament's power to amend the Constitution by insisting that any legislative alterations could not materially affect the basic structure of the document. In a second development, the Court expanded subjects it deemed fit for judicial intervention. This practice led to the rise of new instruments like "public interest litigation," whereby any citizen could petition the apex Court if they believe the public interest is at stake (Mehta 2007).

The BJP's rise to power tested the Court's independence. A critical warning sign of the Court's growing dysfunction emerged unexpectedly in January 2018, when four sitting Supreme Court justices sounded alarm bells about the behavior of then Chief Justice of India (CJI) Dipak Misra. The justices accused Misra of not only sitting in judgment in a corruption case implicating him personally, but also using his prerogative as the "master of the court's roster" – which allows him to unilaterally assign benches to hear specific cases – to influence the outcome at the behest of the executive (Bhatia 2018).

Another manifestation of executive interference involves the appointment of judges to the Supreme Court and regional High Courts. In India, a *collegium* – comprised of the CJI and the four most senior justices – recommends appointments to the Supreme Court and the state-level High Courts. Customarily, the judiciary consults the executive on its recommendations before appointments are finalized. In recent years, this informal system has deteriorated. The Modi government attempted to amend the Constitution to create a judicial appointments commission with representation from the executive and judicial branches. Though the Court struck the bill down as unconstitutional, it acknowledged that the *collegium* system suffered several infirmities, such as a lack of transparency (Robinson 2016).

Since then, the judiciary and the executive negotiated a Memorandum of Procedure to regulate appointments. Still, the executive has often undermined the spirit, if not the letter, of this agreement. Once the *collegium* finalizes its recommendations, the government should approve appointments within a few weeks. However, A. P. Kumar (2022) has found that the median appointment time is nearly twice that long. The government has also adopted a "pick and choose" model whereby it expedites the processing of some names, while sitting on others. In extreme cases, the *collegium* has been forced to revisit appointments in the wake of executive disapproval on questionable grounds. In still others, judges who clash with the executive branch have been inexplicably transferred to less prestigious courts (Shah 2019). This practice has given the government the ability to exercise a "pocket veto" over appointments.

A second discernible pattern has to do with judicial deference to the executive. This practice involves the Court willfully declining to take up controversial matters that might place it in opposition to the ruling party. In August 2019, the government unilaterally nullified Article 370 of the Constitution, which had long granted partial autonomy to the state of Jammu and Kashmir. Furthermore, it bifurcated the state into two parts and changed their status to that of federally administered "union territories." In October 2019, the Court refused to entertain a stay on this constitutionally contentious move. In fact, it adjourned the hearing to a future date following the bifurcation and demotion, rendering the challenge moot. In December 2023 – more than four-and-a-half years after the change in status – the Court upheld the abrogation with the caveat that statehood should be restored "at the earliest" and fresh elections should be held by September 2024.

The apex Court's deference does not stop with dithering on the legality of the constitutional change. When the government altered Jammu and Kashmir's status, it preemptively detained hundreds of political leaders across the state in the name of public order and security. Those detentions prompted hundreds of habeas corpus petitions to be filed before the Jammu and Kashmir High Court and the Supreme Court.[1] But neither the High Court nor the Supreme Court demonstrated any semblance of urgency to defend one of the most fundamental rights democratic citizens enjoy (Bhatia 2019). The Kashmir case is an apt example of the judiciary using national security to justify deference to the executive branch.

Another example of deference pertains to political finance. One of the Modi government's most touted electoral reforms was the introduction of a political funding instrument known as "electoral bonds." Using this instrument, associations, individuals, or firms wishing to donate to political parties could purchase time-limited bearer bonds that would be deposited into parties' registered bank accounts. The transactions occur through the banking system and, therefore, produce a digital paper trail. However, neither donor nor

---

[1] According to a report by the Jammu and Kashmir Coalition of Civil Society (2020), 412 habeas corpus petitions were filed between August 5 and December 31, 2019.

recipient must publicly report the transaction. Thus, there is no public record of who bought each bond and to whom the funds were given (Vaishnav 2024a).

While the government introduced such bonds under the dubious guise of "enhancing transparency," the bonds are shrouded in opacity. The Supreme Court, which had amassed an admirable record of supporting efforts to promote electoral transparency, refused to grant a stay on the scheme in advance of the 2019 general elections. The Court claimed the issue was a "weighty" one and lamented having "limited time" before the poll. In February 2024, half a decade after the bonds' introduction, the Court finally ruled that the scheme was unconstitutional and demanded that all transaction-level details be made public immediately (Vaishnav 2024b).

While it can be argued that the Court eventually held the government to account, its rulings on Kashmir and electoral bonds came years after new realities were created on the ground. In the case of electoral bonds, the BJP – as the principal beneficiary of the new scheme – was able to maintain and then expand its financial advantage over its competitors, tilting the playing field in its favor. Although granular details of the bonds were not made public prior to the Supreme Court's ruling, because the purchases and subsequent deposits were processed by India's largest public sector bank, the government (as regulator) had access to this information, leading to a form of asymmetric transparency. On Kashmir, given how much time had elapsed since the abrogation of Article 370, it would have been politically difficult, if not practically impossible, to restore the erstwhile state's previous status before the constitutional alterations. As the saying goes, "justice delayed is justice denied."

In sum, within just a few years, an apex Court that was uninhibited in confronting political power turned deferential in the extreme. What is striking about this abrupt shift is that it was not the result of any constitutional reimagination of its powers, but rather a complex mix of political hardball and an unwillingness or inability to confront a popular executive.

2.2.2 Election Commission of India

Given India's record of electoral vibrancy, it is not surprising that its apex elections agency, the ECI, has traditionally been one of the most revered federal institutions in the country. Under India's Constitution, the ECI is given wide berth to prepare, supervise, and conduct all aspects of election management at the state and national levels. Since the early 1990s, strong-willed election commissioners upset incumbents and challengers in equal measure when cracking down on electoral malpractice, impropriety, or undue government influence (Sridharan and Vaishnav 2017).

However, the ECI's shine has dulled in recent years. In several high-profile cases, its judgment has been questioned. Most of these cases fit the pattern of deference. In October 2018, the agency broke from established convention by announcing election dates in one state (Himachal Pradesh) while staying silent on polls in another (Gujarat), even though polling was to take place roughly simultaneously. Although the incumbent Chief Election Commissioner (CEC) claimed the delay was due to flood relief work in Gujarat, it escaped few people's attention that the delay allowed the BJP government there to hastily roll out several electorally lucrative welfare schemes before the election-time "Model Code of Conduct" [MCC], which prohibits the announcement of new public schemes, kicked in (S. Kumar 2022).[2]

A second deferential move is the ECI's sudden reversal on electoral bonds. When the scheme was first announced in 2017, the commission told Parliament it was a "retrograde step" that would "compromise" electoral transparency. Yet, a year later, then CEC A. K. Joti suddenly changed his tune, publicly proclaiming that the bond scheme was a "step in the right direction" (*Financial Express* 2018).

Leaked government documents reveal that some within the ECI privately attempted to derail the scheme, citing concerns on foreign funding, the consolidation of a corrupt business-politics nexus, and the potential of dubious shell companies to make political donations (Sethi 2019). However, the ECI's reluctance to make its objections public damaged its cause and allowed the executive to circumvent the body.

Not all election commissioners have been equally deferential. In the run-up to the 2019 general election, several complaints of violating the MCC were filed against BJP leaders – including the prime minister and BJP President Amit Shah. The ECI exonerated Modi and Shah of any wrongdoing despite objections from one of the three election commissioners, Ashok Lavasa. Although Lavasa was outvoted, he requested that the CEC publicly release his dissenting opinions; his requests were denied (Chopra 2019a). Lavasa later clarified that he was following through on a Supreme Court directive that the commission urgently resolve MCC violations during elections (Chopra 2019b).

After the Modi government returned to power, retribution against Lavasa began immediately. In August 2019, the government searched for evidence of "undue influence" that Lavasa might have exerted during his earlier stint in the power ministry (Sarin 2019). The next month, the media reported that tax and anti-money laundering authorities initiated investigations in Lavasa, his wife, sister, and son (Siwach et al. 2019). After no wrongdoing was uncovered, Lavasa was reassigned to a foreign posting. This punishment demonstrates that those who stand apart from their deferential colleagues find themselves actively undermined by the executive, strengthening the latter's rule.

In the 2024 general election campaign, the ECI was also noticeably flat-footed in pursuing allegations that the Modi and other BJP campaigners had

---

[2] The Model Code of Conduct, or MCC, is a voluntary set of principles promulgated by the ECI that guide the conduct of candidates, parties, and incumbent governments during election time (Bhat 2021). The BJP narrowly won the 2017 Gujarat elections, although one cannot make a causal connection between the welfare schemes and their victory.

openly flouted the MCC, especially its provisions prohibiting divisive speech. After one notable campaign speech in which Modi used inflammatory language castigating Muslims, the ECI eventually sent a show cause notice to the BJP party president, but without naming Modi personally (Chakrabarty 2024).

2.2.3 Accountability Institutions

This section considers the fate of three accountability institutions, two relatively recent creations – the Lokpal and the Central Information Commission (CIC) – and the much older Central Bureau of Investigation (CBI). The varied ages of these institutions shed light on how the Modi government approaches three types of bureaucracies: one it created (Lokpal), another that was young when the BJP rose to power (CIC), and a third (CBI) that has been around for decades. While the party has largely neglected the Lokpal and CIC, the CBI continues to be a venue for political interference.[3]

2.2.3.1 *Lokpal*

In 2011, India was rocked by powerful street protests provoked by a series of high-profile corruption scandals facing the incumbent, Congress-led United Progressive Alliance (UPA) government. Those protests spawned a nationwide anti-corruption movement that lobbied for a federal "Lokpal" or anti-corruption ombudsman to ensure timely and fair investigation and prosecution of public corruption cases. The agitation successfully pressured Parliament into legislating the new position (Johri, Bhardwaj, and Singh 2014) and fueled the BJP's rise to power in 2014 on a platform of anti-corruption, clean governance, and inclusive development.

Ironically, having profited from the Lokpal agitation, the BJP steadfastly marginalized the new ombudsman. Indeed, it took the government more than five years to set up a committee to name a chairperson and subordinate members of the Lokpal (Bhatnagar 2018). It only deigned to do so in March 2019 after the Supreme Court entertained a contempt petition challenging its deliberate inaction. Once the government-sponsored committee selected the Lokpal's inaugural leadership, the government again threw sand in the gears by slow-walking the formalization of the rules and regulations governing the Lokpal's operations. These rules were finally promulgated in March 2020 (*Scroll.in* 2020).

The story of the Lokpal is one of calculated neglect – intended to deactivate a potential check on executive power (Johri and Bhardwaj 2020). The ruling party campaigned in favor of the Lokpal when it was in the opposition and the ombudsman's attentions would be trained on its rivals; it has been less passionate since coming to power and is considered an object of the watchdog's vigilance.

---

[3] For an aligned account of the weakening of "fourth branch" institutions in India, see Khaitan (2020).

2.2.3.2   *Central Information Commission (CIC)*

Another tale of neglect lies with the CIC. In 2005, the Congress-led UPA government passed comprehensive legislation to improve government transparency. Under the Right to Information (RTI) Act, public servants are financially penalized if they do not respond promptly or adequately to citizen requests for information about government operations. The CIC acts as the ultimate appellate authority in RTI cases (Jha 2020).

The Modi government has purposefully undermined the CIC by neglecting to fill key vacancies. As of July 2023, more than 20,000 cases were pending before the CIC, which struggled to resolve the backlog as its leadership ranks thinned. At the time of this assessment, only four commissioners (out of eleven) were in place, with the remaining posts (including that of the agency's chief) lying vacant (Satark Nagrik Sangathan 2024). The government has consistently dawdled on making new appointments to fill vacancies as information commissioners retired. As Bhardwaj (2020) points out, "not a single information commissioner has been appointed in the CIC since May 2014 without the intervention of the courts."

The executive has also interfered in the operations of the CIC. In July 2019, Parliament amended the RTI Act to grant the central government power to decide matters of tenure, salary, and allowances for information commissioners. This move was problematic for at least two reasons (Aiyar 2019). First, the amendment undermines the status of the commissioners, who previously enjoyed a fixed, five-year term and a salary tied to that of election commissioners. Second, the executive indirectly granted itself power to interfere in the operations of the commission by claiming the authority to set the terms of members' appointment and removal, a not-so-subtle message encouraging independent-minded commissioners to stay onside.

2.2.3.3   *Central Bureau of Investigation (CBI)*

The government's actions with regard to the CBI, India's analogue to the United States' Federal Bureau of Investigation, shows it is not only culpable of sins of omission, but has also actively interfered with the function of accountability institutions.

There is a backstory worth recalling here, however; every central government – regardless of partisan affiliation – has sought to undermine the credibility and independence of the CBI. Indeed, successive governments used the CBI as a carrot or stick to keep allies in line and enemies on the backfoot (Wasan 2024). Thus, the CBI has often been called "the handmaiden of the sitting government," or in the more colorful language of the Supreme Court, "a caged parrot." It is with good reason that the CBI used to be colloquially known as the "Congress Bureau of Investigation"; multiple Congress prime ministers wielded the agency as a political cudgel (Srivastava 2013).

Though the BJP pledged to abstain from such machinations, it doubled down on them once in power. The most stunning example of interference took place in October 2018 when the government authorized a midnight raid of the CBI's headquarters. That endeavor ended with the abrupt ousting of the CBI chief Alok Verma (Venkataramakrishnan 2018).

The Modi government deflected resulting negative press by claiming it acted at the behest of the Central Vigilance Commission (CVC), a federal agency that oversees the CBI. This explanation did not pacify critics, who argued that the CVC's powers are limited to investigative, as opposed to administrative, issues, rendering the CVC an implausible scapegoat. To compound matters, Verma was entitled to a protected tenure of two years (which had not been completed) (Yamunan 2018).

A similar story could be told about the Enforcement Directorate (ED), a central agency established to investigate and prosecute economic crimes, such as money laundering. Previous governments have relied on the ED's powers to pressure opposition politicians through the selective filing (or withdrawal) of corruption charges, but the BJP government has doubled down on this strategy. Between 2014 and 2022, there was a fourfold increase in ED cases lodged against politicians – 95 percent of whom belonged to opposition parties (Tiwary 2022).

2.3 UNPACKING INSTITUTIONAL ABDICATION

Section 2.2 paints an unflattering picture of referee institutions under the Modi government. In certain cases, as with the ECI, the agency seems to have almost willingly ceded ground to the executive through inaction or deference. In other cases, the executive has pursued policies of explicit interference or neglect to undermine the autonomy and performance of the institution.

The preceding analysis suggests two difficult puzzles. First, why have some institutions willingly abdicated their responsibilities? Second, is the current era of institutional weakening distinct from the Congress era?

2.3.1 What Explains Institutional Abdication?

Of the three mechanisms at work – deference, interference, and neglect – the first is the hardest to explain. In many troubled democracies, the executive branch uses its authorities to alter appointment powers, rewrite the constitutional mandate of referee institutions, or simply terminate meddlesome institutions. In India, however, many institutions have ceded ground without formal changes to their powers. Why?

While answers to this question are necessarily speculative, there is suggestive evidence for at least four explanations. First, leaders of referee institutions might be ideologically aligned with the ruling party and thus see no reason to oppose potentially majoritarian, illiberal, or antidemocratic policy measures since they work in their preferred party's favor. Indeed, there is evidence for Supreme Court justices allowing ideological considerations to shape their jurisprudence (Vakil 2022). For instance, former CJI Tarun Gogoi enthusiastically sided with the ruling party's desire to hastily implement a National Register of Citizens (NRC) in the northeastern state of Assam, Gogoi's home state. The NRC was intended to distinguish between rightful citizens of India and undocumented immigrants predominantly from neighboring Bangladesh. Gogoi drove the NRC process in "messianic" fashion even prior to becoming CJI (Bhatia 2023), betraying deep sympathy for an expeditious NRC and inserting the Court into a highly consequential *administrative* process with explosive political ramifications. Perhaps as a sign of his ideological alignment with the ruling party, the BJP nominated Gogoi as a Member of Parliament in India's upper house after his retirement (Chhibber 2020).

Second, senior officials might have careerist incentives not to cross a powerful executive. For instance, government officials in India face a mandatory retirement age of sixty-five. This requirement forces officials facing the end of their government careers to look for postretirement work. The practice has led some scholars to speak of a "sinecure state," in which pliant bureaucrats and officials are gifted comfortable postretirement posts in exchange for policy or regulatory forbearance (Dubash 2017). Indeed, Aney, Dam, and Ko (2021) uncovered systematic evidence that Supreme Court decisions in India are directly affected by judges' career concerns. Judges who decide cases in favor of the incumbent government are more likely to be appointed to postretirement jobs in the public sector.

A third possibility is that officials worry about executive branch retribution. In the Lavasa case, the former election commissioner became the subject of investigative scrutiny as soon as he publicly expressed a willingness to sanction Modi and other top BJP leaders. The example of Justice Akil Kureshi, who developed a reputation for fierce independence while serving on the Gujarat High Court, is also instructive. He ruled against the desires of the BJP government several times when Modi was the state's chief minister. When the *collegium* recommended Kureshi be appointed to the Madhya Pradesh High Court, the BJP central government objected. After considerable delay, the *collegium* instead named him to the Tripura High Court, a less prestigious post. Kureshi was also never elevated to the Supreme Court, a decision some have interpreted as retribution (Tripathi 2022).

Fourth, officials associated with referee institutions might be reluctant to be perceived as opposing a popular government. For instance, although there is robust debate about the mechanisms of transmission, some scholars have found that public opinion has a direct causal impact on US Supreme Court decisions (see Casillas, Enns, and Wohlfarth 2011). It is plausible that public opinion could have a similar effect on India's apex Court.

2.3.2 Mean Reversion?

A second vexed question is whether the current weakening of checks and balances under the BJP is fundamentally different from the machinations of the Congress era. Indeed, under the Congress, many referee institutions ceded ground to a dominant, popular executive. For instance, the president has often been seen as an important bridge-builder and figure of national unity. But, just hours after a meeting with Prime Minister Indira Gandhi in 1975, President Fakhruddin Ali Ahmed famously issued a proclamation declaring a national emergency that allowed the prime minister to rule by decree, suppress political opposition, and muzzle the media. Similarly, the Supreme Court also legitimized many of Gandhi's antidemocratic maneuvers by upholding the constitutionality of draconian internal security laws, the politically motivated dissolution of state governments, and limits to habeas corpus (Bhuwania 2017).

Indeed, India has often struggled to live up to the liberal values embedded in its constitution. Time-series data from virtually all democracy league tables indicate that India's commitment to electoral democracy far exceeds its adherence to liberal principles. This does not mean that the era of Congress dominance and the present period of BJP hegemony are equivalent. While the similarities are striking, there is one significant difference: the BJP's Hindu nationalist vision for India, or what Khosla and Vaishnav (2021) have called the "ethnic state."

Taken together, the unwillingness of the ECI to punish candidates who flout hate speech regulations, the Supreme Court's dithering on the Modi government's decision to alter Jammu and Kashmir's status, and the weaponization of investigative agencies against dissidents who criticize *Hindutva* bolster the ideological hegemony of Hindu nationalism. While the weakening of referee institutions today may mirror the process of institutional decay that took place during the era of Congress hegemony, the ideological component of today's processes creates unique conditions for their operation (Mehta 2022).

Therefore, the blatant misuse of, or disregard for, institutions in the current era is not simply about political opportunism and the narrow pursuit of power; rather, it is intimately related to the ideological worldview of the ruling party.

2.4 CONCLUSION

In the presence of a new political hegemon, India's referee institutions have been largely tamed by a powerful executive. Whether through deference, interference, or neglect, the credibility of these institutions stands diminished. Referee institutions, which performed admirably under fragmented power and coalition governance, have faltered with the return of single-party dominance.

In the wake of India's 2024 general election, the BJP emerged as the single largest party in parliament though it failed to win a majority of seats. Thus, for the first time since the party's ascendance under Modi, the BJP was forced to rely on coalition allies to form the government. The electoral weakening of the BJP has led some to argue that the BJP's era of dominance has come to an end, marking a potential period of institutional regeneration. But this hypothesis is premised on the as-yet-untested assumption that the BJP's political allies will significantly constrain its behavior in office. The first few months of the new government's tenure suggest that the BJP's coalition partners are more interested in steering public funds and foreign investment dollars to their states than standing up for liberal principles or advancing institutional renewal.

However, referee institutions are far from the only actor that could halt, slow down, or reverse democratic backsliding. Other backstops do exist – the media, civil society, political opposition, and foreign pressure. Yet, the available evidence suggests that all four actors suffer from infirmities that limit their ability to act as an effective check.

The media, ostensibly dedicated to holding government accountable, faces deep structural and regime-specific challenges (Ninan 2019, 2023). In structural terms, mainstream media in India is deeply beholden to the government; the regime can wield its power as a principal ad buyer to keep the media in check. The government also exerts multiple regulatory levers to shape a private firm's media behavior, resulting in increased self-censorship and, occasionally, actual censorship (Dev 2018).[4]

Civil society in India, more generally, works under severe constraints. Through the selective application of the Foreign Contribution Regulation Act (FCRA), the government can deny organizations foreign funding – an important source of income. These restrictions have squeezed civil society coffers.[5] Another hindrance to civil society is the absence of an absolute right to free speech in India. Individual speech is subject to a wide range of "reasonable restrictions," which allows the ruling party to use defamation or sedition charges to curb inconvenient speech (Singh 2020). This power is not new to the Modi government but has been applied with greater alacrity than in the past (Purohit 2021).

Furthermore, not all civil society actors are concerned with restraining the ruling incumbent's power, as Weiss and Hicken's chapter (Chapter 3) in this volume makes clear in the case of Southeast Asia. Greskovits (Chapter 8, this

---

[4] Beyond the world of advertising, the media also faces real challenges in its day-to-day job or reporting and newsgathering. The Modi government is skeptical about the intentions and biases of mainstream media. As a result, it has pursued a communications strategy that largely eschews it: the Prime Minister's Office has no media advisor; the prime minister has yet to address a single press conference; and the prime minister travels only with official (state-run) media on overseas visits.

[5] An amendment to the FCRA law, passed in 2020, further tightened restrictions on civil society organizations' ability to receive foreign funding. See Robinson (2024).

volume), too, highlights the way in which right-wing civil society in Hungary helped pave the way for Viktor Orban's transformation from opposition figure to entrenched incumbent. In India today, the country's most influential civil society actors are part of the BJP's ideological coalition; they represent the more than three dozen affiliate organizations of the BJP known as the "Sangh Parivar," or family of Hindu nationalist-oriented organizations. The potency of the BJP's hegemony is buttressed not simply by its dominance of state institutions but also by its ability to direct and influence raw "people" power.

Another potential guardrail is the political opposition. The BJP's principal national rival, the Congress Party, suffers from deficits of leadership, ideological vision, and organizational capacity. In the 2024 general election, the Congress experienced a revival, nearly doubling its parliamentary seat tally. The principal opposition party's reversal of fortune was inextricably linked to its willingness to stitch together a pan-Indian grand opposition coalition comprising dozens of smaller opposition parties known as the Indian National Developmental Inclusive Alliance (INDIA). Nevertheless, it remains too early to say whether the opposition can overcome regional divisions, differences over leadership, and ideological disputes to act collectively over the long term.

A final guardrail worth considering is foreign pressure. As a large democracy with a history of resisting foreign meddling, India has rarely proved vulnerable to international pressure. But efficacy questions aside, it is unclear whether foreign countries would press India on issues of democracy and rights given the foreign policy, economic, and security dimensions of their relationships with India.

For many of India's diplomatic partners in the West, the calculation to accommodate Modi is grounded in realpolitik. Led by the United States, the West has made significant bets on India: that it presents the only viable challenger to China in the Asia–Pacific; that its economy represents the consumer market of the future; that bilateral trade and investment ties are lucrative and enduring; and that, as a democracy, it will pursue policies largely in sync with Western democracies (Blackwill and Tellis 2019).

India's domestic churn may represent a new set of irritants but, given the larger stakes surrounding the "India bet," a move to punish India (as was the case after India's controversial 1998 nuclear tests) is highly unlikely (Markey 2023). Furthermore, given ongoing crises in Ukraine, Israel/Palestine, and elsewhere, not to mention their own domestic politics, Western powers are also likely to be consumed by other matters for the foreseeable future.

REFERENCES

Ahuja, Amit, and Susan L. Ostermann. 2018. "From Quiescent Bureaucracy to 'Undocumented Wonder': Explaining the Indian Election Commission's Expanding Mandate." *Governance* 31, no. 4: 1–18.

Aiyar, Yamini. 2019. "Why the RTI Amendments Must Be Opposed." *Hindustan Times.* July 26.

Aney, Madhav S., Shubhankar Dam, and Giovanni Ko. 2021. "Jobs for Justice(s): Corruption in the Supreme Court of India." *The Journal of Law and Economics* 64, no. 3: 479–511.

Bhardwaj, Anjali. 2020. "The War on Information." *India Today.* January 31.

Bhat, M. Mohsin Alam. 2021. "Governing Democracy outside the Law: India's Election Commission and the Challenge of Accountability." *Asian Journal of Comparative Law* 16: S85–S104.

Bhatia, Gautam. 2018. "Master and the Roster." *Indian Express.* January 15.

Bhatia, Gautam. 2019. "The Absentee Constitutional Court." *Hindu.* September 12.

Bhatia, Gautam. 2023. *Unsealed Covers: A Decade of the Constitution, the Courts, and the State.* New Delhi: HarperCollins, 402–416.

Bhatnagar, Gaurav Vivek. 2018. "In RTI Replies, Evidence of How Modi Dragged His Feet on Lokpal Appointment." *The Wire.* December 21. https://tinyurl.com/yekp2bx3.

Bhuwania, Anuj. 2017. "P. N. Bhagwati's Legacy: A Controversial Inheritance." *Hindu.* June 27.

Blackwill, Robert D., and Ashley J. Tellis. 2019. "The India Dividend: New Delhi Remains Washington's Best Hope in Asia." *Foreign Affairs* (September/October): 173–83.

Casillas, Christopher J., Peter K. Enns, and Patrick C. Wohlfarth. 2011. "How Public Opinion Constrains the US Supreme Court." *American Journal of Political Science* 55, no. 1: 74–88.

Chakrabarty, Sreeparna. 2024. "Election Commission Sends Notice to BJP Chief Nadda for Complaints against PM Modi." *Hindu.* April 26.

Chhibber, Maneesh. 2020. "The Reasons Former CJI Ranjan Gogoi Will Give for Accepting Rajya Sabha Nomination." *The Print.* March 18. https://tinyurl.com/3jt9ud9a.

Chopra, Ritika. 2019a. "Election Commissioner Lavasa Opposed Five Clean Chits to Amit Shah, PM Modi." *Indian Express.* May 5.

Chopra, Ritika. 2019b. "Sought Prompt Action after Supreme Court Frowned on Delays: Ashok Lavasa." *Indian Express.* May 21.

Dev, Atul. 2018. "Same Old News," *Caravan.* December 1. https://tinyurl.com/mr2wtuy6.

Dubash, Navroz K. 2017. "New Regulatory Institutions in Infrastructure: From De-Politicization to Creative Politics." In Devesh Kapur, Pratap Bhanu Mehta, and Milan Vaishnav, eds. *Rethinking Public Institutions in India.* New Delhi: Oxford University Press, pp. 225–68.

Financial Express. 2018. "Electoral Bonds: Election Commission Changes Stance, from Retrograde Move to Step towards Right Direction." January 19.

Guha, Ramachandra. 2015. "There's More to Democracy than Holding Elections," *Hindustan Times*, December 6.

Jammu and Kashmir Coalition of Civil Society & Association of Parents of Disappeared Persons. 2020. *Annual Review of Human Rights Situation in Indian Administered Jammu and Kashmir.* Srinagar: Jammu Kashmir Coalition of Civil Society & Association of Parents of Disappeared Persons. https://tinyurl.com/ynanu9kf.

Jha, Himanshu. 2020. *Capturing Institutional Change: The Case of the Right to Information Act in India.* New Delhi: Oxford University Press.

Johri, Amrita, and Anjali Bhardwaj. 2020. "Six Years On, Lokpal Is a Non-Starter." *Hindu.* February 12.

Johri, Amrita, Anjali Bhardwaj, and Shekhar Singh. 2014. "The Lokpal Act of 2014: An Assessment." *Economic and Political Weekly* 49, no. 5: 10–13.

Kapur, Devesh. 2007. "Explaining Democratic Durability and Economic Performance: The Role of India's Institutions." In Devesh Kapur and Pratap Bhanu Mehta, eds. *Public Institutions in India: Performance and Design.* New Delhi: Oxford University Press, pp. 28–76.

Khaitan, Tarunabh. 2020. "Killing a Constitution with a Thousand Cuts: Executive Aggrandizement and Party-State Fusion in India." *Law & Ethics of Human Rights* 14, no. 1: 49–95.

Khosla, Madhav, and Ananth Padmanabhan. 2017. "The Supreme Court and India's Judicial System." In Devesh Kapur, Pratap Bhanu Mehta, and Milan Vaishnav, eds. *Rethinking Public Institutions in India.* New Delhi: Oxford University Press, pp. 104–38.

Khosla, Madhav, and Milan Vaishnav. 2021. "The Three Faces of the Indian State." *Journal of Democracy* 31, no. 1: 111–25.

Kumar, Alok Prasanna. 2022. "Appointing High Court Judges—I." *Economic and Political Weekly* 57, no. 4: 10–11.

Kumar, Sanjay. 2022. "Election Commission's Partisan and Controversial Functioning." In M. G. Devasahayam, ed. *Electoral Democracy? An Inquiry into the Fairness and Integrity of Elections in India.* New Delhi: Paranjoy Guha Thakurta, pp. 148–72.

Markey, Daniel. 2023. "India As It Is: Washington and New Delhi Share Interests, Not Values." *Foreign Affairs* (July/August): 128–41.

Mehta, Pratap Bhanu. 2007. "India's Unlikely Democracy: The Rise of Judicial Sovereignty." *Journal of Democracy* 18, no. 2: 70–83.

Mehta, Pratap Bhanu. 2022. "Hindu Nationalism: From Ethnic Identity to Authoritarian Repression." *Studies in Indian Politics* 10, no. 1: 31–17.

Ninan, Sevanti. 2019. "How India's Media Landscape Changed over Five Years." *The India Forum.* June 6. www.theindiaforum.in/article/how-indias-media-landscape-changed-over-five-years.

Ninan, Sevanti. 2023. "Contours of Media Control in India." *The India Forum.* March 14. www.theindiaforum.in/society/contours-media-control-india.

Palshikar, Suhas. 2018. "Towards Hegemony: BJP beyond Electoral Dominance," *Economic and Political Weekly* 53, no. 33: 36–42.

Purohit, Kunal. 2021. "Our New Database Reveals Rise in Sedition Cases in The Modi Era." *Article 14.* February 2. https://tinyurl.com/mrxup5sz.

Robinson, Nick. 2016. "Judicial Architecture and Capacity." In Sujit Choudhry, Madhav Khosla, and Pratap Bhanu Mehta, eds. *The Oxford Handbook of the Indian Constitution.* New York: Oxford University Press, pp. 340–8.

Robinson, Nick. 2024. "The Regulation of Foreign Funding of Nonprofits in a Democracy." *Virginia Journal of International Law* 65, no. 1: 57–112.

Sarin, Ritu. 2019. "Check if EC Ashok Lavasa Used Influence during Power Stint: Govt to PSUs." *Indian Express.* November 5.

Satark Nagrik Sangathan. 2024. *Report Card of Information Commissions in India 2022–23*. New Delhi: Satark Nagrik Sangathan.

Scroll.in. 2020. "Entire Lokpal Bench to Decide on Complaints against Any Former or Current Prime Minister." March 4. https://tinyurl.com/yc82nanv.

Sethi, Nitin. 2019. "Electoral Bonds: Seeking Secretive Funds, Modi Govt Overruled RBI." *Huffington Post India.* November 18. https://tinyurl.com/3mxftcn2.

Shah, Ajit Prakash. 2019. "All Is Not Well in Court." *Indian Express.* February 12.

Singh, Tripurdaman. 2020. *Sixteen Stormy Days: The Story of the First Amendment of the Constitution of India*. New Delhi: Vintage.

Sircar, Neelanjan. 2021. "The Welfarist Prime Minister: Explaining the National-State Election Gap." *Economic and Political Weekly (Engage)* 56, no. 10: 1–11.

Siwach, Sukhbir, Ritika Chopra, Ritu Sarin, and Sandeep Singh. 2019. "Not Just Lavasa's Wife, His Sister and Son Too Are Under Tax Dept Scanner." *Indian Express.* September 25.

Sridharan, Eswaran, and Milan Vaishnav. 2017. "Election Commission of India." In Devesh Kapur, Pratap Bhanu Mehta, and Milan Vaishnav, eds. *Rethinking Public Institutions in India*. New Delhi: Oxford University Press, pp. 417–63.

Srivastava, Mihir. 2013. "The Congress Bureau of Investigation," *Open.* March 26.

Stepan, Alfred, Juan J. Linz, and Yogendra Yadav. 2011. *Crafting State-Nations: India and Other Multinational Democracies*. Baltimore: Johns Hopkins University.

Tiwary, Deeptiman. 2022. "Since 2014, 4-Fold Jump in ED Cases against Politicians; 95% Are from Opposition." *Indian Express.* September 21.

Tripathi, Ashish. 2022. "Justice Kureshi: An 'Upright Judge's' Journey Ends in HC." *Deccan Chronicle.* March 19.

Tushnet, Mark. 2021. *The New Fourth Branch: Institutions for Protecting Constitutional Democracy*. New York: Cambridge University Press.

V-Dem Institute. 2024. *Democracy Winning and Losing at the Ballot: Democracy Report 2024*. Gothenburg: V-Dem Institute.

Vaishnav, Milan. 2018. "India's Elite Institutions Are Facing a Credibility Crisis." *Mint.* February 20.

Vaishnav, Milan. 2024a. "Political Finance in India." In Sumit Ganguly and Eswaran Sridharan, eds. *The Oxford Handbook of Indian Politics*. Oxford: Oxford University Press, pp. 349–68.

Vaishnav, Milan. 2024b. "On Electoral Bonds, a Short-Lived Celebration." *Hindustan Times.* February 17.

Vaishnav, Milan, and Jamie Hintson. 2019. "The Dawn of India's Fourth Party System." Carnegie Endowment for International Peace. September 5. https://tinyurl.com/4x8txc6p.

Vaishnav, Milan, and Caroline Mallory. 2024. "The Resilience of India's Fourth Party System." Carnegie Endowment for International Peace. September 24. https://tinyurl.com/2d8ync52.

Vakil, Raeesa. 2022. "Representation and Legitimacy in the Supreme Court: Adjudicating Law and Religion in India." *Studies in Indian Politics* 10, no. 1: 48–61.

Varshney, Ashutosh. 2013. *Battles Half Won: India's Improbable Democracy*. New York: Penguin Random House.

Varshney, Ashutosh. 2022. "India's Democratic Longevity and Its Troubled Trajectory." In Scott Mainwaring and Tarek Masoud, eds. *Democracy in Hard Places*. New York: Oxford University Press, pp. 34–72.

Varshney, Ashutosh, and Connor Staggs. 2024. "Hindu Nationalism and the New Jim Crow." *Journal of Democracy* 35, no. 1: 5–18.

Venkataramakrishnan, Rohan. 2018. "Scroll Explainer: What You Need to Know about the Dramatic Midnight Action within the CBI." *Scroll.in*. October 24. https://tinyurl.com/yeyrx87m.

Wasan, Navneet R. 2024. "India's Central Bureau of Investigation and the National Investigation Agency." In Rudra Chaudhuri and Milan Vaishnav, eds. *Institutional Roots of India's Security Policy*. New Delhi: Oxford University Press, pp. 279–302.

Yadav, Yogendra. 1999. "Electoral Politics in the Time of Change: India's Third Electoral System, 1989–99." *Economic and Political Weekly* 34, no. 34/35: 2393–9.

Yamunan, Sruthisagar. 2018. "By Sending the CBI Director on Leave, the Centre Has Stretched the Law to Its Limits." *Scroll.in*. October 24. https://tinyurl.com/2s36ayvn.

3

The (De)Democratizing Tango: Why It's Hard to Get Democracy to Stick in Southeast Asia

Meredith L. Weiss and Allen Hicken

Long-time followers of Southeast Asia might be excused for feeling a bit of whiplash. The region seems locked endlessly in a boom-and-bust cycle of democratizing, then regressing, then democratizing again, then ... One gets the idea. It's not that the region lacks committed democrats. The vehemence of prodemocracy protests among students and youths, middle-class segments, sundry minorities, and other groups in Thailand, Myanmar, Indonesia, Malaysia, and elsewhere, who take to the streets at least every decade or so, makes clear that liberalizing sentiment has its constituents across the region. But the region also has its committed autocrats. These include members of armed forces, royalists, technocrats, supremacists of various stripes, different middle-class segments, and others who would be happy to retain or restore their preferred brand of illiberalism.

We suggest that this mix makes Southeast Asia an ideal, if perhaps less than inspiring, region in which to investigate the dynamics of democratization and its flip side, autocratization. Here, we seek to understand what works, or could work, for or against systemic political reform, understood as an ongoing dance toward some reasonably stable democratic equilibrium. Our examination considers three (interdependent) lenses. First, we look to a hard-to-please cast of dancers, the precise mix varying by country and time. We focus in particular on the military and its allies, interest-driven middle classes, and grievance-stoking and -addressing civil society – all of whom need to be convinced to stick to the democratic choreography. No one player is sufficient. For instance, while the stubborn persistence of coup-making makes Thailand an outlier, we should not let coups overshadow that fact that the military has partners and allies in its efforts to roll back liberalization. Second, we have institutional reforms, including for such critical objectives as party-strengthening. Some of these reforms may work as planned; others may backfire or present counterproductive externalities – for instance, if party system reform fosters polarization or exclusivity. And third, we have a range of tropes that frame the effort, from technocratic elitism as *the* fix for governance, to scrappy rights-protection, to single-minded populism. This analysis will not allow us to crack the puzzle of how to make democratization work, but it will at least offer insight into why careening seems so inescapable, by understanding democratization and autocratization as always sharing a stage.

Our review of the history of democracy and autocracy in Southeast Asia underscores this volume's core themes. First, Southeast Asia reminds us that support for democracy is always contingent. We show how readily factors such as political polarization and the failure of democracy to deliver on its promises can produce receptive audiences, if not full-on partners, for aspiring autocrats. Second, we explore the ways in which institutions can keep autocratic sympathizers in the wings or on the dancefloor itself, and how institutional reforms, particularly those that seek greater political openness and broader empowerment, can, under some circumstances, stoke political divisions and provide fodder for these reactionary forces. Importantly, we suggest, formal liberalization may elevate antidemocratic impulses, in ways we (scholars, democracy promoters, policymakers) *should* by now anticipate. Finally, we note how seldom prodemocracy forces, even when present and active, command center stage – though when they do, their influence can be powerful.

In short, our brief foray into Southeast Asian experience aims to offer insight into what conditions or factors might help democrats maintain and expand access to political space and voice, without imperiling the very institutional forms and ideological convictions that make such opening possible. We focus first on key actors and their interests, and then turn to the role of political institutions.

3.1 ACTORS AND THEIR INTERESTS

As we know from experience across Southeast Asia, the fact of a change of government through elections or otherwise tells us fairly little about which social forces win or lose, or how extensively governance changes. Regular elections can, of course, open up the possibility of real accountability, but it is also not uncommon for elections consistently to return the same set of political elites, albeit sometimes in different configurations and sporting shiny new party/coalition labels. Likewise, nominal transitions to democracy may amount to little more than a new coat of paint on an aging edifice if underlying political patterns do not fundamentally change. As long as major actors fail to view democracy as the "only game in town" (Linz and Stepan 1996), democratic norms or institutions are at risk of remaining ephemeral window dressing.

In part, understanding how democracy develops and (dis)functions in post-transitional states requires attention to the extent to which authoritarian legacies segment, channel, or otherwise shape institutions and societies in ways encouraging of or antithetical to penetrating political liberalization. The issue is not only what sorts of authoritarian regimes are stable or brittle (e.g., Geddes 1999), but a more fine-grained examination of how well those prior regimes equip citizens to push the envelope once they have the chance, what expectations citizens have of institutional functioning, and what leaders are likely to emerge. In both Indonesia and Myanmar, for instance, we see old-guard figures' finding advantage in conforming to new rules of the game, and at least for a time, allowing continued predation by other means (Aspinall 2010; Hadiz 2003). Also in Indonesia, in contrast to less aggressively disabling Malaysia, the Suharto regime's program of atomizing potentially worrisome challengers left civil society at a disadvantage in regrouping for a new democratic era (Weiss 2007), and poorly equipped to defend democracy in the face of new threats (Mietzner 2021). A reading of democratic "transition" and "consolidation" focused even largely on elections and who wins them misses much of what is crucial in analyzing the health of and prognosis for democracy in Indonesia.

The issue is not simply whether "democratic values" must precede or might follow "democratic transition." Rather, the question is what needs to happen in state and society for democracy to work – cultivating interpersonal trust and social capital, yes; but also perhaps inculcating attention to the greater good (presuming communitarian norms are not actually innate to Asians any more than to others; Chua 1995); understanding the array of ways one might participate politically; and ensuring that the most likely spoilers (military, bureaucrats, monarchists) have found niches in which to survive and thrive within a liberal democratic framework. Opening and actively promoting political space, from making it easy for advocacy-oriented, identity-based, and other civil society organizations (CSOs) to form and operate; to relaxing residual controls on speech, press, and association; to taking conscious steps to retrain and remove from everyday sight the security forces perhaps previously involved in enforcing authoritarian rule – all these measures may encourage democratization . . . but may also jostle authoritarians and their allies into (re)action.

In other words, while democratic transitions can bring new dancers onto the floor, they often compete alongside rather than displace existing actors. Thus, the gamut of actors post-transition incline toward different directions. Rather than simply skulk away when they lose a battle, all are likely to regroup for the continuing campaign. The question, then, is not whether autocratic incumbents and their supporters continue in some form. We know that autocrats and their parties or other vehicles often remain active after a democratic transition, which they may even engineer themselves (Riedl 2014; Loxton 2015; Slater and Wong 2022). The question is, rather, whether or not they at least conditionally, if not unreservedly, adapt their strategies and tactics to a democratic framework or whether they retain ambitions to return to the prior authoritarian status quo and maintain illiberal weapons in their arsenal.

In addition, dividing democracy-supporting from democracy-opposing actors is not always a straightforward exercise. Most groups – even purported liberal champions – are contingent democrats. They support democratic reform under many circumstances, and may be even willing to sacrifice marginally for it, but when their core interests are threatened, they are willing to sacrifice democracy to defend them, clearing a path for would-be autocrats (Svolik 2019). We illustrate with examples from three groups: the military, the middle class, and civil society.

3.1.1 The Military and Its Allies

In several states in Southeast Asia (Myanmar, Thailand, Indonesia, the Philippines), the armed forces represent an especially important, if not *the* most important, player when it comes to leading, spoiling, or going along with regime change. Officers may adapt to play (and win) by democratic rules, but cannot readily be coerced to do so, and they retain the capacity to flip if they see themselves better served, especially in a corporate sense, by playing a different game. Or they may stand pat with, or take the lead in expanding, authoritarianism. However, just as nonmilitary democrats need allies, so do military autocrats. Among these allies could well be monarchs and monarchists (as in Thailand), Islamists or other religiously identified forces (as in Indonesia), technocratic bureaucrats who value efficient management over procedural niceties (as in Singapore), and/or economic elites disinclined toward labor/land rights, redistribution, or other concessions (as in various states).

Thailand offers one example. The country receives justifiable attention for its propensity for coup-making. While the comparative literature reveals that military coups have become increasingly rare globally since the end of the Cold War, Thailand has stubbornly averaged a coup every decade since 1990. Overlooked, however, are the ways in which Thailand's conservative forces (military, bureaucracy, monarchy) have used institutional reforms to secure and defend their interests during and in between periods of military rule. Indeed, in the wake of military–civilian clashes in 1992, the discredited Thai military retreated to the barracks, seemingly content to remain in the background while counting on their capacity to advance and defend the interests of the conservative elite via democratic channels. The pledge to stay on the sidelines was not a front – the military passed up tempting opportunities to intervene in politics during periods of instability – but it was contingent. As the landscape of democratic politics changed, and conservative forces found themselves at a systematic disadvantage and under increasing threat, they reevaluated their support for democracy, culminating in a coup in 2006. These forces have since attempted to undermine the threat from democratic challengers and circumscribe the influence of elected officials via institutional reform (more on this in Section 3.2).

Events in Myanmar are also illustrative. In 2003, General Khin Nyut announced a seven-step "Roadmap to Democracy" that included convening a National Convention to write a new constitution and holding free and fair elections for a national legislature. By liberalizing the junta, his administration hoped to generate new economic opportunities and undermine opposition to the regime both at home and abroad. Recognizing that democratization entailed risks, the junta designed a constitution with a number of reserve domains to protect its interests and preserve its influence. These reserve domains offered sufficient protection that the junta agreed to abide by the results of the 2015 election, even though its party lost in a landslide to the democratic opposition. The 2020 election largely reproduced the results of 2015, yet this time the junta responded with allegations of election fraud, and, ultimately, a military coup.

Why the change of heart? For the junta, support for democratic institutions was always contingent on its ability to continue to advance and protect its core interests. Two factors between 2015 and 2020 caused the military to reevaluate, Megan Ryan and Darin Self (2021) explain. Most importantly, after the results of the 2020 election, it was clear that the military's party was not electorally viable, and thus could not serve as an effective advocate of military interests within the legislature.[1] In addition, over the course of those five years, the elected government Aung San Suu Kyi led revealed that it held different preferences from the military, and that it was willing to use its power to push for those priorities over military objections (culminating in rejecting military claims of electoral fraud). Faced with this new reality, the junta calculated that the costs of seizing power were less than the risks of tolerating the democratically elected government.

3.1.2 The Motley Middle Classes

Classic theories of democratization – most obviously "modernization theory" – posit a link (causal or correlational) between the cultivation of a middle class via socioeconomic development and support for political liberalization. It is not the structural position of the middle classes per se that one might expect to drive their preference, but their interests. And yet in reality, where middle classes may be dependent on the state (Gainsborough 2002), might be outnumbered and thus outvoted in a democratic system, or might otherwise see value in authoritarianism, the bourgeoisie need not always support democracy. As the chapters in this volume show, a variety of factors, from cultural conflicts to representational failures, can undermine middle-class enthusiasm for democracy and/or democratic deepening.

Several cases in Southeast Asia underscore that middle-class support for democracy is, again, at best contingent. These citizens like democracy, as long as they are on the winning side and their interests are respected and protected.

---

[1] On the importance of strong military-linked parties for democratic transition, see Self 2022.

However, if some other regime type appears better able to deliver on their interests, including their preferences for goods like stability and good governance, they are willing to jump ship. In Thailand, for instance, middle-class and wealthy voters have been a core part of groups calling for the military to intervene and for abrogation or suspension of democracy. Middle-class and wealthy voters were also among the strongest supporters of Duterte in the Philippines and have been an important part of Prabowo's coalition in Indonesia. In Malaysia, the structuring of economic rewards along ethnic lines has made these patterns especially obvious – not surprisingly, a substantial share of Malay Malaysians (or more broadly, *Bumiputera*, inclusive of other Indigenous groups) reliably back parties and leaders focused on their group interests, not on "progressive" values. Nor has middle-class growth in the remaining formally communist states of the region (Vietnam especially, but also less prosperous Laos) corresponded with political opening, reflecting, among other factors, the fact that many citizens have prospered under communist party governance (and in many cases, owe their employment to the state).

We can home in on the Thai case to see this dimension more clearly: Thai experience challenges the notion that good governance and performance necessarily bolster democratic stability, particularly among the middle classes. By most objective standards, Thailand's pre 2014 coup democratic government performed well. Thailand registered impressive rates of economic growth as it recovered from the Asian Financial Crisis of 1997–98, and the state provided unprecedented levels of public goods. Allegations of corruption certainly accompanied that progress – but these were not unusual in the Thai context (nor, indeed, in many other democracies). And yet, huge numbers of Thais took to the streets, especially in 2006–14, demanding the ousting of several elected governments and calling for the military to intervene. The military did so in 2006, and again, definitively, in 2014, granting their wish.

The collapse of democracy in Thailand reminds us that while good economic and policy performance may increase prospects for democratic stability, government performance is not the only salient issue for citizens. Also, citizens' assessments of performance in the first place are at least partially a function of their partisanship – and those affiliations reflect a range of other interest and identity factors. In this case, Thaksin Shinawatra (and his sister and other successors) pitched their appeals less at the urban middle classes than at the poorer, but more numerous voters in the north and northeast. Although Thailand as a whole prospered, most voters weigh their options less per a national aggregate than in terms of their own opportunity costs and alternatives.

3.1.3 Civil Society

The positive, verging on necessary, role of civil society in democratization and democratic functioning hardly bears repeating. In Southeast Asia specifically, apart from movements for expressive identity or recognition goals, we find manifold movements for instrumental objectives at the core of democratic praxis: against corruption, for civil liberties and social justice, and so forth. And yet we also find movements that either advocate for goals more exclusive than a "democratic" premise might allow, or are fundamentally illiberal – for instance, for clearly exclusive identity-based interests. CSOs may elevate and amplify issue-based appeals, and help inculcate new political norms, as a means of fracturing the image or reality of monolithic identity-based voter-segments – or they may well entrench that way of slicing and dicing the voting public (viz., Weiss 2006 on Malaysia, or Tomsa and Setijadi 2018 on Indonesia). Needing votes, parties can be expected to support whatever appeal woos voters best, even if potentially antithetical to core democratic values. So, rather than eschew attempts by some CSOs to define voters' interests and alignments in narrow, exclusivist terms – since not all CSOs prioritize inclusivity – parties may embrace such appeals as part of their mobilization strategy.

Even movements that seem, on face, constructive, may not have the positive impact on democracy one might hope for or anticipate. For one thing, a focus on the democratic shortcomings of the status quo (e.g., anti-corruption movements) may heighten sentiments that democracy has failed and is beyond repair. Moreover, a new democratic regime does not necessarily mean more space or greater voice for civil society. Democratic governments may continue to operate absent meaningful input from civil society, or co-opt and embrace only contained, unthreateningly incorporated participation (Lorch 2017; Rodan 2018). In consequence, however commonly (and largely unquestioningly) lauded as harbinger of and impetus to democratization, civil society is actually more ambiguous an actor (Weiss and Hansson 2023). Hence, although a strong, active civil society is good for democracy (Bernhard et al. 2020), decades of regular, large-scale mass mobilization by civil societal actors in places like Thailand, Indonesia, and Malaysia has emboldened or provoked would-be authoritarians as often as not.

Here we might turn to Malaysia as an example. When Malaysia's Barisan Nasional (BN) government lost power in 2018 for the first time since elections began there in the 1950s, civil society took no small part of the credit. Amplified by structural changes to the public sphere – not least the proliferation and extension of online news and social media – social movements had pressed cases for electoral probity, civil liberties, anti-corruption, more sustainable and equitable development, and more for decades. Allying strategically with opposition parties, particularly since the late 1990s, these efforts finally forced a breakthrough: the optimistic, upstart Pakatan Harapan coalition took control of the federal government. The transition failed to thrive, however: Reforms proved slow in coming, then two parties fractured, legislators jumped ship, and Pakatan's government capsized less than two years later, in late February 2020. Liberal democracy had not yet had a chance to consolidate by that point; plans for electoral-system, judicial, parliamentary, and other reforms to liberalize Malaysia's electoral-authoritarian politics remained on the drawing board. An especially fragile new coalition, inclusive of what remained of the BN, came to power in early March, tethered by a common interest in holding just enough parliamentary seats to claim a majority, rather than by a coherent common platform. That coalition, too, crumbled, then recoalesced under new management – quite a change from the staunch seeming-permanence of BN rule for Malaysia's first six decades … yet hardly indicative of a compellingly "democratic" turn. And indeed, the BN came back again after elections in November 2022, now in counterintuitive partnership with Pakatan.

We might credit civil society, at least in significant part, for the initial government turnover: A legacy of advocacy and protest campaigns across broad swathes of society served to solidify a coalition around a unifying, distinct platform. The obvious question, given that history, is why the liberalizing effects of those efforts proved so ephemeral in practice. Why did this transition not "catch" in terms of substantial, substantive changes before the alliances activism had forged fractured? An equally important question is what role less "progressive" parts of civil society played: To what extent can they take credit for Malaysia's retreat from liberalizing reforms – since the democratizing zeal of 2018 has remained in abeyance, against a backdrop of right-wing efflorescence?

As Malaysian experience makes clear, alongside that of post-transition Myanmar and Indonesia, or ever-transitional Thailand, "civil society" is not inherently or even necessarily disproportionately "progressive" – and elected politicians' pressing need to woo support may make chauvinist groups a tempting vote-bank. Some of those groups or activists to whom parties and politicians turn for support might well deny broad inclusivity, might champion policies in line with a contested normative vision, or might simply advocate policies that advantage their side in a zero-sum contest.

We might then consider the implications of formal liberalization for civil society – a category in which we include essentially the gamut of nonparty, nonstate, nonbusiness organizations, regardless of structural features or orientation. A successful (or less than successful) transition *might* validate and elevate civil society (or more likely, some portion thereof), especially in the case of a bottom-up process in which nonstate, nonparty actors played significant roles. Just as likely, though, are patterns more of exclusion, transformation, or selective (and perhaps nonprogressive) elevation of CSOs. Understanding the rise or decline, elevation or suppression, broadening or narrowing of civil society is obviously not the only lens through which to analyze post-transition politics, but it is an especially revealing, wide-ranging, and salient lens.

Greg Fealy's inquiry into what he terms "repressive pluralism" under Indonesia's supposed-to-be reformist president from 2014 to 2024, Joko Widodo (aka Jokowi), offers a case in point. As Fealy (2020) explains, Jokowi's administration had "been conducting a concerted and systematic campaign of repression against Islamists" – arguably the best-organized and most-engaged segment in Indonesian civil society. Yet especially vulnerable now are not terrorism-inclined "extremists," but supporters of the Prosperous Justice Party (PKS) and associated organizations, which draw inspiration from the Muslim Brotherhood and other extra-regional, transnational movements. Jokowi may have seen these Islamists as threatening to norms of pluralistic inclusion and tolerance – and indeed, Islamist grandstanding has taken illiberal forms in Indonesia in recent years. But as Fealy clarifies, in reality, "it is hard to make the case that Islamism is imperiling Indonesia's political system," whereas "cracking down on Islamism in fact squeezes civil space and makes Indonesia less democratic."

Other governments, consolidating post-transition or otherwise, might not target any one sector or interest in this way. Singapore's ruling People's Action Party (PAP) leaders, for instance, have sought to channel the full array of "political" challenges into parties, where skewed rules and institutional resources confer a decided PAP advantage, rather than confronting alternatives in the broader public sphere. The fact that new democracies are prone to co-opt and absorb the popular groups that helped them rise, lest their demands prove unwieldy, is hardly a new insight (e.g., Dryzek 1996; Oxhorn 1994). Indeed, it is difficult for CSOs to sustain momentum after a big win; protest does tend to be cyclical, and its impacts may take different forms (Tarrow 1998, chs. 9–10).

This discussion is germane not only for the reminder it offers that transitioning or consolidating democracies might not dance with the ones who brung them (to twist a cliché), but also for the cautionary note it implies about what democratization may (not) do. Change of government is a necessary but not sufficient first step for formal, recognized institutional liberalization and other reform – but it may not be the biggest contributor to opening up the policy process. Democratic leaders might have no more patience for nags from outside (or inside) their own camps or cliques than their authoritarian counterparts do. Meanwhile, just as CSOs are so commonly significant to democratic transitions, they may, depending on their own orientation, offer a bulwark against regime regression (Bernhard et al. 2020). Yet the process of democratization may, perversely, leave CSOs less well equipped or legitimate than they were previously to play that role, may empower the "wrong" sorts of CSOs, or may otherwise intensify voices averse to democracy's premises and promises.

3.2 INSTITUTIONAL REFORMS

Actors aside, as the chapters in this volume emphasize, institutions and their reform may also work against democracy, even when intended otherwise. We highlight two challenges. First is that of institutional renovation – a complicated and uncertain process. Reformers and analysts may have strong expectations about the effects of particular changes, but reforms can interact with existing institutions, social norms, shocks, or other adjustments in unanticipated ways. In short, institutional reforms always have unintended consequences.

A second issue germane to some countries in the region is institutions generally considered above or outside democratic institutions, rather than subject to them. Where such institutions exist, they do not augur well for democratic stability: just note the destabilizing roles monarchy and a politicized military have played in Thailand. But the paradoxes and pitfalls run deeper. Again, we turn to Thailand as a particularly germane case study of institutional design and reform that *might* advance democracy … or might do the reverse, however intended or framed.

Thailand has a long history of institutional engineering – the most cited example being 1997's "people's constitution," the most democratic in Thai history and arguably the first (and only) constitution to be written outside of the shadow of direct military or monarchical influence. The 1997 constitution redesigned core structures of the state, including creating a number of new watchdog institutions designed to boost horizontal accountability: ombudsmen, a constitutional court, human rights and anti-corruption commissions, a new election commission. And yet, as Bleck and van de Walle discuss in Chapter 4, it is often the case that accountability institutions fail where state capacity is low or uneven. This pattern certainly held in Thailand, where such institutions were eventually either sidelined or coopted (Hicken 2013). As is the case in India (see Vaishnav's Chapter 2), institutions designed with multiparty democracy in mind proved ill-suited to a dominant-party environment.

The 2006 coup upended the 1997 constitution, but Thailand's conservative elite, counting on the support of key middle-class segments, have continued to try to engineer their preferred outcomes via constitutional reform. They have made ready use of all of the institutional tools of modern autocrats – and, in fact, pioneered the use of some of them. Like most modern autocrats, this elite relies on strategies beyond just seizing power and governing directly. The also seek to use institutional reforms to secure and defend their interests *between* periods of military rule. The goal of these institutions is to limit the threat from democratic challengers and to contain or circumscribe the power of elected politicians. This strategy includes the most recent 2017 constitution, which went the extra mile to contain vile and venal politicians, while empowering "good people" (almost by definition, unelected people) to manage Thailand's affairs without too much interference from elected politicians – or the public (Hicken 2016). Such reforms make clear that elections can occur, and even be relatively free and fair, while institutional legacies and reserve domains[2] continue to prevent democracy from fully taking root.

---

[2] Valenzuela (1990, 11) coined the term "reserved domains" to refer to areas of governmental authority that elected officials are "prevented from controlling by veiled or explicit menaces of a return to authoritarian rule." As he explains, "reserved domains are products of impositions by

Thailand's neighbor to the west offers another example. Built into the Myanmar military's "Roadmap to Democracy" was a plethora of reserve domains (an appointed upper chamber, reserved seats for the military in the lower house, military control over the government's security agencies, etc.), providing an institutionalized escape hatch ready to be sprung whenever the military saw fit. Other political forces considered these reserve domains such a poison pill that the largest democratic opposition party, the National League for Democracy (NLD), boycotted the 2010 election. Once in power, having ultimately opted to contest, the NLD worked to dismantle or circumvent those institutions, contributing to the military's reassessment of the risks of continued democracy. The endpoint in which Myanmar now flounders was a coup and crackdown even more brutal and relentless than Thailand's.

3.2.1 Political Parties

Looming large in any institutional reform related to democracy or democratization are political parties. These institutions are, without question, critical to channeling input and participation – but they might just as readily foster polarization or exclusivity. We home in further on Thai institutional reform to probe this tension.

Within the ambit of constitutional reform in 1997, a set of provisions aimed to reform the party system, too. One step was to reduce the number of parties, given Thailand's hyper-fractionalized party system and resulting tendency toward unwieldy, unstable, and short-lived coalition governments, as well as poor governance in many domains throughout the 1970–90s. Reforms sought to strengthen the importance of party labels to both voters and candidates. They aimed, too, to reorient parties away from patronage and particularism and toward policies and public goods. In subsequent elections, parties began campaigning on national policy proposals – particularly the winning Thai Rak Thai (TRT) party, with, for instance, a signature 30-baht (about US$0.80) health care scheme (Hicken 2013). Amid a sharp reduction in the number of parties, TRT ended up controlling a majority of seats. The government it formed actually implemented many of TRT's policy promises, as it became the first elected government in Thai history to serve out its full four-year term. TRT won again in a landslide in 2005, securing 61 percent of the votes and 75 percent of the seats. Nevertheless, in the nineteen years since then, Thailand has experienced two military coups, five constitutions (plus another failed draft),

---

political actors – such as the military, the monarch, the judicature, the high civil service, and/or nonstate actors such as capitalists – who are not themselves subjected to electoral accountability but have privileged access to crucial elements of state power to make credible their threat of destabilization" (11).

nine national elections/referenda, the dissolution and banning of several major parties, and thirteen heads of government.

What can we make of this outcome? We know that stronger, more programmatic parties are good for democracy. Yet the breakdown of Thai democracy occurred in the wake of parties' becoming stronger and more programmatic, and just as voters seemed to be developing fairly stable partisan ties. We find that, in this case, the strengthening of political parties and partisan attachments, as well as increased civil society activism in Thailand, occurred alongside growing political polarization – indeed, increasing partisanship helped drive polarization, and vice versa.

The deleterious effects of polarization on democracy and democratic stability are hard to overstate (cf. Drutman 2020). During the 1980s and 1990s in Thailand, fickle partisan attachments combined with large, short-lived governments meant a lot of turnover and volatility. Every major actor could expect to get access to government in the short-to-medium term. This system of no permanent winners or losers, no permanent enemies or friends, was inefficient and prone to corruption, but nearly everyone stood to gain by playing by the democratic rules of the game. But as voters became more firmly attached to political parties, and the rules enabled some of those parties to win near-majorities, Thailand transformed. Politics became a zero-sum game, with permanent winners and losers (Hicken 2013). One side could mobilize to win at the ballot box, feeling decreasingly compelled to exercise winner's restraint. Another, unable to win elections, felt shut out of power, and increasingly refused to give its consent. Crucially, it was the latter group that had the stronger links to the military and palace. Stronger partisanship thus reified and amplified political division. Pulling in threads from the preceding discussion, it was in this context of increasing polarization that we found that many in the middle classes and elite turned against democratic rules of the game under which they were no longer winning, and that civil societal mobilization by groups from both sides – prodemocratic "red shirts" and royalist "yellow shirts" – helped destabilize rather than shore up democracy.

3.3 TROPES OR NORMATIVE FRAMES

Finally, as with any aspect of politics, ideas matter, too. Democratic ideas and ideals exist alongside and compete with notions that are often in tension or outright conflict with democratic norms. The antidemocratic thrust of some frames for political identity or policies may be obvious; for others, these effects are more subtle or contingent. We briefly discuss three of these ideas: rule by technocrats/elite, claiming and protecting political rights, and populism. These ideas can empower aspiring autocrats or can serve as a bulwark against backsliding.

3.3.1   Technocracy and Elitism

Across Southeast Asia, preference for technocratic governance and norms of meritocracy runs especially deep – with Singapore having pride of place among adherents given its especial reverence for these norms, and indubitable economic progress through their application. Yet technocracy, or recourse to bureaucratic management, may reflect antidemocratic attitudes or responses to the challenges and problems of democratic governance: making things "run well" may be easier with the cacophony of voices tamped down. We see these sentiments in appeals to "order" in the Philippines and Indonesia (see Pepinsky 2017), rule by "good people" in Thailand, or a "party you can trust" (as the ruling PAP describes itself) in Singapore. Still, there *are* big issues to solve, and it may well be that fixing those needs to come first – or so advocates of this approach may argue.

Among the "modes of participation" Garry Rodan (2018) identifies as dominant even in comparatively democratic corners of the region, for instance, are forms that favor technocratic problem-solving, absent of and evading political competition or acknowledgement of how "political" decisions are, or that reify only discrete communities' or identities' rights to specific representation. Even those modes more inclined toward opening policy access might make co-optation the cost of getting on the agenda, or might effectively contain voice to the civil society arena, quarantined from the state proper. As such, Rodan calls into question conceptions of democracy that fail to take seriously how the policy or political process works. As depoliticizing consultative and particularist ideologies permeate across Southeast Asia and elsewhere, participatory institutions may serve more to consolidate political and economic elites' control than to empower autonomous voices. Participatory budgeting processes, as in the (pre-Duterte) Philippines (Maravilla and Grayman 2019), for instance, can serve as an alternative arena for democratic praxis if these mechanisms encourage or oblige social-welfare or investment policies that prioritize the poor, or if they favor those actors whose interests are at odds with those of the large firms states court. But this workaround also may offer limited empowerment, while reducing incentives to push for something better.

3.3.2   Rights Protection

Claims for rights may work in similarly ambiguous ways, either promoting or undercutting liberal premises. The presumption may be that all in society enjoy formally equal rights (however much various forms of discrimination undercut these in practice), yet especially where we see the rise of varieties of identity politics, we may encounter zero-sum rights claims. Indeed, such developments continue to challenge Southeast Asia, as claims to recognition, voice, and resources both embody and uphold, as well as undercut and endanger, democracy's promise.

The term "identity politics," rarely clearly defined, has taken on a negative valence in states such as Indonesia, as signaling an antipluralist, exclusionary orientation. Specifically in Indonesia, this term makes reference to "hardline" Islamists intolerant of domestic religious minorities (e.g., Nugroho 2019; Mietzner 2020). Yet the "politics of recognition," including "conceptualizing struggles for recognition so that they can be integrated with struggles for redistribution, rather than displacing and undermining them" (Fraser 2000, 109), has liberal roots, calling for seats at the societal and policy table, plus shares of the plenty for all. That promise of inclusivity is among democracy's key benefits: that all citizens have votes to cast makes each equally valuable, and gives all citizens a stake. Southeast Asian states confront the thorny challenge of how to embrace the good side of identity politics while avoiding the exclusionary flip side.

One way to do so is to consider mechanisms for identity articulation. Malaysia offers the starkest example, in an ethnicized politics that elevates one category above others. Yet even there, the imperative of vote-pooling mitigates in favor of a "bridging" approach, of targeting ethnic or otherwise-defined communities in order to draw each under the same partisan tent (e.g., Aspinall, et al. 2022, ch. 7). Singapore takes the opposite approach, banning most expressions of ethnoreligious sentiment from election campaigns. But this approach, too, may shut out or silence those who demand equity beyond equality: not just the same rules as now, but the ability to reach a common starting point. The mid-pandemic 2020 elections offered a clear example, in official efforts to discredit and sanction a young, female opposition-party candidate who had tweeted previously of the state's privileging Chinese citizens and disfavoring Malay Muslims such as herself. That episode sparked notable pushback among citizens, suggesting real potential for conversation, and for acknowledging differences in lived experiences of identity, with an eye toward broaching structural racism.

In other words, "identity politics" in and of itself lacks normative valence. If pitched toward exclusion, it obviously subverts more pluralist democratic possibilities. The "bad" populism of a glorious "we" opposed to a disentitled "they" remains a risk. Likewise, illiberal state responses to exclusionary identity demands are also a risk (consider Indonesia). But "identity politics" remains also essential. In explaining why narrowly pitched, "bonding" rather than "bridging," appeals to ethnic and religious identities have tipped upwards in Indonesia since 2009 (a decade beyond the country's democratic transition), Colm Fox (2020) raises a key intervening factor: the structure of the electoral and party systems. Reforms as of 2009 instituted open-list proportional representation and, hence, amplified the need for a personal vote. Although Indonesia's constitutional court instituted the shift from closed- to open-list in the name of enhancing democracy, institutional reforms (as we suggest in Section 3.2) carry externalities. One "fix" to this particular worrisome indicator for democratic decline is to think more thoroughly through the ramifications of institutional engineering (and to allow for subsequent retooling, as unexpected consequences emerge). If we know or learn that exclusionary identarian appeals are a problem, we know ways to use mechanisms available to any electoral regime to encourage crossing cleavages.

3.3.3 Populism

Last but not least, we might consider populism: the bugbear of contemporary theorists and practitioners concerned about autocratization, and a recurring theme of this volume. Populism is an issue in Southeast Asia as in many other regions – though here, as elsewhere, its reach is often overstated (Weiss 2020). Populists may present their premises as being fundamentally prodemocratic – as upholding "the people." And indeed, left-wing populisms in particular (common in Latin America) might validate and elevate workers over elites. But right-wing (nativist, exclusionary) populisms are harder to vindicate in the name of democracy, and these are arguably what we find more commonly in Southeast Asia (see Palestini and Kaltwasser's Chapter 15 for a discussion of the characteristics, origins, and global spread of such variants). The claims of Rodrigo Duterte in the Philippines (president from 2016 to 2022), or Prabowo Subianto in Indonesia (*not* elected in 2014 or 2019, but the third try, in 2024, was the charm), may sound quite "democratic" on face, but are, in fact, exclusive and rigid in practice.

3.4 CONCLUSIONS

Across Southeast Asia (and elsewhere), we encounter a long-running tango between actors and forces for and against democracy, with no "natural" or "normal" balance between these. In one context, civil society might take on the prodemocracy role; in another, CSOs might sashay toward a different corner. That fungibility of functions, positions, and goals makes reform inherently and persistently challenging – though if it leaves democracy precarious, at least it leaves authoritarianism equally shaky (albeit with the benefit of a coercive tool kit with which to buy time).

We intend the brief illustrations we have offered from the region not to sketch a comprehensive picture, but to clarify our emphasis on context and contingency. Stronger parties are good for democracy under some conditions, but not all. An active civil society can bolster democracy in some contexts and threaten it in others. Middle-class support for democracy is contingent on its assessments of what these individuals stand to gain or lose from the democratic bargain. All told, Southeast Asia's decidedly broad repertoire of regime types is certainly distinctive, but does more to throw into relief broadly relevant factors than region-specific features. The dance continues, here as elsewhere, with no shortage of dramatic flair.

REFERENCES

Aspinall, Edward. 2010. "Indonesia: The Irony of Success." *Journal of Democracy* 21 (2): 20–34.

Aspinall, Edward, Meredith L. Weiss, Allen Hicken, and Paul Hutchcroft. 2022. *Mobilizing for Elections: Patronage and Political Machines in Southeast Asia.* Cambridge: Cambridge University Press.

Bernhard, Michael, Allen Hicken, Christopher Reenock, and Staffan I. Lindberg. 2020. "Parties, Civil Society, and the Deterrence of Democratic Defection." *Studies in Comparative International Development* 55 (1): 1–26.

Chua, Beng-Huat. 1995. *Communitarian Ideology and Democracy in Singapore.* London: Routledge.

Drutman, Lee. 2020. *Breaking the Two-party Doom Loop: The Case for Multiparty Democracy in America.* Oxford: Oxford University Press.

Dryzek, John S. 1996. "Political Inclusion and the Dynamics of Democratization." *American Political Science Review* 90 (1): 475–87.

Fealy, Greg. 2020. "Jokowi's Repressive Pluralism." *East Asia Forum*, 27 September, www.eastasiaforum.org/2020/09/27/jokowis-repressive-pluralism/.

Fox, Colm. 2020. "Why Have Candidates in Indonesian Elections Increasingly Been Rallying Ethnic and Religious Support?" *The Conversation*, 30 September, https://tinyurl.com/yc5ud9uz.

Fraser, Nancy. 2000. "Rethinking Recognition." *New Left Review* 3 (May/June): 107–20.

Gainsborough, Martin. 2002. "Political Change in Vietnam: In Search of the Middle-class Challenge to the State." *Asian Survey* 42 (5): 694–707.

Geddes, Barbara. 1999. "What Do We Know about Democratization after Twenty Years?" *Annual Review of Political Science* 2:115–44.

Hadiz, Vedi R. 2003. "Reorganizing Political Power in Indonesia: A Reconsideration of So-called 'Democratic Transitions.'" *Pacific Review* 16 (4): 591–611.

Hicken, Allen. 2013. "Late to the Party: The Development of Partisanship in Thailand." *Trans: National and Regional Studies of Southeast Asia* 1 (2): 1–15.

2016. "Thailand's Containment Constitution." *New Mandala.* April 28.

Linz, Juan J., and Alfred Stepan. 1996. *Problems of Democratic Transition and Consolidation: Southern Europe, South America, and Post-communist Europe.* Baltimore, MD: Johns Hopkins University Press.

Lorch, Jasmin. 2017. "State Weakness and Civil Society in the Philippines." In *Civil Society and Mirror Images of Weak States,* pp. 133–97. London: Palgrave Macmillan.

Loxton, James. 2015 "Authoritarian Successor Parties." *Journal of Democracy* 26 (3): 157–70.

Maravilla, Gladys Ann R. and Jesse Hession Grayman. 2020. "Understanding Participatory Budgeting through Formal and Informal Processes of Inclusion: A Case Study in the Philippines." *Development in Practice* 30 (4): 448–58.

Mietzner, Marcus. 2020. "Authoritarian Innovations in Indonesia: Electoral Narrowing, Identity Politics and Executive Illiberalism." *Democratization* 27 (6): 1021–36.

2021. "Sources of Resistance to Democratic Decline: Indonesian Civil Society and Its Trials." *Democratization* 18 (1): 161–78.

Nugroho, Johannes. 2019. "Why Identity Politics in Indonesia Is Here to Stay." *Today*, 6 May, www.todayonline.com/commentary/why-identity-politics-indonesia-here-stay.

Oxhorn, Philip. 1994. "Where Did All the Protesters Go? Popular Mobilization and the Transition to Democracy in Chile." *Latin American Perspectives* 82 (21): 49–68.

Pepinsky, Thomas. 2017. "Southeast Asia: Voting against Disorder." *Journal of Democracy* 28 (2): 120–31.

Riedl, Rachel Beatty. 2014. *Authoritarian Origins of Democratic Party Systems in Africa*. New York: Cambridge University Press.

Rodan, Garry. 2018. *Participation without Democracy: Containing Conflict in Southeast Asia*. Ithaca, NY: Cornell University Press.

Ryan, Megan and Darin Sanders Self. 2021. "Myanmar's Military Distrusts the Country's Ruling Party: That's Why It Staged a Coup and Detained Leaders and Activists." *Washington Post*, February 2.

Self, Darin Sanders. 2022. *Bounded Democracy: How Authoritarian Civilian-military Relations Shape Democratization and Democratic Development*. PhD dissertation, Cornell University.

Slater, Dan and Joseph Wong. 2022. *From Development to Democracy: The Transformations of Modern Asia*. Princeton, NJ: Princeton University Press.

Svolik, Milan W. 2019. "Polarization versus Democracy." *Journal of Democracy* 30 (3): 20–32.

Tarrow, Sidney. 1998. *Power in Movement: Social Movements and Contentious Politics*. New York: Cambridge University Press.

Tomsa, Dirk, and Charlotte Setijadi. 2018. "New Forms of Political Activism in Indonesia." *Asian Survey* 58 (3): 557–81.

Valenzuela, J. Samuel. 1990. *Democratic Consolidation in Post-transitional Settings: Notion, Process, and Facilitating Conditions*. Working paper #150. Helen Kellogg Institute for International Studies, University of Notre Dame, Notre Dame, IN.

Weiss, Meredith L. 2006. *Protest and Possibilities: Civil Society and Coalitions for Political Change in Malaysia*. Stanford, CA: Stanford University Press.

  2007. "What a Little Democracy Can Do: Trajectories of Reform in Malaysia and Indonesia." *Democratization* 14 (1): 26–43.

  2020. "The Limits of 'Populism': How Malaysia Misses the Mark and Why That Matters." *Journal of Current Southeast Asian Affairs* 39 (2): 207–26.

Weiss, Meredith L. and Eva Hansson. 2023. "Civil Society in Politics and Southeast Asia in Civil Society." In Eva Hansson and Meredith L. Weiss, ed. *Routledge Handbook of Civil and Uncivil Society in Southeast Asia*, pp. 1–22. London: Routledge.

4

State Capacity and Accountability in Low-Income States

Jaimie Bleck and Nicolas van de Walle

4.1 INTRODUCTION

One consequence of the Third Wave of democratization has been the generalized emergence in Africa and the rest of the low-income world of regular competitive elections and some significant degree of political liberalization in the last three decades. Though some of these states can be viewed as genuine democracies, perhaps most are better characterized as electoral autocracies, or highly imperfect competitive electoral regimes, with a combination of an overreaching executive branch, regular multiparty elections and the occasional transfer of power (Bleck and van de Walle, 2018). In most of these states, the winners and losers' dilemmas described in the Introduction of this volume can be observed. Incumbents and oppositions are enmeshed in a dialectical interplay, with the former using the powers of office to increase their hold on power, and the latter mobilizing emerging domestic and international resources to resist autocratization and compete effectively in elections.

In the low-income world, the modal result of this dialectic has so far been the resilience of very imperfect democracies or electoral autocracies, and not a broad trend of backsliding, representing something of a puzzle, since low-income states with few long-standing democratic traditions have been generally viewed as the most vulnerable to autocratization. In this chapter, we offer some tentative hypotheses for one possible reason for this apparent stability, by focusing on the relationship between state capacity and democracy.

In this chapter, we argue that the relationship between state capacity and democracy in these low-income electoral autocracies can better be understood

We thank Rachel Riedl, Trevor Lwere, and Arsène Brice Bado as well as participants in Cornell's "Global Challenges for Democracy" conference for comments on earlier drafts. We thank Tavin Martin and Brian Olemo for research assistance.

by disaggregating the different components of state capacity and democracy, in order to clarify the ways that they are linked (or not). Vertical accountability can exist with limited state capacity, while processes of horizontal accountability are much more dependent on state capacity to function effectively. However, we show that elite-led processes can generate substantial gains in horizontal accountability in environments with relatively limited capacity.

Going back to Huntington's (2006) foundational work, political scientists have taken for granted the thesis that state capacity has a profound effect on the nature of the regime. This literature has largely adopted a "no state, no democracy" hypothesis, arguing that in the absence of a minimal threshold of state capacity, there can be no democracy (Linz and Stepan 1996). Debates have focused on the capacity side of the equation, from how it is defined to the impact of specific forms of capacity such as Mann's *despotic* and *infrastructural power* (1984, emphasis in original) or Soifer's further disaggregation of *national capabilities, weight of the state, and subnational variation* (2008, emphasis in original). However, the existing literature has failed to distinguish between the different components of democracy, though it seems intuitive that different democratic institutions or procedures might require different levels and types of capacity.

We make two primary hypotheses about how we should understand the relationship between state capacity and democracy. First, we argue that institutions of vertical accountability can generally exist (or in some cases flourish) with limited state capacity. These include formal political participation, such as elections and voting, which is often incentivized and subsidized by the international community, or citizen and civil society action that are made possible by freedom of association and freedom of the press, which do not rely on state capacity (Bleck and Logvinenko 2018). While elections may remain imperfect due to a variety of factors including an uneven playing field (Levitsky and Way 2010) and international monitors' bias toward approving them (Kelley 2009), weak state capacity in organizing and executing elections can be buttressed by donor support as well as by domestic civil society networks of electoral monitoring.[1] If anything, weak state capacity makes it harder, though not impossible, for the regime to control electoral results or makes it more difficult to conceal meddling.

On the other hand, we hypothesize that the consolidation of political institutions that advance horizontal accountability will be constrained by deficient state capacity. Judicial independence and legislative power as well as other independent checks on the executive branch of government will typically be more undermined by low capacity than the incumbent regime itself. We anticipate that decisions about investing in bureaucratic and military capacity will prioritize institutions that favor the executive, thus facilitating abuses of

---

[1] Though we acknowledge that such support could be problematic if it favors a particular candidate or enables the incumbent to leverage the resources for his advantage.

power. In addition, legislatures and the judiciary are complex organizations for which processes of institutionalization and legitimation require time and cannot easily be accelerated or imported from the outside.

In addition, we argue that it is important to look at how these relationships play out over political geography: in the capital and periphery as well as in the citizen and elite spheres. In environments with low levels of state capacity, elite-driven accountability in the capital is much more likely than broader accountability in the periphery.

We start with a brief review of the literature, then turn our attention to the impact of low state capacity on different democratic institutions, schematically divided into whether they promote horizontal or vertical accountability. Our empirical examples come from sub-Saharan Africa, but we believe our argument extends more widely to all low-income countries.

4.2 STATE CAPACITY AND DEMOCRACY

The relationship between the state and the political regime has been problematized by scholars since World War II and the emergence of postcolonial states, with young and relatively weak political institutions. There has been very rich literature about the nature of capacity, but it has generally not focused much on the nature of democratic institutions. Huntington's seminal analysis of political development famously began with the proposition that "the most important political distinction among countries concerns not their form of government but their degree of government" (1968, p. 1). The explosion in political participation brought on by modernization would put enormous stress on the weak institutions in the postcolonial world, not least because many of them did not have a strong sense of national unity and were riven by ethnic, religious, and regional divisions. Ensuring order was the foremost priority, at least until state institutions were strong enough to process popular participation.

The Third Wave of democratization focused this debate specifically on the emerging democratic regimes and a large number of scholars have since weighed in (Andersen et al. 2014; Bratton and Chang 2006; Fukuyama 2001; Linz and Stepan 1996; Mazzucca and Munck 2014; Slater 2008). Without undertaking a comprehensive review of this literature, several comments are useful.

First, could really low-income states be fully democratic? Linz and Stepan (1996, p. 14) argued categorically that no modern polity can become democratically consolidated unless it is first a state. In sum, they argued, there can be no democracy in the absence of a state that is capable of projecting power across the territory, of establishing law and order, and of carrying out the policies of the elected government. This "no state, no democracy" argument has been widely adopted in the literature. Observers noted that it follows the historical patterns of the West, since a good deal of *stateness* was gained in most of these nation states before they broadened the franchise and democratized (for discussion, see Bäck and Hadenius 2008).

Second, while accepting the broad argument that low capacity could undermine the process of democratic consolidation in low-income states, the literature has differed on the extent to which democratic governance could have a positive effect on state capacity over time. As Carothers has argued (2007), the "no state, no democracy" hypothesis can lead to what he calls the "sequencing fallacy," according to which the policy prescription for low-income states is that they should defer democratization until a strong state has been fully established. Way has argued that many hybrid regimes are the result of "pluralism by default" as aspirational autocrats do not have the ability to fully implement authoritarian regimes; however, this same weakness also impedes democratic consolidation (2015).

On the other hand, Carbone and Memoli (2015), Bratton and Chang (2006), and Mazzucca and Munck (2014) all have countered that the introduction of democratic institutions itself promotes state capacity over time, which suggests that there is a democratic path to a strong state, and thus no requirement for every state to go first through a phase of authoritarian state building. Organizing elections, for instance, they argue, helps strengthen the reach of the state. Being responsive to voters helps motivate governments to build their capacity to deliver various social services to the population, and so on. For instance, in their analysis of leaders and leadership transitions in Africa since 1960, Carbone and Pellagatta (2020) find that presidents elected in the context of multiparty elections are more likely to increase state capacity.

Third, most of the discussion has focused on the appropriate way of thinking about and disaggregating state capacity. How important was coercive capacity? Did different kinds of capacity have different impacts on democratic governance? Was the important factor the more organic concept of stateness or legitimacy, rather than specific forms of capacity within the state? Was the state's ability to gain public authority or legitimacy more important than the actual capacity to get stuff done?

On the other hand, this literature has relatively little to say about the democracy side of the equation. Much of the literature appears to adopt a minimalist procedural definition of democracy, following Dahl (1973), and alludes to elections and sometimes basic civil rights. However, it often falls back into substantive definitions of democratic governance, when it discusses the failures of low-income democracies. For instance, the high levels of corruption allowed by low capacity are said to be a consequence of some properties of democracy. Or, the failure to reduce inequality or poverty is viewed as making the country less democratic. In making such claims, the literature has tended to conflate democracy with governance quality, thus forgetting Schmitter and Karl's (1991) admonition about "what democracy is ... not." We need to remind ourselves that "governability is a challenge for all regimes, not just democratic ones" as Schmitter and Karl (1991), put it (p. 86), and low-income authoritarian regimes hardly have a better record in these regards. If we adopt a strictly procedural definition of democracy, then a state's substantive achievements or sociological makeup are not necessarily relevant to our assessment of the quality of the democracy, even if we readily admit that they may seriously undermine the long-term evolution of democratic deepening and can provoke regime crises.

In addition, and more immediately useful to our purpose in this chapter, this literature fails to disaggregate the different institutions necessary for basic procedural democracy, though they do not all have similar implications for state strength, as we now argue. One quick way to disaggregate procedural democracy and its relationship with state capacity is to compare and contrast vertical and horizontal accountability issues.

For the purposes of this chapter, we primarily focus on Mann's infrastructural capacity defined as "the capacity of the state to actually penetrate civil society, and to implement logistically political decisions throughout the realm" (1984, p. 189). This would include functions of fiscality (taxation), bureaucratic administration (service provision), and coercion (military/police) capacity. We hypothesize and attempt to show in the next section that institutions of vertical accountability tend to be less vulnerable to low-capacity environments than institutions of horizontal accountability.

While horizontal accountability is typically more dependent on state capacity, we hypothesize that elite-level factors of vertical and horizontal accountability can move states toward democratic progress in environments of relatively little capacity. The continent has witnessed some significant judicial rulings that have significantly swayed the balance of power away from the executive: The annulation of election results in Kenya (2017) and Malawi (2019–20) by the courts provides a good example of this. The brave members of government who abide by their professional duty to their country are a testament to the human capital in these countries, but their training and success are less dependent on broad increases in state capacity. Assemblies, typically limited by the resources they control, have also managed to pass term-limit laws that have significantly shaped the trajectory of politics (McKie 2019). Despite the very real impact of these rulings and laws, these achievements do not automatically trigger more far-reaching increases in state capacity. The processes of democratic deepening that involve citizens and elected officials, bureaucracy, and political parties rely more heavily on state capacity. Citizens may continue to struggle to achieve transparent, fair, and consistent rulings in courts across the country, due, in part, to deficits in capacity. Insufficient capacity to overhaul, professionalize, and provide adequate pay to a police force means that citizens, even those residing in the capital, will continue to contend with corruption. Experiences of poor governance could dampen citizens' trust in state institutions as well as their engagement with the state.

One key difference between institutions of vertical and horizontal accountability in low-capacity states, we hypothesize, is related to their degree of autonomy from the state. Civil society and political actors tend to be autonomous from the state, relying on private and international support to survive. On the other hand, judiciaries and legislatures tend to lack budgetary and organizational autonomy. They typically rely on the central state for all of their funding. As a result, the actors in the vertical accountability sector tend to thrive from the neglect of the central state, whereas limited state capacity is typically one of the weapons that executives use to emasculate legislatures and judiciaries.

Similarly, we suggest that political will can compensate for low capacity, so that inexpensive gains in democracy sometimes rely on policy choices more than state capacity. Moreover, popular will or desire for democratic governance can push regimes to concede to terms limits or maintain electoral timetables or, by contrast, support junta leaderships' continued presence in power. Prodemocracy political and popular will can happen throughout these political systems, but we hypothesize that it is more likely to constitute a significant factor for the institutions of vertical accountability. There are many times when moves toward (or stagnation in respect to) democratization and representation can be triggered by a change in political will and a series of committed reforms in a singular sector. Efforts at decentralization in the early 1990s were often stymied by a failure to actually transfer the control of resources to newly created entities rather than a dearth of resources to transfer. By contrast, constituency development funds, taken away from the general operating budget, have proven effective vehicles to connect voters with their MPs (Kimenyi 2005). Both represent questions of political will rather than state capacity.

Our research has implications for the understanding of the democratic achievements and their limitations in low-income pluralist regimes, which typically include both genuinely participatory politics and competitive party politics, with a largely unaccountable executive branch of government, and substantial incumbency advantages. Low-income states are likely to exhibit "uneven pluralism" (Bleck and Logvinenko 2018). While pockets of democracy can flourish within poor states, democratic deepening or consolidation will be nearly impossible without commensurate improvements in horizontal institutions.

4.3 VERTICAL ACCOUNTABILITY

First, we hypothesize that elements of vertical accountability are relatively less dependent on state capacity. We draw on Bleck and Logvinenko (2018) who describe low-income states as characterized by "uneven pluralism," where certain aspects of "democracy" are more probable than others. Drawing on case studies of Mali and Kyrgyzstan, they argue that certain components of pluralism are more common in low-income states because they are relatively "cheap." These include freedom of the press and freedom of association, which require little state support or intervention in order to flourish. Valued by the population, the availability of these freedoms allows leaders to gain favor with their constituencies; conversely, low-income states have limited capacity to clamp down on these freedoms and efforts to do so are met with popular protest and dissent, which these low-income states have difficulty containing. They argue that these freedoms are consequential and describe multiple instances of protest changing government policy (2018, p. 813). While they may be effective in changing specific policies, these types of ad hoc government concessions do nothing to strengthen political parties or institutions of horizontal accountability because they remain in the contentious sphere.

To be clear, we recognize that even very weak governments can and do repress civil society actors, particularly in the capital and other big cities. The internet gets shut down, journalists arrested, and so forth. The contemporary situation in Mali or the ruling junta in Burkina Faso has shown that some leaders may be able to leverage ideology and external threats to quell domestic criticism about restricted freedoms – at least in the short term. Nonetheless, unlike institutions of horizontal accountability, weakening civil society actors requires active repression, which is unpopular both with domestic actors and with international ones. The decentralized nature of civil society, the entrepreneurship of countless individuals who will privately benefit from building successful civic bodies, unions, newspapers, or radio stations helps to explain why, despite an increase in repression in recent years, cross-national data suggests continued increases in political participation and civic activism in low-income countries (Dupuy 2023).

The independent flourishing of journalists (freedom of expression) and civil society (freedom of expression and association) is less dependent on state capacity than the horizontal institutions that we will describe in the next section. While state capacity might limit communication technologies or infrastructure that could further strengthen civil society or journalism to contribute to freedom of expression or freedom of association, these actors can exist in the space outside of the state and do not rely on its support to achieve their goals. For instance, for many years local, rural radio networks in the Sahel region have flourished in localities with very limited infrastructure and state presence. We concede that if communications networks remain localized, it is harder to coordinate large-scale protest; however, telephony has become a very lucrative private sector – incentivizing corporate pushes for network expansion. At the same time – state weakness limits the regimes' ability to monitor and censor information flows. We do note that many states seek to control the expansion of online communication and coordination and limit freedom of association through internet shutdowns.[2] In this sense, capacity

---

[2] For instance, the Ethiopian government shut the internet down more than six times between 2016 and 2019 (Ayalew 2019).

may aid a state's ability to monitor its population, control phone and internet, and to participate in a cycle of political learning, as citizens seek to respond and innovate with tactics such as the adoption of VPNs (virtual private networks).

Elections, perhaps the most important institution of vertical accountability, also require relatively low amounts of state capacity to be a fair reflection of citizen preferences, and – just as important – be perceived as such by the citizenry. The empirical evidence suggests tentatively that they are more likely to be institutionalized in low-income states, and the ability and motivation of incumbents to steal the elections are not closely correlated with state capacity. Even though elections can generate significant costs, a host of external donors have proven willing to subsidize them during this period (Gelb and Diofasi 2019; Wrong 2013).[3] As a focal point for democratic scrutiny, elections are also highly incentivized for elites – particularly those with aid-dependent economies (Peiffer and Englebert 2012). Election cycles typically have greater salience and visibility to the international community than other types of democratic reforms. Ruling elites face international and domestic incentives to hold elections; states who cease regular multiparty elections face harsh sanctions (Bleck and Logvinenko 2018, p. 811). Like freedoms of the press and association, most populations with experience of regular multiparty elections value this form of governance,[4] and the habituation of electoral practice garners support from the mass public.

Elections operate on punctuated timelines – with resources and attention pouring into elections once every four or five years – rather than the steady flow of resources and routinized procedures required for something like equitable application of the rule of law. Further, elections can borrow capacity and funding from international and regional organizations, as well as from parties and civil society, which are willing to devote manpower to the electoral exercise. In cases like the Gambia, youth organizing and significant flows of resources from the diaspora were significant factors to defeat the long-standing incumbent at the ballot box (Keita 2023). In this case, a third-party security provider, ECOWAS (Economic Community of West African States), rather than an institution of the state, stepped in to make sure that the former ruling president actually left power. In some countries, coalitions of domestic observers helped ensure that there was a parallel vote count; in Ghana the Coalition of Domestic Observers deployed more than 4,400 observers from 42 civil society groups to polling stations throughout Ghana.[5]

We are not suggesting that elections in low-income states are very likely to be free and fair. Low-income governments often steal elections, particularly

---

[3] Though donors prefer to concentrate on technical support of election preparation rather than activities like civil society sensitization and training negotiation capacity in the lead-up to elections (Bado 2016).

[4] The most recent round of Afrobarometer data revealed nearly three-quarters of respondents wanted good quality, regular elections to choose the leaders (M'Cormack-Hale and Dome 2021).

[5] See more information about these efforts on their website at: www.codeoghana.org.

presidential ones (Bleck and van de Walle 2018). Certainly, at the lowest levels of state capacity – infrastructure deficits may hinder expressions of vertical accountability – particularly in more remote areas in the country's periphery. When resources and infrastructure do not make it out to rural areas, mechanisms of accountability can be hindered: Communication between citizens is difficult, voting might require an arduous journey across bad roads, or guarantees of security might be insufficient for citizens to assemble or participate in democracy, in a manner which is not a concern in the main urban areas. Still, we suggest that a minimal threshold of state capacity and infrastructure is met over most of the territory in the overwhelming majority of low-income countries today, and that even very low-capacity countries can deliver free and fair participatory exercises.

4.4 HORIZONTAL ACCOUNTABILITY

Accountability is related to both autonomy and capacity. Effective accountability requires organizational autonomy, regardless of the level of capacity that exists. Mechanisms of horizontal accountability are primarily constituted by the checks and balances that an independent judiciary and legislature provide relative to the executive branch. A striking characteristic of low-income electoral regimes is how weak these institutions are and how little genuine autonomy they enjoy relative to the executive, to which they are subordinate and dependent, even in relatively democratic countries. In part this results from long-standing constitutional provisions that often go back to the colonial era, long predating the transition to democracy in the 1990s and that have left an institutional legacy of an overbearing bureaucracy and dominant presidency (Prempeh 2008; Soumano 2023), that undercuts the independence of the judiciary and the legislature. Most obviously, the number of low-income states with parliamentary forms of government is exceedingly low.[6] In the hyperpresidential systems that predominate the low-income countries, the executive branch can use its institutional power to control the national narrative and emasculate the other branches of government.

Three factors distinguish the impact of low state capacity on horizontal accountability, compared to vertical accountability. First, legislatures and judiciaries rely on the support and funding that the executive branch is willing to grant them. Even when the latter does not mean to weaken and control the former, which is often the case in these imperfect electoral systems, the executive is likely to prioritize capacity building in its own branch of government, over the legislature and judiciary. For instance, the work of the Supreme Court in Zambia appears to be directly undermined by basic resource problems.

---

[6] Of some forty-seven countries identified by DFID (Department for International Development) as low-income states in 2017, only four had a parliamentary form of government (Nepal, Ethiopia, Lesotho, Papa New Guinea).

One recent report noted systematic problems of inadequate funding in the judiciary, arguing that, "These financial, technological, and human resource challenges have led to crippling inefficiencies, including case backlog and court congestion, all of which have cascading social and economic effects on ordinary litigants and defendants interfacing with the judicial system?" (The World Bank 2022, p. 6). It goes on to indicate the extent to which the lack of support influenced the ability of the Constitutional Court to function at all:

From the time the Constitutional Court was established in 2016, it has had no infrastructure of its own. Therefore, the Court [has] had to share courtrooms and office space, among others, with the Supreme Court … [T]he Court of Appeal, despite having its own infrastructure at the former IRC building, had no holding cell and [is], therefore, restricted to hearing civil appeals in its premises. Criminal appeals [have] to be heard at the Supreme Court, thereby exerting more pressure on the already stretched Supreme Court resources. In addition, given the criminal jurisdiction of the Court, the security of Judges [is] compromised by the Court's location in a busy area with a consequently high concentration of potential wrongdoers. (The World Bank 2022, p. 6)

The failure of legislatures and judiciaries to enforce accountability is in part caused by constitutional provisions that empower the executive, but it is sustained over time, by issues of capacity within these institutions, and the consequences of low capacity within the state more generally.

In theory, the Western donors could provide them support and compensate for the lack of central state support, but in practice, the donors have shied away from supporting them, with most of the governance assistance focusing on elections (Resnick and van de Walle 2013).

Second, enhancing the capacity of the legislature and judiciary is linked to complex processes of institutionalization, in addition to individual issues relating to human capacity, in a manner that is more likely to have a critical influence on democracy than is the case for the organizations of vertical accountability discussed above. Surely, no modern state lacks the resources to successfully train a couple of dozen judges every decade or so to make up the top tier of the justice system. On the other hand, creating an *esprit de corps* among these judges, building a critical culture in the judicial bodies in which they labor, and establishing their credibility and legitimacy is difficult and time-consuming at the best of times. In addition, retaining the services of well-trained jurists can prove to be a Sisyphean task, given the many alternative and often more lucrative career opportunities available to them. Much the same can be said about the top echelons of the civil service, well-trained and experienced technocrats who are regularly offered higher salaries to work in the private sector or for NGOs or international agencies.

Third, processes of horizontal accountability do not play out evenly across geographic territory or across the realms of elite and lived politics. It is very important to consider subnational variation in state capacity (Soifer 2006). Since most revenue continues to come from the central state, areas in the periphery, particularly in large low-population density spaces, are more affected by deficiencies in capacity than is the capital. Relatedly, in the absence of capacity, it is easier to make progress on horizontal accountability at the elite level, typically circumscribed to the capital city, rather than the citizen level – dispersed throughout the country. We discuss these types of variations through the lenses of the judiciary and legislature.

The Judiciary. The small number of well-trained judges and lawyers limits the power of the judiciary at every level in low-income states. Prominent judges who could easily move to the private sector or abroad are more likely to resist the pressures from the presidency, but in the poorest countries fewer such opportunities are available for judges, who are as a result more vulnerable to pressures from the executive branch. It is true that in countries like Senegal, Benin, Kenya, Nigeria, or most recently Malawi, the judges in high courts have asserted their independence loudly and powerfully, whether on the issue of the third presidential term or invalidating fraudulent elections. The small size of apex courts means that they are less likely to be constrained by capacity issues, or can more easily compensate for them. Broad state capacity is not a necessary condition for this elite-driven accountability in the highest courts.

At lower levels of the judiciary, long-standing inadequate funding and problems of oversight have plagued the lower levels of the court system: Alou's characterization of judicial organizations in West Africa is devastating: "the absence of political independence, subordination of justice to political, venality of judges, insufficient and inappropriate training of magistrates, financial and bureaucratic poverty of courts, excessive formalism of rules and procedures, alienation of the judiciary from the population"[7] (Alou 2001, p. 61).

Outside of the capital, the problems with the justice system are typically exacerbated, with inconsistent norms of impartiality and professionalism, and less independence relative to local elites or government officials. For instance, several recent studies of the legal system in Zambia (Banda 2019; Ndulo 2011) emphasize that the financial and organizational deficiencies of the legal system in Zambia are pervasive, but worse in the lower courts across the territory. Banda (2019, pp. 81–84) notes problems linked to poor infrastructure, poor lighting, the absence of microphones, lack of working air-conditioning, and repeated interruptions due to power failures, all with negative impacts on the efficiency of the judicial system. In other countries, problems of corruption are often noted in routine cases, in which favorable judgments require a payoff (for instance, Bierschenk 2008 for the case of Benin).

Among other consequences of these weaknesses in the periphery is the likelihood that the independent decisions of high-level judges in the capital are

---

[7] Original in French: "*Absence d'un pouvoir judiciaire indépendant, subordination de la justice au pouvoir politique, vénalité des juges, insuffisance et inadéquation de la formation des magistrats, misère financière et documentaire des tribunaux, excessif juridisme des règles et procédures, éloignement de l'appareil judiciaire par rapport à la population.*"

not implemented across much of the territory. In Dakar, the capital of Senegal, for example, the high courts have long played an active and key role in checking executive power, but its ability to reach the troubled province of Casamance and limit human rights abuses there is probably quite limited (Alou 2001, for examples of these kinds of deficiencies in Senegal and French West Africa more specifically).

In addition to these capacity and funding issues, the judiciary finds it hard to assert its institutional prerogatives vis à vis the executive. Culturally predisposed to discretion and the avoidance of partisanship, the judiciary is poorly understood and rarely appreciated by the electorate, and must use its limited social capital carefully. In many instances it is thus easily outflanked and manipulated by autocratic rulers who have found they can weaponize the law to enhance their own power (Glopen et al., 2022).

Lack of consistent rule of law has far-reaching consequences for how citizens experience governance, but it also generates secondary effects on the political ecosystem. Bratton and Chang (2006) argue that rule of law, including the widespread sense of personal security and leaders respecting the constitution, is critical for democracy. Consistent application of the rule of law is also really important for the development of the private sector, which is important for economic growth (Feld and Voigt 2003; Haggard et al. 2008) and relatedly for the development of opposition political parties (Arriola 2013).

Moreover, in most postcolonial low-income states, the judiciary retains many of the characteristics of colonial justice. Often inappropriate norms and procedures have remained unchanged in the books since before independence. Colonial systems tended to be hybrid, with a modern justice system coexisting with the persistence of customary law, and/or colonial "native courts." This hybridity has typically persisted to this day, introducing ambiguity about jurisdiction and conflict. At the macro level, the authoritarianism or at least paternalism of colonial systems remains embedded in the culture of current judicial institutions, which emphasize the rights of citizens less than the need to punish and discipline subjects (Alou 2001; Roberts and Mann 1991; Tambedou 2008).

In Francophone countries, in addition, a culture of judicial independence is all the harder to institute because of the civil law tradition, that has the judiciary more closely linked to the executive and magistrates treated as civil servants (see Joireman; Tambedou 2008), which makes it even harder to break away from old colonial traditions. Similar issues of institutionalization confront fledgling legislatures before they can become effective constraints on the executive.

The Legislature. The other key institution for horizontal accountability is the legislature. The literature has long argued that the power of African legislatures to serve as an effective check on the executive branch is undermined by the various institutional mechanisms that reinforce presidential supremacy in many countries of the region (Barkan et al. 2010; Ochieng'Opalo 2019). Here, however, we are concerned by the capacity issues that could weaken legislatures. The power of legislatures is also surely related to the skills and training of individual legislators, and the evidence suggests they have been slowly but surely increasing (Barkan 2009; Ochieng'Opalo 2019). But the evidence also suggests African legislatures to be seriously underfunded with most legislators constrained by inadequate office space, and secretarial and research staff, a problem that has been exacerbated by the steady growth in the number of legislators for many African legislatures, since the onset of electoral competition in the early 1990s (Gerzso and van de Walle 2022). Many African legislatures do not have the capacity to use member committees to review bill proposals from government before they vote on them (Barkan et al. 2010, pp. 19–20). Few legislatures have a proper library. The poorest countries in some cases lack a comprehensive Hansard, or its equivalent, that provides a record of all legislative activities since independence.

Like all legislators in the world, African representatives understand that they need to undertake constituency service, monitor the performance of the government in their home district, and perform to the expectations of their constituents to get reelected. However, these tasks are made comparatively more difficult when there is poor infrastructure. Just getting to and from the constituency may not be easy for many legislators representing districts far from the capital. In the rainy season, in many countries, the ability to drive to one's rural constituency may be seriously compromised, given the state of the roads. Communications technologies have improved dramatically, but may still be constraining, particularly in times of emergencies.

Poor rural infrastructure in low-income states favors better-funded incumbent parties. Opposition parties may shine in key moments, but might fail to consistently win seats, given resource imbalances, low party institutionalization, and the low esteem in which they are held in the overwhelming majority of low-income countries (Bleck and van de Walle 2018). Poor public infrastructure, such as bad roads, increases the cost of citizens outreach and will create a disproportionate advantage in favor of incumbent parties, which can tap into state resources and local administration to enhance their presence in remote areas during campaigns as well as outside of the political business cycle (Paget 2019; Wahman and Boone 2018). These inequities limit responsiveness of all representatives to rural populations, but also enhance incumbency advantage for parties in power.

Finally, in a resource poor environment, the ability of the executive to wield state resources for partisan purposes weakens both the legislature and individual legislators, particularly of the opposition. It is harder for the legislature to assert and broadcast its own narrative in periods of legislature–executive contention, and the unity of the legislature is systematically undermined by the ability of the executive to co-opt its members with selective promises of positions in government and pork barrel spending in their districts. Opposition legislators are particularly at a disadvantage if the administration chooses to starve their districts of spending since voters may pragmatically view voting for the opposition as a material disadvantage. As Lindberg (2010) and others have noted, in an environment in which the state towers over other actors in terms of reach and wealth, voters expect and demand a generosity from their representatives that few are able to afford. Indeed, the ability to appear responsive to voters has led opposition parties to enthusiastically support "constituency development funds," which provide each legislator with a financial allocation to spend in their district on development activities, and in effect makes them less reliant on gaining the good graces of the administration.

4.5 CONCLUDING REMARKS

Disaggregating democratic institutions into mechanisms of vertical and horizontal accountability provides a useful frame with which to hypothesize about the impact of low state capacity on democratic politics, as it allows us to explain suggestive recurring patterns that we observe in many low-income electoral regimes. These regimes often combine reasonably free and fair elections, a free press, and a relatively active civil society in the big urban areas, as well as some occasional judicial independence the capital; with weak and pliant legislatures, incumbent presidents that dominate the political scene and appear largely above the law, and the quality of rights declining sharply the further away from the capital one travels.

We conclude this essay with a brief discussion of several factors that can complicate our narrative.

First, in low-income countries, there is a heightened possibility that issues of political stability can have a significant impact on democratic regimes that they do not have on low-income authoritarian regimes. We should note that this chapter simplifies the analysis by assuming that there are no active insurgencies; our scope conditions exclude regimes with active challengers. Insecurity can render electoral competition entirely infeasible if insurgent groups close polls, kidnap candidates, or dissuade participation. Limited state presence and state weakness allow room for these groups to make arguments for their leadership and simultaneously make it difficult for the government to combat and resist these groups. We readily concede that low-income states which do not project power or maintain a monopoly on the legitimate use of violence across the majority of the territory can witness a significant decline in the level of procedural democracy as a result of an insurgency or a climate of general lawlessness in the state's periphery, since they clearly undermine civil and political rights for a segment of the population.

Second, it is important not to conflate political will and political capacity. Often enough, certain actions are not taken or certain institutions are not supported, not from a lack of capacity, but because powerful actors do not think it in their interest to do so. The comparative literature also underscores the role of political will. In their analysis of regime trajectories in Latin America since 1900, Mainwaring and Pérez-Liñán argue that political actors and their "normative preferences about democracy and dictatorship, their moderation or radicalization in policy preferences" are key factors in understanding regime survival or failure (2013, pp. 5–6). These political factors are largely questions of political will, but they also suggest that it is important to explore how variation in state capacity might affect the salience of actors' preferences for democracy or other regimes. As we have suggested, the lack of political will to govern democratically by the incumbent government is more likely to weaken institutions of horizontal accountability than those of vertical accountability.

On the other hand, there are plenty of examples of political decisions to act resulting in the manufacturing of capacity to carry out significant policy shifts, across a large number of sectors. Elischer (2021) provides a useful example of this in his discussion of how a number of states with very low capacity proved able to regulate religious actors in their territory in order to prevent the rise of fundamentalist Muslim groups, while other states with similar or greater levels of state capacity could not do so. Another example is provided by the emergence of effective, independent electoral commissions to oversee free and fair elections. In these cases, the commitment to a policy resulted in the progressive emergence of capacity to ensure the policy's effective implementation. The logical counterfactual to such successes is that often when certain democratic practices are not achieved, it is equally likely that it was not so much due to low state capacity as it was to low political will. Most low-income countries have the human capital needed to establish effective electoral commissions (Gazibo 2006; Kerr 2013). Many more have failed to do so because some proportion of the political elite found it in its interest to undermine such a body. Yet, the political will that creates and supports an independent electoral commission makes a significant difference in the likelihood of well-administered and free and fair elections, as suggested by Piccolino's interesting comparison between elections in Ghana and Côte d'Ivoire (Piccolino 2016). It is not clear whether or not this is a cause of celebration, given how few effective independent electoral commissions have emerged in low-income countries; but, here as well, it does confirm that the easy relationship between state capacity and democracy posited in much of the literature needs to be reexamined.

Third, this chapter has hinted at the role of the international community and its relationship to capacity and democracy. In the Latin American context, Mainwaring and Pérez-Liñán discuss the ways that international and regional effects can impact capacity and/or regime trajectories through norm diffusion, material resources, sanctions, or military intervention favoring incumbent or opposition actors (2013, pp. 211–15). In some recent instances in West Africa, the state's inability to fulfill its basic functions and the international community's emphasis on elections can build popular discontent with the governing regimes as well as domestic support for these military regimes. Indeed, analysts point to the tremendous gap between procedural and substantive democracy as a primary obstacle to regime stability and governance in places like Mali (Soumano 2023). A productive future research agenda could look at the impact of the international political influences on state capacity and democracy.

REFERENCES

Alou, Mahaman Tidjani. "La justice au plus offrant: les infortunes du système judiciaire en Afrique de l'Ouest (autour du cas du Niger)." *Politique Africaine* 83, 2001: 59–78.

Andersen, David, Jørgen Møller, and Svend-Erik Skaaning. "The State-Democracy Nexus: Conceptual Distinctions, Theoretical Perspectives, and Comparative Approaches." *Democratization* 21 (7), 2014: 1203–1220.

Arriola, Leonardo R. *Multi-ethnic Coalitions in Africa: Business Financing of Opposition Election Campaigns*. Cambridge: Cambridge University Press, 2013.

Ayalew, Yohannes Eneyew. "The Internet Shutdown Muzzle(s) Freedom of Expression in Ethiopia: Competing Narratives." *Information & Communications Technology Law* 28 (2), 2019: 208–224.

Bäck, Hanna, and Axel Hadenius. "Democracy and State Capacity: Exploring a J-Shaped Relationship." *Governance* 21 (1), 2008: 1–24.

Bado, Arsène Brice. *Building Peace by Supporting Post-Conflict Electoral Processes*. PhD Dissertation, The University of Laval, 2016.

Banda, Tinenenji. *Access to Justice: Court Efficiency in Zambia* (Spring 2020, Ser. No. 17). The Occasional Paper Series of The Cornell Institute for African Development, 2019.

Barkan, Joel D., ed. *Legislative Power in Emerging African Democracies*. Boulder: Lynne Rienner Publishers, 2009.

Barkan, Joel D., Robert Mattes, Shaheen Mozaffar, and Kimberly Smiddy. "The African Legislatures Project: First Findings." 2010, CSSR Working Paper No. 277.

Bierschenk, Thomas. "The Everyday Functioning of an African Public Service: Informalization, Privatization and Corruption in Benin's Legal System." *The Journal of Legal Pluralism and Unofficial Law* 40 (57), 2008: 101–139.

Bleck, Jaimie, and Igor Logvinenko. "Weak States and Uneven Pluralism: Lessons from Mali and Kyrgyzstan." *Democratization* 25 (5), 2018: 804–823.

Bleck, Jaimie, and Nicolas van de Walle. *Electoral Politics in Africa Since 1990: Continuity in Change*. Cambridge: Cambridge University Press, 2018.

Bratton, Michael, and Eric C. C. Chang. "State Building and Democratization in Sub-Saharan Africa: Forwards, Backwards, or Together?" *Comparative Political Studies* 39 (9), 2006: 1059–1083.

Carbone, Giovanni, and Vincenzo Memoli. "Does Democratization Foster State Consolidation? Democratic Rule, Political Order, and Administrative Capacity." *Governance* 28 (1), 2015: 5–24.

Carbone, Giovanni, and Alessandro Pellegata. *Political Leadership in Africa: Leaders and Development South of the Sahara*. Cambridge: Cambridge University Press, 2020

Carothers, Thomas. "How Democracies Emerge: The 'Sequencing Fallacy.'" *Journal of Democracy* 18 (1), 2007: 12–27.

Dahl, Robert Alan. *Polyarchy: Participation and Opposition*. New Haven: Yale University Press, 1973.

Dupuy, Kendra. "Political Participation and Regime Responses," in Leonardo R. Arriola, Lise Rakner, and Nicolas van de Walle (eds.) *Democratic Backsliding in Africa?: Autocratization, Resilience, and Contention*. Oxford: Oxford University Press, 2023, pp. 37–57.

Elischer, Sebastian. *Salafism and Political Order in Africa*. Cambridge: Cambridge University Press, 2021.

Feld, Lars P., and Stefan Voigt. "Economic Growth and Judicial Independence: Cross-Country Evidence Using a New Set of Indicators." *European Journal of Political Economy* 19 (3), 2003: 497–527.

Fukuyama, Francis. *State-Building: Governance and World Order in the 21st Century.* Ithaca: Cornell University Press, 2001.

Gazibo, Mamoudou. "The Forging of Institutional Autonomy: A Comparative Study of Electoral Management Commissions in Africa." *Canadian Journal of Political Science/Revue canadienne de science politique* 39 (3), 2006: 611–633.

Gelb, Alan, and Anna Diofasi. "Biometric Elections in Poor Countries: Wasteful or a Worthwhile Investment?" *Review of Policy Research* 36 (3), 2019: 318–340.

Gerzso, Thalia, and Nicolas van de Walle. "The Politics of Legislative Expansion in Africa." *Comparative Political Studies* 55 (14), 2022: 2315–2348.

Gloppen, Siri, Marja Hinfelaar, and Lise Rakner. "Zimbabwe: Contested Autocratization," in Leonardo R. Arriola, Lise Rakner, and Nicolas van de Walle (eds.) *Democratic Backsliding in Africa? Autocratization, Resilience, and Contention.* Oxford: Oxford University Press, 2022, pp. 235–257.

Haggard, Stephan, Andrew MacIntyre, and Lydia Tiede. "The Rule of Law and Economic Development." *Annual Review of Political Science* 11, 2008: 205–234.

Huntington, Samuel P. *Political Order in Changing Societies.* New Haven: Yale University Press, 1968.

Joireman, Sandra Fullerton. "Inherited Legal Systems and Effective Rule of Law: Africa and the Colonial Legacy." *The Journal of Modern African Studies* 39 (4), 2001: 571–596.

Keita, Lamin. "Youth and Protest: How '#Gambia' Ended Decades of Autocratic Rule." *Canadian Journal of African Studies/Revue canadienne des études africaines* 57 (3), 2023: 585–604.

Kelley, Judith. "D-Minus Elections: The Politics and Norms of International Election Observation." *International Organization* 63 (4), 2009: 765–787.

Kerr, Nicholas N. The Causes and Consequences of Electoral Administrative Reform in Africa. PhD Dissertation, Michigan State University, 2013.

Kimenyi, Mwangi S. "Efficiency and Efficacy of Kenya's Constituency Development Fund: Theory and Evidence." 2005, Economics Working Papers No. 200542, https://digitalcommons.lib.uconn.edu/econ_wpapers/200542.

Levitsky, Steven, and Lucan A. Way. "Democracy's Past and Future: Why Democracy Needs a Level Playing Field." *Journal of Democracy* 21 (1), 2010: 57–68.

Lindberg, Staffan I. "What Accountability Pressures Do MPs in Africa Face and How Do They Respond? Evidence from Ghana." *The Journal of Modern African Studies* 48 (1), 2010: 117–142.

Linz, Juan J., and Alfred C. Stepan. "Toward Consolidated Democracies." *Journal of Democracy* 7 (2), 1996: 14–33.

Mainwaring, Scott, and Aníbal Pérez-Liñán. *Democracies and Dictatorships in Latin America: Emergence, Survival, and Fall.* Cambridge: Cambridge University Press, 2013.

Mann, Michael. "The Autonomous Power of the State: Its Origins, Mechanisms and Results." *European Journal of Sociology/Archives européennes de sociologie* 25 (2), 1984: 185–213.

Mazzuca, Sebastián L., and Gerardo L. Munck. "State or Democracy First? Alternative Perspectives on the State-Democracy Nexus." *Democratization* 21 (7), 2014: 1221–1243.

McKie, Kristin. "Presidential Term Limit Contravention: Abolish, Extend, Fail, or Respect?" *Comparative Political Studies* 52 (10), 2019: 1500–1534.

M'Cormack-Hale, Fredline, and Mavis Zupork Dome. "Africans Want Elections, but Fewer Believe They Work." *The Washington Post*, 2021.

Ndulo, Muna. "Judicial Reform, Constitutionalism and the Rule of Law in Zambia: From a Justice System to a Just System." *Zambia Social Science Journal* 2 (1), Article 3, 2011.

Ochieng'Opalo, Ken. *Legislative Development in Africa: Politics and Postcolonial Legacies*. Cambridge: Cambridge University Press, 2019.

Paget, Dan. "The Rally-Intensive Campaign: A Distinct Form of Electioneering in Sub-Saharan Africa and Beyond." *The International Journal of Press/Politics* 24 (4), 2019: 444–464.

Peiffer, Caryn, and Pierre Englebert. "Extraversion, Vulnerability to Donors, and Political Liberalization in Africa." *African Affairs* 111 (444), 2012: 355–378.

Piccolino, Giulia. "Infrastructural State Capacity for Democratization? Voter Registration and Identification in Côte d'Ivoire and Ghana Compared." *Democratization* 23 (3), 2016: 498–519.

Prempeh, H. Kwasi. "Progress and Retreat in Africa: Presidents Untamed." *Journal of Democracy* 19 (2), 2008: 109–123.

Resnick, Danielle, and Nicolas van de Walle, eds. *Democratic Trajectories in Africa: Unravelling the Impact of Foreign aid*. Oxford: Oxford University Press, 2013.

Roberts, Richard, and Kristin Mann, eds. *Law in Colonial Africa*. Vol. 199. Portsmouth: Heinemann, 1991.

Slater, Dan. "Can Leviathan Be Democratic? Competitive Elections, Robust Mass Politics, and State Infrastructural Power." *Studies in Comparative International Development* 43 (3), 2008: 252–272.

Schmitter, Philippe C., and Terry Lynn Karl. "What Democracy Is … and Is Not." *Journal of Democracy* 2 (3), 1991: 75–88.

Soifer, Hillel David. Authority over Distance: Explaining Variation in State Infrastructural Power in Latin America. PhD Dissertation, Harvard University, 2006.

Soifer, Hillel David. "State Infrastructural Power: Approaches to Conceptualization and Measurement." *Studies in Comparative International Development* 43 (3), 2008: 231–251.

Soumano, Moumouni. *L'intervention internationale à l'épreuve de la crise malienne*. Paris: Harmattan, 2023.

Tambedou, Malick. "De l'indépendance du pouvoir judiciaire au Sénégal." *Revue juridique et politique des états francophones* 62 (3), 2008: 271–314.

Wahman, Michael, and Catherine Boone. "*Captured countryside? Stability and change in sub-national support for African incumbent parties.*" *Comparative Politics* 50 (2), 2018) 189–216.

Way, Lucan A. *Pluralism by Default: Weak Autocrats and the Rise of Competitive Politics*. Baltimore: Johns Hopkins University Press, 2015.

The World Bank. "Zambia Judicial Sector Public Expenditure and Institutional Review (PEIR)" Report No: AUS0002884. Final Report (June 22, 2022). The World Bank, Washington DC.

Wrong, M. "Africa's Election Aid Fiasco." 2013. *The Spectator Online*, www.spectator.co.uk/2013/04/the-technological-fix/.

5

Democratic Backsliding and the Politicization of Public Employment

Frances Cayton and Bryn Rosenfeld

5.1 INTRODUCTION

When Viktor Orbán took office in Hungary in 2010, his Fidesz party quickly passed a new law allowing for the immediate dismissal of all government civil servants without any explanation. At first, the new rule applied only to those working in the central state administration. Later, it was extended to civil servants in regional and local self-government. Although the courts eventually struck down the new law, later reforms – including a 2013 amendment to the national security law that, among other things, increased surveillance of public servants and introduced loyalty into the measurement of performance – had a similar effect.

Under Orbán, Hungary has renationalized or otherwise increased state control over scores of companies across the energy, natural gas, and other utilities sectors as well as telecommunications and banking (Moldicz 2021). These nationalizations have brought within the state's purview thousands of new patronage jobs (Voszka 2018). The national oil company alone, over which Fidesz moved to assert greater control shortly after coming to power, employed more than 28,000 people, or 0.7 percent of Hungary's total workforce (Voszka 2018: 6).

Upon winning an outright majority in Poland's 2015 parliamentary election, Jarosław Kaczyński's Law and Justice (PiS) party followed a similar playbook. Just one month after PiS came to power, it pushed through a legal amendment, which changed the recruitment process and standards of the Polish civil service, undermining the existing requirements of open and competitive recruitment (Frank Bold 2016). It also removed all barriers to politically motivated dismissals. What followed was a massive purge of the civil service, local administration, and publicly owned companies (Tworzecki and Markowski 2017). While simultaneously moving against the judiciary to prevent challenges to its dismissals from gaining traction in the courts, PiS installed its own loyalists into these vacancies.

Besides the civil service law that PiS passed in December 2015, the party used new personnel statutes to place its loyalists across state-controlled institutions (Sadurski 2019: 137). Thirty-seven new statutes yielded over 11,000 new vacancies, which PiS immediately filled with its own cadres. In addition, PiS quickly replaced the top executives of Poland's largest state companies further extending the reach of its patronage. As Sadurski (2019: 138) concludes, "This was perhaps the most thorough, and at the same time least publicly and internationally visible, aspect of the state capture by PiS."

In the United States, the Heritage Foundation, working with a Budapest-based think tank funded by the Hungarian state, published detailed plans in 2023 to quickly capture control of the federal civil service (Shortis 2024). The Presidential Transition "Project 2025" – which runs to nearly 1,000 pages – lays out how the Republican administration should spend their first 180 days in office, with special emphasis on what Paul Dans, a former Trump administration official and director of Project 2025, describes as "flooding the zone with conservatives" (PBS 2023). Following Orbán's playbook, the plan recommends gutting the civil service through rule changes that would permit mass firings and appointments made on an acting basis to circumvent Congress (Skocpol 2024). The plan calls for the President to revive a Trump-era policy, known as Schedule F, that made it easier to fire career federal employees. If successful, the plan would reclassify tens of thousands of the two million federal employees and, its critics allege, "return the federal workforce to a 19th-century 'spoils system' with major turnover" (Heckman 2024). Up to 50,000 federal workers could be let go, with a chilling effect on those who remain in their jobs (PBS 2023).[1]

Although reorganization of the public sector and purges of public-sector payrolls have not been a central area of scholarly attention within the study of democratic backsliding (though see e.g., Bauer et al. 2021), activist groups opposing democratic erosion have recognized the bureaucracy as a crucial area of contention. Soon after PiS came to power, the Polish Committee for the Defense of Democracy (KOD) focused its efforts on the judiciary, state media, and the civil service. Within the Biden administration and in the US Congress, efforts to enhance protections for federal employees and make it tougher for a new administration to bring back Schedule F began before Trump's 2024 election victory.

This chapter's central argument is that politicization of public employment is an important, if understudied, component of the institutional landscape that makes democracy vulnerable to autocratic challenges. Politicization of public employment makes it more likely that backsliding becomes endogenous by generating electoral advantages for incumbents (i.e., by giving aspiring autocrats economic leverage to extract support and hamper the power of opposition forces) and, also, by raising the stakes of control over government. When the stakes of elections increase, and winning allows an incumbent to capture (or maintain their capture of) the bureaucracy, so too do the incentives

---

[1] This chapter went to press in the first days of the second Trump administration.

to grab power. Building on this volume's aim of untangling the relationship between institutional subversion and backsliding, we give particular attention to the timing and sequencing of these processes.

Empirically, we draw on several types of evidence primarily from Eastern Europe, but also contextualize our discussion using data from a broad global sample. We begin by exploring the relationship between public-sector politicization and democratic backsliding in Hungary and Poland over the past decade using Varieties of Democracy (V-Dem) project data. We then analyze turnover in public employment following the election of backsliders in Hungary and Poland, documenting the depth of politicization of the civil service that resulted in both countries. Next, we use cross-national data from V-Dem to consider the timing and sequencing of public-sector politicization and democratic backsliding across Eastern Europe and globally. These analyses show that changes in the impartiality of public administration both precede and predict subsequent changes in the quality of democracy. We then illustrate, using the example of Hungary's "Pathway to Work" program, how preexisting public-sector institutions that lack strong protections against politicization can make it easier for aspiring autocrats to grab and hold onto power. Finally, we examine the conditions in which politicization of public bureaucracies sometimes fails to result in significant democratic erosion. Using a case study of PiS's first term in Poland – an instance where state politicization was attempted but did not lead to a significant erosion of democracy and was instead followed by electoral turnover – we find evidence that the sequencing and form of politicization is crucial.

This evidence lends a better understanding of how governments in countries such as Poland and Hungary that once seemed to be the front-runners of democratization in the region have over the past decade succeeded at concentrating political and economic power. It also suggests that institutional changes which undermine the independence of public bureaucracies and extend the reach of the state leave a political system vulnerable to democratic erosion. Altogether, this chapter draws attention to the illiberal political economy that supports backsliding regimes and their capture of key levers of political power.

5.2 POLITICIZATION AND DEMOCRATIC BACKSLIDING

5.2.1 Definitions and Concepts

Some challenges to democracy occur from outside the democratic order, while others emerge endogenously from within democratic regimes themselves, as noted in this volume's Introduction. We are concerned with the latter class of threats to democracy and, specifically, with how politicization of public bureaucracies contributes to "the subversion of democracy by democratically elected incumbents" (Svolik 2019: 20). Backsliding, or incremental dedemocratization, represents incumbents' successful efforts to concentrate power, marginalize opponents, and free themselves of checks and balances.

Meanwhile, politicization, as we use the term here, refers to a lack of transparency in hiring and lack of protection from politically motivated dismissal that gives political actors discretion over jobs and other benefits in the public sector. According to Peters and Pierre (2004: 2), it is "the substitution of political criteria for merit-based criteria in the selection, retention, promotion, rewards, and disciplining of members of the public service."

5.2.2 The Relationship between Politicization and Backsliding

As framed by Wilson (1887) in his classic work on public administration, a competent, politically neutral bureaucracy is essential to democratic governance. Such neutrality is best achieved when legal constraints insulate bureaucrats from political pressures (Weber 1921). Following in this tradition, an extensive literature in comparative politics illustrates how bureaucratic quality affects party development and competition (see, for example, Shefter 1977, 1994; van de Walle 2003; Bustikova and Corduneanu-Huci 2017). While many studies consider how neutral, competent public bureaucracies are built and contribute to consolidating democratic gains, scholars have paid less attention to how they are dismantled. We still have much to learn about the timing and tactics of public-sector reform that encourage and advance democratic erosion.

Yet, empirically, the politicization of public employment institutions is often a core component of the strategy that authoritarian leaders use to win, expand, and keep power – and, in the process, gut democracy. Meyer-Sahling and Toth (2020), for example, explore the impact of democratic backsliding in Hungary on the management of top officials in public administration. In their framework, politicization and volatility in top official positions are a consequence of Hungary's democratic backsliding under Orbán (Bánkuti, Halmai, and Lane Scheppele 2012). Political control over public employment is part of an aspiring autocrat's tool kit.

At the same time, public-sector politicization may not only be a consequence of democratic backsliding, but also a risk factor – increasing the likelihood that backsliding becomes endogenous. Bauer and Becker (2020), for example, investigate how populist public administration policies make democracy more susceptible to erosion. Focusing on top officials, Ginsburg and Huq (2018) argue that politicization removes key obstacles to prospective efforts by incumbents to entrench themselves in the state. Such arguments predict that politicization of public employment will increase the likelihood of subsequent democratic backsliding.

Politicization also encourages anti-democratic power grabs by raising the stakes of elections. Because politicization ensures that a change in government also entails a change in politically dependent employment for public-sector bureaucrats and officials, it increases the costs of losing and the payoffs of winning an election. Moreover, as antidemocratic forces intervene in the bureaucracy, reshaping the state, they risk sharpening ideological divisions. Such polarization in turn also raises the stakes of elections with respect to policy.

In short then, politicization of public employment can be a consequence of democratic erosion, part of the tool kit by which illiberal incumbents are able to lock in electoral advantage and implement their policy agenda. But it can be a risk factor as well. By raising the stakes of elections, undermining their competitiveness, and giving incumbent governments an unfair electoral advantage, politicization of public bureaucracies encourages incumbents to grab power and hold onto it.

Finally, the close association between democratic backsliding and public-sector politicization may be a function of some other more fundamental factor, such as weak party competition. For example, Grzymala-Busse (2007: 63) argues that lack of competition limits checks on governing parties' power and lowers a governing party's incentives to submit to constraints that would check their opposition in the event it took power. And O'Dwyer (2006) shows that differences in the strength of party systems affect parties' incentives to politicize the state through patronage appointments (though see Haughton 2008 and Meyer-Sahling and Veen 2012 for critiques of this argument).

In sum, existing literature suggests several different approaches to the relationship between public-sector politicization and democratic backsliding, with no clear consensus. This chapter revisits these contrasting frames with the aim of contributing a better understanding of the causal processes and sequencing underlying this association. The evidence we present suggests that reforms which undermine the neutrality of public bureaucracies and extend the state's reach can immediately follow but also often *precede* democratic backsliding, suggesting that politicization is both a factor that makes democracy vulnerable as well as a tool that helps aspiring autocrats make backsliding processes endogenous.

5.2.3 Mechanisms: How Does Politicization Matter?

Scholars have long recognized that public-sector independence – and specifically, a professional, merit-based civil service – reinforces democracy (Wilson 1887; Weber 1921; Levitan 1942; Suleiman 2003). Indeed, a large body of work in public administration focuses on building less politically dependent bureaucracies in service of democratic consolidation. Although public bureaucracies often remain politically dependent in new democracies, scholars typically explain politicization as a function of weak party competition or an underdeveloped party system (O'Dwyer 2006; Grzymala Busse 2007). Politicization is thus viewed as a feature of bureaucracies in newly democratized states that will fade with fully fledged competitive democracy (though see e.g., Meyer-Sahling 2008). What happens when it does not? Does politicization of public bureaucracies make democracy more vulnerable to attack by elected authoritarians? What impact does it have as part of the arsenal of an elected autocrat?

Classic work on communist one-party systems underscores that political control over the bureaucracy and avenues of upward mobility play a crucial role in regime durability. Hence, János Kornai's (1992) account of Soviet political economy shows how universal state employment ensured communist regimes a high degree of social control and relative longevity. By giving the party control over appointments and making political loyalty the chief criterion for all senior posts in the economy and state administration, the Soviet *nomenklatura* system ensured elite loyalty over many decades of communist rule.

A large and politicized public sector appears equally important for the survival of contemporary autocracies. Studying Mexico's dominant-party system, Greene (2010; 2007) finds that a politically pliant public sector helped the PRI (Institutional Revolutionary Party) mobilize voters and extract resources to win elections. By limiting both private support and public expressions of support for democratization among politically pivotal middle-class professionals, Rosenfeld (2021) argues that a large, politically dependent public sector aids authoritarian survival in postcommunist countries today. Indeed, scholars studying regime transition link retrenchment in the size of the public economy to successful democratization (Greene 2010, 2007).

Building on this literature, we argue that politicization of public employment may contribute to subsequent democratic decline through several mechanisms. First, politicization of public employment allows incumbents to gain a more durable partisan advantage by doling out patronage jobs to supporters and withholding them from opponents. A politically dependent public sector generates the popular support that helps to make backsliding processes endogenous. For example, Orbán's expansion of Hungary's workfare policies created a large new base of politically dependent Fidesz voters (Vidra 2018), while his purges of the public sector after coming to office created vacancies that were filled by Fidesz loyalists among the Christian national middle class (Greskovits 2020). The presence of such loyalists in official positions has helped Fidesz's maintain its partisan electoral advantage.

Second, politicization of public bureaucracies furthers democratic erosion, because it allows an aspiring autocrat to direct civil servants to conduct their business on a pay-to-play basis or to apply political loyalty tests as a precondition for citizens to access basic government services. Beginning in 2010 in Hungary, further politicization of public employment allowed Fidesz to expand the range of nonprogrammatic strategies that it could deploy. With social assistance benefits conditioned on participation in the country's public employment program, politicization allowed Fidesz to direct its intermediaries in local administrations to exercise discretion over valuable economic and policy resources (Mares and Young 2019: 1–2).

Third, politicization of public bureaucracies gives incumbents power to press public employees into public displays of loyalty. It gives them the ability to recruit public employees for campaign-related work, from informing and mobilizing voters to falsifying the vote. As Mares and Young (2019: 2) write, "employees in [Orbán's] workfare program became a reserve army of voters whom the mayor can mobilize to achieve a particular electoral goal." And fourth, incumbents may use their control over politicized ministries and state enterprises to divert funds for political purposes.

As these examples make clear, autocratic challenges to democracy are more likely to succeed, more likely to produce the popular support and electoral advantages that make backsliding processes endogenous, and therefore more likely to result in meaningful dedemocratization, when incumbents wield wide discretion over the public sector. At the same time, a politically dependent public payroll increases the gains of winning an election and the costs of losing it. High-stakes elections can be bad for democracy, as Valerie J. Bunce notes in this volume's Conclusion, because they encourage incumbents to grab power in hopes of maintaining their position and preventing the opposition from winning in the future. A politicized public sector raises the stakes of elections, making electoral cheating and executive aggrandizement more appealing.

Finally, as Chiopris, Nalepa, and Vanberg (2024) argue, democratic backsliding is most likely to occur when voters are initially uncertain about an incumbents' intentions. From the voters' perspective, growth of the state apparatus and turnover favoring political loyalists may be ambiguous signals of an incumbent's intentions. Actions that politicize public bureaucracies could be consistent with the behavior of a closet autocrat or an ideological incumbent, since personnel changes can be political, policy motivated, or both. This makes public-sector politicization a particularly insidious risk factor for democratic erosion.

Two prominent cases of democratic backsliding illustrate these points.

5.3 THE EMPIRICAL LANDSCAPE, EASTERN EUROPE IN COMPARATIVE PERSPECTIVE

Figure 5.1 plots deterioration in the quality of democracy in two countries – Hungary and Poland – that have been a major focus of the growing literature on democratic backsliding (e.g., Bánkuti, Halmai, and Lane Scheppele 2012; Lane Scheppele 2013; Diamond 2015; Varol 2015; Grzymala-Busse 2019).[2] The solid black lines show the V-Dem rigorous and impartial public administration score, while the red dot-dash lines show liberal democracy scores (Coppedge et al. 2022).[3] Vertical lines reflect the entrance of backsliding parties. At first glance, the two metrics appear to move together. Though it remains hard to ascertain whether changes in one trend precede

---

[2] Though see Cianetti, Dawson, and Hanley (2018) for a perspective on democratic backsliding in Central and Eastern Europe that extends beyond the paradigmatic cases of Hungary and Poland.

[3] For a critique of these data, see Little and Meng (2024).

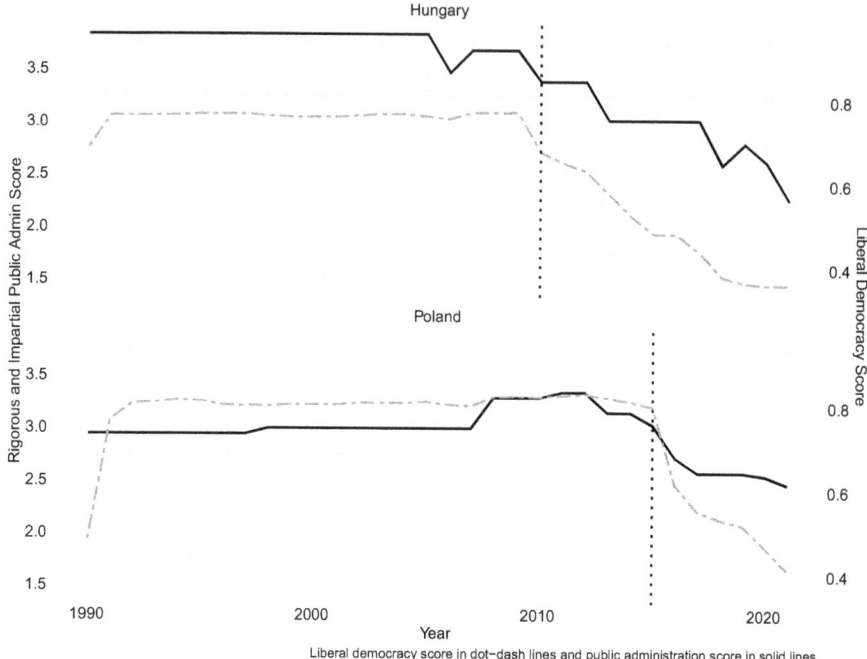

FIGURE 5.1 V-Dem rigorous and impartial public administration and liberal democracy scores for Hungary and Poland.[4]
Source: Coppedge et al. (2019).

changes in the other, it does appear that, in both Poland and Hungary, ratings of the impartiality of the country's public administration began to decline before liberal democracy was eroded – in Hungary around 2009[5] and in Poland around 2013.

In Hungary, significant and prolonged democratic decline is evident under Viktor Orbán and his Fidesz-led government from its election in 2010. Fidesz has remained Hungary's ruling party with Orbán as prime minister for four consecutive terms. In the parliamentary election of 2022 – for the fourth time since 2010 – Fidesz secured a constitutional majority, winning 83 percent of the single member district seats with just 53 percent of the vote.

---

[4] The V-Dem Liberal Democracy Index includes three subcomponents: equality before the law and individual liberty, judicial constrains on the executive, and legislative constrains on the executive. Among the indicators for the first of these subcomponents is rigorous and impartial public administration. The closeness of the concept of politicization and the operationalization of the outcome, democratic backsliding, raises several potential concerns – though it is also worth noting that the component regarding public administration is but one among a great many used to measure liberal democracy (Coppedge et al. 2019).

[5] Though with some earlier deterioration and then subsequent recovery around 2006.

In Poland, we see a marked decline in liberal democracy in 2015 after the PiS won an absolute majority of seats in the Sejm. Writing on the global decay of democratic institutions in an article published earlier that year, Diamond (2015: 148) described Poland's democracy as "firmly consolidated and secure" – while remarking ironically in hindsight that "the pace of decay in democratic institutions is not always evident to outside observers."

Although these are among the best-known and most widely studied cases of recent reversion, again there has been relatively little attention to the role of public-sector politicization in their democratic decline. While recent studies (see e.g., Hajnal 2015; Bauer and Becker 2020; Meyer-Sahling and Toth 2020; Bauer et al. 2021) have begun to address this gap, much remains to be done. In the realm of comparative research, our investigations into the "prime sites" for democratic backsliding have more often focused on the media and on judicial autonomy (e.g., Diamond 2015; Varol 2015; Blauberger and Kelemen 2017; Surowiec and Štětka 2020). Accordingly, scholars have often inquired into the effects of an independent press or an independent judiciary and less often into the consequences of politicization of public administration on democratic erosion.

One task of this chapter is to show that replacement of public-sector employees, politicization of their tenure and promotion, and growing centralization of state administration are frequently part of the playbook that accompanies democratic reversals. Politicization of the state bureaucracy is, as Singer (2018) puts it, one of the ways that leaders transform the transitory institutional leverage of incumbency into a source of permanent competitive advantage.

Less well understood, however, is the efficacy of bureaucratic autonomy and personnel protections in preventing regime reversals toward authoritarianism and, conversely, the degree to which the expansion of a pliant public sector increases the risk of democratic decline. We turn to this task in the second half of the chapter.

5.3.1 Politicization: Part of the Playbook in Eastern Europe's Democratic Backsliders

In this section, we consider politicization as part of the backsliding tool kit, looking at how it manifests *following* changes in government. Here we are less concerned with the long-term causes of democratic decline and more with the politicization of public employment as a key mechanism *by which* democracy declines.

To measure the extent to which recruitment and promotion in the public sector is politically dependent, scholars have used a variety of indicators. These include the relative weight of skills and merit versus political connections (Lapuente and Suzuki 2020), the absolute number (or alternately share) of positions in public administration that are subject to direct political appointment (e.g., Lewis 2008; Meyer-Sahling and Toth 2020), control by top political officials over dismissal (Lapuente and Suzuki 2020), the extent of turnover after government changes[6] (Meyer-Sahling and Toth 2020), and the absence of civil service laws (Grzymala-Busse 2007).[7]

In the analyses that follow, we focus on turnover after government changes, using an ordinal measure from the OECD. We also draw on data regarding the size of employment in the government sector, both in absolute terms and as a share of total employment – recognizing that the number of state employees may reflect changes in the functions and capacity of the state rather than politicization. In the present cases, however, there is strong evidence that fluctuations reflect the growth of patronage appointments.

5.3.1.1 *Hungary*

Hungary provides a striking case of democratic erosion and politicization of the government sector. In both absolute terms and as a share of total employment, jobs in public administration, defense, and social security expanded sharply in the years after Fidesz assumed power. By contrast, the trend across OECD countries was decidedly in the opposite direction (OECD 2017: 91).[8] To put the size of this increase in comparative perspective, Hungary (alongside Turkey) had in 2015 the highest annual growth rate of government employment of the 28 OECD countries for which data are available.

In Hungary, this trend has been especially marked among senior government civil servants whose ranks increased under Fidesz following each of its three election victories in 2010, 2014, and 2018. Using data on more than 1,600 top officials, Meyer-Sahling and Toth (2020) show that the number of appointments to top positions rose significantly with Fidesz's election in 2010 and continued to rise in subsequent years – testament to the growing political dependence of the top ranks of Hungary's civil service.

---

[6] Most measures of turnover could in theory reflect either rotation of cadres (i.e., reappointment of the same individual to a different position within government) or the dismissal of people appointed under the previous government in favor of people who are politically loyal to the new government.

[7] Several of these measures, such as the relative weight of skills and merits over political connections, are typically assessed using expert surveys. A drawback of these surveys, like all expert surveys, is that experts may not in fact have a clear view of the actual workings of bureaucratic appointment and promotion practices. Surveys of senior civil servants and in-depth interviews (e.g., Hanjal and Csengodi 2014) provide an insider perspective but may be biased in other ways if some individuals are reticent about taking part or are insincere in their responses. However, more quantitative/administrative measures do not necessarily provide a clear solution. And coding based on legal statutes may fail to capture actual practice (i.e., where existing formal civil service protections are disregarded).

[8] Though growth in the size of state bureaucracies has often been used as an indicator of state politicization, one obvious alternative explanation is that the number of state employees might reflect changes in the functions and capacity of the state rather than political motives.

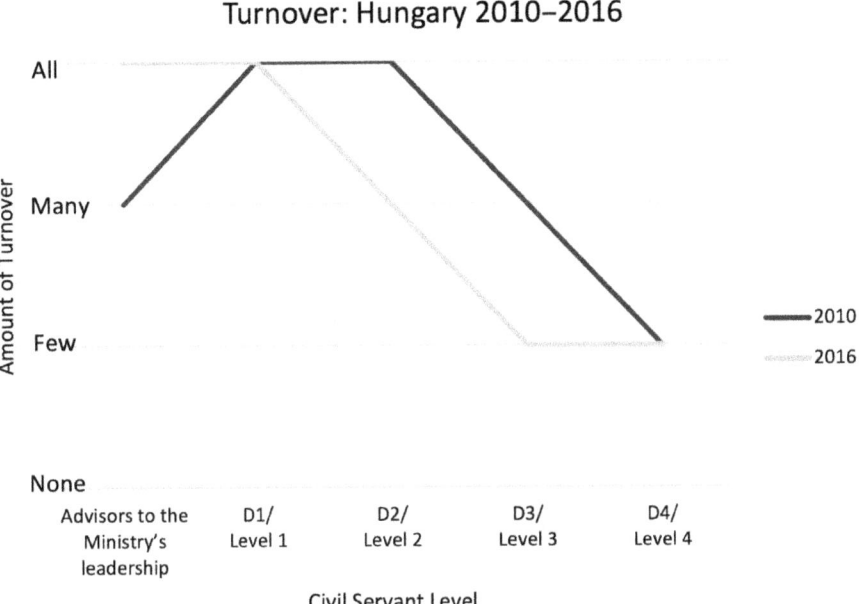

FIGURE 5.2 Civil service staff turnover with a change in government, Hungary.
Source: OECD 2011; 2017.

The political dependence and vulnerability of Hungarian public servants are reflected in their high rates of turnover. Figure 5.2 displays data from the OECD. After the election of Hungary's new Fidesz-led government in 2010, *all* positions changed systematically in the top two echelons of the civil service (i.e., Level 1 and Level 2) (OECD 2011). Such extensive turnover in the top ranks of civil servants after changes in government occurred only in Turkey and the Czech Republic among the thirty-five countries for which the OECD reports data. Turkey under Erdoğan is indeed another paradigmatic case of democratic erosion. Meanwhile, attention has recently turned to the Czech Republic, which experienced backsliding under the Babiš government between 2017 and 2021 (Hanley and Vachudova 2018).

Looking below the top ranks of Hungary's civil service, Figure 5.2 shows that turnover extends well into lower levels of the bureaucracy, too. In five categories out of six, there was turnover of civil servants with Fidesz's initial election victory in 2010 – a pattern shared after changes in government only in Turkey and Ukraine. Although following Fidesz's second victory in 2014, staff turnover below the top ranks declined somewhat as compared with 2010, turnover continued to filter down to the lower ranks of middle management. This pattern again sets Hungary apart from three-quarters of the countries for which the OECD reports data (OECD 2017: 145).

Last, it is noteworthy that in Hungary centralization of public administration has continued to increase since Fidesz's initial victory. Between 2011 and 2017, the share of government staff employed at the central level increased by 27 percentage points (OECD 2019: 86). This sizable shift is explained largely by the reorganization during this period of Hungary's territorial public administration. Schools and hospitals were again brought under the supervision of the central government, as they were in Soviet times. Funding for local governments has been cut by up to 80 percent. Various ministries and agencies were also merged, while a new type of agency was introduced that could be established by decree of the government without parliamentary legislation. These new agencies are not subject to the same accountability as the old agencies and are more susceptible to political meddling (Bauer and Becker 2020: 25).

Putting in historical context the turnover patterns just discussed, Meyer-Sahling and Toth (2020: 107–8) note that the degree of turnover in top positions under Fidesz is significantly higher than under any previous government during Hungary's first two postcommunist decades. Turnover remained high after the 2014 and 2018 elections – consistent both with continual vetting on political criteria and rotation of cadres to ensure loyalty.

At the same time, it is important to note that the trend toward rising politicization did not begin with the Fidesz-led government. Meyer-Sahling and Veen's (2012: 11) interviews from 2007 to 2009, before Fidesz's election, indicated that "many positions of strategic importance" within Hungary's senior civil service had "increasingly become politicised." Meanwhile, the preceding socialist government's workfare policies created important new opportunities for clientelism which aided the consolidation of Fidesz's authoritarian rule in rural Hungary after 2015 (Szombati 2021). We take up the question of how these trends toward rising politicization helped to enable subsequent democratic erosion under Orbán in the next section.

5.3.1.2   Poland

The strong association between politicization and backsliding evident in the V-Dem data of Figure 5.1 is corroborated by OECD data on turnovers for Poland, as well, pictured in Figure 5.3. Comparing statistics on turnover of civil servants[9] with a change in government before PiS took power and after (2010 vs. 2016), we see that previously there was turnover only in

---

[9] The OECD reports data on the turnover in civil servants following a change of government for 2016 and 2010 in its 2011 and 2017 reports, respectively. In the 2011 report, this information is broken down into seven categories: "Advisors to the Ministry's leadership," and then levels 1 through 6 with 6 being the lowest. In the 2017 report, there are only five categories: "Advisors to the Ministry's leadership" and D1 through D4, with D4 being the lowest. As D3 and D4 of the 2017 report are listed as "Middle Management" and Level 6 is listed as "Lowest," I assume for the purposes of this comparison that D3 and D4 are comparable to Level 3 and 4 respectively, and that Level 5 and 6 (not displayed in Figures 5.2 and 5.3) do not have counterparts in the 2017 report.

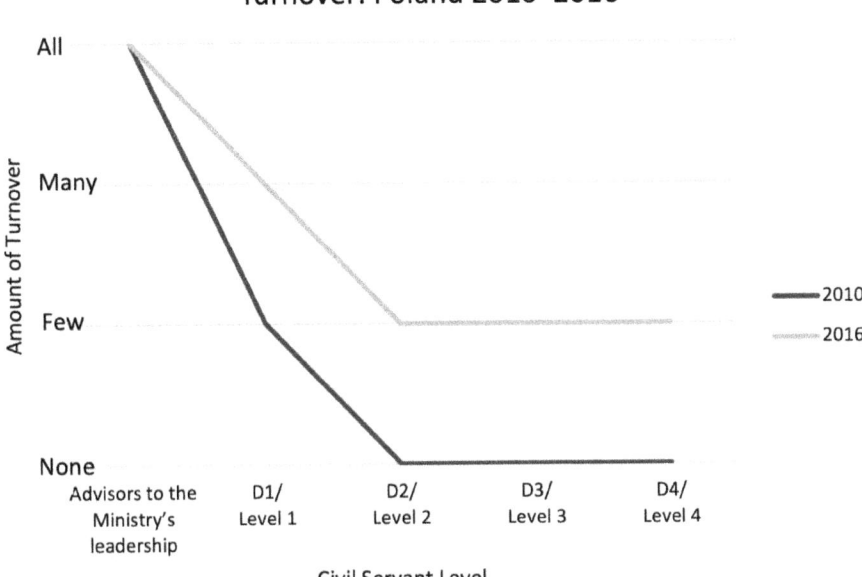

FIGURE 5.3 Civil service staff turnover with a change in government, Poland.
Source: OECD 2011; 2017.

advisors to a ministry's leadership and at the highest rank of civil servants. After PiS came to power turnover extended down to even the lower levels of middle management. For comparison: In seventeen OECD countries there is no turnover or very little in any of the four levels of senior civil servants when a change in government occurs (OECD 2017: 145). Relative to the level of turnover in other OECD countries, the extent to which PiS has doled out appointments to reward party loyalists is striking. Beyond these changes within the civil service, PiS also renationalized banks and power companies under its program of "repolonization," expanding the ranks of state enterprise workers on the government payroll in these and other industries.

What is unclear from the OECD data, however, is whether turnover began to rise under the Civic Platform government following the 2011 parliamentary election – that is, before PiS took power – or only after. Both the V-Dem data in Figure 5.1 and qualitative evidence on government turnover suggest that, in fact, the growth in politicization evident in Figure 5.3 is not due *entirely* to policies PiS enacted after its 2015 election victory. Instead, Heywood and Meyer-Sahling (2013: 197) observe a similar pattern of high turnover and many patronage appointments – which "reached further down into the ministries under their control" – during the first PiS government under Prime Minister Kaczyński between 2005 and 2006. And interviews that

Meyer-Sahling and Veen (2012: 11) conducted for their study *before* PiS came to power indicated that "the positions of Director General and director of department have also become increasingly political over the last few years." In short, then, while a longer series of OECD data on turnover is, unfortunately, not available, the V-Dem data in Figure 5.1 appear to indicate that politicization was already trending upward prior to 2015, a trend that accelerated under the second PiS government. Tracing the extent to which precedents such as rising politicization prior to the election victory of an aspiring autocrat may increase a country's subsequent susceptibility to democratic reversal remains an important task – one that we take up and test using cross-country evidence from V-Dem in the next section.

5.4   TIMING AND SEQUENCING OF PUBLIC-SECTOR POLITICIZATION AND DEMOCRATIC DECLINE

5.4.1   Cross-Country Analysis

Following the electoral victories of authoritarian challengers in Eastern Europe, attacks on public-sector independence quickly became part of the backsliding tool kit – a mechanism by which aspiring autocrats undermined democracy and aimed to secure lasting electoral advantage. However, the question still remains: Does a country's prior experience with politicization of the public sector heighten the risk of democratic reversal? To gain leverage on this question, we return to the V-Dem data, which provide time-series, cross-sectional measures of both "rigorous and impartial public administration" and a country's liberal democracy score.

   To start, the public administration score measures the "extent to which public administration is characterized by arbitrariness and biases (i.e., nepotism, cronyism, or discrimination)" (Coppedge et al. 2022: 178). This is measured on a 0 to 4 ordinal scale, with 0 indicating that "The law is not respected by the public officials. Arbitrary or biased administration of the law is rampant" and 4 "the law is generally fully respected by the public officials. Arbitrary or biased administration of the law is very limited" (Coppedge et al. 2022: 179). We operationalize backsliding using V-Dem's Liberal Democracy Index on a scale from 0 to 1, with higher values coded as more democratic (Coppedge et al. 2022).

   To explore the relationship between the politicization of public employment and democratic backsliding – and, in particular, whether weak public-sector independence may also be a structural factor in democratic decline – we next conduct a test of Granger causality in broader regional and global samples. A variable X_t Granger-causes Y_t if adding past values X_{t-1} (…) X_{t-k} alongside past values Y_{t-1} (…) Y_{t-k} has greater predictive capacity than just those values Y_{t-1} (…) Y_{t-k} (Granger 1969; Hood, Kidd, and Morris 2008). One may also rule out that Y_t Granger-causes X_t through the same test (Cromwell et al. 1994).[10]

Turning to the results, we find that lapses in a rigorous and impartial public administration routinely predict lower liberal democracy scores in the future. This holds across a series of specifications that vary the number of lags. Table 5.1 shows our results among a sample that includes East-Central Europe and the Balkans from 1990 to 2021.[11] In Table 5.1, we see that the inclusion of lagged values of a country's rigorous public administration score routinely increases our ability to account for variation in a country's liberal democracy score. We, therefore, conclude that impartial public administration Granger-causes democratic quality.

Meanwhile, politicization of the public sector is more tenuously predicted by prior years' liberal democracy score. At lower lags, there is a statistically significant relationship, but this effect disappears at higher lags. In other words, backsliding tends to produce growing politicization within a short timeframe, but there is little evidence that – all else equal – past episodes of backsliding make politicization more likely after several years. Taken together, this evidence suggests that politicization of the public sector may immediately follow but, importantly, also *precedes* democratic backsliding.

Next, to help parse the directionality of this relationship further, we turn to a global sample of V-Dem scores for the same 1990–2021 period for all global third-wave democratizers (Table 5.2).[12] The results remain very similar to those observed in the East-Central European countries. Across third-wave democratizers, declines in rigorous public administration tend to predict subsequent declines in liberal democracy. While in this global sample liberal democracy scores also predict subsequent changes in the impartiality of public administration, the results are again mixed. At some lags, they are significant and at others not, suggesting a more tenuous relationship.

---

[10] To carry out Granger tests, we must first establish that our data is stationary. We employ two comparable tests to detect unit roots: the Im–Pesaran–Shin and Fisher procedures (Maddala and Wu 1999). Appendix Table A5.1 presents statistics from these tests, which indicate that our data are stationary.

[11] The East-Central Europe and Balkan sample includes Bulgaria, Bosnia and Herzegovina, Croatia, Czechia, Estonia, Hungary, Latvia, Lithuania, Poland, Romania, Serbia, Slovakia, Slovenia, and Turkey.

[12] Third-wave sample includes: Albania, Argentina, Armenia, Barbados, Belarus, Benin, Bhutan, Bolivia, Bosnia and Herzegovina, Botswana, Brazil, Bulgaria, Burkina Faso, Cape Verde, Chile, Colombia, Croatia, Cyprus, Czechia, Dominican Republic, Ecuador, El Salvador, Estonia, Georgia, German Democratic Republic, Ghana, Greece, Guatemala, Guyana, Hungary, India, Indonesia, Israel, Italy, Jamaica, Japan, Kosovo, Latvia, Lesotho, Liberia, Lithuania, Malawi, Maldives, Mali, Malta, Mauritius, Mexico, Moldova, Mongolia, Namibia, Nepal, Nicaragua, Niger, Nigeria, North Macedonia, Panama, Paraguay, Peru, Philippines, Poland, Romania, Senegal, Serbia, Seychelles, Sierra Leone, Slovakia, Slovenia, Solomon Islands, South Africa, South Korea, Sri Lanka, Suriname, Taiwan, Thailand, Timor-Leste, Trinidad and Tobago, Tunisia, Turkey, Uruguay, Vanuatu, Venezuela, and Zambia.

TABLE 5.1 *Granger causality in East-Central European and Balkan sample*

	Years of lags				
	1	2	3	4	5
Rigorous public administration Granger causes liberal democracy score					
F statistic	13.918	4.9401	6.1529	3.7972	2.5845
p-value	<.001***	.0076**	<.001	.0049**	.0259*
Party strength control					
F statistic	14.22	3.3469	4.5474	3.1702	1.8414
p-value	<.001***	0.0362*	.0038**	.014*	.1042
Liberal democracy score Granger causes rigorous public administration					
F statistic	9.8644	6.7974	2.7663	1.7488	1.423
p-value	.0018**	.0013**	.042*	.1387	.2152
Party strength control					
F statistic	13.517	11.278	5.9133	4.1511	1.9896
p-value	<.001***	<.001***	<.001***	.0026**	.0797

Note: * $p<0.05$; ** $p<0.01$; *** $p<0.001$

TABLE 5.2 *Granger causality among third-wave democratizers*

	Years of lags				
	I	2	3	4	5
Rigorous public administration Granger causes liberal democracy score					
F statistic	58.374	46.427	34.837	25.505	18.789
p-value	<.001***	<.001***	<.001***	<.001***	<.001***
Party strength control					
F statistic	50.799	40.756	25.148	19.53	14.444
p-value	<.001***	<.001***	<.001***	<.001***	<.001***
Liberal democracy score Granger causes rigorous public administration					
F statistic	1.7314	9.6058	6.4171	3.5487	2.6177
p-value	.1884	<.001***	<.001***	.0068 **	.0229*
Party strength control					
F statistic	.8757	8.9182	5.8753	3.9326	2.6505
p-value	.3495	<.001***	<.001***	.0034**	.02142 *

Note: *p<0.05; **p<0.01; ***p<0.001
In both tables, column 1 displays results from the model with a lag of 1 year. Column 2 displays results from the model with lags up to 2 years. Column 3 with lags up to 3 years, column 4 with lags up to 4 years, and column 5 with lags up to 5 years.

An obvious potential confounder is the strength of the party system. We conduct a follow-up Granger test controlling for party strength via the V-Dem party institutionalization metric (Bizzarro, Hicken, and Self 2017). These results, which are very similar to those reported above, are also given in Tables 5.1 and 5.2, for both the regional and global samples. In sum, the party strength control does not change the consistent, statistically significant Granger relationship between a rigorous and impartial public administration and subsequent democratic performance.

Overall, these findings suggest that, across space and time, patronage-based public sectors make democracy vulnerable and should be viewed as an early warning sign for potential democratic erosion. Political systems that concede significant "spoils" to the victor are generally more prone to democratic degradation – and not only because they also suffer from weakly institutionalized parties. That US democracy was durable (if flawed) in the period of Jacksonian democracy and following Eisenhower's creation of Schedule C appointments, should not, considering this evidence, inspire confidence in the resilience of US democracy to new threats to public-sector independence. This evidence thus aligns with accounts of what has been termed variously as "sultanism," "patrimonialism," or simply "clientelism" – all of which conclude that a politically dependent public sector is pernicious for democracy.

5.4.2 When Public-Sector Policies Make Democracy Vulnerable: Hungary's Workfare Program

In this section, we explore how the nature of existing public-sector institutions shapes the likelihood that an aspirational autocrat succeeds at rolling back democracy. We aim to show how public-sector policies adopted by a prior government can make it easier for an aspiring autocrat to engage in executive aggrandizement.

One of the reasons Fidesz has been electorally successful is the support it has extracted from a public works program, introduced by the preceding socialist government in 2009. At the time the program was adopted, Ferenc Gyurcsány called it "the most important Social and Labor Reform Act since [communism's collapse]" (Vidra 2018: 73). The "Pathway to Work Program," passed by the socialists was itself built on earlier legislation that established a "work for benefit" principle but had been chronically underfunded. The socialists' workfare program extended the link between public work and social benefit conditionality and dramatically increased participation rates, quadrupling public work participants in the first year of the program (Vidra 2018: 76). Workers in the scheme do low-skill physical labor in public infrastructure and maintenance – from construction to street cleaning (IMF 2017).

Fidesz continued these programs and further expanded participation, gaining a massive electoral benefit from them among low-skilled voters, particularly in disadvantaged regions. Rule changes that Fidesz imposed in

2011 stipulated new conditions under which recipients could lose their entitlements. They also gave the local governments that were responsible for implementing the program broad discretion to determine ongoing eligibility. Together these changes only increased the program's coercive power.

Orbán's workfare program has failed as a policy for dealing with the problem of long-term unemployment. The IMF notes that it actually worsens participants' chances of becoming employed on the open labor market (IMF 2017). However, it both allows Fidesz to claim economic improvements, by pushing the unemployment rate down, and to benefit electorally from the patron-client relationships the program provides. By 2016, Hungary's public works scheme employed about 5 percent of the country's labor force (IMF 2017).

In their study of everyday electoral practices in postcommunist Hungary, Mares and Young (2019) note that control over employment allows Fidesz a broad range of coercive electoral strategies. Because social assistance benefits are conditioned on participation in the workfare program and Fidesz mayors control access, employees in the workfare program can be readily conscripted as loyal voters (Mares and Young 2019: 2). Meanwhile, the rents that accrue to mayors helps to ensure their continued loyalty. In sum, the expansion of Hungary's pliant public-sector workforce, a policy that preceded Orbán's rise to power, illustrates how public-sector policies and institutions may increase the risk of subsequent democratic decline.

5.4.3 The Dog that Didn't Bark: Poland 2005–2007

Having established that political control over employment can precede and potentially aid democratic reversal, the question remains: Can bureaucratic politicization increase without producing backsliding? Understanding these "near misses" can help to establish when and how politicization of the state bureaucracy proves a threat to democracy (Peters and Pierre 2022). Through process tracing of the Polish case, we find that while the first PiS government sought greater political control over public administration between 2005 and 2007, its reforms were limited in uptake due to unpopular but politically necessary coalition partners, strong checks from the courts, and a largely independent media. In turn, public administration reforms were reversible when PiS exited power in 2007.

By contrast, when PiS returned to power in 2015, it prioritized the politicization of certain elements of the state bureaucracy – in particular, the courts and state media – before others like the civil service and state ministries. This approach proved more dangerous for Poland's democracy – a danger that was magnified by PiS's outright majority in the 2015 parliamentary election. PiS governed for the second time in a less competitive environment in which it no longer had to rely on coalition partners. In this final section, we draw lessons about the relationship between politicization of the public bureaucracies and democratic backsliding from closer study of a case in which politicization increased, but democratic backsliding did not follow.

5.4.3.1 *Politicization without Backsliding*

As in Hungary, PiS inherited an already politicized bureaucracy in 2005. Despite reforms in the 1990s to ensure a politically neutral public sector, PiS's immediate predecessors also used patronage jobs to their benefit (Dziewanowski and Makarucha 2016: 105). While an apolitical public sector was *de jure* law, this was not de facto practice (Gwiazda 2008). Formalizing the status quo, PiS adopted a new Civil Service Act in 2006, which eliminated the Head, Office, and Council of Civil Service and filled these bureaus with cronies and copartisans (Kopińska 2018). Examination requirements to fill state positions were also relaxed and loopholes written so that acting managers hired into vacancies could assume their roles full time without passing any examination or going through a competitive recruitment process (Heywood and Meyer-Sahling 2008).

With the urging of its extreme right-wing coalition partners, PiS also undertook a series of attacks on government ministries. These reforms met harsh public backlash. Targeting cultural institutions, PiS passed a controversial schooling reform which installed ex-military officers in the Ministry of Education alongside controversial curriculum changes (Pankowski 2009: 183). With over 968,000 education employees in the public sector – 94 percent of all education employees nationally – these reforms made Poland's educational apparatus dependent on the state (Oleński et al. 2007: 239). Hiring for positions within the education ministry became personalistic, with pipelines running from right-wing student organizations. This practice also occurred in the state treasury and local governments (Kornak 2006).

Pressure from PiS's coalition partners also led to the resignation of PiS-appointed Foreign Minister Stefan Meller. When asked about his departure, Meller urged that PiS "wanted for me to stay but entering into government with Samoobrona and LPR [PiS's far-right coalition partners] put an end to my presence" (Milewicz 2006). Meller's comment points to tensions between the center-right and bombastic Eurosceptic factions of PiS and their coalition partners. Like the party's attacks on public education, these reforms reflect how niche interests within the party's coalition lacked popular backing.

Elsewhere, PiS adopted new lustration laws requiring individuals across a variety of professions to declare previous collaboration with communist authorities (Nalepa 2010). Some staff at the Institute for National Remembrance (IPN), which verified each declaration, overlapped with local-level PiS candidates and supporters. Critics claimed the law targeted political opponents and sought to control historical narrative. Public backlash from members of the targeted professional groups was swift. And many of the law's provisions were ultimately overruled by the Constitutional Tribunal (Pankowski 2010: 179–80).

Indeed, few of PiS's public-sector reforms outlasted the party's 2007 exit from power. The opposition party PO centered their 2007 campaign on reversing politicization of the civil service and public administration (Kópinska 2018: 30). Grassroots opposition was active, partly coalescing around critiques of PiS's educational reforms (Lempicka 2006). The 2007 election had the highest turnout of any previous Polish parliamentary election since 1989. Making good on their campaign promises, PO reversed many of the 2005–7 reforms with the adoption of a new Civil Service Act in 2008 (Dziewanowski and Makarucha 2016: 105; Kopińska 2018).

Why did the 2005–7 efforts to politicize public administration fail to further PiS's attempted consolidation of power? First, working with two fringe coalition partners who were politically necessary to sustain their coalition, PiS was trapped into unpopular and highly visible reforms. It was those reforms that went beyond existing norms of party patronage and advanced specific ideological aims that garnered the most public ire. Second, a free media environment facilitated public discourse and subsequent opposition. PiS's coalition tried – but failed – to bring the National Broadcasting Council (NBC) under presidential control. That effort was ruled unconstitutional by the Constitutional Tribunal (Jakubowicz 2008: 39–40). In this case, as in the case of the lustration laws, courts challenged public-sector politicization before it could stick.

5.4.3.2 *Politicization with Backsliding: Lessons Learned*

What lessons did PiS learn from its 2007 defeat, and how did these inform the success of public-sector politicization after 2015? When the party returned to power with an outright majority in November 2015, it sequenced its public-sector reforms differently. By mid-December, PiS had already launched an initiative to pack the courts and censor independent media (Połońska 2019; Sadurski 2019: 62–3). By April 2016, PiS restructured the public service broadcaster to be overseen by presidential and parliamentary appointees (Połońska 2019: 233). PiS also removed journalists critical of the party from the main public television station. Thus, politicization began not in the ministries but in the courts and public media – removing crucial obstacles to PiS's consolidation of power more effectively than in 2005–7.

After securing politically pliant courts and media, and without the challenge of coalition rule, PiS subsequently relaunched its more controversial reforms. In late December 2015, after the court and media reforms, PiS adopted a new Civil Service Act that limited the role of career public servants in hiring, ended competitive hiring, and eliminated the public posting of upper-level civil service positions (Dziewanowski and Makarucha 2016; Mazur 2021). Major public education reforms, mirroring those of 2005–7, started only after voters reelected PiS in 2020 (Kononczuk 2022).

5.4.3.3 Implications

Are some forms of politicization more dangerous for democracy than others? Or is it just a matter of degree? Further exploration of the Polish case suggests, first, that politicization of the public sector is more likely to advance backsliding in permissive environments, when competition is low or aspiring autocrats win with an outright majority. By contrast, it is more likely to fail when the environment is less permissive, that is when there is greater electoral competition or coalition government. Popular backlash – both electoral and from organized interests – may in such circumstances contribute to democracy's resilience. Second, while public-sector politicization may be a standard part of the executive aggrandizement tool kit, the sequencing of such reforms affects the efficacy of these reforms in a party's efforts to consolidate power. Undertaking unpopular public administration policies after coopting the judiciary and state media allows aspiring autocrats to hedge against institutional backlash and better secure the longevity of their reforms.

In short, political competition and strong guardrails in the courts and free media can hinder the success of efforts to politicize public administration and state industries. When backsliders first target employment in the judiciary and state media, they create a more permissive environment for further attacks on the independence of career public servants and state ministers. The sequencing of state politicization dictates the success of autocratic challenges to democracy and creates a more permissive environment for subsequent democratic erosion.

5.5 CONCLUSION

To sum up, a politicized public sector enhances vulnerability to democratic backsliding by making it easier for aspiring autocrats to sidestep bureaucratic backlash for their antidemocratic actions, and by creating patronage pipelines that help them to maintain the popular support that makes backsliding endogenous.

If we want to understand how governments in countries that once seemed to be the front-runners of democratization in Eastern Europe have succeeded in concentrating political and economic power over the past decade, we need to pay more attention to their public-sector policies. Both Hungary and Poland's governments have purged managers and professionals of the state sectors, replacing them with loyalists, on a scale unseen since the communist era. Similar efforts to extend executive power through politicization of the civil service have occurred in Turkey under Erdoğan and in the Czech Republic under Babiš. Indeed, Turkey and the Czech Republic are the only other OECD countries with rates of turnover that match Hungary's after 2010. The first Trump administration's policies, particularly Schedule F, an executive order which made it easier to fire tens of thousands of federal employees, reflect the same aims. One could likewise extend this investigation to the historical rise of fascism in Portugal, Germany, Italy, and Austria, which was also in each case accompanied by the politicization and purging of the public bureaucracies.

We illustrate that public-sector politicization can both precede democratic backsliding – acting as a facilitating condition – and, form part of an aspiring autocrat's tool kit, a mechanism by which democratic checks and balances are further dismantled. Utilizing V-Dem data, we show across a regional and global sample of third-wave democracies that decreases in rigorous public administration regularly precede declines in liberal democracy. Liberal democracy scores sometimes also predict changes in the impartiality of public administration, though these findings are more mixed. These results are consistent controlling for party system strength.

We underscore that the sequencing of attacks on the bureaucracy matters as does the competitiveness of the political environment. We illustrate how the public-sector policies of a previous government can facilitate an aspiring autocrat's own attacks on the bureaucracy, as in the case of Hungary. We also show that when incumbents face resistance from media and the courts – as in Poland under the first PiS government – attempts to undermine public-sector independence may be less likely to result in significant erosion. This may be true especially when incumbents face a more competitive electoral environment and/or rule in coalition. Under such conditions, aspiring autocrats may be drawn into pursuing unpopular public-sector policies. This may spur opposition from organized interests, removing backsliders from power before they can engage in substantial democratic reversal.

It is worth noting, by way of conclusion, some implications for governments that defeat backsliding parties. A government that seeks to put democracy back on track must also reverse the illiberal political economy that supports backsliding regimes and their capture of key levers of political power. Addressing the fears of dependent public employees, whose support helped maintain backsliders' electoral advantage, can help these new governments consolidate democratic gains. Donald Tusk's 2023 campaign promised to support pay raises for public employees, a move that was ratified in the formal coalition agreement adopted between Tusk's Koalicja Obywatelska party and its partners Lewica and Trzecia Droga (Szymczak 2023). Since entering office, this coalition has emphasized pay raises for teachers, civil servants, and administrators in ministries like the social service administration (ZUS) and state agricultural insurance fund (KRUS) (Cieślak-Wróblewska 2023a; 2023b). Such policies may reassure public employees following backsliders' exit, reducing public support for an aspiring autocrat's return to power.

Altogether, public administration remains a crucial venue of democratic contestation. Discerning whether and how the public sector can be leveraged to insulate regimes from democratic threats is a vital task for parties seeking to improve democratic resilience.

APPENDIX

TABLE A5.1 *Unit-root tests*

Test	ECE and Balkans		Third-wave Democratizers	
	test statistic	*p*-value	test statistic	*p*-value
Liberal democracy score				
Im, Pesaran, and Shin (2003)	−14.462	<.001***	−43.533	<.001***
Fisher Test (Choi 2001)	−22.96	<.001***	−75.191	<.001***
Rigorous public administration Score				
Im, Pesaran, and Shin (2003)	−11.946	<.001***	−45.969	<.001***
Fisher Test (Choi 2001)	−16.79	<.001***	−82.314	<.001***

Note: $*p<0.05$; $**p<0.01$; $***p<0.001$

REFERENCES

Bánkuti, Miklós, Gabor Halmai, and Kim Lane Scheppele. 2012. "Hungary's Illiberal Turn: Disabling the Constitution." *Journal of Democracy* 23(3): 138–46.
Bauer, Michael W. and Stefan Becker. 2020. Democratic Backsliding, Populism, and Public Administration, *Perspectives on Public Management and Governance* 3(1): 19–31.
Bauer, Michael W., B. Guy Peters, Jon Pierre, Kutsal Yesilkagit, and Stefan Becker (eds.). 2021. *Democratic Backsliding and Public Administration: How Populists in Government Transform State Bureaucracies*. Cambridge: Cambridge University Press.
Bizzarro Fernando, Allen Hicken, and Darin Self. 2017. "The V-Dem Party Institutionalization Index: A New Global Indicator (1900–2015)." *SSRN Electronic Journal*. www.ssrn.com/abstract=2968265 (accessed January 30, 2023).
Blauberger, M. and R. Daniel Kelemen. 2017. "Can Courts Rescue National Democracy? Judicial Safeguards against Democratic Backsliding in the EU." *Journal of European Public Policy* 24(3): 321–36.
Bustikova, Lenka and Cristina Corduneanu-Huci. 2017. "Patronage, Trust, and State Capacity: The Historical Trajectories of Clientelism." *World Politics* 69(2): 277–326.
Chiopris, Caterina, Monika Nalepa, and Georg Vanberg. 2024. "A Wolf in Sheep's Clothing: Citizen Uncertainty and Democratic Backsliding." The Journal of Politics. Forthcoming. https://doi.org/10.1086/734253.

Choi, In. 2001. "Unit Root Tests for Panel Data." *Journal of International Money and Finance* 20(2): 249–72.

Cianetti, Licia, James Dawson, and Seán Hanley. 2018. "Rethinking 'Democratic Backsliding' in Central and Eastern Europe: Looking Beyond Hungary and Poland." *East European Politics* 34(3): 243–56.

Cieślak-Wróblewska, Anna. 2023a. "Pracownicy budżetówki mają się gorzej za rządów PiS." *Rzeczpospolita.* https://tinyurl.com/cx9za5md (accessed May 16, 2024).

Cieślak-Wróblewska, Anna. 2023b. "Rząd Tuska zwiększa deficyt zaplanowany przez PiS. Wystarczy na obietnice?" *Rzeczpospolita.* https://tinyurl.com/3r4t37ea (accessed May 20, 2024).

Coppedge, Michael, John Gerring, Carl H. Knutsen, Joshua Krusell, Juraj Medzihorsky, Josefine Pernes, Svend-Erik Skaaning, Natalia Stepanova, Jan Teorell, Eitan Tzelgov, Steven L. Wilson, and Staffan L, Lindberg. (2019). "The Methodology of 'Varieties of Democracy' (V-Dem)[1]." *Bulletin of Sociological Methodology/ Bulletin de Méthodologie Sociologique* 143(1): 107–33.

Coppedge, Michael, John Gerring, Carl H. Knutsen, Staffan I Lindberg, Jan Teorell, David Altman, Michael Bernhard et al. 2022. "*V-Dem Codebook V12.*" Varieties of Democracy (V-Dem) Project. Gothenburg: Varieties of Democracy (V-Dem) Institute.

Cromwell, Jeff, Michael Hannan, Walter Labys, and Michel Terraza. 1994. *Multivariate Tests for Time Series Models.* Thousand Oaks: SAGE Publications, Inc.

Diamond, Larry. (2015). "Facing Up to the Democratic Recession." *Journal of Democracy* 26(1): 141–55.

Dziewanowski, Artur and Aleksandra Makarucha. 2016. "Ustawa o Służbie Cywilnej. Prawne Instrumenty Zapobiegania Korupcji." In *Korupcja w Administracji,* eds. Małgorzata Myśliwiec and Agnieszka Turska-Kawa. Katowice: Fundacja Akademicka IPSO ORDO, 103–20.

Frank Bold. 2016. "Briefing on the Polish Civil Service Act: Risk of politicization in Polish civil service." https://tinyurl.com/bdhjrv46 (accessed May 20, 2024).

Ginsburg, Tom and Aziz Huq. 2018. "Democracy's Near Misses." *Journal of Democracy* 29(4): 16–30.

Granger, Clive W. J. 1969. "Investigating Causal Relations by Econometric Models and Cross-Spectral Methods." *Econometrica* 37(3): 424–38.

Greene, Kenneth F. 2007. Why Dominant Parties Lose: Mexico's Democratization in Comparative Perspective. New York: Cambridge University Press.

Greene, Kenneth F. 2010. "The Political Economy of Authoritarian Single-Party Dominance." *Comparative Political Studies* 43(7): 807–34.

Greskovits, Béla. 2020. "Rebuilding the Hungarian Right through Conquering Civil Society: the Civic Circles Movement." *East European Politics* 36(2): 247–66.

Grzymala-Busse, Anna. 2007. Rebuilding Leviathan: Party Competition and State Exploitation in Post-Communist Democracies. New York: Cambridge University Press.

Grzymala-Busse, Anna. 2019. "How Populists Rule: The Consequences for Democratic Governance." *Polity* 51(4): 707–17.

Gwiazda, Anna. 2008. "Party Patronage in Poland: The Democratic Left Alliance and Law and Justice Compared." *East European Politics and Societies* 22(4): 802–27.

Hajnal, György and Sándor Csengődi. 2014. "When Crisis Hits Superman: Change and Stability of Political Control and Politicization in Hungary." *Administrative Culture* 15(1), 39–57.

Hajnal, György. 2015. "Illiberalism in the Making: Orbán-Era Governance Reforms in the View of the Administrative Elite." In *Contemporary Governance Models and Practices in Central and Eastern Europe*, eds. Polonca Kovač and György Gajduschek. Bratislava: NISPAcee Press, 133–56.

Hanley, Seán and Milada Anna Vachudova. 2018. "Understanding the Illiberal Turn: Democratic Backsliding in the Czech Republic." *East European Politics* 34(3): 276–96.

Haughton, Tim. 2008. "Parties, Patronage and the Post-Communist State." *Comparative European Politics* 6(4): 486–500.

Heckman, Jory. 2024. "OPM defends rule to hamper Schedule F's return" 22 May. *Federal News Network*. https://tinyurl.com/bt4wyz36 (accessed May 24, 2024).

Heywood, Paul and Jan-Hinrik Meyer-Sahling. 2008. "Corruption Risks and the Management of the Ministerial Bureaucracy in Poland." Sprawne Państwo Program Ernst-Young. https://tinyurl.com/4bb3msvf.

Heywood, Paul and Jan-Hinrik Meyer-Sahling. 2013. "Danger Zones of Corruption: How Management of the Ministerial Bureaucracy Affects Corruption Risks in Poland." *Public Administration and Development* 33(3): 191–204.

Hood, M. V., Quentin Kidd, and Irwin L. Morris. 2008. "Two Sides of the Same Coin? Employing Granger Causality Tests in a Time Series Cross-Section Framework." *Political Analysis* 16(3): 324–44.

Im, Kyung So, Mohammad Pesaran, and Yongcheol Shin. 2003. "Testing for Unit Roots in Heterogeneous Panels." *Journal of Econometrics* 115(1): 53–74.

International Monetary Fund. European Dept (IMF). 2017. "Hungary: Selected Issues." *IMF Staff Country Reports* 124, A003. https://doi.org/10.5089/9781484300473.002.

Jakubowicz, Karol. 2008. "Going to Extremes? Two Polish Governments Deal with the Media." *Global Media Journal: Wydanie Polskie* 4(1): 24–50.

Kononczuk, Peter. 2022. "New Bill to Centralise Control over Polish Schools Sparks Protests inside and outside Parliament." *Notes from Poland*. https://tinyurl.com/yc3hpa7z (accessed January 29, 2023).

Kopińska, Grażyna. 2018. *Polityka personalna w okresie od 16 listopada*. Warszawa: Fundacja Batorego.

Kornai, János. 1992. *The Socialist System: The Political Economy of Communism*. Oxford: Oxford University Press.

Kornak, Marcin. 2006. "Młodzież Wszechpolska u Władzy." *Midrasz* 6(110).

Lane Scheppele, Kim 2013. "Commentary: The Rule of Law and the Frankenstate." *Governance* 26: 559–62.

Lapuente, Victor and Kohei Suzuki. 2020. "Politicization, Bureaucratic Legalism, and Innovative Attitudes in the Public Sector." *Public Administration Review* 80(3): 454–67.

Lempicka, Marta. 2006. "Protests against the Minister of Education." Human Rights House Foundation. https://tinyurl.com/24whp938 (accessed November 19, 2022).

Levitan, David M. 1942. "The Neutrality of the Public Service." Public Administration Review 2(4): 317–3.

Lewis, David E. 2008. *The Politics of Presidential Appointments: Political Control and Bureaucratic Performance*. Princeton: Princeton University Press.

Little, Andrew T. and Anne Meng. 2024. "Measuring Democratic Backsliding." *PS: Political Science & Politics* 57(2): 1–13.

Maddala, G. S. and Shaowen Wu. 1999. "A Comparative Study of Unit Root Tests with Panel Data and a New Simple Test." *Oxford Bulletin of Economics and Statistics* 61 (S1): 631–52.

Mares, Isabela and Lauren Young. 2019. *Conditionality and Coercion: Electoral Clientelism in Eastern Europe*. Oxford: Oxford University Press.

Mazur, Stanisław. 2021. "Public Administration in Poland in the Times of Populist Drift." In *Democratic Backsliding and Public Administration*, eds. Michael W. Bauer, B. Guy Peters, Jon Pierre, Kutsal Yesilkagit, and Stefan Becker. Cambridge: Cambridge University Press, 100–126.

Meyer-Sahling, Jan-Hinrik. 2008. "The Changing Colours of the Post-Communist State: The Politicisation of the Senior Civil Service in Hungary." *European Journal of Political Research* 47: 1–33.

Meyer-Sahling, Jan-Hinrik and Tim Veen. 2012. "Governing the Post-Communist State: Government Alternation and Senior Civil Service Politicisation in Central and Eastern Europe." *East European Politics* 28(1): 4–22.

Meyer-Sahling, Jan-Hinrik and Fanni Toth. 2020. "Governing Illiberal Democracies: Democratic Backsliding and the Political Appointment of Top Officials in Hungary." *NISPAcee Journal of Public Administration and Policy* 13(2): 93–113.

Milewicz, Ewa. 2006. "Meller do Kaczyńskiego: Ja, sprzedawczyk?" *gazetapl*. https://wiadomosci.gazeta.pl/wiadomosci/7,114873,3397023.html (accessed January 29, 2023).

Moldicz, Csaba. 2021. "Hungary Economy Briefing: State-Owned Enterprises in Hungary." China-CEE Institute Weekly Briefing 37(2). https://china-cee.eu/wp-content/uploads/2021/02/2021e02_Hungary.pdf (accessed May 19, 2024).

Nalepa, Monika. 2010. *Skeletons in the Closet: Transitional Justice in Post-Communist Europe*. Cambridge: Cambridge University Press.

Nalepa, Monika. 2021. "Transitional Justice and Authoritarian Backsliding Constitutional Crises and Human Rights." *Constitutional Political Economy* 32 (3): 278–300.

O'Dwyer, Conor. 2006. *Runaway State-Building: Patronage Politics and Democratic Development*. Baltimore: Johns Hopkins University Press.

OECD. 2011. Government at a Glance 2011. Paris: OECD Publishing. https://doi.org/10.1787/gov_glance-2011-en.

OECD. 2017. Government at a Glance 2017. Paris: OECD Publishing. http://dx.doi.org/10.1787/gov_glance-2017-en.

OECD. 2019. Government at a Glance 2019. Paris: OECD Publishing. https://doi.org/10.1787/8ccf5c38-en.

Oleński, Józef et al. 2007. *Rocznik Statystyczny Rzeczypospolitej Polskiej 2007*. Warsaw: Ministerstwo Edukacji Narodowej.

Pankowski, Rafał. 2010. *The Populist Radical Right in Poland: The Patriots*. London; New York: Routledge.

PBS. 2023. "Conservatives Aim to Restructure US Government and Replace It with Trump's Vision" 29 Aug. https://tinyurl.com/yc3yz3fs (accessed May 20, 2024).

Peters, B. Guy and Jon Pierre. 2004. *Politicization of the Civil Service in Comparative Perspective: The Quest for Control.* London: Routledge.

Peters, B. Guy and Jon Pierre. 2022. "Politicisation of the Public Service during Democratic Backsliding: Alternative Perspectives." *Australian Journal of Public Administration* 81(4): 629–39.

Połońska, Eva. 2019. "Watchdog, Lapdog, or Attack Dog? Public Service Media and the Law and Justice Government in Poland." In *Public Service Broadcasting and Media Systems in Troubled European Democracies*, eds. Eva Połońska and Charlie Beckett. Cham: Springer International Publishing, 227–55. https://doi.org/10.1007/978-3-030-02710-0_11.

Rosenfeld, Bryn. 2021. *The Autocratic Middle Class: How State Dependency Reduces the Demand for Democracy.* Princeton: Princeton University Press.

Sadurski, Wojciech. 2019. *Poland's Constitutional Breakdown.* Oxford: Oxford University Press.

Shefter, Martin. 1977. "Party and Patronage: Germany, England, and Italy." *Politics & Society* 7(4): 403–51.

Shefter, Martin. 1994. *Political Parties and the State: The American Historical Experience.* Princeton: Princeton University Press.

Shortis, Emma. 2024. "Friday Essay: Project 2025, the Policy Substance behind Trump's Showmanship, Reveals a Radical Plan to Reshape the World," *The Conversation.* https://tinyurl.com/mm4azf26 (accessed May 20, 2024).

Singer, Matthew. 2018. "Delegating Away Democracy: How Good Representation and Policy Successes Can Undermine Democratic Legitimacy." *Comparative Political Studies* 51(13): 1754–88.

Skocpol, Theda. 2024. "Rising Threats to US Democracy: Roots and Responses." Lecture at Cornell University. www.cornell.edu/video/theda-skocpol-2024 (accessed May 20, 2024).

Svolik, Milan W. 2019. "Polarization versus Democracy." *Journal of Democracy* 30(3): 20–32. https://dx.doi.org/10.1353/jod.2019.0039.

Suleiman, Ezra. 2003. *Dismantling Democratic States.* Princeton: Princeton University Press.

Surowiec, Paweł and Václav Štětka. 2020. "Introduction: Media and Illiberal Democracy in Central and Eastern Europe." *East European Politics* 36(1): 1–8.

Szombati, Kristóf. 2021. "The Consolidation of Authoritarian Rule in Rural Hungary: Workfare and the Shift from Punitive Populist to Illiberal Paternalist Poverty Governance." *Europe-Asia Studies* 73(9): 1703–25. DOI: 10.1080/09668136.2021.1990861.

Szymczak, Jakub. 2023. "Podwyżki dla budżetówki w umowie koalicyjnej. Szef OPZZ: 'Za mało konkretów'." *OKO Press.* https://tinyurl.com/mrx68fw9 (accessed May 16, 2024).

Tworzecki, Hubert and Radosław Markowski. 2017. "Why Is Poland's Law and Justice Party Trying to Rein in the Judiciary?" *The Washington Post Monkey Cage Blog* 26 Jul. https://tinyurl.com/3dmacnmh (accessed May 16, 2024).

van de Walle, Nicolas. 2003. "Presidentialism and Clientelism in Africa's Emerging Party Systems." *The Journal of Modern African Studies* 41(2): 297–321.

Varol, Ozan. 2015. "Stealth Authoritarianism." *Iowa Law Review* 100(4): 1673–742.

Vidra, Zsuzsanna. 2018. "Hungary's Punitive Turn: The Shift from Welfare to Workfare." *Communist and Post-Communist Studies* 51(1): 73–80. https://doi .org/10.1016/j.postcomstud.2018.01.008.

Voszka, Éva. 2018. "Nationalisation in Hungary in the Post-Crisis Years: A Specific Twist on a European Trend?" *Europe-Asia Studies* 70(8): 1–22.

Weber, Max. 1921. *Economy and Society*, Vol 2. Berkeley: University of California Press.

Wilson, Woodrow. 1887. "The Study of Administration." *Political Science Quarterly* 2 (2): 197–222.

6

Election Administration and Democratic Fragility in the US

David A. Bateman, Robert C. Lieberman, and Aaron Childree

6.1 INTRODUCTION

The election of 2020 was a significant watershed in the evolution of US democracy and its slide toward vulnerability (Mettler et al. 2022). After decades of rising and converging threats to democracy and eroding norms and four years of a tumultuous presidency, the 2020 election spawned a divisive controversy over the election itself. The sitting president participated in a nationwide campaign challenging the emergency procedures that many states adopted to make voting safe and widely accessible during a global pandemic. As it became clear that the president had lost the election, his allies in and outside the administration sought to overturn the results, looking for ways to manipulate the procedures for counting votes and certifying the results and to twist the legal and constitutional process of presidential selection in his favor. These efforts culminated in a violent insurrection at the US Capitol that sought to disrupt the final step in that process.

Years later, despite the lack of evidence and the revelations of illegal actions inside and around the previous administration, a substantial majority of Republicans, voters and candidates alike, continued to claim that the election was fraudulent (Cuthbert and Theodoridis 2022; Gardner 2022; Monmouth University Poll 2022). Although the former president and his coconspirators ultimately failed to overturn the election, they continued after leaving office to press for changes in the processes governing US elections and in the personnel who direct them. These developments highlight the potential fragility of the structure of US elections (Hasen 2020) and prompt us to consider what might make them vulnerable to this kind of assault in the future.

Free and fair elections may not be sufficient to define a country as a democracy, as Joseph Schumpeter (1942, 269) postulated, but they are surely a necessary condition for that designation. Defined most succinctly by Adam Przeworski (1991, 10) as "as system in which parties lose elections," democracy requires not just that citizens and officials go through the mechanics of casting and counting ballots but also that the process actually generates a reasonable likelihood that those in power will lose and thus be induced to relinquish the reins of government to someone else. It is this inherent uncertainty in elections that potentially gives democracy a dynamic of accountability between rulers and ruled (Schmitter and Karl 1991; Manin, Przeworski, and Stokes 1999; Bateman 2022).

Much of the recent anxiety about democratic fragility, both in the United States and elsewhere, has revolved around the integrity of election systems and the erosion of their capacity to effect meaningful political and governmental change. Bermeo (2016) identifies "strategic electoral manipulation" – deliberate actions intended to undermine free and fair elections without the need to resort to outright election-day fraud – as a key form of democratic backsliding. If elected officials can successfully rig the electoral system in order to maintain themselves in power, then democracy decays precisely because elections lose their characteristic uncertainty and thus their ability to induce accountability and confer legitimacy (Levitsky and Ziblatt 2018).

Of course, elections might not disappear altogether. "Competitive authoritarian" regimes often hold elections that are highly participatory, effectively run, and even accurately counted but that still do not serve this key accountability function (Levitsky and Way 2002). Elections may fail along either of Robert Dahl's (1971) two critical dimensions of democratization: liberalization (or public contestation) and inclusiveness (or participation). On the inclusiveness dimension, elections might fail because key electoral processes – of voter access, counting, and reporting – are either restrictive or corrupt, resulting in the exclusion of some citizens' voices and preferences from collective decision-making. On the liberalization dimension, they may fail because challengers are suppressed, through restrictions on speech and information channels or suppression of political parties and other forms of collective action. If any of these conditions are violated, elections are neither free nor fair.

We focus here on the apparent challenge to free and fair elections that is currently occurring in the United States. For elections to be considered "free and fair," they should have several characteristics that we might, following Dahl, also classify along two overlapping dimensions. First, free and fair elections require the protection of ballot *access*. Access, in turn, has several components. It begins with widespread and well-enforced voting rights, ideally universal adult suffrage without categorical exclusions. Access also depends on low and equal procedural barriers to the exercise of voting rights; rules and procedures that impose undue burdens of time or other resources might inhibit voting by citizens who might otherwise be inclined to participate, and do so differentially (Herd and Moynihan 2018). Policies regarding voter registration and the maintenance of voter rolls can make voting either more or less accessible. Policies that impose additional costs on registered voters can also be construed as impeding access; common examples include ID requirements for casting a vote or laws limiting the provision of assistance to would-be voters. Access can also be restricted by policies that govern what the US Constitution (Article 1, Section 4) calls the "time, place, and manner of holding elections": the location and opening hours of in-person polling places, the availability of early voting (before the date designated as "election day"), the means of voting other than in person (by mail or in ballot drop boxes), for example. Beyond policy, access can be restricted through the discretion of "street-level bureaucrats" such as local election officers (White, Nathan, and Faller 2015).[1]

In the current deeply polarized and highly competitive electoral environment in the United States, ballot access has become a central axis of partisan competition (Bentele and O'Brien 2013; Hicks et al. 2014; Rocha and Matsubayashi 2014; McKee 2015). Democrats tend to favor more open access rules, especially on the suspicion that access restrictions disproportionately limit voting by groups that typically vote Democratic, such as racial and ethnic minorities, young people, and lower-income voters. Republicans, on the other hand, claim that liberal access rules result in fraudulent votes being cast and counted, and thus favor more restrictive access laws. Partisan polarization on this dimension has deep historical roots but has extended in recent years to include policies such as early voting or liberal absentee voting that historically had bipartisan support (Oliver 1996; Gronke 2008; Biggers and Hanmer 2015).

Changes in all of these access rules, in various combinations, have been increasingly common in the United States in recent years, especially since the Supreme Court's decision in *Shelby Counter v. Holder* 570 U.S. 529 (2013) (affirmed and amplified in *Brnovich v. Democratic National Committee* 594 U.S. 647 [2021]) relaxed the Voting Rights Act's limitations on state and local policy change. These changes are the subject of a growing literature that seeks to understand their causes and consequences and to connect them to the long history of racialized voter suppression and democratic vulnerability in the United States (Bentele and O'Brien 2013). Such policies might impede access directly, by making it more difficult for voters without the required identification or registration status to cast a ballot, or indirectly, by generating disparities in the quality and speed of election administration, producing long lines in some precincts and not others (Barreto, Cohen-Marks, and Woods 2009; Stewart and Ansolabehere 2015; Stein et al. 2020). There is little consensus on their net electoral impact, but wide recognition that the stipulated motivation of preventing voter fraud is not compelling and that whatever burdens these impose are likely to fall heaviest on poorer voters

---

[1] Discretion can be used to facilitate or impede access, and there is likely no a priori basis for establishing the right amount or use of discretion beyond a guiding principle that discretion should be used to facilitate access only up to the point where it interferes with maintaining the integrity of the electoral process.

who lean Democratic (Highton 2017; Hajnal, Kuk, and Lajevardi 2018; Burden 2018; Pryor, Herrick, and Davis 2019; Mickey 2022).

The second defining dimension of free and fair elections is the prevention of electoral *malfeasance*. Public confidence in electoral processes underlies even a minimal understanding of democracy: Elections can be biased, and even subject to a certain amount of malfeasance, but not so extensively that they throw into doubt the anticipated possibility of candidates' winning future elections. Aspirants to office, as well as citizens more generally, can accept electoral uncertainty and the possibility of losing if they believe that the process is not so rigged as to make winning impossible (Przeworski 1999; Bateman 2022). Ensuring that all votes are counted equally and correctly, that the rules are universally observed and fairly applied to all ballots and all candidates, and that the reported outcomes are accurate are essential to this calculation.

The evolution of professional election administration, with experienced or professional administrators and an increasingly thick and standardized body of procedures, has generally provided an important foundation for the impartial and reliable canvassing of ballots and the prevention of electoral malfeasance (James et al. 2019; Persily and Stewart 2021; Gaughan 2020, 252). The norms and practices of election administration are critical for ensuring that both principles are respected and trade-offs between them minimized. State and local election administrators in particular proved to be important bulwarks of access and electoral accuracy in the face of widespread partisan assault on the outcome of the 2020 presidential election (Jacobs and Choate 2022). Requests by the president to "find" votes went unheeded because the targeted administrators had sufficient regard for the integrity of the process as well as sufficiently circumscribed legal authority that acquiescence would have been neither administratively nor legally straightforward.

But as Jaimie Bleck and Nicolas van de Walle (Chapter 4 this volume) observe, this kind of effective state capacity can be double-edged; while it can facilitate free and fair elections and vertical accountability when effectively administered, it is also ripe for partisan capture. This is no less true in the United States than in the African settings that Bleck and van de Walle examine. Organized efforts to deny the election results have focused political and legal attention on the administration of elections. There are now a large number of candidates and elected officials who deny the outcome of the elections and argue, without evidence, that election administrators either committed malfeasance or failed to prevent it. This sentiment has widespread support among Republican voters and has encouraged an unprecedented level of intimidation and threats against election officials and workers (Hasen 2021; Stein and Hamburger 2022; Wines 2020). The appearance of an organized movement denying the integrity of the elections, often associated with fraudulent attempts to "audit" the vote, and campaigning for positions that would have authority over election administration, has prompted substantial worries that future elections might see a deliberate and partisan effort to make malfeasance easier to commit and conceal, and even to alter the results of elections.

The questioning of electoral integrity has fueled new political conflict over election authority, especially over who is entitled to change established processes or the conditions under which results are certified. For example, some states have shifted authority away from secretaries of state or local election boards and transferred it to newly created agencies or officials under the control of the state legislature. Journalists, as well as nonpartisan advocacy organizations, have documented widespread efforts across states to significantly change how elections are conducted, altering both access rules as well as election authority more broadly. Such moves seemingly create more opportunities for the strategic partisan manipulation of elections that Bermeo (2016) describes as a key pathway of democratic backsliding, and this has been a prominent theme in national coverage.

A critical backdrop to the attacks on election integrity is the flurry of rule changes instituted at the height of the COVID-19 pandemic, intended to protect voter access given public health concerns. In some states these changes were relatively consensual, but many others saw heated contestation among governors, state legislatures, local election officials, and state and federal courts (e.g., Zhang 2021). The timing of the pandemic's emergence in the United States was paradoxically fortuitous. A considerable number of states were still conducting their primaries, and the considerable disruptions in states such as Ohio and Wisconsin served as a "warning shot" that other states heard loud and clear (Persily and Stewart 2021, 161). The overall result was a triumph for access and integrity: Despite the pandemic, 2020 saw the highest turnout in a national election since 1900; states and localities successfully adapted to the pandemic; and the election was conducted with essentially zero credible and verifiable instances of fraud or error. The pandemic and the contested election, however, were a shock to the system, and the changes undertaken to ensure access, often under murky or ambiguous statutory authority, provided grist for conspiracy theories while also prompting legislative efforts to statutorily overturn or recognize them going forward.

6.2 WINNERS AND LOSERS

In their introductory essay to this volume, Kenneth M. Roberts, Valerie J. Bunce, Thomas B. Pepinsky, and Rachel Beatty Riedl emphasize the dual winners' and losers' dilemmas that confront actors in a democracy and shape the resilience or fragility of democratic regimes. For the losers of an election, the challenge is how to induce compliance and further democratic participation rather than reach for election chicanery or violence (Przeworski 1991). For the winners, on the other hand, the challenge is to restrain them from manipulating the system from within to tilt the playing field, lock in electoral gains, and stay in power (Levitsky and Ziblatt 2018). When either winners or losers, or both, are unwilling to accept the inherent uncertainty of democratic processes, democracy is at risk.

But the federated US electoral system introduces a new layer of complexity to these twinned dilemmas. National (i.e., presidential) elections in the United States are not single elections, but multiple elections, conducted in different places, under different rules, under the authority not of a national election management body (James et al. 2019) but of state governments and the local level administrative bodies they have established to manage the elections. Election administration is one of the principal "referee institutions" that Milan Vaishnav (Chapter 2 this volume) identifies, in which neutral competence acts as a key safeguard for democratic legitimacy and accountability against partisan assault. But the paradox of accountability that Vaishnav identifies in India also plagues the United States: These institutional safeguards are most at risk when they are challenged by a locally dominant party.

We generally think of the instruments of election administration as tools that are available to the winners in a democratic election, but in the United States, *national* losers may in fact be *local* winners; that is, the losing party in a presidential election will likely control (or share in the control of) the governments of some states and will inevitably have significant representation in the local administration of elections. In this way, the winners' and losers' dilemmas can be intermingled. A party that loses a national election might be tempted to use its control of state governments to try to ensure that it does not lose again, essentially acting out the winners' and losers' dilemma scripts simultaneously. And since the states where there is a discrepancy between the national and local result are perhaps especially likely to be pivotal for the national outcome, the opportunity for local winners to overturn a national loss is concentrated.

While it has to some degree always been present as a potential challenge to democracy in the United States, this state-level connection between winners' and losers' dilemmas is especially pertinent in contemporary US politics given the increasing nationalization of partisan conflict (Hopkins 2018; Mickey 2022). Historically, US parties were federated, rooted primarily in local cleavages and patterns of behavior; at the national level, they were aggregated "catch-all" parties. This helped push US politics toward the center and restrain antidemocratic extremism in national winner-take-all elections (Linz 1990), but it also meant that local winners were less invested in the success or failure of their national allies. But over the past few decades, partisan cleavages have become more nationally uniform, especially as white voters gravitated toward the Republican Party and partisanship itself became a key social identity for many Americans (Achen and Bartels 2016; Mason 2018). State politics has evolved to reflect and reinforce national conflicts rather than cutting across them. And whereas we often think of contentious political issues "bubbling up" from the states (Schickler 2016), it seems that national conflicts now increasingly "trickle down" to state and local arenas. In this context, state elected officials frequently use their positions to pursue national partisan agendas, as in recurring controversies over transgender rights, the teaching of history in schools, and the September 2022 stunt in which Florida Governor Ron DeSantis arranged for fifty Venezuelan migrants to be shipped to Massachusetts against their will. In the extreme, partisan control of state governments can undermine democracy (Grumbach 2022).

In the wake of the frenzy over false accusations of election fraud in the 2020 US presidential election, this framework suggests a particular focus on states controlled by Republicans, who faced both the winners' and losers' dilemmas at the same time. Several features of the 2020 election made state election authority a particularly inviting target for state-level Republicans. First, the COVID-19 pandemic prompted many states to alter their voting procedures to accommodate the public health crisis – often on the fly and sometimes on dubious legal or administrative authority. Many of these emergency changes were designed to ease early or absentee voting in order to lower newly raised barriers to participation for people affected by the pandemic and allow voters to avoid congregating indoors at in-person polling sites. As a result, nearly half of those who voted in 2020 cast absentee or mail-in ballots, more than double the share in 2016 (Stewart 2020). Republican and conservative activists were extensively involved in litigation to prevent these changes. Because Republican voters were less likely to vote early or remotely and because early and absentee ballots are often counted and reported more slowly than in-person election-day ballots, early election-night reports that appeared to show Donald Trump ahead in several pivotal states gave way over several days to more complete and accurate counts that favored the eventual winner, Joseph Biden.

This pattern fueled the chaos sown by the second key feature of the 2020 election: an incumbent president who refused to concede. Having warned against absentee balloting on the campaign trail, President Trump promoted increasingly extravagant claims of electoral fraud after the election day tallies left him unable to declare victory credibly. His rhetoric and the actions of his lawyers and supporters stoked mistrust in the election administration of battleground states not only as the count was happening but also long after the result was apparent. Trump and his team's postelection behavior notoriously included verbal assaults on state election administrators, Trump's own request to Georgia Secretary of State Brad Raffensperger to "just find 11,780 votes," and ultimately of course violent interference with the congressional certification of the presidential vote. These actions have placed state election administration squarely in the crosshairs of partisan politics after decades of hard-won political independence and carefully constructed capacity (Jacobs and Choate 2022).

This approach, based on nested winners' and losers' dilemmas in the distinctive US institutional context, suggests several empirical implications. First, we should expect to see the most strenuous efforts to assert partisan control over election administration in heavily contested battleground states.

In a partisan context in which most states' voters predictably choose one party or the other by fairly wide margins, the last two presidential elections in particular have heightened the importance of a few closely divided states whose electoral votes often prove decisive, where margins are often close, and where it is more likely that national losers will be local winners. In 2016, for example, three states – Pennsylvania, Wisconsin, and Michigan – supported Trump by a combined margin of fewer than 78,000 votes and tipped the Electoral College in his favor despite a national popular vote margin for Hillary Clinton of more nearly 2.9 million votes. Similarly, in 2020 four close states – Arizona, Georgia, Pennsylvania, and Wisconsin again – proved decisive, supporting Biden by a total of fewer than 124,000 votes (out of Biden's popular margin of more than 7 million). Such states, where the ability to shift small numbers of votes could have large electoral consequences, should prove especially fertile ground for partisan challenges to election administration. Second, these challenges should be more likely in states where the government is controlled by the national losing party, which has a stronger incentive to sow skepticism of the results and to seek future electoral advantages.

But these propositions assume some kind of partisan symmetry; if both parties are equally committed to upholding democracy, neither party should challenge evidently accurate and fair election results. Conversely, if both parties are equally intent on winning at all costs (even if it means subverting democratic norms), we should observe both parties succumbing to the losers' temptation to capitalize on state government control. There is, in fact, some suggestive experimental evidence that members of both parties are willing to accept antidemocratic behavior from their copartisans (Graham and Svolik 2020). But evidence has mounted in recent years of a weakening Republican commitment to democracy (Levitsky and Ziblatt 2018; Mettler and Lieberman 2020; Kalmoe and Mason 2022). Jacob M. Grumbach (2022) has shown that the commitment to democracy varies substantially across US states, and in particular that Republican control of state governments is associated with sharp declines in state-level democratic institutions, especially since 2010. These trends suggest that the parties might not be equally likely to engage in this kind of electoral hardball and that we should expect Republicans to be more likely to seek to shift election authority in order to influence election outcomes. In the contemporary era of effectively nationalized partisanship, which renders states effectively staging grounds for national partisan conflict, this effect should be even further apparent.

6.3 THE LANDSCAPE OF ELECTION REFORM, 2021–2022

6.3.1 The Data

To examine the partisan and other dynamics of post-2020 election reforms, we use a data set compiled from the State Voting Rights Tracker produced by the

Voting Rights Lab (VRL).[2] The VRL is an advocacy organization that aims to promote free and fair elections and voter access through a combination of research, analysis, and advocacy. The virtue of VRL's legislative data is that they are comprehensive and accurate; the organization has registered and coded all state legislation relating to voting rights beginning in 2021, 4,113 bills in all (as of May 2022), and they update bill changes and legislative status in real time. VRL codes each bill for both subject matter and policy impact (whether it improves or restricts voter access or election administration). At the same time, VRL's advocacy mission might bias its coding decisions, so we have independently verified the topic and impact coding of a sample of legislation included in our data set. We also developed our own coding scheme for the subset of bills coded by VRL as shifting election authority and have further verified this coding through case studies of selected states.

Additionally, we have compiled state-level political and demographic data in order to assess the political correlates of state-level election reform and have begun to test our hypotheses about the democratic dynamics of election reform as a window on democratic backsliding. Several measures identify a state's political leanings: the 2020 presidential election winner; the two-party vote margin in 2020 (a measure of electoral competitiveness); partisan control over state government; and the distribution of partisan affiliation in the state electorate as measured by Gallup. Over the past few decades, the urban–rural partisan balance has shifted dramatically, with rural areas leaning more heavily Republican and cities and increasingly suburbs tilting Democratic; this pattern has reshaped political competition, particularly in states that are relatively evenly divided between urban and rural populations (Mettler and Brown 2022). Thus, we include a US Department of Agriculture measure of a state's rurality. Finally, partisan conflict has increasingly fused with racial antagonism in recent decades, so we also include the racial and ethnic composition of the state population, as well as the change in the non-Hispanic white proportion of the population between the 2010 and 2020 censuses. The latter measures taps into both academic research highlighting the significance of demographic change (Hicks et al. 2014; McKee 2015; Parker 2021), as well as rhetoric on the right that frames immigration as "voter replacement" (Keveney 2021).

We also consider two additional political variables that bear on the particular circumstances of the post-2020 election context: the number of individuals from each state charged with criminal activity in connection with the January 6, 2021, insurrection at the US Capitol, and the aggregate number of hate groups located in the state, as measured by the Southern Poverty Law Center.[3] The intuition is that right-wing extremism and the overlapping Trumpist "stop the steal" movement might have encouraged state-level

---

[2] Information about bills provided by the Voting Rights Lab via tracker.votingrightslab.org.
[3] The insurrectionist measure comes from The Chicago Project on Security and Threats (the January 2022 report). https://cpost.uchicago.edu/publications/american_face_of_insurrection/.

partisans to take aim at election administration, whether by directly encouraging policy change or by helping sustain a political context in which these measures were more attractive. Finally, we conducted case studies of legislative activity in several representative states, both to verify the VRL's substantive coding and to assess the substance and potential consequences of state election authority measures.

The VRL legislative data reveal that states have considered legislation on a wide range of election law concerns since the 2020 election. Table 6.1 displays the count of the VRL's major topic categories among bills introduced.[4] There is considerable geographic variation in legislative activity; states have ranged from 10 bills introduced to nearly 1,000. At the same time, there is not much of a discernible geographic pattern; states east of the Great Plains have been somewhat more active than those to the west, but this is not a universal pattern. The most active states have been Texas and Arizona, where Republican state legislatures have been very active, passing both sweeping omnibus reform bills as well as more targeted measures. But Democratic-controlled New York and New Jersey and divided Minnesota have also been extremely active. While both parties have been roughly equally active in introducing legislation (Democrats have introduced 2,155 bills to the Republicans' 1,912), some partisan patterns emerge. While public attention has been directed primarily toward Republican efforts to alter voting and election procedures, both parties have been roughly equally likely to propose bills on these procedures, particularly on the issues that arose in 2020 as a result of the COVID-19 pandemic, such as absentee and mail-in voting and the process of returning, verifying, and "curing" (correcting errors in) those ballots. (As Table 6.1 shows, these are also the issues that received the most overall legislative attention.) General registration procedures have also attracted considerable bipartisan attention, although with some partisan difference in emphasis (Democrats are more likely to focus on automatic voter registration, while Republicans tend to emphasize list maintenance and general registration issues).

The largest area of partisan divergence is on the topic of "shifts in election authority." Under the VRL's definition, this category encompasses efforts to "shift the allocation of power in election administration." Proposed shifts in election authority might include limiting officials' emergency powers (such as those that were frequently invoked to expand voting access in the pandemic), replacing appointed offices with elected ones, expanding the authority of more clearly partisan actors, increasing state oversight of local election officials, and in the extreme giving state legislatures the power to overturn election results (which would be further bolstered if the Supreme Court were to accept the "independent state legislature" theory, a novel argument (Zhang 2021) that would make the

---

[4] The counts in Table 6.1 sum to more than the total number of bills (4,113) because most bills cover more than one topic.

TABLE 6.1 *Major topics in the Voting Rights Lab Bill Tracker*

Count of major topics in the Voting Rights Lab Bill Tracker			
Automatic voting registration	*168*	List maintenance	*364*
Absentee	*1,326*	Permanent automatic voter list	*131*
Ballot return, verification, and cure	*927*	Proof of c	*40*
COVID-19 and states of emergency	*108*	Redistricting	*597*
Criminal and civil enforcement	*547*	Registration – general	*739*
Electronic voting	*435*	Restoration	*252*
Election day	*262*	Same day registration	*175*
Emerging issues	*263*	Shifts in election authority	*303*
In-person voting	*560*	Vote by mail	*179*
Incarcerated voting	*58*	Voter ID	*309*

state legislature, rather than the full legislative system as established by the state constitution, the unique authority over elections). Even more directly than provisions aimed at limiting ballot access, these measures are a particular area of concern for democratic backsliding. Proposed shifts in election authority account for 7.4 percent of all the proposed bills, but only 3 percent of Democratic bills propose to shift election authority, versus 13 percent of Republican bills. Republicans have also been much more likely to introduce legislation that imposes criminal or civil penalties for violations of voting regulations, including penalties for local election officials who might previously have had authority or discretion to expand access.[5]

In general, these patterns confirm widely held expectations that Democrats are concerned more with facilitating ease of access and Republicans more with preventing malfeasance (real or imagined) while potentially raising barriers to access.[6] They also make clear that the issue agenda is at least partially reactive to the emergency changes in election procedures, most clearly in the attention given to absentee voting. Finally, they provide preliminary evidence that

---

[5] Other areas of significant partisan divergence are registration list maintenance and voter identification (more Republicans than Democrats) and the restoration of voting rights to formerly incarcerated persons, electronic voting, and automatic voter registration (more Democrats than Republicans).

[6] We have validated the VRL's coding of the direction and anticipated impact of policy change in our sample and conducted supplementary analyses available upon request. The clear pattern is that Republican bills are more likely to have an expected restrictive impact and that states where non-Hispanic whites are a declining share of the population are more likely to see Republicans introduce more restrictive bills.

authority over election administration has become an important area of policy attention and political contestation. While inextricably connected to the pandemic, the partisan imbalance in this attention suggests that the roots go deeper than simply trying to reestablish lines of authority that the emergency disrupted.

6.4 SHIFTS IN ELECTION AUTHORITY

The degree to which election administration has become overtly politicized is one of the more worrying features of the discourse and politics since the November 2020 election. To better understand the policy terrain in this domain, we examine more closely the 303 bills that have been tagged as shifting election authority, as well as the 167 of those bills that had received serious legislative consideration at the time of coding.[7]

Arizona and Texas legislators have been the most active in this policy area, introducing thirty-seven and thirty-one bills, respectively. These two states have to date enacted four of these bills, which we discuss in more detail below. Fourteen of the bills introduced in Arizona would shift election authority horizontally (between officials or agencies that have equal or independent authority), while thirteen would shift it vertically (between higher and subordinate or devolved agencies or officials); Texas has introduced bills with seventeen and nineteen such provisions. These amount to wholesale efforts to reconfigure elections in these states, and while these two states are outliers in this area, they are not unique in the degree to which they are looking to alter or redesign electoral authority.

6.4.1 What Do These Bills Do?

Our case studies suggest that shifts in election authority can take a variety of forms. The most concerning are shifts that would move authority toward actors under the control of or aligned politically with the state legislature, whether by shifting authority horizontally or vertically. At issue here is not whether or to what extent states legislatures should control the broad contours of elections, but the extent of control or influence a partisan body can bring to bear on critical election officials during the administration of their electoral duties (i.e., the degree to which the state legislature is able to exercise a role in election management rather than election design (James et al. 2019)). It is especially concerning when the shift in authority is clearly associated with partisan considerations. Since the 2020 elections, it very clearly has been.

---

[7] This is measured by whether they have been enacted, passed but vetoed, passed one legislative chamber, or been advanced out of the committee stage. Coding was conducted in March and April of 2022.

Arizona, Pennsylvania, and Georgia, three of the most competitive and closely watched states in the 2020 election (that all have Republican-controlled legislatures), have passed legislation that shifts election authority horizontally. Arizona's S1819, for example, took authority over election-related litigation and voter list maintenance away from the Democratic secretary of state and instead gives it to the Republican attorney general.[8] This law was found unconstitutional by Arizona's state supreme court and therefore is not currently in effect. Pennsylvania's legislation, passed by the Republican legislature but vetoed by the Democratic governor, would have limited the secretary of the commonwealth's authority in elections to that which was explicitly authorized in the Pennsylvania Statutes or Pennsylvania Consolidated Statutes, limiting authority claimed on the basis of court orders or the state constitution. This was an effort to establish a variant of the "independent state legislature" theory, removing the legislature from state constitutional controls. Georgia's omnibus election bill, SB (Senate Bill) 202, similarly removed authority from the secretary of state, replacing the secretary as the chair of the State Election Board with an official named by the legislature. In this case, the target was Republican Secretary of State Brad Raffensperger, who maintained that Biden was the legitimate winner of Georgia's Electoral College votes despite pressure from Donald Trump and his allies to "find" votes that would overturn the results. The legislation effectively put the State Election Board heavily under the influence of the state legislature.

Georgia's SB 202, as well as Pennsylvania's vetoed election legislation, also provides representative examples of vertical shifts in electoral authority. One of the Georgia bill's provisions requires the secretary of state's office and Election Board to appoint an independent performance review board if there is evidence regarding the competence of a local election official. This gives statewide institutions increased oversight over local election administrators, and Georgia Republican legislators have already used this provision to initiate a review of heavily Democratic Fulton County (Atlanta) that could under the new law lead to the removal and replacement of the county's board and superintendent of elections.[9] Pennsylvania Republicans have also attempted to establish a Bureau of Election Audits in the auditor general's office, shifting authority over newly expanded auditing practices from county boards of elections and the Department of State to the auditor general.[10] One potential worry, true of many of the expansions of audit requirements, is that these would not conform to best practices, but would be more akin to a "partisan election review."[11] The auditor general is an elected partisan official while county

---

[8] https://ballotpedia.org/Arizona_Secretary_of_State_election,_2022.

[9] https://tinyurl.com/49jhvay7.

[10] www.spotlightpa.org/news/2021/06/pa-election-overhaul-voter-id-wolf-veto/.

[11] The change might reflect capacity concerns. The expansion of results-confirming auditing requirements and a pilot program of risk-limiting audits, as well as new requirements for preelection equipment testing and performance auditing, may or may not improve auditing practices, but it would impose significant resource requirements on county boards of election.

boards are bipartisan, and the auditor general when the legislation was passed by the legislature was – unlike the secretary of the commonwealth who has authority over the Department of State – a Republican. Similarly, Missouri enacted a law allowing the secretary of state to audit voter rolls, again providing state-level oversight of some election administration functions that primarily occur at the local level.[12]

A related shift in election authority concerns litigation. While the run-up to every election cycle sees a considerable amount of litigation, the courts were especially active during the pandemic. Republican legislatures, exclusively, have sought to require any district that is considering entering into a consent order to first inform the legislature, which could then intervene to prevent it. The Republican state legislature in Pennsylvania has attempted to claim authority to intervene in any lawsuit contesting the constitutionality of its proposed bill, and under legislation vetoed by the Democratic governor the legislature would have been explicitly named as the authority prescribing election authority in the commonwealth. This aim was to limit the authority of courts and other election officials. Other states have effectively limited the authority of local officials to respond to potential judgments requiring changes to secure access or comply with federal election law.

Other changes in election authority are less about shifting it between levels and more about imposing new regulations that effectively deprive local officials of authority that they might previously have been able to use. Texas, for instance, has passed several pieces of legislation targeting Harris County (Houston), whose election officials pushed the limits of their statutory authority during the pandemic to expand access. While recently-passed Texas legislation establishes a framework for mail-in and early voting that is expansive across much of the state it is highly restrictive relative to what Harris County had pursued in 2020. The county created drive-through voting centers, mailed every registered voter a mail-in ballot application (other counties sent unsolicited applications to persons aged sixty-five, who are automatically eligible to vote by mail under Texas law), and created popular twenty-four-hour early-voting centers (Bradner 2021; Corasaniti 2021). Most of these measures were overturned by new statutes that restrict county authority to devise new procedures or modify existing ones.

At the same time, the state has required that local election officials and judges give more leeway to partisan poll watchers, threatening officials with criminal charges if they remove poll watchers they believe to be intimidating voters. Failure to accept a poll watcher, obstructing their view, or relegating them to an ineffective distance has been made a misdemeanor. Election judges are not allowed to remove watchers for violating the law unless the judge observes the violation, and the watcher has been warned that the conduct violates the law.

---

[12] See Voting Rights Tracker summary for MO H 1878: https://tracker.votingrightslab.org/pending/search.

The empowerment of poll watchers in Texas points to another, more subtle consequence of changes in election authority, one that was evident across a number of states. Officials throughout the state and local bureaucracy are being required to interpret discrepancies as evidence of possible criminal conduct and to report this to legal authorities. Some states – most notably Florida – have gone so far as to create special policing agencies tasked with election crimes (Pennsylvania Republicans have sought to do the same but have been stymied by the governor's veto). Florida's new Office of Election Crimes and Security, lodged within the Department of State, is headed by a director appointed by the secretary and staffed with investigators who are not sworn law enforcement officers. The office oversees the voter fraud hotline and investigates complaints, initiates and conducts investigations based on information from the hotline and any other source, refers matters to prosecutors, and provides reports to the governor, president of the Senate, and speaker of the House with information on the investigations. The governor quickly used the activities of the office for political gain, using minor violations of the law – almost none of which involved criminal intent – to sustain false notions of widespread malfeasance. In a similar vein, the Florida governor and Department of Law Enforcement now need to appoint at least one special officer to conduct election-related investigations in each region, with election-related investigations taking precedence over any nonelection-related duties the officer might have (under existing law the governor could appoint a special officer, but did not need to). In the case of the Office of Election Crimes, an institutional incentive is created to find and publicize instances of failure to abide by the rules, regardless of whether these were motivated by malfeasance or not.

The end result is grist for the mill in terms of creating a public and political perception of election malfeasance, regardless of the extent or severity of its occurrence. A similar possibility exists with expanded auditing requirements, especially when these are being lodged in partisan-controlled offices. Auditing is an essential function of election administration, but the partisan election reviews that followed 2020 are more a threat to the perceived legitimacy and possible integrity of the system than a cure. Even professionally conducted audits can be made into tools of partisanship, if partisan officials are entitled – as new legislation in some states establishes – to select which counties are audited, or if the resulting reports are presented to the media through a partisan lens.

The bulk of the shifts in election authority that we examined in closer detail do give partisan officials discretion over certification.[13] The threat from this dimension primarily concerns the widespread election of local officials who have rejected the results of the 2020 election, who have explicitly called for measures such as state legislatures appointing presidential electors, or who have

---

[13] One provision of Texas's legislation that would have made it easier for judges to overturn election results was ultimately removed (Nichols 2021; Inskeep and Lopez 2021).

already begun refusing to certify results as required under existing law. That threat, at least, is political rather than legal.

The legal changes we are witnessing are instead more about providing state-level partisan officials with greater control over the procedural implementation of elections and their review while restricting the ability of local election officials to alter procedure in order to protect access or facilitate election administration. The increased partisan and centralized control over list maintenance, over auditing, and, in the possible case of Fulton County, over the entire administration of the election, complements legal and rhetorical efforts to establish the state legislature as the unique authority over election law and over the officials tasked with administering the law. The heightened criminal and civil penalties, and the more stringent reporting requirements of discrepancies to law enforcement officials, function to restrict local election officials' discretion, possibly to restrict access through fear of legal consequences for mistakes, and perhaps most importantly to create an evidentiary basis, however thin, for claims of electoral malfeasance that can justify increased restrictions or invalidation of election results. These laws have been passed almost exclusively by Republican state legislatures and were enacted into law only where there was unified Republican control.[14]

6.4.2 State-Level Correlates of Shifts in Election Authority

We expect that the underlying motivations for bills shifting election authority are the invidious claims of election fraud and malfeasance advanced by the losers of the 2020 presidential election and their state allies. Two factors, however, might act as complementary or alternative explanations. The first is the intense litigation and conflicts over election authority that were produced during the frantic efforts to adapt election procedures to the challenges of the COVID-19 pandemic. Governors, local election boards and officials, and federal and state courts acted aggressively within the scope of their authority, or sometimes beyond it, to secure access. State legislatures were at times active participants in the process, but in some cases opposed changes being implemented by other actors. The Trump campaign, however, quickly decided that changes to secure access were likely to be harmful electorally, and early on started attacking absentee or mail-in voting as likely to facilitate coordinated electoral fraud. As the campaign's loss became clear, this claim was pushed even more aggressively. It is plausible that Trump would have denied the validity of any election he lost, but pandemic-motivated changes provided the frame around which conspiracy theories were spun. The other factor is the preexisting calculations of partisan actors concerned with how demographic

---

[14] The only Democratic-led shift in election authority of significance was in New York, which limited the ability of parties to get court orders to stop a ballot from being opened and made it so that lawsuits can be filed only to challenge the rejection of ballots rather than their acceptance.

TABLE 6.2 *Negative binomial regression of count of bill introductions*

	All bills
Biden won	0.588 (0.408)
Two-party margin, 2020	−0.0339* (0.0144)
GOP-controlled legislature	1.705*** (0.498)
Divided legislature	0.992 (0.743)
Insurrectionists	−0.00771 (0.00918)
Hate groups	0.572** (0.205)
% Non-Hispanic white	−0.00845 (0.0116)
Change in non-Hispanic white	−0.253* (0.102)
% in union	0.0162 (0.0338)
Rurality	−0.00464 (0.0122)
Observations	50

Note: $^{*}p < 0.05$, $^{**}p < 0.01$, $^{***}p < 0.001$
Standard errors in parentheses.

and political changes in the states might affect the parties' relative position. Attacks on election authority might simply be a state-level escalation of earlier efforts to restrict access in the name of rooting out malfeasance.

We interpret the pandemic and demographic changes as intersecting factors that might shape the propensity of actors to take up the Trump campaign's claims about electoral malfeasance. COVID-19 might have been a common shock, but variation in state legislative responses were driven not solely by the shock itself but by state-level factors. Similarly, we interpret legislative activity in this domain as descriptive evidence about where partisan and activist networks have been more responsive to and active in driving claims of 2020 election malfeasance.

The analysis in this section focuses on a negative binomial regression of bill introductions in each state. Our dependent variables are simply the count of all bills introduced in the area of election authority. The results are reported in Table 6.2.

A Biden victory is not significantly associated with greater bill introductions, while the two-party margin is significant; electorally close states saw more proposed shifts in election authority. Republican control over state legislatures is also important. Since introducing legislation is relatively costless, there is no obvious reason to expect that GOP-controlled legislatures would see more bills introduced than those that were divided or controlled by the Democratic party, even in an issue area such as election authority where most bill authors have been

Republican. Shifts in election authority, however, are especially sensitive to which branch of government is controlled by which party. And it has been state legislatures that have been most consistently the beneficiaries of state-level shifts in election authority. Indeed, much of the substance of these shifts involves restrictions on local election officials' authority, whether in litigation, in ballot handling, or through the imposition of criminal or civil penalties for deviating from state-imposed regulations. These penalties significantly raise the cost of local election officials acting to expand access, even if in doing so they were entirely in accordance with state regulations. They serve, potentially, as a form of intimidation. These results are consistent with the nested winners'/losers' dilemma scenario, in which it is the national losers who control state governments that are most likely to seize opportunities to reorganize the electoral machinery in defiance of democratic norms.

Two other variables that stand out as important are the change in the non-Hispanic white population, and the number of hate groups in the state. A state seeing increasing racial and ethnic diversity is especially likely to restrict local election authority or to shift the institutional location of authority. This suggests some continuity with the pre-2020 period, where voter identification laws were similarly associated with demographic changes that diminished the number of non-Hispanic white voters. The relationship between hate groups and shifts in election authority is a more novel finding. States where there are a greater number of hate groups are especially likely to see a greater number of bills looking to shift the institutional location of election authority. Our case studies, however, were unable to find evidence that the legislators who were most active on these issues had any known ties to hate groups (which is not true of all state legislators). We expect instead that hate group activity and legislators' activism on election authority are reflective of deeper and more widespread activism and extremism on the right and far right, which has been benefiting hate groups and radicalizing the Republican party even when direct connections between these are lacking. In any event, this connection bears further study, especially given what we increasingly know about the role that far-right hate groups have played in the assault on democracy in the United States.

6.5 CONCLUSION

In February 2020, legal scholar Richard L. Hasen (2020) warned that the country was at risk of democratic breakdown, with the losing party refusing to accept the results of the election. Hasen (2005) had long noted that election law had become a core political strategy, but the urgency was greater than ever. While the quality of election administration continued to improve year after year, the political cause of the voting wars had only intensified: "the extreme partisanship and close division of the American electorate" (2005, 944) had created a situation in which either party might squeeze a victory through sympathetic courts or voter suppression and would at least seriously entertain the possibility of denying the outcome to their followers. By 2020, this approach had become clearly concentrated in the Republican Party.

The analysis we have presented provides one perspective on a vital threat to the resilience of US democracy. Recent legislation continues a pattern of restricting access, but also indicates a willingness to treat election administration as a tool for partisan gain. This has no doubt always been true to some extent (James 2012), and it remains the case that most election officials are elected (and thus usually partisan) officials. But it is easy to miss the profound improvement and professionalization of election administration that has occurred nonetheless. The losing candidate and movement in the 2020 election have threatened to reverse this progress and to make the people who have achieved it objects of attack (Jacobs and Choate 2022).

Just as important as the policies we have focused on is the widespread adoption within the Republican Party of election denialism and the championing of candidates who refuse to commit to accepting the results of future elections. As these candidates become office holders, in many places they will likely be met by a Republican electorate that echoes their skepticism of the legitimacy of the 2020 election. Due to the changes we document here, they may also encounter a policy environment more amenable to efforts to undermine election integrity.[15]

In this volume's Introduction, Roberts, Bunce, Pepinsky, and Beatty Riedl highlight the respective dilemmas of the losers and winners, but also the dialectical character of democracy and backsliding. While this might often appear in the form of backlash – an effort to roll back recent gains – we also see a dialectic in the patterns across states. There has been no uniform rolling back of voting rights and the quality of election administration. The pattern is bifurcated by party and varies by state. It remains the case that there are few democratic countries where it is as easy and as difficult to vote as the United States (Bateman 2016), while perceptions about electoral integrity have reached new lows at the moment when its objective performance has never been better.

These are manifestations of the deeper problem confronting US democracy. Not only has one party become willing to subvert the essential institutions of democracy for its own gain, but polarization has also become sufficiently severe that there is no broad, institutionally recognized majority that can consign such political tendencies to the margins.[16] The winners' and losers' dilemmas are, in the United States, intermingled, while the dialectic of democratic advances and authoritarian backsliding is simultaneous, diffused across the country's political geography and one more symptom of its tearing apart.

---

[15] The Brookings Institution identified 345 Republican candidates in 2022 who denied the legitimacy of the 2020 election (https://tinyurl.com/56maphxw).

[16] In an Ipsos poll conducted in December of 2021, only 26 percent of Republicans agreed with the statement "Joe Biden legitimately won the 2020 presidential election," while 47 percent disagreed (https://tinyurl.com/4hj52xj9).

REFERENCES

Achen, Christopher H., and Larry M. Bartels. 2016. *Democracy for Realists: Why Elections Do Not Produce Responsive Government*. Princeton: Princeton University Press.

Barreto, Matt A., Stephen A. Nuño, and Gabriel R. Sanchez. 2009. "The Disproportionate Impact of Voter-ID Requirements on the Electorate: New Evidence from Indiana." *PS: Political Science & Politics* 42, no. 1 (January): 111–116.

Bateman, David A. 2016. "Race, Party, and American Voting Rights." *The Forum* 14, no. 1: 39–65.

Bateman, David A. 2022. "Elections, Polarization, and Democratic Resilience." In *Democratic Resilience: Can the United States Withstand Rising Polarization?* eds. Robert C. Lieberman, Suzanne Mettler, and Kenneth M. Roberts. Cambridge: Cambridge University Press, 343–368.

Bentele, Keith G., and Erin E. O'Brien. 2013. "Jim Crow 2.0? Why States Consider and Adopt Restrictive Voter Access Policies." *Perspectives on Politics* 11, no. 4 (December): 1088–1116.

Bermeo, Nancy. 2016. "On Democratic Backsliding." *Journal of Democracy* 27, no. 1 (January): 5–19.

Bradner, Eric. 2021. "The New Texas Voting Law Includes These 7 Major Changes." *CNN.com.*, September 8.

Brnovich v. Democratic National Committee. 2021. 141 S. Ct. 2321.

Biggers, Daniel R., and Michael J. Hanmer. 2015. "Who Makes Voting Convenient? Explaining the Adoption of Early and No-Excuse Absentee Voting in the American States." *State Politics & Policy Quarterly* 15, no 2 (June): 192–210.

Burden, Barry C. 2018. "Disagreement over ID Requirements and Minority Voter Turnout." *Journal of Politics* 80, no. 3 (July): 1060–1063.

Corasaniti, Nick. 2021. "Abbott Signs Texas Election Law, Ending a Fierce Voting Rights Battle." *New York Times*, September 8, A20.

Cuthbert, Lane, and Alexander Theodoridis. 2022. "Do Republicans Really Believe Trump Won the 2020 Election? Our Research Suggests that They Do." *Washington Post*, January 7. www.washingtonpost.com/politics/2022/01/07/republicans-big-lie-trump/.

Dahl, Robert A. 1971. *Polyarchy: Participation and Opposition*. New Haven: Yale University Press.

Gardner, Amy. 2022. "A Majority of GOP Nominees – 299 In All – Deny the 2020 Election Results." *Washington Post*, October 6. https://tinyurl.com/2fvxfjch.

Gaughan, Anthony J. 2020. "American Democracy Is Healthier than It Appears." *Boston University Law Review Online* 100: 249–267.

Graham, Matthew H., and Milan Svolik. 2020. "Democracy in America? Partisanship, Polarization, and the Robustness of Support for Democracy in the United States." *American Political Science Review* 114, no. 2 (May): 392–409.

Gronke, Paul. 2008. "Early Voting Reforms and American Elections." *William & Mary Bill of Rights Journal* 17, no. 2 (December): 423–451.

Grumbach, Jacob M. 2022. *Laboratories against Democracy: How National Parties Transformed State Politics*. Princeton: Princeton University Press.

Hajnal, Zoltan, John Kuk, and Nazita Lajevardi. 2018. "We All Agree: Strict Voter ID Laws Disproportionately Burden Minorities." *Journal of Politics* 80, no. 3 (July): 1052–1059.

Hasen, Richard L. 2005. "Beyond the Margin of Litigation: Reforming US Election Administration to Avoid Electoral Meltdown." *Washington and Lee Law Review* 62, no. 3 (Summer): 937–999.

Hasen, Richard L. 2020. *Election Meltdown: Dirty Tricks, Distrust, and the Threat to American Democracy.* New Haven: Yale University Press.

Hasen, Richard L. 2021. "Identifying and Minimizing the Risk of Election Subversion and Stolen Elections in the Contemporary United States." *Harvard Law Review Forum* 135: 265–301.

Herd, Pamela, and Donald P. Moynihan. 2018. *Administrative Burdens: Policymaking by Other Means.* New York: Russell Sage Foundation.

Hicks, William D., Seth C. McKee, Mitchell D. Sellers, and Daniel A. Smith. 2014. "A Principle or a Strategy? Voter Identification Laws and Partisan Competition in the American States." *Political Research Quarterly* 68, no. 1(March): 18–33.

Highton, Benjamin. 2017. "Voter Identification Laws and Turnout in the United States." *Annual Review of Political Science* 20: 149–167.

Hopkins, Daniel J. 2018. *The Increasingly United States: How and Why American Political Behavior Nationalized.* Chicago: University of Chicago Press.

Inskeep, Steve, and Ashley Lopez. 2021. "Some Texas Lawmakers Disown Part of Their Plan to Change Voting Rules." *npr.com Morning Edition* [online transcript], June 2.

Jacobs, Lawrence R., and Judd Choate. 2022. "Democratic Capacity: Election Administration as Bulwark and Target." *ANNALS of the American Academy of Political and Social Science* 699, no. 1 (January): 22–35.

James, Toby S. 2012. *Elite Statecraft and Election Administration: Bending the Rules of the Game?* London: Palgrave Macmillan.

James, Toby S., Holly Ann Garnett, Leontine Loeber, and Carolien van Ham. 2019. "Election Management and the Organisational Determinants of Electoral Integrity: Introduction." *International Political Science Review* 40, no. 3 (June): 295–312.

Kalmoe, Nathan P., and Lilliana Mason. 2022. *Radical American Partisanship: Mapping Violent Hostility, Its Causes, and the Consequences for Democracy.* Chicago: University of Chicago Press.

Keveney, Bill. 2021. "Tucker Carlson Doubles Down on Voter 'Replacement' Comments after ADL Calls for his Firing." *USA Today.* April 12.

Levitsky, Steven, and Lucan A. Way. 2002. "The Rise of Competitive Authoritarianism." *Journal of Democracy* 13, no. 2 (April): 51–65.

Levitsky, Steven, and Daniel Ziblatt. 2018. *How Democracies Die.* New York: Crown.

Linz, Juan J. 1990. "The Perils of Presidentialism." *Journal of Democracy* 1, no. 1 (Winter): 51–69.

McKee, Seth C. 2015. "Politics Is Local: State Legislator Voting on Restrictive Voter Identification Legislation." *Research and Politics* 2, no. 3: 1–7.

Manin, Bernard, Adam Przeworski, and Susan C. Stokes. 1999. "Elections and Representation." In *Democracy, Accountability, and Representation,* eds. Adam Przeworski, Susan C. Stokes, and Bernard Manin. Cambridge: Cambridge University Press, 29–54.

Mason, Lilliana. 2018. *Uncivil Agreement: How Politics Became Our Identity*. Chicago: University of Chicago Press.

Mettler, Suzanne, and Trevor Brown. 2022. "The Growing Rural-Urban Political Divide and Democratic Vulnerability." *ANNALS of the American Academy of Political and Social Science* 699, no. 1 (January): 130–142.

Mettler, Suzanne, and Robert C. Lieberman. 2020. *Four Threats: The Recurring Crises of American Democracy*. New York: St. Martin's.

Mettler, Suzanne, Robert C. Lieberman, Jamila Michener, Thomas B. Pepinsky, and Kenneth M. Roberts. 2022. "Democratic Vulnerabilities and Pathways for Reform." *ANNALS of the Academy of Political and Social Science* 699, no. 1 (January): 8–20.

Mickey, Robert. 2022. "Challenges to Subnational Democracy in the United States, Past and Present." *ANNALS of the American Academy of Political and Social Science* 699, no. 1 (January): 118–129.

Monmouth University Poll. 2022. "National: Faith in American System Recovers after Summer Jan. 6 Hearings." September 27. www.monmouth.edu/polling-institute/documents/monmouthpoll_us_092722.pdf/.

Nichols, John. 2021. "It's Not Just Voter Suppression: Texas Republicans Want to Overturn Elections." *The Nation*, June 3.

Oliver, J. Eric. 1996. "The Effects of Eligibility Restrictions and Party Activity on Absentee Voting and Overall Turnout." *American Journal of Political Science* 40, no. 2 (May): 498–513.

Parker, Christopher S. 2021. "Status Threat: Moving the Right Further to the Right?" *Daedalus* 150, no. 2: 56–75.

Persily, Nathaniel, and Charles Stewart III. 2021. "The Miracle and Tragedy of the 2020 US Election." *Journal of Democracy* 32, no. 2 (April): 159–178.

Pryor, Ben, Rebekah Herrick, and James A. Davis. 2019. "Voter ID Laws: The Disenfranchisement of Minority Voters?" *Political Science Quarterly* 134, no. 1 (Spring): 63–83.

Przeworski, Adam. 1991. *Democracy and the Market: Political and Economic Reforms in Eastern Europe and Latin America*. Cambridge: Cambridge University Press.

Przeworski, Adam. 1999. "Minimalist Conception of Democracy: A Defense." In *Democracy's Value*, eds. Ian Shapiro and Casiano Hacker-Cordón. Cambridge: Cambridge University Press, 23–55.

Rocha, Rene R., and Rodolfo Espino. 2009. "Racial Threat, Residential Segregation, and the Policy Attitudes of Anglos." *Political Research Quarterly* 62, no. 2 (June): 415–426.

Rocha, Rene R., and Tetsuya Matsubayashi. 2014. "The Politics of Race and Voter ID Laws in the States: The Return of Jim Crow?" *Political Research Quarterly* 67, no. 3 (September): 666–679.

Schickler, Eric. 2016. *Racial Realignment: The Transformation of American Liberalism, 1932–1965*. Princeton: Princeton University Press.

Schmitter, Philippe C., and Terry Lynn Karl. 1991. "What Democracy Is . . . and Is Not." *Journal of Democracy* 2, no. 3 (Summer): 75–88.

Schumpeter, Joseph A. 1942. *Capitalism, Socialism and Democracy*. New York: Harper & Brothers.

Shelby County v. Holder. 2013. 570 U.S. 529.

Stein, Perry, and Tom Hamburger. 2022. "Over 1,000 Election-Worker Threats Reported in Past Year, Official Says." Washington Post, August 3. https://tinyurl .com/yc9c9uwt.

Stein, Robert M., Christopher Mann, Charles Stewart III, Zachary Birenbaum, Anson Fung, Jed Greenberg, Farhan Kawsar et al. 2020. "Waiting to Vote in the 2016 Presidential Election: Evidence from a Multi-County Study." *Political Research Quarterly* 73, no. 2 (June): 439–453.

Stewart, Charles, III. 2020. "How We Voted in 2020: A First Look at the Survey of the Performance of American Elections." MIT Election Data + Science Lab, December 15. https://tinyurl.com/59w42scd.

Stewart, Charles, III, and Stephen Ansolabehere. 2015. "Waiting to Vote." *Election Law Journal: Rules, Politics, and Policy* 14, no.1 (March): 47–53.

White, Ariel R., Noah L. Nathan, and Julie K. Faller. 2015. "What Do I Need to Vote? Bureaucratic Discretion and Discrimination by Local Election Officials." *American Political Science Review* 109, no. 1 (February): 129–42.

Wines, Michael. 2020. "Here are the Threats Terrorizing Election Workers." *New York Times*, December 3. www.nytimes.com/2020/12/03/us/election-officials-threats-trump.html.

Zhang, Emily Rong. 2021. "Voting Rights Lawyering in Crisis." *City University of New York Law Review* 24, no. 2: 123–44.

PART II

CIVIL SOCIETY, SOCIAL MEDIA, AND POLITICAL
MESSAGING

7

Civil Society Mobilization against Equal Citizenship in Latin America

Lindsay Mayka

Much of the literature on democratic backsliding and illiberal democracy focuses on developments at the level of elite institutions. However, illiberalism does not only occur at the elite level: we also see its creep in citizens' experience of democratic rights in their everyday life. At that micro level, civil society groups can play a key role in promoting illiberalism by redefining what citizenship entails and who can claim it.[1] Who is understood to be part of the collective "us," and who is seen as the disloyal "them"? Who has rights? Which rights are valid, and which rights are perceived to be dangerous special privileges? Battles over the boundaries and content of citizenship are at the core of populist claims (Goodman 2019) and are central to our understandings of democratic backsliding, since citizenship is the level at which individuals experience democracy most directly. Given that only 15 percent of Latin Americans believe that they truly experience the full package of political, civil, and social rights (Luna and Medel 2023: 182), the region offers important insights into threats that liberal democracy can face on the level of citizenship.

This chapter examines civil society activism in Latin America around two broad issue areas: opposition to inclusion on the lines of gender identity and sexuality, and support for repressive policing. I explore these groups' role in undercutting a core component of liberal democracy: the enjoyment of

---

[1] There is a rich literature examining the politics behind the causes and consequences of extending *formal* membership into citizenship through naturalization processes, see Sara Wallace Goodman, "Citizenship Studies: Policy Causes and Consequences," *Annual Review of Political Science*, 26 (2023). In this chapter, I analyze citizenship as a social category that goes beyond legal status, see Evelyn Glenn, "Constructing Citizenship," *American Sociological Review*, 76/1 (2011), 1–24, focusing on the experience of "differentiated citizenship" for people who have formal membership as citizens, yet experience diminished rights due to their social status and identities, see James Holston, *Insurgent Citizenship: Disjunctions of Democracy and Modernity in Brazil* (Princeton: Princeton University Press, 2008) at 5 and Iris Marion Young, Justice and the Politics of Difference (Princeton: Princeton University Press, 2011).

universal and equal citizenship rights backed by rule of law. First, some right-wing civil society groups delineate marginalized groups – such as low-income and racialized youth, people experiencing homelessness, and LGBTQ+ individuals – not as rights-bearing citizens, but rather as existential threats to the physical, social, and moral survival of "good citizens." Second, these civil society groups redefine the content of rights: They both exclude marginalized groups from the protections of existing legal rights, and also argue that violating the formal rights of marginalized groups *is required* to protect the rights of "good citizens." These civil society groups assert that this illiberal and unequal approach to citizenship is essential to protect the true essence of democracy: responsiveness to "good citizens," and protection of their rights above all else.

7.1 HOW CIVIL SOCIETY CAN UNDERMINE LIBERAL DEMOCRACY

While a vibrant civil society can play a crucial role in slowing, halting, or reversing democratic backsliding (Bernhard Chapter 9 this volume; Beissinger Chapter 10 this volume), civil society groups can also advance backsliding if they pursue illiberal or antidemocratic agendas (Armony 2004; Chambers and Kopstein 2001; Payne 2000). Civil society groups can deepen fragmentation and polarization (Berman 1997; Smith and Boas 2023), advocate policies that restrict the rights of marginalized groups (Reuterswärd 2021; Sosa-Villagarcia and Rozas Urrunaga 2021), and support the candidacies of illiberal politicians (Berman 1997; Gold and Peña 2021, Greskovits Chapter 8 this volume). Here, I focus on civil society's involvement in a prior step in the political process: promoting discourses that identify certain populations as not only outside the boundaries of citizenship, but also as active threats to the rights of true citizens.

The meanings of citizenship are not determined just by formal rules, but also by how these rights operate for citizens in practice – a point first established by T. H. Marshall (1950). The actual experience of citizenship is "a fluid status that is produced through everyday practices and struggles" (Glenn 2011: 1). I analyze how citizenship is constructed (and reconstructed) through discursive practices and informal institutions that shape the lived experience of citizenship on the ground. This view of citizenship mirrors the dialectical approach laid out by the editors in Chapter 1, seeing democracy not as a fixed state or teleological conclusion, but rather a terrain that is constantly subject to contestation.

In Latin America today, some right-wing civil society groups challenge the tenets of universal and equal citizenship at the heart of liberal democracy, as part of what Chambers and Kopstein (2001: 839) refer to as "bad civil society": associations that reject the moral standing of their targets (see also Greskovits, Chapter 8 this volume). As Chambers and Kopstein explain, these groups threaten liberal democracy not just because they hold illiberal tendencies or values; instead, "[t]he question is whether their stated values, beliefs, creed, agenda, ideology, or platform is clearly incompatible with a belief in equal moral consideration" (Chambers and Kopstein 2001: 840).

Civil society groups play a key role in crafting and legitimating the ideational infrastructure that justifies unequal citizenship, developing frames that sanitize authoritarian demands in the more palatable language of democracy and human rights. Over time, civil society groups can normalize and legitimate illiberal and violent ideas that might otherwise seem shocking. This ideational infrastructure can later be harnessed by illiberal politicians, making their agendas seem within the mainstream of political ideas (Collins 2014: 62).

Latin America's illiberal civil society groups attack equal citizenship in two ways. First, they seek to restrict de facto membership in the polity only to those designated as "deserving." Second, they actively define marginalized groups as existential threats to the very survival of "good citizens," meaning that their exclusion and repression is deemed essential to protect the public interest.

7.1.1 Equal and Unequal Citizenship

Equal citizenship regimes set (and follow) clear and neutral criteria to determine belonging, and extend a series of rights that are premised on individual equality before the law (Shklar 1991; Smith 1997). By contrast, unequal citizenship regimes extend membership only to those who are seen as deserving, and/or make individual rights binding for privileged groups but discretionary for those from a lower social status (Caldeira and Holston 1999: 692–93; O'Donnell 1993: 1361). To understand how right-wing groups can advance unequal citizenship, we must first define two key dimensions that distinguish equal and unequal citizenship: the boundaries of who is considered to have membership in the citizenry, and the rights included in citizenship.

First, what are the boundaries of citizenship? Who is considered a citizen, and who is excluded from membership? What criteria determine belonging? Boundaries are established by both formal requirements, as well as informal processes that signal whose formal citizenship actually counts. Under equal citizenship practices, a range of criteria might be used to determine membership, such as birthright citizenship, bloodline citizenship, and/or various conditions required for naturalization. While formal criteria for membership may reflect and reinforce societal hierarchies and yield unequal results, they do not threaten equal citizenship as long as the rules are predetermined and applied equally. By contrast, with unequal citizenship, belonging is determined by deservingness (Holston 2011: 345). Privileged groups are recognized as citizens because they are seen as virtuous, while groups considered to be deviant or inferior are excluded from full membership. Marginalized groups are not only excluded from membership, but also are viewed as threats to the physical safety and moral integrity of true citizens (González and Mayka 2023: 266–67). Marginalized groups are not just non-citizens – they are *anti*-citizens.

Second, what is the content of citizenship?[2] What rights are considered inviolable for citizens? Once again, it is important to consider not only the rights conferred by laws and jurisprudence, but also how these rights are experienced in practice. Deep social inequalities can shape which rights matter, and which rights only exist on paper for marginalized groups (da Matta 1987). With unequal citizenship practices, the rights of marginalized groups are disposable if they clash with the "public interest," as determined by those who wield power (Mitchell and Wood 1999: 1006) – a view that rejects the basic premise of the rule of law (Holston 2011: 345; O'Donnell 1993: 1357). Basic civil or social rights established in the law for all citizens are portrayed as "special rights" when accessed by marginalized groups – loopholes that cause harm to deserving citizens. The state need not – and indeed, *should* not – universally respect rights established through the law. Instead, public officials should use discretion to determine who deserves the protections of the rule of law, and who merits repression (González and Mayka 2023: 267). Any formal rights targeted for minoritized populations – such as gender quotas, antidiscrimination laws, or same-sex marriage – are a trojan horse to allow the infiltration of these groups into respectable spheres of society, where they can cause further harm.

7.1.2   When Do Civil Society Groups Threaten Equal Citizenship?

Civil society groups advance unequal citizenship when they not only defend traditional hierarchies, but go further to present marginalized groups as existential threats whose inclusion or even existence endangers the rights of deserving citizens. This often takes the form of what Yanilda González and I term "asymmetric citizenship": when expanding the rights of one group requires the contraction of another group's citizenship rights (González and Mayka 2023).

Right-wing movements *can* mobilize in defense of traditional social, racial, economic hierarchies without imperiling liberal democracy.[3] Within the bounds of liberal democracy, it is natural and even healthy to see contestation over the boundaries and content of citizenship. After all, different rights are in tension with one another, and sparring movements often claim competing rights when articulating grievances and making demands (Bob 2019). Women's rights to control their bodies clash with the rights of fetuses to live. The rights of

---

[2] While content typically refers to both rights and duties, I focus just on rights for simplicity's sake in this chapter.

[3] Other scholars – most notably, Payne, Escoffier, and Zulver, *The Right against Rights in Latin America* (New York: Oxford University Press, 2023) – contend that any right-wing mobilization that seeks a contraction in the rights of marginalized groups as being fundamentally against rights and therefore illiberal. I see such a view as too sweeping. This perspective fails to distinguish between "normal" debates over how to define belonging and the content of citizenship, and an approaches that define certain groups as existential threats.

racialized groups to economic opportunities through affirmative action after centuries of violent exclusion clash with other individuals' right to equal competition today. Social rights, including the right to health, can come at the expense of property rights and economic liberties. Fights over which of these rights are most valid are the substance of healthy political debates in liberal democracies. Moreover, greater inclusion of right-wing groups can alleviate gaps in representation (Boas and Smith 2019; Boas 2021; Mayka and Smith 2021: 13), and give right-wing actors a stake in democratic processes, which is essential for the stability of democracy (Gibson 1996; Ziblatt 2017).

Movements that oppose abortion rights, affirmative action, or economic redistribution to deepen social rights may oppose the rights-based claims of movements defending the interests of marginalized groups without threatening the tenets of equal citizenship, as long as they do so in a way that does not cast those groups as existential threats to the public.[4] For instance, a group may oppose same-sex marriage, as long as it does not depict LGBTQ+ individuals as perverted groomers of children who should be stripped of rights afforded to all, such as freedom of speech or assembly. Once a civil society group denies the tenet of reciprocity – "the recognition of other citizens, even those with whom one has deep disagreement, as moral agents deserving civility" – it crosses a line by rejecting the basic principles of equality to contest ideas that lies at the root of democracy (Chambers and Kopstein 2001: 839).

7.2 THE RISE OF ILLIBERAL CIVIL SOCIETY ON THE RIGHT IN LATIN AMERICA

In the past thirty years, progressive social movements in Latin America have expanded the boundaries and content of citizenship for marginalized groups, eroding deep-seated patterns of hierarchy and exclusion (Rich et al. 2019). Feminist movements have promoted reproductive rights, laws combating gender-based violence, and quotas for women in politics (Alvarez 1990; Daby and Moseley 2022; Ewig 1999; Thayer 2009; Walsh and Xydias 2014). LGBTQ+ movements successfully advocated legalization of same-sex marriage and civil unions, adoption rights, and prohibitions against discrimination (Corrales 2021; Díez 2015; Encarnación 2016; Hummel and Velasco-Guachalla 2024; Wilson and Gianella 2019). Movements representing indigenous and Black people have secured new land rights, plurinational recognition, and affirmative action programs (Lucero 2008; Paschel 2016; Van Cott 2005; Yashar 2005). New, intersectional labor movements expanded economic inclusion for informal-sector workers, including street vendors, waste pickers, sex workers, and domestic workers, who often have intersecting marginalized

---

[4] Depending on how movements frame their grievances and demands, each of these issues *could* undermine equal citizenship, if done in a dehumanizing way that presents beneficiaries as an existential threat.

identities, especially on race and class lines (Acciari 2021; Blofield 2012; Garay 2016; Hummel 2017, 2022; Murray et al. 2018). Of course, progressive movements experienced many failures along the way – yet on net, they have upset Latin America's entrenched inequalities and social hierarchies.

Unsurprisingly, countermovements on the right emerged to contest these rights expansions (Mayka and Smith 2021: 2; Smith and Boas 2023). Civil society groups have organized around two causes – the protection of traditional gender and sexual hierarchies, and the promotion of repressive, hardline policing – in ways that promote the contraction of equal rights for marginalized groups and thus the erosion of democracy.

7.3 ANTIGENDER MOVEMENTS

In the first two decades of the 2000s, Latin America experienced an explosion in mobilization around issues of gender and sexuality. Right-wing groups arose to combat what they call "gender ideology": the idea that gender is socially constructed, rather than biologically determined (Corredor 2019).[5] These antigender activists collapse feminist and LGBTQ+ movements as essentially the same force: groups that seek to disrupt "natural" gender roles, promote promiscuity, and threaten the moral foundations of the family (Biroli and Caminotti 2020: 3; Corredor 2021: 52). Moreover, the use of the word "ideology" casts a conspiratorial tone, suggesting these ideas are artificial, foreign, and imposed on virtuous citizens.

This broad conception of "gender ideology" provides a portable framework to critique a range of different policy and societal developments, including same-sex marriage (Wilson and Gianella 2019), abortion rights (Reutersward 2021), school antibullying programs (Boas 2023; Corredor 2021; Rousseau 2020: 28–29; Sosa-Villagarcia and Rozas Urrunaga 2021), and efforts to promote gender parity in public office (Caminotti and Tabbush 2019). These movements also invoke the specter of "gender ideology" to oppose issues that are not directly connected to gender and sexuality. In Colombia, antigender activists emphasized gender-inclusive language included in a small section of the 2016 Peace Accords, which offered a plan to end the country's decades-long conflict between the military and the FARC guerrilla group, to mobilize voters to oppose and eventually defeat a referendum approving the Accords (Corredor 2021).[6] In Brazil, opponents of "gender ideology" joined forces with other

---

[5] The phrase "gender ideology" is only used by those who oppose it, and thus I write it using quotation marks. Following Corredor "On the Strategic Uses of Women's Rights: Backlash, Rights-Based Framing, and Anti-Gender Campaigns in Colombia's 2016 Peace Agreement," *Latin American Politics and Society*, 63/3 (2021), 46–68, I call these critics "antigender movements" because they reject the concept of gender altogether.

[6] The Peace Accords were later approved through a process that operated through the legislature, though the failed referendum undercut their legitimacy.

right-wing groups in protests supporting the impeachment of President Dilma Rousseff for financial irregularities in 2016 (Biroli 2016).

7.3.1 Constricting Membership

Antigender activists challenge the patriotic loyalty of feminists and supporters of LGBTQ+ rights, portraying them as conspiring foreign agents promoting perversion, rather than as real citizens. These groups are depicted as existential threats because they imperil the traditional family structure, groom and prey upon innocent children, and endanger the moral foundations of society through "cultural Marxism." As they do so, Antigender activists insist that they are not behind the times, but rather are the last defense for human rights and democracy.

Battles against "gender ideology" are never simply about the specific issues at hand, but rather are symbolic struggles for the soul of the country. Brazil's Movimento Brasil Livre (MBL, Free Brazil Movement) issued an alarm that secular public schools were teaching children to be gay. The MBL presented a gender-inclusive curriculum as a symptom of a broader left-wing conspiracy to dismantle traditional families, promote Marxism, and engage in corruption (Payne and de Souza Santos 2020: 35). In Peru, the group called Con Mis Hijos No Te Metas ("Don't Mess with My Children") uses street protests, legal strategies, lobbying, and media campaigns to oppose a gender-inclusive school curriculum (Boas 2023; Rousseau 2020: 28–29; Sosa-Villagarcia and Rozas Urrunaga 2021). Con Mis Hijos No Te Metas interpreted updates to national school curriculum as reflective of a broader "set of ideas that a global leftist conspiracy disseminates intending to 'homosexualise' society through the indoctrination of children from an early age, thus gaining cultural hegemony" (Sosa-Villagarcia and Rozas Urrunaga 2021: 643). Proponents of "gender ideology" make outlandish claims about the danger posed by those defined as sexual predators, resulting in a moral panic.

Antigender activists claim that gender-sensitive and inclusive approaches are ideological constructions, and that science confirms their belief that sex and gender are synonymous (Corredor 2019). Corrales (2021: 40) explains, "By stressing that a pro-LGBTQ agenda is an ideology of belief, they are insinuating that it is not a scientific proposition, and therefore, adults have the right to protect themselves, and more important, their children from exposure to it." In Colombia, Brazil, and Costa Rica, antigender activists embrace bioethical and scientific frames to discredit abortion rights and advocate "complementary" gender roles in the family as grounded in genetics (Morgan 2014). This scientific and secular framing is also strategically useful in appealing to the nondevout who may be wary of an alliance with the religious right (Reuterswärd 2021; Vaggione 2005).

In this accounting, feminist and LGBTQ+ movements are not legitimate groups that seek to protect the rights of minoritized groups, but rather neocolonial vehicles that endanger sovereignty (Biroli and Caminotti 2020: 3; Bob 2012: 162). Brazil's Schools without Parties (Escola Sem Partido) organizes to combat "cultural Marxism" and "radical feminism" in schools, which it claims are backed by globalist forces operating out of the United Nations that seek to undermine the traditional family structure (Biroli and Caminotti 2020: 3). Antigender activists depict their opponents as foreign infiltrators, not legitimate citizens, who therefore should be excluded from political debates. Advocates of women's and LGBTQ+ rights are not just wrong in their claims – they are fundamentally illegitimate interlocutors who imperil the polity.

7.3.2 Redefining Rights

Those mobilized against "gender ideology" reject the premise of rights designed to protect sexual minorities and advance egalitarian gender relations. They propose a view that rights are something to be earned by the deserving, good citizens – contrasting with a liberal view of rights as belonging to individuals, based on the principles of equality and the fundamental worth of each as human beings (Goodman 2022: 35, 39). Antigender activists contend that individual rights do not exist separate from the needs of society and the family. Thus, family rights are more important than individual rights, because family is the foundation of society (Biroli and Caminotti 2020: 3). These movements link the primacy of family rights with Catholic traditions in the region and conceptions of natural rights, and suggest that the notion of the very idea of individual rights is foreign and inappropriate for the Latin American context (Morgan 2014).

   Yet, antigender activists do *not* reject the idea of rights altogether. They frame their grievances and demands in terms of their own rights, which they claim are under attack by advocates of "gender ideology." Most commonly, they invoke the rights of children, at times presenting their claims in the language of the UN Convention on the Rights of the Child. In Mexico, the Pro-Yucatán Network supported legislation banning gay adoption by claiming that it violates children's fundamental right to grow up with both a mother and father (Reuterswärd 2021: 29). Antiabortion activists reframe debates about contraception and abortion by invoking fetal rights (Morgan 2014). Opponents of Colombia's peace process decried the 2016 Peace Accords as an attack on the freedom of religion, right to life, right to a family, and right to human dignity, invoking the specific language for these rights spelled out in Colombia's 1991 constitution (Corredor 2021). This use of rights language subverts allegations that they are prejudiced or backward, and yields strategic advantages by framing their demands as morally righteous and legally nonnegotiable under the constitution (Bob 2019: 14; Mayka 2021).

   Excluding LGBTQ+ individuals from inclusion as citizens necessarily precludes these groups' rights to same-sex marriage, adoption of children, freedom from discrimination, and gender-affirming care for trans people. Thus, initiatives to ensure the safety of LGBTQ+ children should not be seen as protections of their rights to live free from violence and access public services, but rather attacks on family rights and the safety of other children. Any policies extending LGBTQ+ rights become unconstitutional mandates that need not be implemented. These movements challenge the rule of law by demanding that public officials utilize discretion in assessing which legally mandated social rights can be disregarded at will.

7.4 CIVIL SOCIETY MOBILIZATION IN FAVOR OF *mano dura*

Civil society organizations – including NGOs, social movements, business groups, and neighborhood associations – have mobilized to support an ironfisted approach to security, known as *mano dura* in Latin America. *Mano dura* is characterized by militarized policing practices, limits to citizens' due-process rights, and extensive discretion for the police to detain and deploy violence against anyone they suspect to be criminals (Holland 2013: 46).

A range of Latin American interest groups and social movements organized around *mano dura* policies and expanded gun rights for citizens – what Fuentes (2005) calls a pro-order coalition. Many of these groups mirror the victims' rights movement in the United States, arguing that the criminal justice system insufficiently protects the rights of crime victims. In Argentina in 2004, the kidnapping and murder of Axel Blumberg led his father to establish the Fundación Axel Blumberg por la Vida de Nuestros Hijos, which opposed police reform initiatives that sought to reduce abuses by Buenos Aires' *maldita policía* (goddamn police, as it is commonly called). Instead, the foundation advocated an increase in hard-line policing tactics (Eaton 2008: 22–25). Similarly, Chile's Paz Ciudadana – established by news mogul Agustín Edwards after his son was kidnapped – provides research and analysis backing tough-on-crime approaches, which are then amplified through Edwards' newspaper, *El Mercurio* (Bonner 2013: 689). Other groups seek to expand citizens' access to guns, framed as a right in the terms of the United States' second amendment. In Brazil, groups such Movimento Viva Brasil model their activities on the National Rifle Association in the United States and have been instrumental in blocking efforts to pass disarmament legislation, and in advocating access to firearms as a right (Bob 2012: 155–59).

Groups that originally organized for other purposes – including neighborhood associations and business groups – also channel demands for repression to the state. In São Paulo, neighborhood associations and local business groups in wealthy and low-income areas alike mobilize through participatory institutions to demand a tough-on-crime approach to policing (González and Mayka 2023). In Bogotá, local merchants organized through the national merchants confederation (FENALCO) to demand that the police remove people experiencing homelessness and drug users from their neighborhoods, through violent force if necessary (Mayka 2021: 9). Neighborhood associations, business groups, and other civil society groups can quickly evolve into (or hire) "self-defense," vigilante, and paramilitary organizations that take security into their own hands (Moncada 2022; Payne 2000; Ungar 2011: 92–93).

7.4.1 Constricting Membership

Civil society advocates of *mano dura* draw a distinction between deserving, upstanding citizens – *gente de bien* in Spanish, or *cidadão de bom* in Portuguese – and those belonging to the underbelly of society, who must be excluded from citizenship. Mark Ungar explains that "to maintain control and respond to community demands, police divide society into groups they serve, such as elderly people, and those that they control, such as youth" (Ungar 2011: 101), a process reinforced through civil society demands. São Paulo's participatory security councils serve as a site for participants to assert their deservingness of security provision, while defining marginalized groups – such as low-income Black adolescents, sex workers, and drug users – as security threats that cause crime and disorder, rather than as rights-bearing citizens (González and Mayka 2023). Outside of participatory institutions, civil society groups – particularly neighborhood associations and business associations – amplify these messages about those who do and do not deserve citizenship.

Civil society groups assert their contributions to society as "good citizens" that make them worthy of police protections. In São Paulo's poor urban periphery, neighborhood associations define their members as good citizens because they uphold dominant social norms as to who is "a good worker, family provider, and honest person" (Holston 2008: 256). In São Paulo's participatory security councils, participants frequently preface their demands by noting that they are citizens who pay taxes; during an observation of one meeting, an individual equated their status as a taxpayer with citizenship by asserting "I pay my rights" (*eu pago meus direitos*).

By contrast, marginalized groups are denied inclusion as citizens because they are seen as provoking disorder and causing crime. Suspect groups – particularly racialized boys and young men, but also including other groups that violate social norms, including drug users, people experiencing homelessness, and LGBTQ+ individuals – pose "the threat not only of crime but also of social decay" (Caldeira 2000, 32). These individuals serve as an existential threat to society: their very presence endangers the physical well-being of the "good citizens," as well as the moral fabric of society. During meetings of São Paulo's participatory security councils, participants described squatters as "people who do nothing for society," street vendors were called "lowlifes" (*marginais*) who would invite an "air of decay" to the neighborhood, and low-income children were presented as budding criminals who made upstanding residents afraid to even go outside (González and Mayka 2023: 270–71). These groups are not described as citizens in need of protection, despite facing grave threats to their own physical safety. Instead, they are framed as security threats that must be eliminated to defend the virtuous citizens.

7.4.2 Redefining Rights and Rule of Law

Right-wing civil society knits together an ideational infrastructure that justifies a *mano dura* approach as legitimate and essential to protect the rights of "good citizens." As with the antigender activists, those mobilizing in favor of *mano dura* do not reject the notion of rights, but rather adapt it to new purposes. Support for extrajudicial violence and illegal detentions are justified using rights language, with the argument that marginalized groups threaten citizens' rights to property, mobility, and life, and therefore protecting rights means using any means necessary to end criminality and disorder. For the Brazilian gun rights movement, any effort at gun control threatens the "inalienable natural rights of peaceful, law-abiding people," in the words of pro-gun activist Jairo Paes de Lira (Bob 2012: 133). According to Paes de Lira, gun control efforts would go against "the right to keep and bear arms" (Bob 2012: 161) – a right that does not exist in the Brazilian constitution. Argentina's Fundación Axel Blumberg por la Vida de Nuestros Hijos invokes the rights of children in its to justify *mano dura* policing. In São Paulo's participatory security councils, participants frequently referred to their rights to security and mobility as requiring police repression and the removal of marginalized groups deemed to be "security threats." As I argue elsewhere, the adoption of human rights frames, reinterpreted in a highly selective and exclusionary manner, can clear the way for repressive policies that violate rights (Mayka 2021).

For *mano dura* activists, marginalized groups wreak havoc precisely because of the inappropriate protections of due process rights and civil liberties (Caldeira 2002; González and Mayka 2023; Smith 2015). Prohibitions on indefinite and warrantless detention, torture, or fabricated evidence simply prevent police from taking unreformable criminals off the streets. Procedural rights are loopholes and "luxuries" (Caldeira 2002: 242), not rights, that harm the deserving citizens. A common refrain is that criminals have more rights than upstanding citizens, and the protection of criminals' rights interferes with deserving citizens' more legitimate right to security (Caldeira 2002; González and Mayka 2023; Stanley 2005). Similarly, social rights that extend services or protections to marginalized groups are illegitimate and only encourage deviant behavior. In São Paulo's participatory security councils, participants argued that low-income adolescents manipulate protections in Brazil's rights-based child welfare system to evade the justice system and continue criminal behavior. Likewise, programs to help those experiencing homelessness only encourage them to stay on the street, where they threaten the rights of deserving citizens to move about freely (González and Mayka 2023: 274).

From the perspective of *mano dura* advocates, the state, as a duty bearer, has an obligation to protect virtuous citizens' rights by halting crime at any cost.

Following due process and restraining police violence would only enable criminals to continue to violate citizens' rights. In other words, the constraints of the rule of law can be discarded when it comes to the marginalized groups who endanger the citizenship rights of others.

7.5 CONCLUSION

Illiberal politicians may articulate authoritarian views that run counter to universal citizenship rights, yet to understand why these views resonate in a society, we need to move our gaze beyond the elite level to that of civil society organizations. As Sheri Berman warned, civil society groups can deepen societal divides and build support for antidemocratic movements (Berman 1997). This chapter has explored how civil society groups can advance an ideational infrastructure that justifies social exclusion on democratic and rights-based grounds. Antigender movements depict LGBTQ+ individuals as predators who target children and threaten family rights, and thus imperil the fabric of democratic society. Likewise, activists supporting *mano dura* point to repressive policing as the only way to safeguard the rights to mobility and safety that are under attack by dangerous criminals.

To be clear, these illiberal ideas are not recent constructions by these activists. However, right-wing associations play a key role in reproducing these ideas and repurposing them to tackle new "threats," as marginalized groups in Latin America have seen an unprecedented expansion in their social and procedural rights in recent years. Bad civil society sanitizes authoritarian ideas as compatible with and even essential under a democratic system, and creates broader narratives and scripts that politicians can later harness.

In the long run, these attacks on equal citizenship undermine the basic tenets of a procedural, Schumpeterian notion of democracy. When illiberal activists cast marginalized groups as *anti*-citizens who should be further excluded and repressed, they reject those groups' rights to electoral participation and fundamental civil liberties. Advocating further marginalization threatens the foundations behind liberal democracy: a respect for mutual tolerance despite differences, and the recognition that even your political enemies are still rights-bearing citizens who are members of the collective.

REFERENCES

Acciari, Louisa (2021), "Practicing intersectionality: Brazilian domestic workers' strategies of building alliances and mobilizing identity," *Latin American Research Review*, 56 (1), 67–81.

Alvarez, Sonia (1990), *Engendering democracy in Brazil: Women's movements in transition politics* (Princeton: Princeton University Press).

Armony, Ariel C. (2004), *The dubious link: Civic engagement and democratization* (Stanford: Stanford University Press).

Berman, Sheri (1997), "Civil society and the collapse of the Weimar Republic," *World Politics*, 49 (3), 401–29.

Biroli, Flávia (2016), "Political violence against women in Brazil: Expressions and definitions," *Revista Direito e Práxis*, 7 (16), 557–89.

Biroli, Flávia and Caminotti, Mariana (2020), "The conservative backlash against gender in Latin America," *Politics & Gender*, 16 (1), 1–6.

Blofield, Merike (2012), *Care work and class: Domestic workers' struggles for equal rights in Latin America* (University Park,: The Pennsylvania State University Press).

Boas, Taylor (2021), "Expanding the public square: Evangelicals and electoral politics in Latin America," in Diana Kapiszewski, Steven Levitsky, and Deborah J. Yashar (eds.), *The inclusionary turn in Latin American democracies* (New York: Cambridge University Press), 362–97.

(2023), *Evangelicals and electoral politics in Latin America: A kingdom of this world* (New York: Cambridge University Press).

Boas, Taylor and Smith, Amy Erica (2019), "Looks like me, thinks like me: Descriptive representation and opinion congruence in Brazil," *Latin American Research Review*, 54 (2), 310–28.

Bob, Clifford (2012), *The global right wing and the clash of world politics* (New York: Cambridge University Press).

(2019), *Rights as weapons: Instruments of conflict, tools of power* (Princeton: Princeton University Press).

Bonner, Michelle (2013), "The politics of police image in Chile," *Journal of Latin American Studies*, 45 (4), 669–94.

Caldeira, Teresa (2000), *City of walls: Crime, segregation, and citizenship in São Paulo.* (Berkeley: University of California Press).

(2002), "The paradox of police violence in democratic Brazil," *Ethnography*, 3 (3), 235–63.

Caldeira, Teresa and Holston, James (1999), "Democracy and violence in Brazil," *Comparative Studies in Society and History*, 41 (4), 691–729.

Caminotti, Mariana and Tabbush, Constanza (2019), "Más allá del sexo: la ampliación de la oposición conservadora a las políticas de igualdad de género en América Latina," *LASA Forum*, 51 (2), 27–31.

Chambers, Simone and Kopstein, Jeffrey (2001), "Bad civil society," *Political Theory*, 29 (6), 837–65.

Collins, Jennifer (2014), "New left experiences in Bolivia and Ecuador and the challenge to theories of populism," *Journal of Latin American Studies*, 46 (1), 59–86.

Corrales, Javier (2021), *The politics of LGBTQ rights expansion in Latin America and the Caribbean* (Cambridge Elements in Politics and Society in Latin America; New York: Cambridge University Press).

Corredor, Elizabeth (2019), "Unpacking 'gender ideology' and the global right's antigender countermovement," *Signs: Journal of Women in Culture and Society*, 44 (3), 613–38.

(2021), "On the strategic uses of women's rights: Backlash, rights-based framing, and anti-gender campaigns in Colombia's 2016 peace agreement," *Latin American Politics and Society*, 63 (3), 46–68.

da Matta, Roberto (1987), "The quest for citizenship in a relational university," in John Wirth, Edson Nunes, and Thomas Bogenschild (eds.), *State and society in Brazil: Continuity and change* (Boulder: Westview Press), 307–35.

Daby, Mariela and Moseley, Mason (2022), "Feminist mobilization and the abortion debate in Latin America: Lessons from Argentina," *Politics & Gender*, 18 (2), 359–93.

Díez, Jordi (2015), *The politics of gay marriage in Latin America* (New York: Cambridge University Press).

Eaton, Kent (2008), "Paradoxes of police reform: Federalism, parties, and civil society in Argentina's public security crisis," *Latin American Research Review*, 43 (3), 5–32.

Encarnación, Omar (2016), *Out in the periphery: Latin America's gay rights revolution* (Oxford University Press: New York).

Ewig, Christina (1999), "The strengths and limits of the NGO women's movement model: Shaping Nicaragua's democratic institutions," *Latin American Research Review*, 34 (3), 75–102.

Fuentes, Claudio (2005), *Contesting the iron fist: Advocacy networks and police violence in democratic Argentina and Chile* (New York: Routledge).

Garay, Candelaria (2016), *Social policy expansion in Latin America* (New York: Cambridge University Press).

Gibson, Edward (1996), *Class and conservative parties: Argentina in comparative perspective* (Baltimore: Johns Hopkins University Press).

Glenn, Evelyn (2011), "Constructing citizenship," *American Sociological Review*, 76 (1), 1–24.

Gold, Tomás and Peña, Alejandro (2021), "The rise of the contentious right: Digitally intermediated linkage strategies in Argentina and Brazil," *Latin American Politics and Society*, 63 (3), 93–118.

González, Yanilda and Mayka, Lindsay (2023), "Policing, democratic participation, and the reproduction of asymmetric citizenship," *American Political Science Review*, 117 (1), 263–79.

Goodman, Sara (2019), "Liberal democracy, national identity boundaries, and populist entry points," *Critical Review: A Journal of Politics and Society*, 31 (3), 377–88.

(2022), *Citizenship in hard times: How ordinary people respond to democratic threat* (New York: Cambridge University Press).

(2023), "Citizenship studies: Policy causes and consequences," *Annual Review of Political Science*, 26, 135–52.

Holland, Alisha (2013), "Right on crime? Conservative party politics and *mano dura* policies in El Salvador," *Latin American Research Review*, 48 (1), 44–67.

Holston, James (2008), *Insurgent citizenship: Disjunctions of democracy and modernity in Brazil* (Princeton: Princeton University Press).

(2011), "Contesting privilege with right: The transformation of differentiated citizenship in Brazil," *Citizenship Studies*, 15 (3–4), 335–52.

Hummel, Calla (2017), "Disobedient markets: Street vendors, enforcement, and state intervention in collective action," *Comparative Political Studies*, 50 (11), 1524–55.

(2022), *Why informal workers organize: Contentious politics, enforcement, and the state* (New York: Oxford University Press).

Hummel, Calla and Velasco-Guachalla, Ximena (2024), "Activists, parties, and the expansion of trans rights in Bolivia," *Comparative Politics*, 56 (3), 321–43.

Lucero, José Antonio (2008), *Struggles of voice: The politics of indigenous representation in the Andes* (Pittsburgh: University of Pittsburgh Press).

Luna, Juan Pablo and Medel, Rodrigo (2023), "Uneven states, unequal societies, and democracy's unfulfilled promises: Citizenship rights in Chile and contemporary Latin America," *Latin American Politics and Society*, 65 (2), 170–96.

Marshall, T. H. (1950), *Citizenship and social class* (Cambridge: Cambridge University Press).

Mayka, Lindsay (2021), "The power of human rights frames in urban security: Lessons from Bogotá," *Comparative Politics*, 54 (1), 1–25.

Mayka, Lindsay and Smith, Amy Erica (2021), "The grassroots right in Latin America: Patterns, causes, and consequences," *Latin American Politics and Society*, 63 (3), 1–20.

Mitchell, Michael and Wood, Charles (1999), "Ironies of citizenship: Skin color, police brutality, and the challenge to democracy in Brazil," *Social Forces*, 77 (3), 1001–20.

Moncada, Eduardo (2022), *Resisting extortion: Victims, criminals, and states in Latin America* (New York: Cambridge University Press).

Morgan, Lynn M. (2014), "Claiming Rosa Parks: Conservative Catholic bids for 'rights' in contemporary Latin America," *Culture, Health & Sexuality*, 16 (10), 1245–59.

Murray, Laura, Kerrigan, Deanna, and Paiva, Vera Silvia (2018), "Rites of resistance: Sex workers' fight to maintain rights and pleasure in the centre of the response to HIV in Brazil," *Global Public Health*, 14 (2), 1–15.

O'Donnell, Guillermo (1993), "On the state, democratization, and some conceptual problems: A Latin American view with glances at some postcommunist countries," *World Development*, 21 (8), 1355–69.

Paschel, Tianna (2016), *Becoming black political subjects: Movements and ethno-racial rights in Colombia and Brazil* (Princeton: Princeton University Press).

Payne, Leigh (2000), *Uncivil movements: The armed right wing and democracy in Latin America* (Baltimore: Johns Hopkins University Press).

Payne, Leigh and de Souza Santos, Andreza Aruska (2020), "The right-wing backlash in Brazil and beyond," *Politics & Gender*, 16 (1), 32–38.

Payne, Leigh, Escoffier, Simón, and Zulver, Julia (eds.) (2023), *The right against rights in Latin America* (New York: Oxford University Press).

Reuterswärd, Camilla (2021), "'Pro-life' and feminist mobilization in the struggle over abortion in Mexico: Church networks, elite alliances, and partisan context," *Latin American Politics and Society*, 63 (3), 21–45.

Rich, Jessica A.J., Mayka, Lindsay, and Montero, Alfred (2019), "The politics of participation in Latin America: New actors and institutions," *Latin American Politics and Society*, 61 (2), 1–20.

Rousseau, Stéphanie (2020), "Antigender activism in Peru and its impacts on state policy," *Politics & Gender*, 16 (1), 25–32.

Shklar, Judith (1991), *American citizenship: The quest for inclusion* (Cambridge: Harvard University Press).

Smith, Amy Erica and Boas, Taylor (2023), "Religion, sexuality politics, and the transformation of Latin American electorates," *British Journal of Political Science*, 54 (3), 1–20.

Smith, Nicholas Rush (2015), "Rejecting rights: Vigilantism and violence in post-apartheid South Africa," *African Affairs*, 114 (456), 341–60.

Smith, Rogers (1997), *Civic ideals: Conflicting visions of citizenship in US history* (New Haven: Yale University Press).

Sosa-Villagarcia, Paolo and Rozas Urrunaga, Lucila (2021), "From the state to the streets: The debate over the civil union bill and conservative strategic change in Peru," *Bulletin of Latin American Research*, 40 (5), 634–49.

Stanley, Ruth (2005), "Controlling the police in Buenos Aires: A case study of horizontal and societal accountability," *Bulletin of Latin American Research*, 24 (1), 71–91.

Thayer, Millie (2009), *Making transnational feminism: Rural women, NGO activists, and northern donors in Brazil* (New York: Routledge).

Ungar, Mark (2011), *Policing democracy: Overcoming obstacles to citizen security in Latin America* (Baltimore: Johns Hopkins University Press).

Vaggione, Juan Marco (2005), "Reactive politicization and religious dissidence: The political mutations of the religious," *Social Theory and Practice*, 31 (2), 233–55.

Van Cott, Donna Lee (2005), *From movements to parties in Latin America: The evolution of ethnic politics* (New York: Cambridge University Press).

Walsh, Shannon Drysdale and Xydias, Christina (2014), "Women's organizing and intersectional policy-making in comparative perspective: Evidence from Guatemala and Germany," *Politics, Groups, and Identities* 2(4), 549–72.

Wilson, Bruce and Gianella, Camila (2019), "Overcoming the limits of legal opportunity structures: LGBT rights' forking paths in Costa Rica and Colombia," *Latin American Politics and Society*, 61 (2), 138–63.

Yashar, Deborah J. (2005), *Contesting citizenship in Latin America: The rise of indigenous movements and the postliberal challenge* (Cambridge: Cambridge University Press).

Young, Iris Marion (2011), Justice and the politics of difference (Princeton: Princeton University Press).

Ziblatt, Daniel (2017), *Conservative parties and the birth of democracy* (New York: Cambridge University Press).

8

Nationalist Passion, Economic Interest, and the Moral Economy of the Hungarian Civic Right: 2002–2010

Béla Greskovits

In 2010–22, Hungary's increasingly radicalizing national conservative party, Viktor Orbán's Fidesz-Hungarian Civic Alliance (Fidesz), achieved in a row four landslide victories at national parliamentary elections. The party also won all the municipal and European Parliament elections of the period. Declaring victory at the spring 2022 election, Orbán recalled that Fidesz triumphed no matter whether the opposition parties ran on their own (as in 2014), engaged in limited cooperation (as in 2018), or joined an encompassing electoral alliance (as in 2022). Moreover, Fidesz achieved its victories in changing electoral systems. At the Hungarian elections of the past twelve years, then, the formation of a cohesive and united opposition adopting innovative electoral strategies, identified by Bunce and Wolchik (2011) as the winning formula against Eastern Europe's competitive authoritarian rulers, either failed to materialize or failed to be effective.

Orbán attributed the 2022 results to the nationwide presence and patriotic spirit of activists. He emphasized that the 100,000 campaign workers were "volunteers, not robots or mercenaries," and called the victory "the triumph of the heart. We won because we share a passion: the passion for Hungary" (Orbán 2022).[1] Unsurprisingly, most opposition politicians, pundits, and critical scholars have come up with different explanations of Fidesz's continuing success story. They explained the party's strengthening and eventual breakthrough with the initial irresponsible welfare spending and lack of reform commitment of the coalition governments of the Hungarian Socialist Party (MSZP) and the liberal Alliance of Free Democrats (SZDSZ), the right-wing riots of 2006, the social demagoguery of Fidesz, and the financial crisis of 2008. After 2010, the critical perspective shifted to the increasingly authoritarian measures of the Orbán regime coupled with the fragmentation

---

[1] The Hungarian texts cited in the chapter are translated by Béla Greskovits.

of opposition and the ineffective response of the European Union (EU) to democratic backsliding (see Greskovits 2020 for details and references). Lastly, the bulk of the intellectual effort of opposition strategists went into forging an electoral coalition encompassing all the left and liberal parties and even the (formerly) radical right Jobbik, notwithstanding their conflicting values and identity. So far, there is no consensus about the reasons for the new fiasco.

All in all, the critique of Fidesz's lasting rule converged on the following points: (1) it stripped Orbán's power of any benevolent social purpose; (2) it unveiled the regime's claims to uphold national sovereignty and build a native bourgeoisie as mere excuses for rampant corruption and graft; and (3) it demystified the bonds of loyalty within the right-wing camp as products of lies and bribes used to fool the uninformed and uneducated and satisfy those motivated by pure economic calculus. This picture is popular among pundits and academic analysts within Hungary and without, and does have some elements of truth. Even so, it falls short of a nuanced interpretation of the Orbán regime and overlooks a key pillar of its political success. It misses the role of the supportive civic activism of educated conservative middle-class groups claiming moral superiority and leading an unabated *quest for moral leadership*, which, in the eyes of a critical mass of the electorate, has been successful.

My earlier work traced Fidesz's resilience partly to tectonic shifts in civil society, which helped the right accumulate ample social capital well before its political breakthrough in 2010 (Greskovits 2020). The rise of a vibrant right-wing civil sector was decisively advanced by the Civic Circles Movement founded by Orbán when after a term in government his party marginally lost the 2002 elections to the MSZP and SZDSZ. The movement was militant in terms of its hegemonic aspirations and contentious collective practices; massive in terms of its membership and activism; educated middle-class-based in terms of social stratification; and dominantly metropolitan and urban but also transborder on the spatial dimension. Parallel to contentious mobilization, the circles reorganized and extended the right's grassroots networks, associations, and media; rediscovered and reinvented its holidays and everyday lifestyles, symbols, and heroes; and explored innovative ways for cultural, charity, leisure, and political activities. Leading activists, among them patriots, priests, professionals, politicians, and pundits, offered new frames and practices for Hungarians to feel, think, and act as members of a lasting *identity community* with shared values concerning the nation, Christianity, citizenry, and Europe.

Building and expanding on these findings, this chapter focuses on the political economy of the movement. I shall elaborate that the circles viewed the political economy through a markedly moralizing lens that deserves scholarly attention. Accordingly, I adopt a moral economy framework to grasp the ways in which cultural/ethical values and material interests were related in the circles' economic perceptions and activities. I start with situating the moral economy argument in the context of current academic disputes on the salience of cultural and economic factors in the ascendance of antiliberal leaders and agendas. Then I analyze the moral economy vision and related agency of the civic circles' most vocal groups: the Christian national *Bildungsbürgertum*, and the propertied *petit bourgeoisie*. Finally, I propose that the moral economy contributed to the right's moral leadership aspiration partly through enhancing the movement's legitimacy, and partly through providing frames and devoted activists for effective mobilization.

8.1 CULTURE, THE ECONOMY, AND ANTILIBERAL POLITICS: POSSIBLE CONCEPTUALIZATIONS OF THEIR RELATIONSHIP

Currently, liberalism is attacked by its enemies for exacerbating global economic inequality and insecurity, and, simultaneously, for its efforts to educate citizens to respect their societies' diversity and accept the emancipation of women or ethnic and sexual minorities. The double attack inspired a new body of scholarship with different though partly overlapping propositions on the interplay between the cultural and economic dimensions of politics. For the purposes of this chapter, three perspectives are relevant: the cultural backlash and/or status anxiety thesis, the notion of the cultural drivers of voters' distributive preferences, and the moral economy.

The cultural backlash thesis traces the antiliberal tide to the resentment of those left behind by the "silent revolution" of postmaterialist value change, embraced since World War II by the entire Western world (Inglehart and Norris 2016). In this view, persons with traditional attachments to the nation, religion, and family hierarchies experience a "fundamental loss of certainty and the withering of a 'golden age,' when their individual norms were in tune with those in society" (Bornschier and Kriesi 2013: 14). Their status anxiety is fueled by their worsening labor market position and threatening social dislocation, exacerbated by the Global Financial Crisis of 2008, the ensuing Great Recession, and new waves of immigrants viewed as competitors for welfare benefits or, like the emancipated women, jobs (Inglehart and Norris 2016; Gidron and Hall 2017). The explanations based on cultural backlash and economic insecurity share a preoccupation with the grievances of "have-nots," the (not necessarily impoverished) losers of cultural and/or economic modernization, and their electoral mobilization by the nativist, populist, and authoritarian radical right (Mudde 2021; Palestini and Kaltwasser Chapter 15 this volume).

More generally, it has been suggested that "the distinction between the realm of economic and cultural politics becomes blurred, since cultural mechanisms increasingly drive preferences regarding distributive policies," such as welfare schemes, labor market measures, or charity (Häusermann and Kriesi 2015: 207). Similar to the cultural backlash thesis, the notion of cultural drivers of distributional preferences provides a convincing argument on "what voters want" and why, or what is termed the demand side of politics. Yet, both accounts are incomplete in that they neglect the supply side. Specifically, they have little to say about the phenomenon of lasting solidarity, which is "more than an expression of the social and occupational location of any set of individuals," and cannot be forged without "collective identities, grassroots movements and hierarchical organizations" (Hooghe and Marks 2018: 111), that is, a vibrant civil society.

Herein lies the relevance of the moral economy approach for capturing the cultural and ethical rather than merely material dimensions of the civic circles' political economy. This approach is part of a rich and influential tradition of thought represented prominently by Weber's work on the economic ethics of religions (Weber [1904–05] 1958), Polanyi's theory of the embedded economy (Polanyi [1944] 1957), and Thompson's notion of moral economy (Thompson 1971). Critical about Thompson's narrow understanding of the term "as a traditional consensus of crowd rights that were swept away by market forces," Götz recently argued that in an extended form the moral economy could become "a key concept of civil society research" (Götz 2015: 148, 158).

If one concentrates on civil society, the focus on the moral economy will be shifted away from the destitute and towards those employing economic options in moral ways, that is, to the economic supply side ... The moral might then find approval, or it might appear as something self-righteous, ignorant, and fueling destructive forces. It might impose the ideas of the powerful on others. (Götz 2015: 158)

Perceived this way, the moral economy appears to have several analytic advantages. It helps to grasp the interested passions or passioned interests, as it might be the case, of the "haves," that is, members of the educated middle class. This is important, because these actors play a crucial role in creating a vibrant civil society and this way set standards of vision and action even for the "have-nots" of social and cultural capital. Related, the perspective helps to trace the ethical connotations of distinctions between deserving versus undeserving poor, gender roles, and productive versus unproductive, or plainly "good" versus "bad" capital.

However, let me clearly state that although the Hungarian civic right never stopped professing the moral superiority of its economic visions and practices over the "amoral" or "immoral" economy of its political rivals, in my understanding of the term there is no such thing as an amoral economy. In this, I follow the Weberian interpretation, which is echoed by many contemporary economic sociologists. As summarized by Swedberg, in Weber's view "while an economic interest aims at utility, what is seen as utility differs quite a bit according to what values (or culture) are involved" (Swedberg 2003: 227).

Which agents, led by which motifs, crafted the moral economy of the civic circles, and how did they try to make their economic ethic's "practical impulses of action" matter for politics and policymaking (Weber [1915] 1946: 268, cited by Swedberg 2003: 228)? These are the questions to which I now turn.

8.2 TWO ROADS TO THE MORAL ECONOMY

The political economy profile of the Civic Circles Movement was formed by the interacting values and interests of the educated Christian national *Bildungsbürgertum*, or cultural bourgeoisie, and of the propertied *petit bourgeoisie*, the native owners of small and medium-sized businesses. The agendas and practices of both groups also reflected the political opportunities and risks of the social and economic policies of successive left and liberal governments. In 2002 and 2003, the MSZP–SZDSZ government's priorities were the following. A new social policy package labeled the "Program of Transformation with Welfare" was implemented. The modernization of the economy via massive imports of foreign direct investment (FDI) continued. The coalition completed the preparations for EU membership, and from 2004 faced the new tasks and constraints brought by the enlargement.

8.2.1 Transformation with Welfare, and Foreign-Led Economic Modernization

As promised in the 2002 election campaign, in the first 100 days in power, Premier Péter Medgyessy's government implemented a "Program of Transformation with Welfare" with a substantial budget of about 162 billion Hungarian forint (the overview below relies on Kapcsándi 2002; Pethő 2009). Civil servants working in central and municipal administrations and public servants employed in education and healthcare were granted a 50 percent salary raise on average. In addition, for those with a university degree, a special minimum wage was introduced, and their maximum salary limit was significantly raised as well. These measures covered about 600,000 teachers, medical doctors, nurses, lawyers, and other educated professionals employed in the public sector, foundations, or in various institutions affiliated with the churches. As a gesture to the youngest cohort of the educated middle class, the stipends of university students were increased by 30 percent.

The minimum wages of all employee categories were exempted from the personal income tax. The Labor Code was modified to guarantee two days of rest weekly, including one on a Sunday. Firms' social security contributions paid for their casual employed workers were reduced. The government also promised to start a new round of bargaining with the EU to improve the financial conditions of accession for farmers and planned to restore public controls over the management of the National Land Fund.

The social policy measures included a onetime benefit of 19,000 Hungarian forint compensating pensioners for their alleged losses under the Orbán government. Parents were granted two extra monthly installments of family allowance annually to help cover the costs of their children's schooling. Increasing the family allowance and maternity benefit by 20 and 50 percent, respectively, and doubling the amount and duration of childcare benefit for parents raising twins were also on the social policy agenda.

This was not all. The first 100-day program was soon to be followed by a second set of measures, which included increasing the subsidies for housing construction for middle-class families, relief to heavily indebted agricultural producers, and subsidized travel for students visiting museums. In 2003, steps were made toward the introduction of a thirteenth month's pension. Finally, fulfilling the campaign promise of SZDSZ, from 2004 personal income tax was to be lowered.

Rather unusually, then, during its honeymoon period the Medgyessy government went out of its way to appease virtually all strata of society with generous social protection benefits and other distributive measures and cared little about the negative repercussions of fiscal overspending. In the short run, the program brought political dividends: In September 2002 the popularity of MSZP stood at 54 percent, while that of Fidesz only at 38 percent. In the same year, the coalition parties scored a landslide victory at the municipal elections. But even in the following years when the budget deficit spiraled out of control and the government's popularity was on the decline, Hungary stood out for its large social protection expenditure in comparison with the previous Orbán government and the other Eastern European countries (Bohle and Greskovits 2019).

Medgyessy's second priority was to continue the country's economic modernization based on massive FDI. While in this area the administration did not introduce radical changes but rather followed previously established practices, Hungary remained one of the regional leaders as far as its generous FDI incentives, efficient investment promotion, and FDI inflows are concerned (Bohle and Greskovits 2019). How did these policies shape the context of mobilization on the right in general, and the responses of influential groups within or allied with the civic circles in particular?

8.2.2   Cultural and Economic Factors of Right-Wing Civic Activism

Large groups of the educated conservative middle class were among the main beneficiaries of the Medgyessy government's welfarist policies, even if these fell short of satisfying all their pent-up demands. This, and the fact that the movement's rapid expansion occurred well before the Global Financial Crisis, make it likely that the Christian national *Bildungsbürgetum* had more important reasons for flocking to the civic circles than economic grievances. In a seminal essay on the discontents of economic development Hirschman (whose work inspired the title of this chapter) suggests that even the upwardly mobile social strata might remain "disaffected and subversive" if they suspect that despite their rise "along one of the dimensions of social status, such as wealth [or, in our case, income – B. G.] . . . a number of obstacles, rigidities, and discriminatory practices still block their continued ascent along other dimensions as well as their all-round acceptance by the traditional elites" (Hirschman 1981: 46).

In this vein, I trace the right-wing *Bildungsbürgertum*'s discontent primarily to their belief that the collapse of socialism did not bring about the emancipation, let alone dominance, of their conservative values. Indeed, they were convinced that the left and liberal governments' (in fact, only timid) attempts to emancipate women, sexual and ethnic minorities, and promote secular values and nontraditional lifestyles, could only be halted by a vigorous counterattack. Their militancy is illustrated by the call of the Alliance of Christian Intellectuals (KÉSZ) for expanding the organization in the Budapest metro area, and recruiting new squads of competent and experienced activists who were capable of turning the tide of "moral decay and disastrous marginalisation of the values of divine inspiration, the only desirable values for human beings" (Civic Circles Database, 2003).[2]

In turn, the native *petit* and partly even *grand bourgeoisie* feared deprivation and status loss in economic and not only cultural terms. In this respect, the Hungarian case is not exceptional. In Western Europe, the strongest support for illiberal politics was found among "small proprietors like self-employed plumbers, or family-owned small businesses, and mom-and-pop shop-keepers" (Inglehart and Norris 2016: 26). As Skocpol and Williamson observed, small and medium-sized enterprise owners in construction, remodeling, repair, technology, insurance, and real estate businesses, "relatively well educated and economically comfortable compared to Americans in general," have been very active in the grassroots organizations of the Tea Party as well. "Older husbands and wives often attended together [the Tea Party meetings – B. G.], leaving big cars in the parking lot festooned with Tea Party stickers that symbolized their new joint passion" (Skocpol and Williamson 2012: 125). Interestingly, in an interview Csaba Hende, member of parliament for the conservative Hungarian Democratic Forum (MDF) party and chief coordinator of civic circles, also mentioned big cars as the status symbols of activists. "The overwhelming majority of the circles' membership is highly educated, well-to-do, conservative individual. I suggest you to visit any larger civic circle event, and look at the automobiles parked around" (Halász 2004).

---

[2] The Civic Circles Event Database includes about 4,900 events organized, co-organized, or sponsored by the movement and attended by its members between July 2002 and April 2006. I compiled the data from the Electronic Newsletter of Civic Circles and other media sources. Originally collected by civic circle members and preserved by the Open Society Archives, the newsletter consists of civic circle messages. The database does not contain personal, secret, or classified data. According to Hungarian and EU law, the messages are anonymized except for those from persons performing public functions about public matters and used solely for the purposes of historical research.

Similarities aside, while the above examples point to the global financial and economic crisis (and its management) as the main sources of the *petit bourgeoisie*'s radicalizing political orientation in the United States and Western Europe, the Hungarian small and medium-sized entrepreneurs' discontent in the early–mid 2000s originated from a different kind of insecurity. Their main concern was with the country's FDI-based modernization strategy, which in an everexpanding range of activities put them into cutthroat competition with foreign transnational corporations (TNC) and with each other. According to experts, "a remarkable part of this social group – members of which started businesses mostly in the first years of the post-socialist transition – lost its influence and economic power at the end of the first decade of the 21st century" (Laki and Szalai 2015: 14). One reason was that after 2001–02 the economy slowed down. Further, when the impact of onetime specific incentives, such as privatization, deregulation, and nonsaturated markets, faded, the more conventional incentives of entrepreneurship fell short of creating prosperity (Laki and Szalai 2015). Thus, both the boom of startups and the expansion of existing private firms so characteristic of the early transition years became a thing of the past.

Similar to the grassroots entrepreneur activists of the Tea Party, whose "pessimism about the economy is politically tinged" (Skocpol and Williamson 2012: 29), members of the native Hungarian *petit bourgeoisie* tended to distrust the Medgyessy administration, which supposedly turned a blind eye to their problems. Similar to the *Bildungsbürgertum*, the *petit bourgeoisie*'s search for remedies reflected the interplay of cultural values and material interests.

8.2.3   Mobilizing for the Nation's Social and Cultural Reproduction

In his famous speech of May 7, 2002, Orbán recalled his outgoing administration's vision of welfare: "We wanted to create true well-being, material, and spiritual well-being. For many, prosperity means bread, work, school, car, vacation. But prosperity for us also means family, children, friends, national pride, love, togetherness, and holidays. We wanted both together" (Orbán 2002). In the speech Orbán also stressed that the desirable opposition strategy was to lend support to the MSZP–SZDSZ government's social policy measures but at the same time remain alert to dangers of austerity.

Faithful to the Orbán government's vision of well-being but left without real influence over the policies to achieve material prosperity while in opposition, the conservative teachers, doctors, lawyers, social workers, and clergy(wo)men promoted a moral economy of the nation's social and spiritual reproduction. This model served as the intellectual background for the *Bildungsbürgertum*'s critique of liberal education and healthcare reforms and provided the ethical foundations for their own allegedly superior activities. Taking shape gradually, the ideas and practices of this moral economy differed from those of the administration in significant ways.

In contrast to the MSZP–SZDSZ coalition's alleged myopic preference for boosting present consumption via salary increases and social transfers, the movement stressed the need for a future-oriented policy strategy. Hence the educated conservatives' critical engagement with the administration's management and reforms of education, healthcare, culture, family care, and labor market. At a cursory look, their preferred model of investing in people reminded of a "social investment-oriented" welfare state (Beramendi et al. 2015).

However, the aim of advocates of the moral economy of national reproduction was more noble than improving employability: it was to keep the nation's "body and soul" in good health in times of globalization. This, the conservative opinion leaders argued, could not be achieved by liberal education reforms, which, in their eyes, lacked any moral compass. Such distrust was for instance expressed by the Alliance for Education, one of the teachers' organizations associated with the movement: "'Our side' primarily means pedagogical affiliation. There is no right-wing or left-wing pedagogy, only value-centered versus liberal pedagogy. We represent the former and are convinced that the majority of Hungarian teachers is on our side" (Civic Circles Database 2003, see Footnote 2).

There were significant differences between the typical beneficiaries and geographic scope of the two welfare models as well. Assistance to a variety of churchbound cultural, educational, healthcare, and family-related activities and institutions accounted for a large share of the civic circles' charitable activities. Ethnic Hungarians in neighboring states were no less frequently supported by donations. Among those seen as worthy of assistance, children and the young were the most prominent. In addition to the image of the innocent minor, other factors played a role in activating solidaristic emotions. In a nutshell, charitable activities were meant to prepare children for a future life guided by Christian ethics and for serving the ethnic community through honorable work. However, Roma children were only once mentioned as beneficiaries of charity, although many Hungarian poor belong to the Roma minority. In that instance, civic circles covered the schooling costs of pupils, whose parents in 2002 "campaigned for the victory of the national side … despite the risk of retaliation" (Civic Circles Database 2003, see Footnote 2).

Finally, the civic circles' limited resources allowed only relatively modest monetary or in-kind donations or voluntary work. Not infrequently, such activities appeared as complementary to the public welfare system, especially as in the wake of neoliberal state reforms the maintenance of kindergartens, schools, hospitals, and nursing homes was increasingly outsourced to nonprofit organizations. Such organizations, including those related to the civic circles, were offered legal possibilities and generous financial benefits for taking over originally public functions. Furthermore, the movement could utilize the regulatory measures introduced in 1996, 1997, and 2003 by various MSZP–SZDSZ administrations in order to support civic associational life. The most important of these regulations allowed Hungarian citizens to donate 1 +1 percent of their personal income tax to support civil society organizations and initiatives of public interest.

8.2.4   Producing by the Nation, for the Nation: The Sectoral Affiliation, Activities, and Spirit of Native Petty Capitalists

Members of the native *petit bourgeoisie* tried to shelter themselves from the cutthroat competition with TNC by resorting to the moral economy of national production, which, they believed, would fit the nation's communitarian spirit better than the soulless individualism of global capitalism. The vision of producing (to paraphrase Abraham Lincoln) by the nation, for the nation, found a welcoming home in the movement even if "to create, bolster and protect" national production was permanently challenged by "the global economy making it all but impossible to separate by nationality" (Pryke 2012: 281).

The related moralizing language sought to contrast the immorality of the footloose financier and speculator with the loyalty of the economic patriot, and to replace the "homo oeconomicus" ideal of the neoliberal transformation with the "homo laborious." One example of Orbán's recurrent advocacy of a new "work-based society" was his speech inaugurating a new vocational school of the Kolping Society, a Catholic international organization founded to remedy social problems worldwide:

> One of the most important tasks in Hungary today is to restore the dignity of work, and the Kolping movement can help a lot in this. 'During the 15 years of the systemic change ... a distorted idea has developed in Hungary that speculation should be valued more than work' ... and the real talent is to make a good living without work. (Civic Circles Database 2005, see Footnote 2)

Facing the challenge of TNC, the native entrepreneurs tried to distinguish themselves through their sectoral affiliation, entrepreneurial practices, and spirit. Their small and medium-sized businesses were often active in agriculture, winemaking, production and retail of authentic and bio food, publishing, and local media – all attached to Hungarian land, labor, and culture. They invented national brands and advertisement slogans, and were involved in solidaristic local patriotic projects. One cofounder of the Magor commercial and producer network, who was also active in the civic circles, summarized its business ethics as follows:

> the name covers a worldview that manifests itself in our everyday life, as a voluntary commitment ... to the national value, thinking in the nation ... The legal entities participating in the movement are 100 percent Hungarian-owned, so their work, activities, and results serve the country ... The most important goal is to protect Hungarian products, Hungarian small and medium-sized entrepreneurs and traders, and to organize their unified action. (Bencze 2003)

The moral economy of national production is equally well illustrated by the example of transborder service chains of mobility, tourism, transport, and hospitality organized by the native economic bourgeoisie. Of course, journeys to the lost territories of the former Greater Hungary – to Transylvania, Southern and Eastern Slovakia, or the Transcarpathian territory of Ukraine – have never been the right's monopoly. However, as I showed earlier, the civic circles' tourism differed from ordinary excursions in several respects (Greskovits 2020). Dozens of specialist business enterprises offered trips at lower prices to civic circle members and attracted them with professional guides and even trusted bus drivers coming from within the movement. The organizers promised authentic Hungarian hospitality and personal encounters with locals who hosted the travelers in their guest rooms, offered traditional meals of their home cuisine, and entertained the guests with folkloric spectacles. These journeys routinely included stopovers at the very same legendary places of Greater Hungarian history and culture, including, for example, the monument of the 1,000-year-old border, King Mathias Corvinus's birthplace, or the Csíksomlyó Passion. As revealed by the somewhat exalted "travelogues," all these features made these adventures at the headwaters of national identity more reminiscent of pilgrimages to sacred places than the usual experiences of dull mass tourism. Against this background it is hardly surprising that in a keynote address at a tourism summit in 2018, Premier Orbán called successful tourism entrepreneurs "patriots by definition" and proclaimed that earning one's living from tourism qualifies as patriotism (2019).

8.3   ASSETS OF THE MORAL ECONOMY

Above I argued that the moral economies of the civic right were politically conditioned in the sense that their meanings and practices developed in response to the political opportunities and risks shaped by the social welfare and economic modernization policies of the MSZP–SZDSZ governments. But were these moral economies also politically consequential? How far did it matter for Hungarian politics and civil society that the opposition adopted moral economy frameworks to formulate its strategic visions and mobilize for collective action? My answer is that the convergence of the cultural bourgeoisie and the native economic bourgeoisie on the moral economies of the nation's reproduction and economic production (1) created a common ground for the interpenetration between the visions of political leadership and those spreading in popular politics; (2) offered resources for collective contention; and (3) deepened the movement's social embeddedness in other ways as well.

Concerning the first aspect, Orbán's article in the *Magyar Nemzet* daily newspaper deserves to be cited at some length because it aptly illustrates his vision that his followers (ought to) form an identity community distinguished from the organizations of their political rivals by solid moral self-definition.

Neither the liberal nor the socialist ideology is able to envisage good life as a goal and essential value. The liberal mind is captivated by creating freedom but does not care about moral self-determination and livelihood. Socialists neither care about freedom nor about values only about material livelihood. It is only the civic mindset that captures the meaning of good life as a whole . . . Liberals create freedom, socialists modernize, and the civic forces build a community. (Orbán 2006)

Although Orbán's concept of morally defined identity community resonated well with the related visions of the civic camp, his claim about the absent morality of liberals and socialists was pure demagoguery. As I argued above, the extended notion of moral economy does not justify the normative ranking of "moral" versus "amoral" or "immoral" economies, as it considers an economy lacking a moral dimension as an oxymoron. It follows that far from being the sole moral actor in contentious politics the civic circles engaged in a "war of position" (Gramsci 1971) with their leftist and liberal rivals fighting under the banners of their own, different, moral economies. The real difference, then, was in the ways in which the moral economies helped the civic right to have the upper hand in this war. Let me touch upon some of the ways.

Many of the larger protest campaigns in 2002–06, and virtually all the national referenda in 2004–22, were organized about (or were at least related to) broadly defined or more concrete issues of health and healthcare, education, labor markets and mobility, or environment. Accordingly, the moral economies meant ideal foundations for the civic circles to make meanings via frames, identities, and emotion work (Tarrow 2011). Let me illustrate this by comparing the main frames of the government's and the opposition's campaigns prior to the December 2004 referendum on whether ethnic Hungarian citizens of neighboring countries ought to be offered a second, Hungarian, citizenship. In addition, based on the initiative of the communist Workers' Party, which was supported by the civic circles and eventually Fidesz, the citizenry was asked about the government's hospital privatization plans.

The opposition mobilized for the referendum with the message that citizens of the current Hungarian state should be willing to share everything they possessed with the ethnic Hungarian citizens of Romania, Serbia, Croatia, and Ukraine. What was at stake was sharing the EU citizenship and passport, which would allow these minorities to enjoy the single market's EU-wide privileges, such as the coming freedoms of movement, and educational and essential healthcare benefits, without delay. In contrast, the coalition government, and especially the socialists, were not bothered with finding a middle way between the nationalist compassion for the fate of five million ethnic Hungarians in neighboring states and the assumed economic interests of contemporary Hungary's ten million citizens. Instead, adopting a welfare chauvinist exclusionary variant of the moral economy, the campaign threatened the latter with rising taxes, unemployment, and a worsening housing situation due to the mass immigration of their would-be fellow citizens.

Even if the referendum was invalid, the framing battle between the opposition's inclusionary nationalist and the government's exclusionary anti-immigrant campaign was not without political consequences. On the one hand, it buttressed Fidesz's image as the only legitimate representative of all-Hungarian interests. On the other hand, it cast a long shadow on the credibility of any inclusive left and liberal position in future conflicts about immigration, which backfired during and ever since the refugee crisis of 2015.

A related asset stemming from the civic circles' moral economy was that this perspective made it easier to build ideational bridges between the movement and other actors, even if the latter only partly or in specific contexts shared the worldview of the former. Such bridging ideologies, then, enabled the movement and Fidesz to flexibly move between ideological camps and align – whether permanently or on occasion – with national(ist) social democrats, environmental movements, churchbound trade unions, or exceptionally (as shown above) even with the unreformed communists. Such flexibility, again, proved to be important in future political conflicts, especially those triggered by the social and economic consequences of the Global Financial Crisis and the Great Recession.

Besides offering convenient tool kits for making meanings, cementing images, and building ideological bridges, the moral economies also functioned as assets for personnel recruitment. They attracted and triggered the participation of many thousands of educated professional activists – teachers, doctors, nurses, priest, pastors, and entrepreneurs – all endowed with extensive grassroots networks including their students and the students' parents, patients and their relatives, churchgoers, and daily customers of locally produced goods and services. Since in Hungary even many of the smaller settlements are likely to have a nursery, a school, a medical station, at least one church, and a market and/or grocery store catering for local consumption, these same activists were likely to be reputed key actors within the local community.

Last but not least, the advanced feminization of many of the professions directly connected to national reproduction, that is, the broadly conceived care economy, explains the vigorous participation of women in a dominantly masculine movement. The female participation either consisted in reinvigorating and politicizing the traditional family as a container of grassroots network properties or even transcended traditional gender roles.

8.4 CONCLUSIONS

Let me finally reflect on some of the key themes of the volume: the global diffusion of radical right agendas; civil society's role in democracy's dialectic; and the relationship between norms, expectations, and democracy's dilemmas.

The nexus between the cultural and economic aspects of right-wing authoritarianism is addressed in the volume as a factor of the fast global diffusion of the "radical right script." Since the populist radical right "is first and foremost centered on cultural issues," it is argued that it "can be very flexible on the economic dimension," which "can be seen as important comparative advantage" (Palestini and Kaltwasser, Chapter 15 this volume). Not denying that the current right-wing agendas tend to marry concepts from diverse and sometimes contradicting traditions of economic thought (which, however, might also characterize *all* the contemporary mixed economies), the moral economy perspective adopted in this chapter helps us to think about the limits of such flexibility. Instead of assuming that virtually anything goes, the perspective suggests a more structured and patterned nexus between the cultural and the economic dimensions and inspires new inquiry into the concrete nature of their relationship: whether it is purely accidental or represents "elective affinity" (Weber [1915] 1946: 284–285), or even qualifies as causality.

The Hungarian case also contributes to a nuanced understanding of the character of "countervailing forces ... that alternately seek to restrict or expand democratic inclusion" (Roberts, Bunce, Pepinsky, and Riedl Introduction to this volume; Mayka Chapter 7 this volume). The 2004 referendum on the dual citizenship of ethnic Hungarians and hospital privatization is a useful reminder that mobilization for democratic inclusion versus exclusion should not be mechanically associated with left and right identities, as these positions and roles may be reversed in specific conflict situations. Further, even if the referendum brought about a democratic settlement between the advocates of ethnic and civic nationalism, the campaign and its outcome exacerbated the extremist elements of Hungarian political discourse turning democratic rivals into enemies, ethnic Hungarians from neighboring states into welfare parasites and job thiefs, and liberals into landless and soulless traitors of the nation. Complicating our search for categories to clearly distinguish "good" from "bad" or "civil" from "uncivil" society, the walls between the language of healthy democratic contestation of citizenship and dehumanizing discourses (Mayka Chapter 7 this volume) might break down in the circumstances of lasting polarization.

But why and how do such polarizing conflicts endure and pave the way to democratic backsliding? The chapter offers some clues about why the compromises, which Rustow saw feasible even "in the absence of favorable preconditions beyond a shared understanding of the boundaries and composition of the national political economy," failed in Hungary to take root and nurture a democratic civic culture (Roberts, Bunce, Pepinsky, and Riedl Introduction to this volume, with reference to Rustow 1970).

Simply put, by the beginning of the new millennium the key political actors appeared to no longer even share the "understanding of the boundaries and composition of the national political economy." Witness Orbán's 2002 speech, which is rightly considered to be the founding document of the Civic Circles Movement: We "will not and cannot be in opposition, because the country cannot be in opposition" (Orbán 2002). This battle cry questioned the powerholders' "true Hungarian" identity and invited everybody else to join the struggle for reclaiming the nation. After this entry into the political arena, it is hardly surprising that the civic right entered the path of relentless quest for moral leadership. As shown by the dynamic of the 2004 referendum, this quest favored zero-sum games.

However, it takes two to tango. Let me thus conclude with an earlier and more general argument (Greskovits and Wittenberg 2016: 6) on the ways in which the dynamics of civil society development might have negatively interfered with the processes of democratic consolidation. Fidesz's appeal to the people directly through civil society organization and permanent mobilization might have impeded democratic consolidation "from below" by questioning the legitimacy of elected rulers and undermining trust in democratic institutions. In turn, the MSZP–SZDSZ governments' practices of keeping democratic politics and policymaking "above" the sphere of society might have impeded democratic consolidation by discouraging popular democratic engagement, leading to the atrophy of their own social hinterland and to their adversaries' anger at what they experienced as the tyranny of the majority.

REFERENCES

Bencze, Áron. 2003. "Szeretem, mert Magor": Beszélgetés Usztics Mátyással ("I love it because it's Magor": conversation with Mátyás Usztics. September 19 https://tinyurl.com/2s42er8n.

Beramendi, Pablo, Silja Häusermann, Herbert Kitschelt, and Hanspeter Kriesi, eds. 2015. *The Politics of Advanced Capitalism*. New York: Cambridge University Press.

Bohle, Dorothee and Béla Greskovits. 2019. "Politicizing Embedded Neoliberalism: Continuity and Change in Hungary's Development Model," *West European Politics*, 42, 5: 1069–1093.

Bornschier, Simon and Hanspeter Kriesi. 2013. "The Populist Right, the Working Class, and the Changing Face of Class Politics." In: Jens Rydgren ed. *Class Politics and the Radical Right*, London and New York: Routledge, 10–30.

Bunce, Valerie and Sharon Wolchik. 2011. *Defeating Authoritarian Leaders in Postcommunist Countries*. New York: Cambridge University Press.

Gidron, Noam and Peter Hall. 2017. "The Politics of Social Status: Economic and Cultural Roots of the Populist Right," *The British Journal of Sociology*, 68, S1: 57–84.

Götz, Norbert. 2015. "'Moral Economy': Its Conceptual History and Analytical Prospects," *Journal of Global Ethics*, 11, 2: 147–162.

Gramsci, Antonio. 1971. *Selections from the Prison Notebooks*. New York: International Publishers.

Greskovits, Béla. 2020. "Rebuilding the Hungarian Right through Conquering Civil Society: The Civic Circles Movement," *East European Politics*, 36, 2: 247–266.

Greskovits, Béla and Jason Wittenberg. 2016. Civil Society and Democratic Consolidation in Hungary in the 1990s and 2000s. Unpublished Manuscript. February 26.

Halász, Csilla. 2004. Kinek az Élete? (Whose life?) Interview with Csaba Hende. *Heti Válasz*. February 27.

Häusermann, Silja and Hanspeter Kriesi. 2015. "What Do Voters Want? Dimensions and Configurations in Individual-Level Preferences and Party Choice." In: Beramendi, Pablo, Silja Häusermann, Herbert Kitschelt, and Hanspeter Kriesi eds. *The Politics of Advanced Capitalism*, New York: Cambridge University Press, 202–230.

Hirschman, Albert. O. 1981. "The Changing Tolerance for Income Inequality in the Course of Economic Development." In his *Essays in Trespassing: Economics to Politics and Beyond*, Cambridge: Cambridge University Press, 39–58.

Hooghe, Liesbeth and Gary Marks. 2018. "Cleavage Theory Meets Europe's Crises: Lipset, Rokkan, and the Transnational Cleavage," *Journal of European Public Policy*, 25, 1: 109–135.

Inglehart, Ronald F. and Pippa Norris. 2016. Trump, Brexit, and the Rise of Populism: Economic Have-Nots and Cultural Backlash. Faculty Research Working Paper Series RWP 16–026, Harvard University, John F. Kennedy School of Government, Cambridge MA, August.

Kapcsándi, Dóra. 2002. 150 milliárdba kerül a száznapos program (The 100-day program costs 150 billion) www.origo.hu/itthon/20020610150milliardba.html.

Laki, Mihály and Júlia Szalai. 2015. *Tíz évvel később: magyar nagyvállalkozók európai környezetben* (Ten Years After: Hungarian Large Entrepreneurs in a European Environment) Budapest: Közgazdasági Szemle Alapítvány.

Mudde, Cas. 2021. "Populism in Europe: An Illiberal Democratic Response to Undemocratic Liberalism (The Government and Opposition/Leonard Schapiro Lecture 2019)," *Government and Opposition*, 56, 4 (October): 577–597.

Orbán, Viktor. 2002. Orbán Viktor beszéde a Dísz Téren (Viktor Orbán's Speech at Dísz Square). May 7 http://mkdsz1.freeweb.hu/n22/orban020507.html.

Orbán, Viktor. 2006. Vízválasztó 3. (Watershed 3.) *Magyar Nemzet*. September 9.

Orbán, Viktor. 2019. Prime Minister Viktor Orbán's speech at the "Tourism Summit 2019" conference. October 28. https://miniszterelnok.hu/tag/turizmus-summit/.

Orbán, Viktor. 2022. Orbán Viktor beszéde a Fidesz–KDNP választási győzelmét követően (Viktor Orbán's speech after the election victory of Fidesz–KDNP). April 3 https://tinyurl.com/rtacknpw.

Pethő, András. 2009. "Így tették lejtőre Magyarországot I-II" (This is how Hungary was brought down) https://tinyurl.com/2fkzep3t ; and https://tinyurl.com/3298z48f.

Polanyi, Karl. [1944] 1957. *The Great Transformation: The Political and Economic Origins of Our Time*. Boston: Beacon Press.

Pryke, Sam. 2012. "Economic Nationalism: Theory, History and Prospects," *Global Policy*, 3, 3: 281–291.

Rustow, Dankwart. 1970. "Transitions to Democracy: Toward a Dynamic Model," *Comparative Politics*, 2, 3: 337–363.

Skocpol, Theda and Vanessa Williamson. 2012. *The Tea Party and the Remaking of Republican Conservatism*. Oxford: Oxford University Press.

Swedberg, Richard. 2003. *Principles of Economic Sociology*. Princeton: Princeton University Press.

Tarrow, Sidney. 2011. *Power in Movement: Social Movements and Contentious Politics*. Cambridge: Cambridge University Press.

Thompson, Edward. P. 1971. "The Moral Economy of the English Crowd in the Eighteenth Century," *Past and Present*, 50: 76–136.

Weber, Max. [1904–05] 1958. *The Protestant Ethic and the Spirit of Capitalism.* New York: Scribner's.

Weber, Max. [1915] 1946. "The Social Psychology of World Religions." In: Hans Gerth and Charles Wright Mills eds. *From Max Weber*, New York: Oxford University Press, 267–301.

9

Post-Communist Democracy, Civil Society, and the Problem of Accountability

Michael Bernhard

9.1 INTRODUCTION

The durability of democracy among modern political systems is based on its ability to provide for its own self-enforcement without recourse to outside compulsion (North, Summerhill, and Weingast 2000; Przeworski 1991). Recourse to outside enforcement is always dangerous because loss of self-restraint by that authority raises the dilemma of "who guards the guardians" (Hurwicz 2008), and holds out the possibility of dictatorship.

Classic studies of democratic accountability focus on two long-identified types: the vertical and the horizontal. Today, it is essential not to omit a less-discussed variety – social accountability – which I will argue is the ultimate, imperfect, last defense against contemporary populist threats to democracy. This piece will begin with a discussion of the three forms of democratic accountability and their potential shortcomings. That is followed by a series of illustrations of how accountability works through both institutions and actors. The focus of the chapter then shifts to a discussion of the crisis of democratic accountability in Eastern Europe focusing on Hungary and Poland. In Hungary democracy has succumbed to a populist assault, whereas in Poland democratic forces have short-circuited an attempt to do the same. It will then draw lessons from these contrasting outcomes to support some propositions on how social accountability can be a means to stem populist democratic backsliding.

9.2 THE THREE ACCOUNTABILITIES

Vertical accountability is based on the responsiveness of elected politicians to citizens because of the power of the electorate to sanction politicians who perform poorly or misrepresent their interests. While it is quite often seen as the main source of accountability in democracy, it has never been made clear why politicians should be accountable between elections, or why they would always prefer to contest the next election rather than subvert the one they just lost (Przeworski, Stokes, and Manin 1999). On its own, vertical accountability is probably only capable of sustaining a minimal form of majoritarian or Schumpeterian democracy in which relatively autonomous leaders are periodically ratified by the electorate. This was identified by O'Donnell (1994) as a pathology known as delegative democracy. Unsupported by other accountability mechanisms, it can also serve as a basis for nondemocratic plebiscitary rule or a majoritarianism that denies the rights of full citizenship to unprotected minorities.

Horizontal accountability lies in the ability of government institutions to hold each other to the rules. Well-designed democratic institutions include the power to monitor the activities of other power holders and to sanction them for noncompliance with the law (Merkel 2004; O'Donnell 1998). The combination of vertical and horizontal accountability has long been seen as the essence of democracy. Specifically, horizontal accountability serves to contain majoritarian abuses of power. While an independent judiciary is necessary for horizontal accountability, the absence of a formal separation of executive and legislative power, a feature common to parliamentary regimes, can be compensated for by other features of institutional design such as cabinet or coalition government. One potential pathology of democratic rule based exclusively on vertical and horizontal accountability is relative elite autonomy from the electorate, which can lead to what has been termed democratic elitism or elite bias to legislative outcomes (Bachrach 1967; Gilens and Page 2014). Judicial autonomy also has the potential to subvert democracy when minority positions are entrenched in the courts (Raskin 2004).

The significance of the third form of accountability, the social, has been underappreciated.[1] Social accountability is produced through the advocacy and protest activity of citizens in civil society before, during, and after elections. Advocacy allows citizens to convey their demands to the political system between elections, more directly connecting politicians to citizens and cultivating responsive behavior on their part (Chalmers, Martin, and Pister 1997). Protest allows citizens to pressure politicians by focusing on unpopular, unsuccessful, and controversial policies. Such actions impose audience costs on officeholders cutting into their bases of support (McAdam and Tarrow 2010). Civil society organizations can also engage in monitoring of government operations to keep government more transparent and make sure that government agencies are living up to their responsibilities (Smulovitz and Peruzzotti 2000). In cases of policy negligence or failure they can make use of

---

[1] Lührmann, Marquandt, and Mechkova (2020) call this form of accountability "diagonal." I prefer the term "social" because of its extant though underappreciated place in the literature, and the spatial metaphor, suggesting that it is a mix of vertical and horizontal, does not make sense to me. It is a distinct path of accountability, not an admixture.

bureaucratic and legal accountability mechanisms to try to compel the state to live up to its responsibilities (Cornell and Grimes 2015). In cases where popular initiatives exist, civil society groups can also attempt to circumvent elite agenda control (Altman 2019).

There are potential pathologies of social accountability as well. First, there is the problem of what has been called uncivil or bad civil society (Chambers and Kopstein 2001; Kopecký 2003). In several interwar cases there is strong evidence that channels of social accountability are subject to capture by antisystem parties and movements antithetical to democracy (Berman 1997; Riley 2010), and can be a central facet of democratic breakdown. There is a renewed concern on this score with regard to contemporary cases of populist inspired backsliding (Graff and Korolczuk 2021; Greskovits 2020; Ślarzyński 2018). Such concerns are the focus of the essays by Maya and Greskovits (Chapters 7 and 8 in this volume). Second, there is the issue of capture of the state by sectors of civil society leading to biased allocation of state resources and constraints on policy debates and choices (Lowi 1979; Migdal 1988).

Third, governments have shaped civil society by funding supportive organizations and creating simulacra of civil society organizations (GONGOS – government-organized nongovernmental organization) (Ekiert and Perry 2020; Walker 2016). And beyond governments, well-endowed private interests have created their own imitations of grassroots civil society organizations, so called Astroturf organizations (Kohler-Koch 2010; Weiss 2017). Whether powerful interests or the state engage in explicit manipulation of the public space, this has the effect of shutting down discursive space, crowding out grassroots organizations, and denying voice to genuine popular interests (Chambers and Kopstein 2022).

Despite these well-founded and documented concerns about the danger to democracy by the capture of civil society by antidemocratic forces, recent large-n research has shown on balance that the social accountability provided by a strong civil society generally enhances democratic durability (Bernhard et al. 2020; Cornell, Møller, and Skaaning 2020). Further, both robust organization and peaceful protest have been shown to be, on balance, effective in the ability of civil society to promote and defend democracy (Bernhard and Edgell 2022). Even though bad actors in civil society can pose dangers for democracy, it is important to remember that overall, a robust and engaged civil society is an intrinsic part of a working democracy with an effective accountability structure.

9.3 ACCOUNTABILITY AS A SOURCE OF DEMOCRATIC DURABILITY

Regime stability is a product of socio-economic structure, agency, and institutional configuration. Accountability plays a role in this on the basis of institutions and the actors embedded in them. Structure, of course, plays an important role, both as the ultimate disrupter of existing arrangements and a facilitator of outcomes. It remains a crucial part of the problem, but its ultimate impact hinges on the ability of institutions to process change and the reactions of actors to changed circumstances. That is the focus of this section.

In any democracy there will be actors who hold democracy as a cardinal value, others for whom realization of their interests are paramount irrespective of regime, and even some who are outright autocratic. In cases where there is a higher quotient of citizens and elites who are prodemocratic, this obviously helps promote democratic stability and quality (Almond and Verba 1963; Inglehart and Welzel 2005; Putnam 1993). Further, citizens with a strong commitment to democracy will be slower to question its legitimacy in the face of crises provoked by ineffectiveness of rule (Linz 1978; Lipset 1959).

When democracy is self-enforcing, those who lose come to believe that the prospect of winning future elections outweighs the costs of short-term loss (Przeworski 1991). However, history abounds with situations in which losers try to overturn the results. In such scenarios other actors need to deter potential defection from the rules of the democratic game as something that entails high costs. The perception that one's competitors have credible intentions to counteract antisystem activity will affect the anticipated potential costs and calculated probability of success that any potential defector will have to pay in moving against the system.

If we think about the way that institutions promote accountability, we should concentrate on how they enable other actors to sanction those who would subvert the rules of the democratic game. It was Linz (1990) who alerted us to this in his discussion of the perils of presidentialism. From this perspective the different configurations of democratic institutions hold inherent possibilities to deter antisystem behavior by different actors. Depending on the configuration of actors, different varieties of democracy have intrinsic strengths and vulnerabilities in providing for self-enforcement.

Different institutional configurations can affect vertical accountability. Whether electoral rules promote governability or representation has different ramifications. Winner-take-all systems inherently have a greater probability of concentrating power in the hands of one party, and when this is not offset by countervailing powers, as under parliamentary systems, such configurations can endow an aspirational dictator with the power and autonomy necessary to erode democratic norms and rules.

More proportional systems that promote representation over governance prevent the kind of abuse that is possible under single-party government and especially supermajority control. In particular, coalition governments, with their greater fragility, provide partner parties with the capability to obstruct power grabs and other abuses. Further with their promotion of multipartyism, proportional systems make it harder for antidemocratic parties to form governments and allow democratic parties to block their rise through a strategy of cordon sanitaire (Art 2007). Excessive proportionality does have its downsides though. It makes it easier for antisystem parties to enter the legislature, and when society is highly fractionalized or polarized, this is more directly reflected in the legislature, making governments harder to form and more fragile. This can lead to gridlock and weak rule, which is particularly dangerous in crisis situations.

Within a given institutional configuration, the history of the party system and the *ex ante* value commitments of parties themselves are important. The ability of democratically committed parties with competing ideological orientations to compromise in the face of authoritarian threats and govern in defense of democracy can be instrumental in averting a crisis as in interwar Belgium, Finland, and Czechoslovakia (Capoccia 2005).

In terms of horizontal accountability, the three main varieties of democratic institutions – presidential, parliamentary, and executive dyarchy (semipresidentialism) – all offer different mechanisms for checking the abuse of executives and/or ruling parties.[2] Under functioning democracy all three varieties have an independent judicial branch. The extent that the courts are empowered to review the legality and constitutionality of legislation determines the role and effectiveness of the judiciary in compelling the executive and legislature to observe the rule of law.

The relationship of the executive to the legislature varies across democratic systems. Under presidentialism, there is a strong separation between executive and legislative power, and separate sources of electoral legitimacy. Divided government provides a strong check on the executive, but even when the president's party controls the legislature, differences in interests between the two branches can constrain presidential overreach.

Under parliamentary systems, the power of the executive and legislature are unified. Single ruling parties with majorities, and especially supermajorities that can pass constitutional legislation, are the least constrained form of power. In the hands of a would-be autocrat, this presents a strong danger. In contrast, government based on a coalition of parties introduces a strong measure of constraint on the power of the executive, as partners in the government can withdraw their support to block legislation with which they do not agree.

In the executive dyarchy of semipresidential systems both the president and prime minister have substantial powers. A second executive, in principle, constitutes a check on the ability of the other to act in an arbitrary antidemocratic fashion. When the president and prime minister come from the same party, the ability of the legislative opposition to constrain the government is diminished. When they come from competing political camps, cohabitation, the president is more likely to try to impose constraints on the government and vice versa. In cases of executives from the same party, the dyarchy could still be constrained by coalition government as in parliamentary systems.

---

[2] This discussion of horizontal accountability is based on readings of Shugart and Carey (1992) and Sartori (1994).

Finally, there are other institutional features common in many democracies that can work to constrain the ability of governments to pursue their agendas unchecked. Bicameralism means that the legislative process can entail the control of two rather than one legislative house, which opens another pathway to divided government. More modest constraints can also be exercised by independent regulatory and oversight bodies such as central banks, media boards, inspectors general, and ombudspersons.

Social accountability is provided by the actions of civil society. It is uniquely positioned between the private sphere and the state and is distinct from the parties and coalitions that directly compete for state power (political society). Civil society is the realm through which other organizations pursue their interests, both material and the ideal, via the provision of support for and the imposition of costs upon actors in the state and in political society. The understanding used here entails a more expansive understanding of civil society, encompassing two different behaviors, organization, and contention.

Civil society organizations engage in a range of activities that constrain the actions of the government. Civil society groups routinely raise opposition to policies. This can affect the visibility of issues. It also offers the opportunity to work with political parties that share that opposition. Civil society organizations also monitor the state to file objections, complain, appeal decisions, and raise awareness of noncompliance with the law and abuse of power. They also use the legal system to contest state actions with which they do not agree. Some organizations also raise money to materially support politicians and parties which they feel are sympathetic to their interests.

Contentious behaviors in opposition to government policies are much more common than demonstrations in support of the government, but the latter do occur (Hellmeier and Bernhard 2023). Contentious political protest is geared to imposing audience costs on the incumbent in power, either by damaging their reputation or by focusing attention on potentially unpopular measures that have not received substantial exposure in the public sphere. In this, civil society's ability to contest government is enhanced by media independence and the free flow of information.

9.4 THE CONSTRUCTION OF DEMOCRACY IN EASTERN EUROPE

In postcommunist Eastern Europe, transitions with democratic outcomes were confined to a small set of countries. Immediately after 1989, reform efforts in this direction were mounted in Poland, Hungary, and Czechoslovakia, and they were joined by Slovenia after the collapse of Yugoslavia, and Latvia, Lithuania, and Estonia following the collapse of the USSR.[3] Several countries moved in this direction following inauspicious or stalled transitions, or even short bouts of dictatorship through a combination of internal and external pressures including

---

[3] I omit the former DDR (Deutsche Demokratische Republik) due to German unification.

Slovakia, Romania, Bulgaria, and Croatia (Bunce and Wolchik 2011). The remainder of the region has alternated between electoral democracy and competitive authoritarianism over time, with the exceptions of Azerbaijan, Belarus, and Russia, which all became consolidated dictatorships.

The countries that undertook democratic reform earliest did so on the basis of strong domestic democratic movements. These countries quickly received the greatest degree of Western attention and aid per capita, and the fastest consideration from the European Union (EU) as potential candidates for membership (Vachudova 2005, chapter 2). In the early movers, democracy and market reforms were put in place in relatively short order. A full range of formal accountability mechanisms were also put in place quickly – regular free and fair elections, an independent judiciary, other independent regulatory agencies, and coalition government as the norm. The starting point for civil society in some of these countries was quite low (Howard 2003; Linz and Stepan 1996) due to the antecedent communist regime's monopoly on political and social organization. However, this was already under challenge in some countries under late communism and the deinstitutionalization of the party's leading role led to a regeneration of civil society in the region to levels no different from global norms for new democracies (Bernhard et al. 2017; Foa and Ekiert 2017).

In the countries in which reform proceeded fastest, the ability of the postcommunist successor parties to shape the political system following extrication were minimized by strong opposition movements which forced and won competitive foundational elections (Bernhard 2016; Fish 1998). This compelled postcommunist successor parties to learn to compete democratically to survive. Those that did largely took a reformist stance,[4] in which they embraced the opposition's agenda – democratization, marketization, and NATO and EU membership (Grzymala-Busse 2002).

Postcommunist democracy was created by consensus not contention, and thus spawned a party system in which the policy differences between parties on major issues were exceptionally narrow. Further, once these countries became applicants for membership in the EU, the variation in the way that democracy could be constructed was subject to further constraint. Once they joined the EU, the policy options open to national governments, particularly with regard to fiscal, monetary, and regulatory policy, were again constrained by the supranational framework of the EU. Eastern European democracy was constructed with a full set of accountability mechanisms but in an environment in which there was limited room for political parties to signal and implement meaningfully different domestic agendas. However, prior to the

[4] With some variation – for instance in the Czech Republic the Communist Party of Bohemia and Moravia remained relatively orthodox, but the left of center reformist space was occupied by a legacy Social Democratic Party that reclaimed a good part of its property from prior to its forced merger with the communists in the 1940s.

global financial crisis of 2008, this was a price that the democratic states of Eastern Europe and their populations seemed willing to pay.

9.5 SUCCESSIVE EXOGENOUS SHOCKS: THE GLOBAL FINANCIAL CRISIS OF 2008 AND THE REFUGEE CRISIS OF 2015

The great irony of the crisis of democracy in Eastern Europe is that it broke out in the two countries that were the first movers in the collapse of communism, had been regional leaders in its building, and had been considered consolidated democracies (Freedom House 2023: 29).[5] A further irony is that entry into the EU in 2004 for both countries helped to enable democratic regress. Once in, the EU has less leverage to sanction antidemocratic behavior in members than it has with candidates. Prior to accession, right-wing extremism was a much more marginal phenomenon in both countries (Kelemen 2017). And as Bohle and Hozić show in this volume (Chapter 14), the European People's Party, to which Fidesz belonged, and elements in the German CDU (Christian Democratic Union)/CSU (Christian Social Union), played a critical role in shielding Hungary from sanctions. And finally, it is important to note before accession, this was not a supply-side problem. There were committed reactionary nationalists or opportunists who tried to gain electoral traction, but none of them really broke through until the mid-2000s. The demand side only picked up after EU accession and the exogenous shocks of the Great Recession and the European immigration crisis.

Hungary was a classic case of populist backlash triggered by economic crisis. While the crisis predated the global economic meltdown by a couple of years, it was exacerbated by it. The impact of the recession was intensified as well by a major scandal. The Hungarian Socialist Party (MSzP) government won reelection in 2006, but the celebration was short-lived. A confession by Prime Minister Gyurcsány, surreptitiously taped at a closed meeting, that he lied about the state of the economy during the electoral campaign triggered the system's social accountability mechanisms in a big way. The main opposition party Fidesz and other activists further to their right, including the incipient far-right Jobbik party, took to the streets and this led to several weeks of social unrest. On several occasions, the demonstrations deteriorated into riots and clashes with the police (Seleny 2014: 48). Despite calls for the government to resign, it managed to weather this crisis.

In 2007 and 2008, Hungary went into a drastic economic slowdown with growth falling from a sustained rate around 4 percent for a decade to less than 1 percent in both years. This was followed by an intense contraction of over 6 percent in 2009 (World Bank 2024). When the full brunt of the contraction hit, the Gyurcsány government finally resigned. It was replaced by a minority

---

[5] Hungary moved from consolidated democracy to semiconsolidated democracy in 2016, to hybrid in 2020, whereas Poland moved from consolidated to semiconsolidated in the 2020 rankings.

government under Gordon Bajnai composed of independents and MSzP ministers.

Following the utter failure of their second term in power, the MSzP was trounced in the general elections of 2010. The Fidesz–Christian Democratic coalition won 263 of 386 seats in the parliament, giving them a constitutional majority. The MSzP experienced a loss of 133 seats falling to a total of 59 seats and Jobbik came in third with 47 seats. Jobbik's performance was the first example of a far-right party gaining sustained traction; it had burst onto the scene, winning three seats in the elections for the European Parliament in 2009.[6] Its ultimate impact on the party system was centrifugal, drawing Fidesz to the right with the center left in disarray.

The crisis of MSzP rule of 2006–2010 was a sterling demonstration that the accountability mechanisms of Hungarian democracy worked as designed. The MSzP was caught in a lie to get reelected, and this led to a scandal which triggered social accountability via intense protest. When the economic crisis hidden by the lie fully manifested itself, horizontal accountability mechanisms kicked in and a new government with a diminished mandate was chosen. Finally, the government was replaced electorally in a classic exercise of vertical accountability by the electorate.

In Poland economic crisis played little role as the economy had grown at a healthy clip since 1992. The precipitating crisis that brought down and propelled Poland's populist Law and Justice (PiS) Party to power was the European refugee crisis of 2015. As in Hungary, the ruling party at that juncture, the Civic Platform (PO), had been damaged by a scandal despite ruling for two consecutive terms with robust economic results. Several prominent PO leaders were illegally tape-recorded in a restaurant in 2014 speaking in ways that were highly contemptuous of the public and cynical of politics and public service generally. This led to several high-profile resignations from the parliament and cabinet (Popielec 2017).

The precipitating anxiety that crystalized populist backlash in Poland was social rather than economic (Kucharczyk and Fomina 2016: 66). Parts of Polish society are very traditional in orientation and the stance of the Catholic Church is very hostile to the kind of social diversity routinely tolerated in the West. A large part of support for PiS is based on resistance to the kind of rapid social change that has accompanied economic prosperity. There has been extensive public agitation against LGBTQ+ rights, feminism, and potential immigration from Muslim countries, not unlike the types of campaigns described by Mayka in Latin America in Chapter 7 in this very volume (Ekiert 2019; Graff and Korolczuk 2021; Kotwas and Kubik 2019). By the time the general election campaign of 2015 was underway the government of Ewa Kopacz was under pressure from the EU to take a quota of refugees. In the parliamentary elections

---

[6] An earlier fat-right party, Justice and Life, won fourteen seats in 1998. However, it was eliminated in 2002. In contrast Jobbik has stayed on the scene.

of October, PiS was able to win 38 percent of the vote and take a majority of seats in the Sejm and form the first single-party government in the history of the Third Republic. Once again vertical accountability had worked, a two-term government which was seen as unconcerned about popular anxiety and was prepared to accommodate the EU on refugee policies, despite intense domestic resistance on this issue, suffered a loss of popularity, lost power, and was replaced.

9.6 POPULISTS IN POWER

While both Fidesz and PiS made use of the accountability mechanisms afforded by democracy to come to power, once in power they moved to dismantle those very mechanisms as constraints on their exercise of power. Whereas Fidesz has been remarkably successful, PiS was unable to fully dismantle the mechanisms of accountability and was ejected from power after two terms. In contrast Fidesz is already in its fourth consecutive term in power, and it has had a supermajority throughout, allowing it to change the constitution at will. PiS never had more than a simple majority.

If we examine the extent to which the populists were able to dismantle democratic accountability, the damage was much worse in Hungary. Starting with the dimension of vertical accountability, Fidesz has been able to change the electoral system to its advantage, use overseas Hungarian populations to increase its electoral margins of victory, and perhaps even falsify election results in small ways (Bazsofy and Goat 2019; Magyar and Madlovics 2022; Notz 2018). Its control of the state media and the preponderance of pro-Fidesz outlets in the private media sphere has put the opposition at a marked disadvantage to the ruling party. Despite the creation of a unified opposition coalition in the 2022 parliamentary elections, Fidesz won a mandate to rule again with a constitutional majority. The report of the OSCE (Organization for Security and Co-operation in Europe) monitors pointed out serious problems, which have led many to conclude that while the elections were still free, they were no longer fair (OSCE 2022: 2).

In contrast, PiS was not able to change the electoral system to its advantage. The competitive nature of elections under PiS rule gives little reason to doubt that the mechanisms of vertical accountability were preserved. PiS was able to defend its Sejm majority in the elections of 2019 but lost its majority in the Senat. In the presidential election of 2020, Warsaw Mayor Rafał Trzaskowski came close to unseating the incumbent, Andrzej Duda. PiS was unable to undermine vertical accountability to the extent Fidesz did and never had the kind of legislative control that Fidesz has so long enjoyed.

In terms of horizontal accountability, both governments have been able to reduce the independence of the judiciary. In the case of PiS, they were able to pack the Constitutional Tribunal with their own judges. They were also able to pack the National Council of the Judiciary (Krajowa Rada Sądownictwa) with party

partisans by taking the selection process away from judges and giving it to the
Sejm. This gave them greater control over judicial appointments and disciplinary
actions against judges (Sadurski 2019, chapters 3 & 4). Fidesz established an even
greater degree of control over the judicial branch, effectively disempowering the
Constitutional Court, curtailing the independent power of judges, and giving
control of case assignments to the head of a new National Judicial Office
(Országos Bírói Tanács), who is appointed for a nine-year term. Fidesz also has
been more systematic in stacking other regulatory bodies with their appointees
for long terms of service and limiting the power of parliament to undo legislation
by the designation of certain laws as "cardinal" requiring a two-thirds majority to
repeal them (Bánkuti, Halmai, and Lane Scheppele 2012; Bugarič and Ginsburg
2016, 72–74).

Finally, in terms of social accountability, both parties have worked to create
a public space that gives priority to their partisan messages. PiS has done so by
turning state television into a propaganda arm of the party (Chapman 2017).
Fidesz has not only accomplished this but has had friendly oligarchs buy the
remaining large news outlets in the country and install pro-Fidesz editorial
policies and news coverage (Bánkuti, Halmai, and Lane Scheppele 2012;
Dragomir 2017). Both governments used state advertising revenues to support
sympathetic outlets, while starving those seen as more aligned with the position
of the opposition.

Fidesz went much further than PiS in asserting control of the academic sector
in its attacks on the Central European University (driving its instructional arm
out of the country) and taking control of the Hungarian Academy of Sciences.
PiS was active in the cultural sphere as well, pushing a nationalist point of view
in the revision of standardized school curricula and replacing directors of
museums seen as sympathetic to viewpoints not congruent with their view of
history.[7]

Finally, both governments have used the state treasury to support
organizations and think tanks sympathetic to their positions. However, the
most drastic action against civil society occurred in Hungary, the so-called
Lex NGO was passed in 2017. Civil Society organizations that received more
than 20,000 euros in funding from overseas had to register with the government
as "foreign-funded." This law had a chilling effect, reminiscent of the Russian
Foreign Agents Act which has been used to harass and shut down independent
organizations and media outlets. The measure was declared illegal by the
European Court of Justice in June 2020 but was not finally revoked by the
Hungarian parliament until May 2021. A law passed in 2018 that makes it
illegal for Hungarian NGOs to help asylum seekers remains on the books. Such
efforts have been bolstered recently by the creation of a new Sovereignty

[7] Notably Dariusz Stola at the Polin Museum, and Paweł Machcewicz at the Museum of the Second
World War.

Protection Office charged with investigating foreign influence on parties, civil society organizations, and other institutions (Ésik 2024).

Both the Hungarian and Polish cases show that building electoral systems to bolster governability over representation are not without potential costs for democracy. In these cases of backsliding, compensating populist parties with seats that exceed their popular vote has allowed Fidesz to undermine mechanisms of vertical, horizontal, and social accountability, whereas the damage in Poland has been more confined – effecting horizontal and, to a lesser extent, the organizational side of social accountability. In the Hungarian case, Fidesz has maintained a two-thirds majority in parliament, sufficient to amend the constitution as it sees fit. In 2018 they won these seats on the basis of an electoral plurality, and not a majority of votes as in the other three instances. The ability to move constitutional legislation that allows it to alter the rules of the game to its advantage helps to explain both the greater success of Fidesz in eroding democratic accountability mechanisms in comparison to Poland, as well as ongoing its electoral juggernaut.

In Poland, PiS won two consecutive elections with pluralities which converted into majorities in the Sejm. Their ability to take control of the judiciary and turn the state media into their own mouthpiece would have been harder to achieve under a coalition government. Its recent time in power was much more successful than its first stint in government in 2005–7, when disputes within the ruling coalition made them less effective and led the Sejm to dissolve itself. So, while Polish democracy was under threat, vertical accountability was never undermined. Another reason why PiS has been less successful is that Polish civil society was more effective in mobilizing opposition to the government and its policies than its counterpart in Hungary. PiS was not able to contain the contentious nature of the civil society opposition.

9.7 SOCIAL ACCOUNTABILITY: DEMOCRACY'S FIREWALL?

The final issue that I will address here is what can be done between elections when executive and legislative power is firmly under the control of populist leaders who are actively trying to undermine democratic accountability. Because populists use democratic mechanisms to take power and legitimize their holding of it, in the short run they are constrained in their ability to dispose fully of elections, abolish competing parties, and undermine the range of civil and political rights necessary for those elections to be credible (Schedler 2006). As long as periodic vertical accountability holds there will be a modicum of room for civil society to contest attempts to curtail democratic accountability.

I agree with Mark R. Beissinger's assessment in Chapter 10 of this volume that the ability of civil society on its own to make some sort of insurrectionary stand against encroaching dictatorship in control of the state is slim. Beissinger's contribution takes an important step toward trying to systematize the conditions that facilitate such resistance. His major finding concerns the combination of strong horizontal accountability and the declining popularity of the populist strongman as a favorable scenario for executive replacement. And the recent fates of PiS in Poland and Bolsonaro in Brazil are certainly congruent with the argument on popularity. However, horizontal accountability is where PiS made its strongest inroads against democracy. And this dimension is where the cases of Poland and Hungary most resemble each other in terms of democratic backsliding. Furthermore, most removals of aspiring autocrats have occurred electorally, and for this reason I want to make sure that we do not overlook the relationship between social and electoral accountability. Cases where we have strong horizontal accountability are more likely to survive backsliding. It is important to understand if there are other paths to democratic durability in the face of duress.

An important dimension where Poland differed from Hungry is in the strength of civil society resistance and the failure of PiS to undermine vertical accountability to the same extent that the Hungarians did. Social accountability can play a key role in bolstering horizontal and vertical accountability in the face of attempts to undermine them. This is the sense in which it can play a firewall role. For instance, civil society can bolster horizontal accountability by contesting policy, either by warning politicians that support may bring costs at election time, protesting to undermine policies or those who support them, or by challenging them in the courts. PiS did not pass its infamous rollback of reproductive rights through legislation. When it provoked a major contentious response, it then relied on the courts to create it through judicial fiat. Civil society's agitation and organization can also bolster vertical accountability. As Bunce and Wolchik (2011) made manifest over a decade ago, parties increase their chances for electoral victory by building and securing the support of civic networks and social movements. Unfortunately, authoritarians took notice of this. Part of the success of Fidesz and PiS is connected to their cultivation of such connections. This authoritarian learning has meant that democratic forces in civil society contesting authoritarianism are not only engaged in struggle with the state, but also with pro-regime competing organizations. Where they prove stronger in winning the hearts and minds of the citizenry, they can help keep vertical accountability viable.

The kind of authoritarian right-wing organization documented by Maya and Greskovits in this volume (Chapters 7 and 8) has persistently provoked contentious political action in defense of democracy by other civil society groups. It is highly visible all over Central Europe, not just in Hungary and Poland. On several occasions (including a demonstration of a quarter of a million people in Letna Park in Prague in the summer of 2019) the "Million Moments for Democracy" movement protested against corruption by Andrej Babiš and his government (Guasti 2020). In Slovakia the protests against the murder of journalist Jan Kuciak and his partner led to the resignation of the government of Prime Minister Robert Fico in 2018

(Bakke and Sitter 2022: 26; Vachudova 2020: 335). Attempts by the government in Romania to reduce prosecutorial autonomy to pursue corruption and reduce penalties for conviction led to two large waves of demonstrations in the winter of 2017 and summer of 2018 (Mungiu-Pippidi 2018). Serbia experienced a year-and-a-half-long protest campaign (from 2018 until it was shut down by the COVID-19 pandemic) organized by the "One out of Five Million" movement which protested the violent suppression of opposition activism and the curtailment of freedom of speech under President Aleksandar Vučić (Jovanović 2019; Pešić and Petrović 2020). And we have seen it clearly in Ukraine, where there has been a general social mobilization in defense of the country from below, buttressing a weak and vulnerable state from the onslaught of the Russian invasion.

In Hungary there were protests of many antidemocratic actions taken by the Orbán regime. Notable were the movements and protests to defend CEU, the Academy of Science, and against the so-called slave law suspending the protection of workers against excessive overtime (Abbott 2019; Enyedi 2018: 1068; Hopkins and Shotter 2018). However, they have been in many respects concentrated in the capital Budapest, the one area where the opposition consistently wins elections.

In Poland we have also seen numerous protests to defend the courts and constitution (Bakke and Sitter 2022: 28; Bernhard 2020: 354), as well as the rights of women (Graff and Korolczuk 2021, chapter 6; Korolczuk and Jacobsson 2017: viii–ix). The protests were sustained over time, larger, and spread across the country. The internationally orchestrated attacks on "Gender ideology" that Mayka highlights in her chapter on Latin America turned out to be PiS' electoral Achilles' heel. The two-day Black Protests of 2016 and the massive Women's Strike protests from October 2020 to January 2021 imposed high audience costs on the government. These were the work of a sustained campaign of organization, mobilization, and contention (Korolczuk et al. 2019).

PiS lost to an electoral coalition of three parties running from left to center-right (The Left, Civic Coalition, and Third Way) which went on to form a government under Donald Tusk, with majorities in both the Sejm and Senat. That outcome was built on the ability of the coalition to mobilize voters from two key groups, women and youth. Overall turnout jumped from 62 percent in 2019 to almost 73 percent. In this sense the work of the movement in defense of reproductive rights and women's health which mobilized women, including many young women, was key to the victory. PiS and its electoral allies took less than 40 percent of women's votes, while taking close to 47 percent of men's votes. For voters younger than 29, turnout increased from 46 percent in 2019 to 69 percent. Participation of women increased from 63 percent to 75 percent, outstripping the participation of men by 2 percent (McMahon 2023; Ptak 2023).

9.8 CONCLUSION

As much as populists would like to shut down their opponents in civil society, their rhetoric of democracy has the effect of constraining their ability to do so in the short to medium term. Thus, civil society often remains the last refuge of democrats to wage a struggle against the antidemocratic practices of populists. The example of Poland shows that where horizontal accountability has been diminished, the social accountability that civil society provides can be an effective means to resist ruling populists and sway the electorate or the next scheduled election that allows for the exercise of vertical accountability. The Poles sustained this sort of resistance across two electoral cycles.

The ability to impose audience costs and inflict reputational damage on aspiring dictators for inept and unpopular policies allows civil society to constrain their autonomy and set the stage for their future defeat at the polls. However, for it to succeed there has to be effective coordination between opposition parties to stop aspiring populist dictators from being reelected (as first argued by Bunce and Wolchik (2011) in their account of the Color Revolutions). But even this may not be enough if the dictator has already undermined vertical accountability. Here the differences between the turning of PiS out of power in Poland and Orbán's repeated reelections in Hungary are instructive. Polish vertical accountability remained intact, and the combination of civil society mobilization and electoral coordination remained potent. In Hungary, Fidesz' ability to pass constitutional acts at will, control of the press, its manipulation of the electoral system, and weaker mobilization by civil society meant that a strategic electoral alliance of opposition parties could not unseat the incumbent.

Thus, while social accountability may be the last refuge for democratic resistance in cases of acute backsliding, it by no means guarantees success. Autocrats who decide that they no longer need the façade of democratic emulation to legitimize their rule and adopt the repressive practices of closed authoritarianism can close down civic space. We have observed this incrementally in Russia since Putin's accession to power, to the point where he can invade the neighbors and murder the leader of the opposition without consultation and with impunity. With backsliding and deployment of state power by aspiring autocrats, civil society becomes a realm of contestation between supporters of the incumbent and the opposition. It is only with a concerted effort by the opposition in a war of position to control the public space can democrats in civil society push back against state power and the supporters of authoritarianism in civil society (see Bohle and Hozić (Chapter 14 in this volume) and Greskovits (Chapter 8 in this volume) on this war of position).

The result in Hungary is disturbing. Fidesz has successfully inaugurated a stable form of electoral authoritarian rule. With its combination of plebiscitary ratification and patrimonial practices, it is hard to see how the party will lose in the near future without some massive external shock disrupting the present configuration of power. The EU is the external actor best positioned to take steps to help restore democracy in Hungary. However, the record to date is not encouraging. What is most disheartening is Orbán's ability to maintain his stranglehold on power using plebiscitary ratification without fully repressing civil society. In contrast, the Polish case shows that as long as vertical accountability remains viable, concerted civil society mobilization when channeled effectively by a united electoral opposition stands a better chance of stemming the erosion of democracy.

REFERENCES

Abbott, A. (2019). Hungarians Protest against Proposed Government Takeover of Science. *Nature* [online] (05 June). www.nature.com/articles/d41586-019-01756-9 [Accessed May 23, 2022].

Almond, G. & S. Verba. (1963). *The Civic Culture: Political Attitudes and Democracy in Five Nations*. Princeton: Princeton University Press.

Altman, D. (2019). *Citizenship and Contemporary Direct Democracy*. New York: Cambridge University Press.

Art, D. (2007). Reacting to the Radical Right: Lessons from Germany and Austria, *Party Politics*, 13(3), 331–349.

Bachrach, P. (1967). *The Theory of Democratic Elitism: A Critique*. New York: Little Brown.

Bakke, E. & N. Sitter. (2022). The EU's *Enfants Terribles*: Democratic Backsliding in Central Europe since 2010, *Perspectives on Politics*, 20(1), 22–37.

Bánkuti, M., G. Halmai, & K. Lane Scheppele. (2012). Hungary's Illiberal Turn: Disabling the Constitution, *Journal of Democracy*, 23(3), 138–146.

Bazsofy, R. & E. Goat. 2019. Fresh Evidence of Hungary Vote-Rigging Raises Concerns of Fraud in European Elections. *openDemocracy*. https://tinyurl.com/4u42jey2.

Berman, S. (1997). Civil Society and the Collapse of the Weimar Republic, *World Politics*, 59(3), 401–29.

Bernhard, M. (2016). The Moore Thesis: What's Left after 1989? *Democratization*, 23(1), 118–140.

Bernhard, M. (2020). What Do We Know about Civil Society and Regime Change after 1989? *East European Politics*, 36(3), 341–362.

Bernhard, M. & A. B. Edgell. (2022). Democracy and Social Forces. In M. Coppedge, A. B. Edgell, C. H. Knutsen, and S. I. Lindberg, eds., *Why Democracies Develop and Decline*. New York: Cambridge University Press, 185–214.

Bernhard, M., D. Jung, E. Tzelgov, M. Coppedge, & S. I. Lindberg. (2017) Making Embedded Knowledge Transparent: How the V-Dem Dataset Opens New Vistas in Civil Society Research, *Perspectives on Politics*, 15(2), 342–360.

Bernhard, M., A. Hicken, C. Reenock, & S. I. Lindberg. (2020). Parties, Civil Society, and the Deterrence of Democratic Defection, *Studies in Comparative International Development*, 55(1), 1–21.

Bugarič, B & T. Ginsburg. (2016). The Assault on Postcommunist Courts, *Journal of Democracy*, 27(3), 69–82.

Bunce, V. J. & S. L. Wolchik. (2011). *Defeating Authoritarian Leaders in Postcommunist Countries*. Cambridge: Cambridge University Press.

Capoccia, G. (2005). *Defending Democracy: Reactions to Extremism in Interwar Europe*. Baltimore: Johns Hopkins University Press.

Chalmers, D. A., S. B. Martin, & K. Pister. (1997). Associative Networks: New Structures of Representation for the Popular Sectors? In D. A. Chalmers, C. M. Vilas, K. Hite, S. B. Martin, K. Piester, & M. Segarra, eds., *The New Politics of Inequality in Latin America: Rethinking Participation and Representation*. Oxford: Oxford University Press, 543–582.

Chambers, S. & J. Kopstein. (2001). Bad Civil Society, *Political Theory*, 29(6), 838–866.

Chambers, S. & J. Kopstein. (2022). Wrecking the Public Sphere: The New Authoritarians' Digital Attack on Pluralism and Truth, *Constellations*, 30(3), 225–240.

Chapman, A. (2017). *Pluralism under Attack: The Assault on Press Freedom in Poland*. Washington, DC: Freedom House.

Cornell, A. & M. Grimes. (2015). Institutions As Incentives for Civic Action: Bureaucratic Structures, Civil Society, and Disruptive Protests, *The Journal of Politics*, 77(3), 664–678.

Cornell, A., J. Møller, & S. Skaaning. (2020). *Democratic Stability in an Age of Crisis*. Oxford: Oxford University Press.

Dragomir, M. (2017). The State of Hungarian Media: Endgame. *LSE Media Policy Project* [online]. https://tinyurl.com/y6umaxtp [Accessed March 25, 2023].

Ekiert, G. (2019). The Dark Side of Civil Society. *Concilium Civitas* [online]. www.conciliumcivitas.pl/en/almanac/item/97-the-dark-side-of-civil-society [Accessed September 1, 2019].

Ekiert, G. & E.J. Perry. (2020). State Mobilized Movements: A Research Agenda. In G. Ekiert, E. J. Perry, & X. Yan, eds., *Ruling by Other Means: State-Mobilized Movements. Cambridge Studies in Contentious Politics*. Cambridge: Cambridge University Press, 1–23.

Enyedi, Z. (2018). Democratic Backsliding and Academic Freedom in Hungary, *Perspectives on Politics*, 16(4), 1067–1074.

Ésik, S. (2024). Viktor Orbán's Newest Tool for Crushing Dissent. *Journal of Democracy* [online]. https://tinyurl.com/y5jmj4xz [Accessed March 15, 2024].

Fish, M. S. (1998). The Determinants of Economic Reform in the Post-Communist World, *East European Politics and Societies*, 12(1), 31–78.

Foa, R. & G. Ekiert. (2017). The Weakness of Postcommunist Civil Society Reassessed, *European Journal of Political Research*, 56(2), 419–439.

Freedom House. (2023). *Nations in Transit 2023: War Deepens a Regional Divide*. Washington, DC: Freedom House.

Gilens, M. & B. I. Page. (2014). Testing Theories of American Politics: Elites, Interest Groups, and Average Citizens, *Perspectives on Politics*, 12(3), 564–581.

Graff, A. & E. Korolczuk. (2021). *Anti-Gender Politics in the Populist Moment*. London: Routledge.

Greskovits, B. (2020). Rebuilding the Hungarian Right through Conquering Civil Society: The Civic Circles Movement, *East European Politics*, 36(2), 247–266.

Grzymala-Busse, A. (2002). *Redeeming the Communist Past: The Regeneration of Communist Parties in East Central Europe*. New York: Cambridge University Press.

Guasti, P. (2020). Populism in Power and Democracy: Democratic Decay and Resilience in the Czech Republic (2013–2020), *Politics and Governance*, 8(4), 473–484.

Hellmeier, S. & M. Bernhard. (2023). Regime Transformation from Below: Mobilization for Democracy and Autocracy from 1900 to 2021, *Comparative Political Studies*, 56(12), 1858–1890.

Hopkins, V. & J. Shorter. (2018). Hungary "Slave Law" Protest Shows Strains of Economic Model. *Financial Times* (20 December) [online]. https://tinyurl.com/22sdtnucwww.ft.com/content/609e64c4-03a3-11e9-99df-6183d3002ee1 [Accessed May 23, 2022].

Howard, M. (2003). *The Weakness of Civil Society in Post-Communist Europe*. Cambridge: Cambridge University Press.

Hurwicz, L. (2008). But Who Will Guard the Guardians? *American Economic Review*, 98(3), 577–585.

Inglehart, R. & C. Welzel. (2005). *Modernization, Cultural Change, and Democracy: The Human Development Sequence*. Cambridge: Cambridge University Press.

Jovanović, S. M. (2019). "One out of Five Million": Serbia's 2018–19 Protests against Dictatorship, the Media, and the Government's Response, *Open Political Science*, 2 (1), 1–8.

Kelemen, R. D. (2017). Europe's Other Democratic Deficit: National Authoritarianism in Europe's Democratic Union, *Government and Opposition*, 52(2), 211–238.

Kohler-Koch, B. (2010). Civil Society and EU Democracy: "Astroturf" Representation? *Journal of European Public Policy*, 17(1), 100–116.

Kopecký, P. (2003). Civil Society, Uncivil Society and Contentions Politics in Post-Communist Europe. In P. Kopecký & C. Mudde, eds., *Uncivil Society? Contentious Politics in Post-Communist Europe*. London: Routledge, 1–18.

Korolczuk, E. & K. Jacobsson. (2017). In E. Korolczuk and K. Jacobsson, eds., *Civil Society Revisited: Lessons from Poland*. New York: Berghahn Books, preface, viii–xi.

Korolczuk, E., B. Kowalska, C. Snochowska- Gonzalez, & J. Ramme, eds. (2019). *Bunt kobiet: czarne protesty I strajki kobiet*. Gdańsk: Europejskie Centrum Solidarności.

Kotwas, M. & J. Kubik. (2019). Symbolic Thickening of Public Culture and the Rise of Right-Wing Populism in Poland, *East European Politics and Societies*, 33(2), 435–471.

Kucharczyk, J. & J. Fomina. (2016). The Specter Haunting Europe: Populism and Protest in Poland, *Journal of Democracy*, 27(4), 58–68.

Linz, J. (1978). Crisis, Breakdown, and Reequilibration. In J. Linz & A. Stepan, eds., *The Breakdown of Democratic Regime*. Baltimore: Johns Hopkins University Press, 1–97.

Linz, J. (1990). The Perils of Presidentialism, *Journal of Democracy*, 1(1), 51–69.

Linz, J. & A. Stepan. (1996). *Problems of Democratic Transition and Consolidation*. Baltimore: Johns Hopkins University Press.

Lipset, S. M. (1959). Some Social Requisites of Democracy: Economic Development and Political Legitimacy, *American Political Science Review*, 53(1), 69–105.

Lowi, T. (1979). *The End of Liberalism: The Second Republic of the United States*. 2nd ed. New York: Norton.

Lührmann, A., K. L. Marquandt, & V. Mechkova. (2020). Constraining Governments: New Indices of Vertical, Horizontal, and Diagonal Accountability, *American Political Science Review*, 114 (3), 811–820.

Magyar, B. & B. Madlovics. (2022). Hungary 2022: Election Manipulation and the Regime's Attempts at Electoral Fraud. CEU Democracy Institute [online]. https://tinyurl.com/5b6e2p4r [Accessed March 31, 2022].

McAdam, D.v & S. Tarrow. (2010). Ballots and Barricades: On the Reciprocal Relationship between Elections and Social Movements, *Perspectives on Politics*, 8(2), 529–542.

McMahon, P. (2023). Young, Female Voters Were the Key to Defeating Populists in Poland's Election. *The Conversation* [online]. https://tinyurl.com/2s4hurt8 [Accessed March 15, 2024].

Merkel, W. (2004). Embedded and Defective Democracies, *Democratization* 11(5), 33–58.

Migdal, J. S. (1988). *Strong Societies and Weak States: State-Society Relations and State Capabilities in the Third World*. Princeton: Princeton University Press.

Mungiu-Pippidi, A. (2018). Explaining Eastern Europe: Romania's Italian-Style Anticorruption Populism, *Journal of Democracy*, 29(3), 104–116.

North, D. C., W. Summerhill, & B. Weingast. (2000). Order, Disorder, and Economic Change: Latin America versus North America. In B. Bueno de Mesquita and H. Root, eds., *Governing for Prosperity*. New Haven: Yale University Press, 17–58.

Notz, A. (2018). How to Abolish Democracy: Electoral System, Party Regulation and Opposition Rights in Hungary and Poland. *Verfassungsblog* [online]. https://tinyurl.com/4dfypz6d [Accessed October 1, 2023].

O'Donnell, G. (1994). Delegative Democracy, *Journal of Democracy*, 5(1), 55–69.

O'Donnell, G. (1998). Horizontal Accountability in New Democracies, *Journal of Democracy*, 9(3), 112–126.

OSCE. (2022). Hungary, Parliamentary Elections and Referendum, 3 April 2022: Statement of Preliminary Findings and Conclusions. www.osce.org/odihr/elections/hungary/515111 [Accessed May 22, 2022].

Pešić, J. & J. Petrović. (2020). The Role and the Positioning of the Left in Serbia's "One of Five Million" Protests. *Balkanologie* [online] 15(2). http://journals.openedition.org/balkanologie/2576 [Accessed May 23, 2022].

Popielec, D. (2017). Afera taśmowa z 2014 roku jako przykład politycznego podziału w mediach: studium przypadku, *Polityka i Społeczeństwo*, 4(15), 72–81.

Przeworski, A. (1991). *Democracy and the Market*. Cambridge: Cambridge University Press.

Przeworski, A., S. C. Stokes, & B. Manin. (1999). *Democracy, Accountability and Representation*. Cambridge: Cambridge University Press.

Ptak, A. (2023). Poland's Election Exit Poll in Charts. *Notes from Poland*. https://notesfrompoland.com/2023/10/16/polands-election-exit-poll-in-charts/ [Accessed March 15, 2024].

Putnam, R. D. (1993). *Making Democracy Work. Civic Traditions in Modern Italy*. Princeton: Princeton University Press.

Raskin, J. B. (2004). *Overruling Democracy: The Supreme Court versus the American People*. New York: Routledge.

Riley, D. J. (2010). *The Civic Foundations of Fascism in Europe: Italy, Spain, and Romania 1870–1945*. Baltimore: Johns Hopkins University Press.

Sadurski, W. (2019). *Poland's Constitutional Breakdown*. Oxford: Oxford University Press.

Sartori, G. (1994). *Comparative Constitutional Engineering: An Inquiry into Structures, Incentives, and Outcomes*. New York: New York University Press.

Schedler, A. 2006. The Logic of Electoral Authoritarianism. In A. Schedler, ed., *Electoral Authoritarianism: The Dynamics of Unfree Competition*. Boulder: Lynne Rienner, 1–23.

Shugart, M. S. & J. M. Carey. (1992). *Presidents and Assemblies: Constitutional Design and Electoral Dynamics*. Cambridge: Cambridge University Press.

Seleny, A. (2014). Revolutionary Road: 1956 and the Fracturing of Hungarian Historical Memory. In M. Bernhard & J. Kubik, eds., *Twenty Years after Communism: The Politics of Memory and Commemoration*. New York: Oxford University Press, 37–59.

Ślarzyński, M. (2018). Rola klubów Gazety Polskiej w sukcesie politycznym Prawa i Sprawiedliwości w 2015 roku. Aktorzy lokalni czy actor ogólnokrajowej sfery publicznej III RP? *Przegląd Socjolgiczny*, 67(2), 139–158.

Smulovitz, C. & E. Peruzzotti. (2000). Societal Accountability in Latin America, *Journal of Democracy*, 11(4), 147–158.

Vachudova, M. A. (2005). *Europe Undivided*. Oxford: Oxford University Press.

Vachudova, M. A. (2020). Ethnopopulism and Democratic Backsliding in Central Europe, *East European Politics*, 36(3), 318–340.

Walker, C. (2016). The Authoritarian Threat: The Hijacking of Soft Power, *Journal of Democracy*, 27(1), 49–63.

Weiss, M. L. (2017). Going to the Ground (or AstroTurf): A Grassroots View of Regime Resilience, *Democratization*, 24(2), 265–282.

World Bank. (2024). World Development Indicators. https://databank.worldbank.org/source/world-development-indicators [Accessed November 19, 2024].

10

Civil Society Resistance to Democratic Backsliding

Mark R. Beissinger

In democracies, violations of democratic norms are supposed to be punished by institutions or electorates. But there are limits to the guardrails that the rule of law, periodic elections, and institutional checks and balances provide for preventing democratic backsliding. Dysfunctional institutions are central to the dynamic that sets backsliding in motion in the first place: party systems that have collapsed, whose legitimacy is eroded, or are captured by societal movements (Haggard and Kaufman 2021); legislatures gripped by gridlock and division and whose authority has declined (Mickey, Levitsky, and Way 2017); electoral rules that can be manipulated or subverted (Bermeo 2016); civil servants who can be replaced (Bauer and Becker 2020); and courts that can be packed or ignored (Lane Scheppele 2018). Much of the functioning of democratic institutions depends on unwritten norms that can be pushed aside by a determined group of politicians (Levitsky and Ziblatt 2018). In short, institutions cannot always be relied upon to save democracy, as democratic backsliding is itself a manifestation of institutional dysfunction.[1]

But if institutions are uncertain and sometimes unreliable defenses against backsliding, what about the other key safeguard that democracies supposedly possess: civil society? Can robust civil society resistance (resistance from social movements, interest and advocacy groups, and ordinary citizens) reverse democratic backsliding once it has emerged?

Two answers predominate within the literature. The neo-Tocquevillian perspective views civil society as the ultimate kryptonite against backsliding – in Daron Acemoglu's words, "the lone true defense we have" (Acemoglu 2017). Active civil societies "intensify the accountability of elected leaders by both reinforcing the formal checks and balances, and imposing audience costs on

---

[1] In most cases, populist movements have ridden to power on a wave of dissatisfaction with traditional political parties. For a contrary view emphasizing the limited capacity of backsliding leaders to overcome the checks and balances within democratic institutions, see Weyland 2024.

would-be democratic defectors" (Bernhard, Hicken, Reenock, and Lindberg 2020: 3).[2] They compel budding autocrats to face backlash from society, making it harder for them to recruit societal support and accomplish their goals. The darker, alternative narrative sees civil society as a cause rather than a cure for backsliding. In this account, backsliding leaders ride a wave of civil society mobilization to power and use it to maintain themselves in office; mobilized civil society represents a threat to democratic institutions, especially when society is polarized and institutions are weak (Berman 1997; Greskovits 2015).[3] Polarization and weakened institutions are closely associated with backsliding (McCoy and Somer 2019).[4] Under these circumstances, is civil society a cure for democratic backsliding or part of the disease?

In some ways, the question is unresolvable, as civil societies have represented both possibilities in various times and circumstances. As Roberts, Bunce, Pepinsky, and Riedl put it in their introduction in Chapter 1 in this volume, "civil society networks can be force multipliers that provide mobilizing resources for both democratic and autocratic political projects." But there is much we do not know about the role (and potential) of civil society for containing or reversing democratic backsliding. Schedler points to "the thinness of our comparative knowledge on possible counterstrategies to illiberal aggressions against democracy" and notes that "existing research on contemporary processes of democratic subversion does not tell us ... how democratic actors might be able to stop illiberal governments before it is too late" (Schedler 2019: 5).[5]

In what follows, I develop a framework for thinking about these issues. Like others, I conceptualize backsliding democracies as an unsettled regime-type between democracy and competitive authoritarianism and explain why backsliding has been such a conducive environment for the growth of societal activism. I identify a series of dilemmas that civil society actors face in resisting backsliding. And through a variety of cases, I examine the conditions that shape civil society activism under backsliding and the roles it has played in containing or reversing autocratization. As I show, civil society resistance has been critical in restraining and reversing backsliding. But it is better able to counter backsliding when popular support for the backsliding leader has eroded and the opposition is able to work through institutions rather than having to work against them.[6] As backsliding proceeds, institutional channels for influence tend

---

[2] See also Michael Bernhard's Chapter 9 in this volume.

[3] See Béla Greskovits's contribution to this volume (Chapter 8) for discussion of the Hungarian case.

[4] Not all backsliding democracies are highly polarized – the Philippines under Duterte constituting an important counterexample. Nevertheless, polarization has been a critical element in fostering constituencies for backsliding leaders within democracies.

[5] Schedler (2019: 6–7) notes that "most democratic demolitions teams, like those headed by Chávez, Erdoğan, and Orbán, have faced massive street protests, to little avail."

[6] On this latter point, see Gamboa 2022.

to deteriorate. As a result, there is a critical window during which civil society resistance stands a better chance of containing backsliding: before electoral processes and institutional constraints are captured. Once capture occurs, civil society resistance moves to the much more dangerous and difficult task of confronting rather than preventing dictatorship – where the odds of success are much lower.

10.1 REGIMES IN-BETWEEN: DEMOCRATIC BACKSLIDING AND SOCIETAL RESISTANCE

Regime-type exercises a deep effect on the organization and political engagement of society; it sets the terms and conditions under which civil societies must function and their relationship to the regimes and states that govern them. It exerts large effects on the goals, forms, timing, and outcomes of societal engagement.

For purposes of simplification, I divide the world of regimes into three types: noncompetitive autocracies; competitive authoritarian regimes; and democracies (Levitsky and Way 2010). In noncompetitive autocracies (such as military governments or one-party regimes), independent civil society is weak and subject to repression and surveillance. Accordingly, much societal resistance is disaggregated, works within the confines of the system, or articulates diminutive goals rather than confronts the regime directly. However, these constraints can shift quickly due to a political opening, a weakening of the regime, or the snowballing of challenges from below.

In competitive authoritarian regimes the electoral moment provides the most important occasions for challenge (Bunce and Wolchik 2011). In rare instances, oppositions win elections. Less rarely but still infrequently, fraudulent elections transform into protests and revolutionary uprisings. Most frequently, societal resistance is repressed. It is difficult to overthrow an authoritarian regime. The risks involved are great, and the chances of success are small.[7]

Backsliding democracies represent a different situation. While de-democratization has assumed various forms, democratic backsliding in the early twenty-first century generally occurred through incremental steps, most of which were legal and carried out within the framework of democracy, but which blurred the line between democracy and competitive authoritarianism (Mickey, Levitsky, and Way 2017: 21). In this respect, a backsliding democracy is a regime in-between, located somewhere between democracy and competitive authoritarianism. The regime has been a democracy and retains many of the features of democracy (how many depends on how far backsliding has proceeded). But democracy is under threat by a would-be autocrat, and

---

[7] Over the last century the odds of successful revolutionary challenge in competitive authoritarian regimes have been worse than in some types of noncompetitive autocracies (especially, military regimes). Beissinger 2022.

the regime may ultimately come to resemble more closely competitive authoritarianism than democracy.[8] As backsliding proceeds, the democratic features of the regime grow more residual and formal. In short, in a backsliding democracy, ambiguity reigns.

Ambiguity similarly permeates regime practices under backsliding. Unlike authoritarian regimes, backsliding democracies do not engage in outright electoral fraud. Rather, they tilt the electoral game in ways favorable to the would-be autocrat. They change the size of electorates by empowering pro-incumbent diasporas to vote or denying felons the franchise. They engage in extreme gerrymandering so as to favor the incumbent party, restrict voting times to demobilize opposition voters, or place fewer polling stations in opposition districts. They weaken the constraints of courts and legislatures over executives, dilute civil liberties and freedoms in order to marginalize opposition, harass and undermine independent media, and alter term limits to perpetuate incumbents in office. These kinds of manipulations are clearly unfair, and they elicit widespread opposition. But they generally occur within the blank spaces of the law.[9] Democratic regimes exercise powers of appointment to manage principal-agent problems; backsliding regimes utilize them to pack institutions and undermine constraints on executive power. Open dissent in authoritarian regimes is marginalized, harassed, and restricted. In backsliding democracies, the personal dangers of public dissent are small at the beginning. But as these regimes slip into authoritarianism, the risks of dissent can grow considerably.

Civil society resistance to backsliding aims to block and reverse this erosion of democratic constraints and rights. In this respect, it is defensive and restorative. Democratic backsliding has on occasion provoked revolutionary uprisings.[10] But these largely occurred in countries with weak democratic traditions, were sparked by the sudden acts by executives to repress oppositions or to seize power, and materialized where institutional channels of influence were unavailable. Nevertheless, revolutions in backsliding democracies are rare. The reasons have to do with the lingering effects of two features of the democratic environment out of which backsliding emerges: constraints on majority rule, and periodic free-and-fair elections. Constraints on majority rule lessen the loser's dilemma by lowering the stakes involved in defeat. Under these conditions, losers have less to fear from losing and less

---

[8] Bangladesh, Turkey, Hungary, Mali (before the coups in 2020 and 2021), Nicaragua, Russia, and Venezuela represent cases in which backsliding tipped into competitive authoritarianism, though the extent to which authoritarianism remains competitive in some of these cases is questionable.

[9] Gandhi (2019) describes the strategy as "following the letter of the law to effectively change the spirit of the law." See also Bermeo 2016; Svolik 2020; Haggard and Kaufman 2021.

[10] Examples include the EDSA II Revolution in the Philippines in 2001, the 2002 Madagascar electoral protests, the 2009 Niger Constitutional Crisis, the 2013 Gezi Park Protests, the 2014 Euromaidan Revolution in Ukraine, the 2014 Burkinabe Uprising, the 2014 Venezuelan protests, the #ResignNow Uprising in Guatemala in 2015, and the 2019 revolt in Bolivia.

reason to rise up. And free-and-fair elections render revolution unlikely by establishing strong incentives for patience within oppositions: why engage in the high-risk collective action that revolution involves when, every four or five years, oppositions have the chance to change who governs through the ballot box? Revolution presupposes a high-stakes game and an impatience that constraints on majority rule and the periodicity of free-and-fair elections undermine. But when these features of democratic life disappear (as can happen as backsliding proceeds), revolution can become more readily imaginable. Revolution, however, is a risky strategy for countering backsliding – one that can easily backfire. Should the attempt fail, it can undermine the legitimacy of the opposition and lead to further consolidation of authoritarian rule.[11] Within a polarized political environment, it incites countermobilization by supporters of the backsliding leader[12] – potentially sparking a descent into a chronic instability that can destroy the democratic project completely.[13] Thus, revolution as a response to backsliding tends to be a strategy of the truly desperate – one appropriate only for those who are permanently locked out of power and lack hope of any institutional or electoral redress.

As "regimes in-between," backsliding democracies are conducive environments for the rapid growth of social movements and mass mobilization. As prior studies tell us, mobilization and movement activity multiply at times of opportunity and threat (Goldstone and Tilly 2001). Democratic backsliding is a situation of threat for those committed to the democratic project and those targeted by backsliding regimes. Indeed, democratic backsliding has produced some of the most spectacular protest mobilizations of recent times: the US Women's March of January 2017 (with between 3 and 5.5 million participating – considered by some the largest single-day of protest in American history); the failed 2017 "Mother of All Protests" campaign against the Maduro government in Venezuela (involving 2.5 million protestors); the 2016–17 Candlelight protests against President Park Geun-hye in South Korea (with one million protesting in Seoul alone); the summer 2021 protests against Bolsonaro in Brazil (mobilizing up to 800,000); Romania's massive protests in 2017–18 against efforts to weaken rules against government corruption (involving up to half a million); the Women's Strike in Poland in fall 2020 against restrictions on abortion rights (mobilizing more than 400,000); and many others. Backsliding regimes have been conducive to the proliferation of all forms of societal activism, including protest, citizen movements, public involvement in electoral campaigns, legal mobilization in the courts, and advocacy groups seeking to contain backsliding and its impact. The resistance to Trump, for instance, began as expressive protests with the

---

[11] On the disastrous attempt to overthrow Chavez in Venezuela, see Gamboa 2017.
[12] The EDSA II Revolution in the Philippines, for instance, was followed by the failed EDSA III incident four months later – an attempt by Estrada's followers to seize back the state.
[13] In the Thai case, repeated mobilizations and countermobilizations in a polarized environment eventually led to the seizure of power by the military.

inchoate goal of "pushing back against Trumpism" (Andersen 2022; Fisher 2019). It soon morphed into a profusion of civil society activism aimed at containing democratic backsliding, securing control of the Democrats over Congress, and defeating Trump at the ballot box. It combined confrontational tactics like protest with institutional tactics like voter mobilization, lobbying, information dissemination, and court challenges.[14] Backsliding is also conducive to mobilization by groups that support backsliding – both in response to opportunities for achieving policy gains and to counter the resistance to which backsliding naturally gives rise. Supporters of backsliding include numerous civil society groups (churches, trade unions, veterans' organizations, and commercial groups) who find common cause with backsliding leaders for policy gains or are drawn to their appeals (Greskovits 2015; Bernhard 2021).

What are the aims of civil society resistance to democratic backsliding? Obviously, the maximalist goal is eviction of the backsliding leader from power and reestablishment of democratic norms and procedures. Removing backsliding leaders is generally easier than overthrowing a full-fledged authoritarian regime: there are simply more channels for exercising control in a backsliding democracy than after authoritarian rule has been consolidated. Removal can occur through impeachment or vote of no confidence, at the ballot box, or as a result of direct pressure from the streets. All three paths involve significant civil society mobilization and have at times proved successful. As backsliding regimes are brought to power through the ballot box, they initially command the support of an electoral or coalitional majority. A key goal of the resistance to backsliding is to alter that situation – to undermine the regime's electoral or legislative coalition and hasten its demise. But even when oppositions are able to remove a backsliding leader through institutional means, the question still remains whether that leader will actually give up power voluntarily. Trump chose not to until forced to do so. Bolsonaro in Brazil pursued a similar strategy. Here, civil society also plays a significant role (in positive and negative ways), with supporters and opponents of backsliding mobilizing. Once a backsliding leader is removed from office, the societal problems that produced backsliding do not magically disappear. They are not simply a matter of institutional control, but are deeply embedded in society and persist beyond the tenure of any single leader, potentially returning to plague politics once more. Leader eviction is only the first step in a process of restoring democracy that is likely to stretch over many years and may never be fully resolved. But if a stable democracy is to be restored, civil society is surely part of the solution, even as it remains part of the problem. The activism that is central to undermining backsliding must be sustained beyond the removal of the leader (when a sense of urgency no longer prevails), while civil society groups associated with backsliding must be co-opted, drawn away from backsliding, or

---

[14] For a sense of the sheer scope of this activity, see Skocpol, Putnam, and Tervo 2020.

marginalized. In the American context after Trump's loss at the ballot box in 2020, these proved to be extremely challenging tasks.

There is also the no less important but more minimalist goal of blocking the implementation of backsliding measures. Civil society resistance can sometimes achieve this by signaling the unpopularity of these measures. In Poland, for instance, massive mobilizations by women in fall 2016 helped to shift public opinion against proposed antiabortion laws and ultimately caused parliament to drop the legislation (Korolczuk 2016). But a onetime blocking of backsliding measures is hardly the end of the story. By 2020 the Polish Constitutional Tribunal, then under PiS control, once again tightened abortion laws, making nearly all forms of abortion illegal. This set off an even more massive wave of protest – one of the largest since the collapse of socialism. This time, however, the government refused to relent and utilized the context of the covid pandemic to repress protestors. Thus, the real question that confronts efforts by civil society to block backsliding measures is: what next? It is not a permanent solution, and ultimately the issue of power must be confronted. Indeed, in the case of Poland a coalition of pro-EU parties was able to win legislative elections in October 2023 and to wrest parliamentary control from PiS, though PiS remained in control of the presidency. The struggle for control over the direction of Polish politics continues.

10.2   DILEMMAS OF RESISTANCE TO DEMOCRATIC BACKSLIDING

While democratic backsliding is conducive to the growth of societal mobilization, there are numerous challenges faced by societal efforts to contain a descent into dictatorship. Many of these are rooted in the circumstances that evoke backsliding in the first place.

One such challenge is the electoral support that backsliding leaders enjoy. Backsliding leaders are elected by a majority (or plurality) of citizens (or, in the American case, enough voters to command control over the Electoral College). One of the challenges faced by civil society resistance to backsliding is how to reverse this and undermine the backsliding regime's electoral or legislative coalition. Economic stagnation and elite corruption can alienate elements of the regime's coalition, demobilizing them or making them potentially available for defection. But polarization greatly complicates these efforts. On the one hand, it reinforces a sense of identity within oppositions and aids in mobilizing resistance. On the other hand, it makes winning over voters from backsliding electoral coalitions more difficult and pushes oppositions toward maximizing voter turnout within their own base of support. However, this does not address (and in some respects, reinforces) the conditions of polarization that underpin backsliding in the first place (McCoy and Somer 2019).

Polarization also weakens the possibilities for a broad-based coalition in defense of democracy in early stages of backsliding. In Indonesia in the late 2010s, for instance, democratic backsliding gained momentum when civil society groups failed to block the regime's efforts to gut anticorruption laws. This failure by what once had been a vibrant civil society committed to democracy was due to increased polarization between secularists and Islamists, who could not cooperate to prevent this from happening (Mietzner 2021). Similarly, in Ecuador, trade unions and indigenous organizations failed to join forces to stop the growing power of Correa, with some even coming to be co-opted by the regime (Laebens and Lührmann 2021: 917–918). And in the United States many Republican-leaning advocacy groups refused to speak out (and still do not speak out) against Trump's dictatorial impulses, preferring partisan advantage to democratic defense. In short, backsliding proceeds in part because of a failure of collective action within civil society: for some sectors of civil society, the personal gains from cooperating with the would-be autocrat outweigh concerns for preservation of the democratic public good.

The polarization underpinning democratic backsliding is magnified as well by the cultural politics that are inevitably intertwined with backsliding. Issues of gender, race, immigration, and ethnic difference have been closely connected with backsliding because of the use of "traditional values" and mobilization against multiculturalism by backsliding leaders for rallying their constituents (Vachudova 2020). Homophobia, Islamophobia, opposition to gender equality and abortion rights, anti-immigration sentiment, and racist dog whistles have figured prominently in the discourse of backsliding regimes in Poland, Hungary, Turkey, the United States, Croatia, and elsewhere.[15] As a result, issues of gender and cultural difference are inevitably drawn into the resistance to backsliding, as groups attempt to protect themselves from encroachments on their rights. This entwinement of cultural politics with backsliding transforms backsliding into a symbolic politics with deeper roots in social and cultural divides, imbuing these divisions with magnified emotional power.

It also complicates the politics of coordinating opposition to backsliding. Civil society resistance to backsliding is in part restorative, aimed at the defense and recovery of democratic norms and practices. These purposes tend to appeal to more moderate opponents of backsliding. But this restorative orientation finds common cause with a wide variety of minority and progressive political groups (immigrant, racial, ethnic, gender, and environmental) who are under attack. The result is that resistance to backsliding tends to consist of a fragile alliance between those motivated simply by defense of democratic norms and a mélange of single-issue groups driven by more particular concerns. This pluralism creates significant tension within the resistance. Backsliding regimes also rely on coalitional alliances among ideological, economic, and religious voters, though these coalitions tend to be somewhat less diverse. Fragile coalitions create coordination issues and can empower radicals over moderates, leading to a politics of outbidding. This has certainly been the case

---

[15] See, for instance, Chapter 7 by Lindsay Mayka in this volume on this phenomenon in Latin America.

within the Democratic and Republican parties in the United States and has been exacerbated by an electoral system that empowers minorities capable of mobilizing numbers within concentrated geographic units.

The connection of gender and cultural issues with the politics of backsliding and the entwinement of backsliding with the international system also play into the nationalist tropes brandished by backsliding leaders. In backsliding regimes "civic organizations representing disadvantaged groups ... [have frequently been] framed and silenced as tools of foreign forces" (Bermeo 2016: 14), especially as the United States and the European Union have come to the defense of the rights of minorities. This foreignization of opposition to backsliding tends to be particularly salient the further backsliding processes proceed (Examples include Hungary, Poland, Russia, Turkey, and Venezuela).

Thus, resistance to backsliding can exert unintended impacts and can have the paradoxical effect of reinforcing identity among supporters of backsliding regimes.[16] It can, for instance, be utilized by backsliding regimes for purposes of destabilization and executive aggrandizement. Studies show that when protestors use disruptive tactics, behave unlawfully, or carry firearms, public support for protest plummets (Wouters 2019). Such situations can play to the advantage of backsliding regimes, allowing them to use the occasion to restrict protest and shore up public support. In Venezuela in 2000–01, for instance, confrontations on the streets between Chavez supporters and opponents escalated into violent conflicts, providing an excuse for the regime to repress the opposition (García-Guadilla 2004). Indeed, backsliding regimes often attempt to provoke violent confrontations in hope of using them to consolidate support.

In part for this reason, civil society groups struggling against backsliding have usually sought to avoid violent protest, relying instead on the power of numbers. In this respect, they present a sharp contrast with civil society groups supporting backsliding leaders, who often have embraced violent tactics. However, utilizing the power of numbers requires forging as broad an alliance as possible across a wide variety of groups, and this contains its own challenges. Such alliances are difficult to maintain over time. There can be significant frictions between left and moderate wings of the opposition that hinder cooperation and problematize electoral mobilization. The opposition to Trump, for instance, was highly fragmented. It first coalesced in the Women's March in January 2017. But due to squabbles within its leadership over racial and ethnic divisions, the Women's March movement fragmented and was never able to replicate the same success (Lang 2020). In Hungary, "links between the women's movement and wider democratization processes and protests were very weak ... and remained incidental even in the context of anti-democratic

---

[16] For one example, note how massive anti-Islamist protests in Turkey in 2007 (coupled with institution-based efforts to contain the AKP's growing grip on the state) backfired and reinforced AKP support (Somer, McCoy, and Luke 2021).

threats from the government." The Hungarian women's movement has been "largely disconnected from wider human rights and democratization protests," and women's rights have been "rarely backed by these groups" (Krizsan and Roggeband 2018: 96). Since the decline of labor's hegemony within the left, fragmentation has been a particular problem for left-wing parties and movements because of the variety of cultural and social issues that the left has absorbed.

The diversity that accompanies reliance on numbers is also exacerbated by the role that digital media play in the twenty-first century in coordinating civil society mobilization. Digital media excel at mobilizing large numbers across disparate groups with minimal organizational presence (Bennett and Segerberg 2013). But they dilute civil society association and have not been adept at generating the kind of strategic coordination that traditional social movement organization was able to supply.

Finally, movements seeking to halt democratic backsliding face a challenge in working through dysfunctional institutions. The resistance to backsliding normally seeks to utilize electoral processes, the courts, and legislative institutions to try to block backsliding and gain back control from backsliding leaders. But these institutions are already dysfunctional to some degree and are part of the underlying causes that brought backsliding into being in the first place. Moreover, as backsliding proceeds, the independence of these institutions is weakened. There is an urgency to civil society resistance to backsliding: action must be taken before already dysfunctional institutions have been fully compromised, for once these institutions are captured, the tactics that the opposition can utilize to contain backsliding narrow considerably.

10.3 THE LOGIC OF CIVIL SOCIETY RESISTANCE TO BACKSLIDING

There is a logic to civil society resistance to backsliding that is largely the product of two factors: (1) the degree of subversion of institutional constraints on backsliding leaders; and (2) the degree of popular support that backsliding leaders command (as refracted through institutional rules). Where a society is located in the backsliding process strongly affects the opportunities and constraints confronting the resistance to backsliding by influencing the degree to which opposition can or cannot work through institutions. As institutional constraints come to be subverted, the possibilities for working through them fade.

The degree of popular support for the backsliding leader also constitutes a separate constraint on civil society resistance by affecting the legitimacy of efforts to remove the leader and the vulnerability of backsliding leaders to electoral challenge or challenges on the streets. As cases like Hungary, Venezuela, India, the Philippines, and Serbia suggest, challenging a backsliding leader who has the allegiance of society is difficult (Bermeo 2016: 11–12). Some backsliding leaders are able to rule with low public support. As of

2022, for instance, Turkish President Recep Tayyip Erdoğan's approval rating was 42 percent, Polish President Andrzej Duda's 40 percent, and Venezuelan President Nicolás Maduro's 15 percent.[17] Public support is necessary for backsliding leaders to gain power, and high levels of popularity insulate them from significant challenge. But as backsliding proceeds and the regime slips toward authoritarianism, institutions are often redesigned to allow leaders to maintain themselves in power even in the face of declining popularity.[18]

Still, as the popularity of the leader slips, backsliding leaders become more vulnerable to institutional and extrainstitutional challenges. In Ecuador, for instance, Presidential Rafael Correa had been largely unassailable for years, having achieved high levels of popularity due to soaring oil prices and redistributive policies, despite curtailing political freedoms. He won reelection twice and even amended the constitution so that he could hold power indefinitely. But in 2015 oil prices collapsed, the economy turned sharply negative, and Correa's popularity began to decline. In summer 2015 a controversial inheritance law proposed by Correa elicited massive protests. In response, Correa chose not to run again for president, instead passing power to his vice president, who subsequently reversed many of Correa's antidemocratic policies (Conaghan 2016).

When backsliding first materializes, politics is heavily shaped by the democratic institutional context out of which backsliding emerges and the recent election of the backsliding leader. Thus, civil society resistance to backsliding is structured by a condition of low institutional subversion/high leader popularity (cell *a* in Table 10.1). Here, institutional constraints to backsliding, though under attack, remain partially (if not wholly) available, and courts, bureaucracies, and legislatures continue to function as channels through which civil society can exercise influence. Under these circumstances civil society resistance is more likely to be channeled through institutions. But because leaders retain public allegiance, informational dissemination aimed at weakening the leader's public support becomes the dominant task of civil society resistance. Street actions may articulate demands for a leader's resignation or removal. But they have little chance of being acted upon and remain largely expressive. The 2017 Women's March, for example, called for Trump's removal but never attempted to compel his resignation. However, should the popularity of the backsliding leader slip (cell *b* in Table 10.1), the weight of civil society activism transfers to elections, impeachment, or vote of no confidence in an attempt to remove the backsliding leader from power.

---

[17] These figures come from https://tinyurl.com/4bfxrm4w; https://morningconsult.com/global-leader-approval/#section-2; https://tinyurl.com/yvkcdyf7.

[18] Institutional design can work in both directions. Federalism, for instance, has helped insulate civil society from backsliding governments in the United States and India, providing a foothold for opposition that has facilitated resistance.

TABLE 10.1 *A logic of civil society resistance to democratic backsliding*

Condition	Low institutional subversion	High institutional subversion
High leader popularity	*(a)* Advocacy in support of institutional constraints, information dissemination, expressive protest	*(c)* Marginalization of oppositional activity, information dissemination, expressive protest
Low leader popularity	*(b)* Advocacy in support of institutional constraints or impeachment, electoral mobilization	*(d)* Confrontational protest on the streets, electoral mobilization

As backsliding proceeds, oppositional civil society is subjected to growing political constraints, and courts, bureaucracies, and legislatures come to function as instruments of regime rule. In this situation, civil society opposition to backsliding can grow more marginalized and isolated within the political system should the leader retain popular support (cell *c* in Table 10.1). If the "losers' dilemma" in democracies consists of the challenge of inducing compliance with electoral outcomes among those who lose or have little expectation of winning, what happens when those who support democracy are the consistent losers and permanently locked out of power by backsliding leaders who have captured institutions? In Hungary, for instance, Viktor Orbán used his majority in the National Assembly to alter the constitution, appoint loyal followers to key institutions, and rig the electoral process so that it was practically impossible to evict Fidesz from power. Once it gained a two-thirds majority in parliament, Fidesz enacted constitutional amendments to further lock in its grip on government. It eviscerated courts, seized control over universities, and forced the closure of opposition press. While Hungarian civil society has not been entirely undermined, it has been marginalized and largely tamed in the political process (Bernhard 2021; Sitter and Bakke 2019; Nagy 2016).

The Venezuelan case represents a similar situation of the marginalization of civil society resistance. Popular support for the Chavez and Maduro governments (particularly among the poor) was buoyed by Venezuela's oil-based economy, the failures of past democratic governance, and redistributive policies. The opposition engaged in multiple tactics: protest, insurrection, recall movements, electoral contestation. Only electoral competition was able to make a dent in the government's grip on power, as the opposition won a foothold in localities and in 2015 gained control over the legislature. But the government reacted by dissolving the legislature, creating an alternative parliament aligned with Maduro, and rewriting the constitution. Protests at times caused the government to postpone policy proposals, but only temporarily. While business and labor organizations were active in challenging the regime, the government eventually built an alternative network of civil society organizations to take their place (Hawkins 2016).

As institutional constraints on dictatorship and the quality of the electoral process grow compromised and backsliding shades into authoritarian rule, a new logic of resistance emerges that more closely resembles the politics of resistance under competitive authoritarianism. In these circumstances, opportunities for reversing backsliding hinge upon public support for the leader (Grzymala-Busse and Nalepa 2022). When institutional constraints on the backsliding leader are weak and the leader commands public allegiance, civil society resistance is marginalized and limited largely to information dissemination and expressive protest. But should support for the regime decline, politics may be pushed in the direction of a more confrontational street politics (cell *d* in Table 10.1). As in competitive authoritarian regimes, open challenges will tend to cluster around electoral campaigns, when authoritarian leaders must renew their legitimacy at the ballot box.

10.4 PATTERNS OF SUCCESS IN CIVIL SOCIETY RESISTANCE TO BACKSLIDING

Judging the influence of movements on political outcomes is difficult (Giugni 1999). Political outcomes depend upon decision-making by government actors and are the products of interactions between movements and regimes in which agency and choice play significant roles. Nevertheless, there are patterns to the outcomes of civil society resistance to democratic backsliding that reflect the larger factors that condition it.

Figure 10.1 provides a mapping of the removal of backsliding leaders across twenty-four backsliding democracies, relative to the degree of subversion of institutional constraints on leaders and the popular support that backsliding leaders commanded. The former is measured by the V-Dem horizontal accountability index (reversed),[19] while the latter measures approval ratings for leaders based on public opinion polls.[20] I have divided the figure into four quadrants analogous to the cells in Table 10.1 and indicated whether leaders were ultimately removed through institutional channels (impeachment or elections) or extrainstitutionally through protest campaigns. Most cases in which leaders were removed by impeachment or elections also involved social movements and protest campaigns; the coding here simply measures whether removal occurred through institutional or extrainstitutional channels.

---

[19] The index measures the power of state institutions to ensure checks between institutions and prevent abuses of power. Coppedge et al. 2022.

[20] For leaders still in power as of the end of 2022, the measurements are from that year. For those removed from power, they are for the year before removal. In Benin and Zambia, Afrobarometer data on whether the country was moving in the right direction was used.

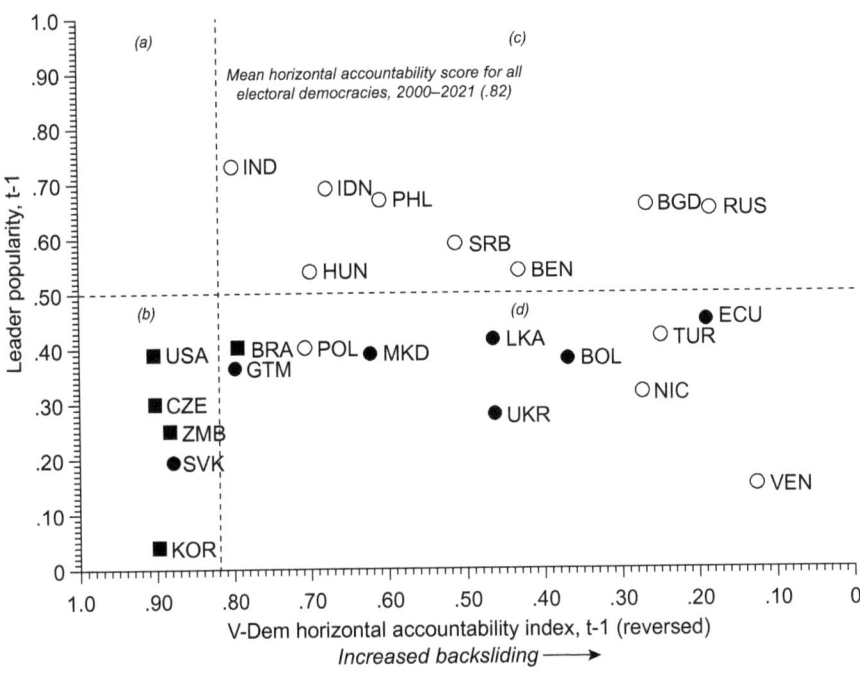

FIGURE 10.1 Horizontal accountability, leader popularity, and leader turnover in backsliding democracies (n=24).

Overall, 50 percent of backsliding leaders in the sample had been evicted from power by the end of 2022. That statistic should provide a degree of hope to those resisting backsliding. But it should also give pause: in half of these cases backsliding leaders not only survived, but on average had been in power for ten years as of 2022 (i.e., most surviving backsliding leaders were reelected at least once or twice). Nearly all of these surviving leaders faced significant waves of protest in response to backsliding, though in none was civil society able to dislodge them.[21] India, for instance, experienced massive waves of protest in response to Modi's anti-Muslim and antidemocratic measures, though these did little to dent his popularity or to stem the BJP's (Bharatiya Janata Party) course toward authoritarianism (Basu 2021). If anything, the BJP deepened its grip on institutions, seizing control over universities, attacking the judiciary,

---

[21] Quadrant *a* in Figure 10.1 (low institutional subversion/high public support) is empty, with most backsliding regimes falling into quadrants *c* (high institutional subversion/high public support) and *d* (high institutional subversion/low public support). As noted earlier, backsliding regimes generally begin in quadrant *a*, but as backsliding proceeds, horizontal accountability declines, pushing regimes toward quadrants *c* and *d*.

and revising citizenship laws. Clearly, popularity (which in the case of Modi, hovered around 70 percent in 2023) insulates backsliding leaders from removal or retreat.

But as leader popularity declines, a variety of outcomes emerge. The five countries located in quadrant *b* in Figure 10.1 (low institutional subversion/low public support) had a perfect rate of success in removing backsliding leaders. Removal in these cases largely came through elections or impeachment, though civil society mobilization also played a role. For example, in the wake of a corruption scandal, massive protests forced South Korea's parliament to impeach Park Geun-hye in 2016. The president's New Frontier Party was the largest in the National Assembly and thus in theory should have been able to halt the impeachment process. But as the president's approval rating fell to 4 percent, the ruling party was itself divided, and almost half of its representatives voted for impeachment. Pressure from civil society widened regional and factional fissures within the party (Shin 2020). In Zambia, falling copper prices severely undercut the popularity of President Edgar Lungu, with record voter turnouts in the 2021 elections sweeping the opposition United Party for National Development to power and putting an end to Lungu's decade-long march toward dictatorship (Resnick 2022). Rocked by corruption scandals and with an approval rating of 30 percent, Czech Prime Minister Andrej Babiš narrowly lost his reelection bid in 2021. Babiš's party received only 2 percent less votes than in the prior parliamentary election in 2017, but as a result of a massive turnout effort by the civil society movement "Million Moments for Democracy" (which also mobilized hundreds of thousands in protests calling for Babiš's removal), 5 percent more voters participated in the elections than in 2017 (the highest turnout in Czechia since 1998) – making the crucial difference (Jurečková 2021). And in the United States in 2020, civil society movements magnified voter turnout in key states, producing the highest participation in an American election since 1960 and partially accounting for Trump's defeat.

At first glance, Slovakia may seem an anomaly: it ranked high on horizontal accountability, yet its regime was felled by protest. The murder of journalist Ján Kuciak in 2018 catalyzed huge demonstrations across the country against the government of Prime Minister Robert Fico that forced his resignation. Fico had attacked media freedoms, and Kuciak was in the midst of investigating Fico's government for embezzlement and links to organized crime. But Fico's resignation was in part a function of Slovak political institutions: His power rested on a fragile coalition of four parties, and he resigned to avoid an early election in the face of his coalition's collapse (Bakke and Sitter 2022). In short, this was a case in which protest combined with institutional accountability to evict a backsliding government.[22]

---

[22] Fico remained active in Slovak politics after his resignation, with the threat of his return to power continuing to hang over the polity.

A slight majority of backsliding leaders in the sample who have been removed were evicted at least in part through extrainstitutional means. A number of backsliding leaders were able to survive declines in public support through extensive institutional manipulation. But where horizontal accountability declined and leader popularity sank (quadrant *d* in Figure 10.1), the likelihood that backsliding leaders would be challenged by significant protest increased. In the Macedonian case, for instance, massive protests took place for the resignation of Prime Minister Nikola Gruevski in May 2015 in response to accusations of electoral fraud and wiretapping the opposition. But Gruevski refused to leave, even in the face of the resignation of a number of his ministers. Eventually, the EU brokered an agreement among Macedonian parties for Gruevski to step down and new elections (which Gruevski's party lost) to be held (Ceban 2015). In the Bolivian case, accusations of electoral fraud by incumbent Evo Morales set off massive urban protests by the opposition, forcing his resignation after almost fourteen years in power. The uprising ultimately came under the control of ultraconservative forces from the Bolivian lowlands. Many of the protests turned violent, as Morales's supporters mobilized in response (Wolff 2020).

The success rate of protest actions to remove backsliding leaders is mixed. There are also cases like Daniel Ortega's Nicaragua, where thousands of protests since 2018 have been forcefully put down, leading to further consolidation of autocratic rule (Buben and Kouba 2020). Brazil, Turkey, and Venezuela also experienced large-scale protests that failed to remove backsliding leaders – leading, in the latter two cases, to further authoritarian consolidation.

10.5 CONCLUSION

Civil society mobilization has played a critical role in nearly all cases in which democratic backsliding has been contained or reversed. But in a significant number of cases, backsliding leaders have survived attempts by civil society to undermine or deter them. There is a naive belief in some circles that civil society resistance is a cure-all for backsliding – the last great hope when all else has failed. The reality is more complex. Failure is as common as success. What is often forgotten in discussions of the role of civil society in countering democratic backsliding is that civil society resistance only works when the targets to be affected (institutions and publics) are themselves vulnerable to influence.

In this respect, the early stages of backsliding (before institutions are fully subverted) are much more propitious for preventing descent into dictatorship than once authoritarian-minded leaders have consolidated their grip over institutions. However, leaders often command public support in these early stages, and that problematizes efforts to hold backsliding leaders accountable. The more institutions come to be captured by backsliding leaders, the less likely civil society resistance can counter de-democratization. In these circumstances, success, when it does occur, depends on an erosion of public support for backsliding leaders. But even here, backsliding leaders have sometimes survived lack of popularity by insulating themselves from society through institutional manipulations and increased reliance on force.

In short, civil society is not a cure-all for the ills of contemporary democracies. It is often deeply polarized, and among opponents of backsliding there are problems of coordination across diverse factions. Working through dysfunctional institutions is difficult. But working against captured institutions is even more challenging.

REFERENCES

Acemoglu, Daron. 2017. "We Are the Last Defense against Trump." *Foreign Policy*, January 18 (https://tinyurl.com/3aecvjet).
Andersen, Kristi. 2022. "Progressive Grassroots Organizing (2016–2020)." In Luke Perry, ed., *The 2020 Presidential Election: Key Issues and Regional Dynamics*. London, UK: Palgrave Macmillan: 71–82.
Bakke, Elisabeth, and Nick Sitter. 2022. "The EU's *Enfants Terribles*: Democratic Backsliding in Central Europe since 2010." *Perspectives on Politics* 20, 1: 22–37.
Basu, Amrita. 2021. "Prefiguring Alternatives to Autocratization: Democratic Dissent in Contemporary India." In Sten Widmalm, ed., *Routledge Handbook of Autocratization in South Asia*. London, UK: Routledge: 35–48.
Bauer, Michael W. and Stefan Becker. 2020. "Democratic Backsliding, Populism, and Public Administration." *Perspectives on Public Management and Governance* 3, 1: 19–31.
Beissinger, Mark R. 2002. *The Revolutionary City: Urbanization and the Global Transformation of Rebellion*. Princeton, NJ: Princeton University Press.
Bennett, W. Lance and Alexandra Segerberg. 2013. *The Logic of Connective Action: Digital Media and the Personalization of Contentious Politics*. Cambridge, UK: Cambridge University Press.
Berman, Sheri. 1997. "Civil Society and the Collapse of the Weimar Republic." *World Politics* 49, 3: 401–429.
Bermeo, Nancy. 2016. "On Democratic Backsliding." *Journal of Democracy* 27, 1: 5–19.
Bernhard, Michael. 2021. "Democratic Backsliding in Poland and Hungary." *Slavic Review* 80, 3: 585–607.
Bernhard, Michael, Allen Hicken, Christopher Reenock, and Staffan I. Lindberg. 2020. "Parties, Civil Society, and the Deterrence of Democratic Defection." *Studies in Comparative International Development* 55, 4: 1–26.
Buben, Radek and Karel Kouba. 2020. "Nicaragua in 2019: The Surprising Resilience of Authoritarianism in the Aftermath of Regime Crisis." *Revista de Ciencia Política* 40, 2: 431–455.
Bunce, Valerie J. and Sharon L. Wolchik. 2011. *Defeating Authoritarian Leaders in Postcommunist Countries*. Cambridge, UK: Cambridge University Press.
Ceban, Elena. 2015. "Democratic Awakening in Macedonia: Expecting the Unexpected." *Journal of Global Politics and Current Diplomacy* 3, 1: 23–33.

Conaghan, Catherine M. 2016. "Delegative Democracy Revisited: Ecuador under Correa." *Journal of Democracy* 27, 3: 109–118.

Coppedge, Michael et al. 2022. "VDem Dataset v12," Varieties of Democracy (V-Dem) Project. https://doi.org/10.23696/vdemds22.

Fisher, Dana R. 2019. *American Resistance: From the Women's March to the Blue Wave*. New York: Columbia University Press.

Gamboa, Laura. 2017. "Opposition at the Margins: Strategies against the Erosion of Democracy in Colombia and Venezuela." *Comparative Politics* 49, 4: 457–477.

Gamboa, Laura. 2022. *Resisting Backsliding: Opposition Strategies against the Erosion of Democracy*. Cambridge, UK: Cambridge University Press.

Gandhi, Jennifer. 2019. "The Institutional Roots of Democratic Backsliding." *The Journal of Politics* 81, 1 https://doi.org/10.1086/700653.

García-Guadilla, María Pilar. 2004. "Civil Society: Institutionalization, Fragmentation, Autonomy." In Steve Ellner and Daniel Hellinger, eds., *Venezuelan Politics in the Chávez Era*. London, UK: Lynne Rienner: 179–196.

Giugni, Marco. 1999. "How Social Movements Matter: Past Research, Present Problems, Future Developments." In Marco Giugni, Doug McAdam, and Charles Tilly, eds., *How Social Movements Matter*. Minneapolis, MN: University of Minnesota Press: xiii–xxxiii.

Goldstone, Jack A. and Charles Tilly. 2001. "Threat (and Opportunity): Popular Action and State Response in the Dynamics of Contentious Action." In Ron Aminzade et al., eds., *Silence and Voice in the Study of Contentious Politics*. Cambridge, UK: Cambridge University Press: 179–194.

Greskovits, Béla. 2015. "The Hollowing and Backsliding of Democracy in East Central Europe." *Global Policy* 6: 28–37.

Grzymala-Busse, Anna and Monika Nalepa. 2022. "How Illiberal Populists Gain and Stay in Power: Programmatic Cohesion and Government Performance." Unpublished paper (https://tinyurl.com/y8d8ejr5).

Haggard, Stephan and Robert Kaufman. 2021. *Backsliding: Democratic Regress in the Contemporary World*. Cambridge, UK: Cambridge University Press.

Hawkins, Kirk A. 2016 "Responding to Radical Populism: Chavismo in Venezuela." *Democratization* 23, 2: 242–262.

Jurečková, Adéla. 2021. "The End of the Babiš Era? The Czech Republic between the Past and the Future." Heinrich Boll Stiftung, October 19 (https://tinyurl.com/ttycupme).

Krizsan, Andrea and Conny Roggeband. 2018. "Towards a Conceptual Framework for Struggles over Democracy in Backsliding States: Gender Equality Policy in Central Eastern Europe." *Politics and Governance* 6, 3: 90–100.

Korolczuk, Elżbieta. 2016. "Explaining Mass Protests against Abortion Ban in Poland: The Power of Connective Action." *Zoon politikon* 7, 7: 91–113.

Laebens, Melis G. and Anna Lührmann. 2021. "What Halts Democratic Erosion? The Changing Role of Accountability." *Democratization* 28, 5: 908–928.

Lane Scheppele, Kim. 2018. "Autocratic Legalism." *The University of Chicago Law Review* 85, 2: 545–584.

Lang, Marissa J. 2020. "'Nobody Needs Another Pink Hat': Why the Women's March Is Struggling for Relevance." *The Washington Post*, January 12 (https://tinyurl.com/3nhm2z9v).

Levitsky, Steven and Lucan A. Way. 2010. *Competitive Authoritarianism: Hybrid Regimes after the Cold War*. Cambridge, UK: Cambridge University Press.

Levitsky, Steven and Daniel Ziblatt. 2018. *How Democracies Die*. New York: Broadway Books.

McCoy, Jennifer L. and Murat Somer. 2019. "Toward a Theory of Pernicious Polarization and How It Harms Democracies: Comparative Evidence and Possible Remedies." *The Annals of the American Academy of Political and Social Science* 681, 1: 234–271.

Mickey, Robert, Steven Levitsky, and Lucan A. Way. 2017. "Is America Still Safe for Democracy: Why the United States Is in Danger of Backsliding." *Foreign Affairs* 96, 3: 20–29.

Mietzner, Marcus. 2021. "Sources of Resistance to Democratic Decline: Indonesian Civil Society and Its Trials." *Democratization* 28, 1: 161–178.

Nagy, Ádám C. 2016. "The Taming of Civil Society." In Bálint Magyar and Júlia Vásárhelyi, eds., *Twenty-Five Sides of a Post-Communist Mafia State*. Budapest: Central European Press: 559–574.

Resnick, Danielle. 2022. "How Zambia's Opposition Won." *Journal of Democracy* 33, 1: 70–84.

Schedler, Andreas. 2019. "What Do We Know about Resistance to Democratic Subversion?" *Annals of Comparative Democratization* 17, 1: 4–7.

Shin, Soon-ok. 2020. "The Rise and Fall of Park Geun-hye: The Perils of South Korea's Weak Party System." *The Pacific Review* 33, 1: 153–183.

Sitter, Nick and Elisabeth Bakke. 2019. "Democratic Backsliding in the European Union." *Oxford Research Encyclopedia of Politics* (https://tinyurl.com/mrxhfswj).

Skocpol, Theda, Lara Putnam, and Caroline Tervo. 2020. "Citizen Activism and the Democratic Party." In Theda Skocpol and Caroline Tervo, eds., *Upending American Politics: Polarizing Parties, Ideological Elites, and Citizen Activists from the Tea Party to the Anti-Trump Resistance*. Oxford, UK: Oxford University Press: 283–316.

Somer, Murat, Jennifer L. McCoy, and Russell E. Luke. 2021. "Pernicious Polarization, Autocratization and Opposition Strategies." *Democratization* 28, 5: 929–948.

Svolik, Milan W. 2020. "When Polarization Trumps Civic Virtue: Partisan Conflict and the Subversion of Democracy by Incumbents." *Quarterly Journal of Political Science* 15, 1: 3–31.

Vachudova, Milada Anna. 2020. "Ethnopopulism and Democratic Backsliding in Central Europe." *East European Politics* 36, 3: 318–340.

Weyland, Kurt. 2024. *Democracy's Resilience to Populism's Threat: Countering Global Alarmism*. Cambridge, UK: Cambridge University Press.

Wolff, Jonas. 2020. "The Turbulent End of an Era in Bolivia: Contested Elections, the Ouster of Evo Morales, and the Beginning of a Transition towards an Uncertain Future." *Revista de Ciencia Política* 40, 2: 163–186.

Wouters, Ruud. 2019. "The Persuasive Power of Protest: How Protest Wins Public Support." *Social Forces* 98, 1: 403–426.

Is Democracy Broken? Disinformation Wants You to Think That It Is

Alexandra Cirone

"Yes, Social Media Really Is Undermining Democracy"
– Headline, *Atlantic*, July 28, 2022[1]

"Don't Be So Certain That Social Media Is Undermining Democracy"
– Headline, *Daily Beast*, Aug. 11, 2022[2]

Social media has a complicated relationship with democracy. In 2022, Pew Research Center surveyed citizens in nineteen advanced economies, to ask their opinions of social media. A majority (57 percent) said that social media has been more of a "good thing" for democracy in their country, citing that social media has made users more informed about politics at home and abroad, and more accepting of people from different ethnic groups, regions, and races (Pew 2022). The rest responded that social media has been a "bad thing' for democracy, and in the US – which has had significant problems with disinformation in politics – the pattern is reversed. Meanwhile, respondents report that access to social media and the internet has made people easier to manipulate with false information and rumors (84 percent), and more divided in their politics (74 percent).[3]

Social media is neither democratic or undemocratic, however, it is an arena where different actors can both promote and undermine democratization (Theocharis et al. 2017). There is also ample evidence that disinformation[4] on

---

[1] https://tinyurl.com/3fnxab83.   [2] https://tinyurl.com/4tsa7ar8.
[3] https://tinyurl.com/mr43p3b5.
[4] Misinformation is defined as false information that is unintentionally shared, while disinformation is false information that is deliberately shared (and fake news is disinformation that resembles journalism) (Tucker 2018).

social media is disrupting democratic elections all over the world (Persily and Tucker 2020). Democracy is also built on a foundation of norms and trust in democratic institutions, where elections are the defining characteristic of the democratic process. Increasingly we worry that disinformation campaigns can undermine democratic elections' ability to ensure fair competition, representation, and accountability. The extent to which disinformation on social media undermines democratic institutions also has severe implications for the "success" of democratic backsliding (Margetts 2019).

This chapter looks at the role of social media and backsliding, but turns the focus to domestic disinformation. It first outlines two ways disinformation can negatively impact democratic elections. First, disinformation narratives try to influence elections by spreading false information about the voting process, or targeting voters, candidates, or parties to alter the outcome. Second, disinformation undermines trust in the integrity of the electoral process (from the ability to have free and fair elections, to expectations about the peaceful transfer of power), which can then erode trust in democracy. Prior work on social media has often focused on foreign election interference efforts, but now it's important to realize electoral disinformation is increasingly originating from domestic, not foreign, political actors.

This chapter, then, argues that an important threat to democracy comes from within – namely, disinformation about democratic elections that is being created and shared by democratic leaders and elites, increasing the reach and false credibility of such false narratives. We know that elites and parties are crucial in determining whether countries become or stay democratic (Levitsky and Ziblatt 2019; Bartels et al. 2023), but elites are now exploiting brand new tools of disinformation on social media to target elections. A running theme through this edited volume is that essential pillars of democracy – in this case, freedom of speech and press and elected representatives – can be weaponized and turned against democracy itself. Given the unique challenge posed by elite disinformation, this chapter concludes by demonstrating how we can take proactive and concrete steps to mitigate the negative impact of elites on elections.

11.1 DISINFORMATION TO MANIPULATE ELECTIONS

"We're making a Woman's Vote Worth more by Staying Home #LetWomenDecide #NoMenMidterm"
– Example of voter suppression post from the 2018 US Midterm Election[5]

"Even the Pope admires Duterte and so do the Filipino"
– Example of a fake endorsement in the 2016 presidential election in the Philippines[6]

---

[5] www.nytimes.com/2018/11/04/us/politics/election-misinformation-facebook.html.
[6] Original post: https://tinyurl.com/r8snpes7; https://tinyurl.com/mvchabku.

Democracy requires active participation in democratic elections by informed citizens (Manin 1997; Przeworski et al. 1999). Fears that voters are too uninformed to meaningfully participate in democratic politics is as old as democracy itself, but now voters might be purposefully and strategically misinformed on a mass scale. McKay and Tenove (2021) also argue that disinformation threatens democracy by undermining citizens' capability to communicate on the basis of "facts and logic, moral respect, and democratic inclusion." This is also in part because many core democratic institutions – such as parties, organized interests, and mainstream media – are being challenged by social media and digital platforms (Persily and Tucker 2020). Democratic election campaigns are now reliant on the use of social media, including Twitter (X) (Jungherr 2015) and Facebook (Aral 2020), all of which are vulnerable to disinformation.

Disinformation is used to manipulate elections, namely in (1) the use of disinformation to target the voting process (election interference), and (2) disinformation that targets election outcomes (election influence).

The most direct attack on the democratic process is fake content created to disrupt political participation in the election – either by giving voters incorrect information about when, where, and how to vote, or engaging in voter suppression tactics designed to depress the turnout of specific groups in society. For example, in the US, voter suppression posts and digital ads were documented in the 2016, 2018, and 2020 US elections (Howard et al. 2018; Roose 2018; Ashok 2019; DiResta et al. 2019; Vandewalker 2020). Such attempts took many forms – some forms of disinformation were less sophisticated than others, and are more obviously fake to the casual viewer; for example, the hashtag #votenovember7th (Kim et al. 2018), or posts encouraging men to stay home so women votes could "count more" (Roose 2018). In particular, communities of color and other historically marginalized groups are being targeted by election falsehoods (Woolley 2022). Sophisticated messaging included incorrect information about voting, while other posts encouraged minority groups to refrain from participating, and some posts even focused on voter intimidation using threats of violence.

It is true that election-influence activities can come from foreign interference – meaning antidemocratic actors are using social media disinformation to attack and influence democratic elections in other countries (with various results). This was the case in the US in 2016 (Eady et al. 2023; Howard et al. 2018), and since then, the US has faced foreign interference attempts from Russia, China, Cuba, Iran, and Venezuela, among others (Crime and Security Research Institute 2021, National Intelligence Council 2021). Recently, China has been found to be engaging in foreign influence campaigns using Facebook, Twitter (X), and YouTube. Such campaigns are wide-ranging – in 2019, the Chinese government used social media to paint prodemocratic figures in Hong Kong as radical and dangerous (Lee Myers and Mozur 2019) in order to influence the 2020 elections in Taiwan (Quirk 2021).

Initially concerns about widescale voter suppression were related to foreign interference, thanks to the Russian IRA's (Internet Research Agency) efforts in using disinformation to influence the 2016 US presidential election (Bail et al. 2019).[7] As a result, governments across the world are now aware and actively combating the threat of foreign interference.

But we should also be aware that election interference campaigns are propagated by both domestic incumbent and opposition actors, and we should be worried about the increase in use of such tactics. Such campaigns are harder to defend against because they often hide behind the activities of normal democratic campaigning. But instead, disinformation campaigns to manipulate elections can discredit candidates or parties, or present false information about policies or platforms. These are organized by domestic actors (including political elites, citizens, and even the media) within a country, to advance partisan interests (Watts and Rothschild 2017; Benkler et al. 2018). A recent Freedom House Report found that domestic digital interference affected 88 percent of countries that held elections or referendums from June 2018 through May 2020.[8] Bradshaw and Howard (2019) similarly found evidence of organized social media manipulation campaigns in seventy countries as of 2019, where at least one party is using social media to shape domestic attitudes. In fifty-two of the countries, cyber troops used disinformation to mislead users, and in forty-five of the countries activities were focused on elections. This involved building an army of government or partisan actors who use strategies such as bots, trolls, or the illegal harvest of data to bully political opposition or journalists online; such cyber armies can also be assembled with minimum investment in infrastructure or personnel. The authors noted that Facebook is the dominant platform for such activity, though other studies have found that disinformation via social media or messaging apps is now playing a disruptive role in elections in developing countries, such as Nigeria (Cheeseman et al. 2020) or India and Brazil (Resende et al. 2019; Pereira et al. 2022).

One example comes from the 2016 presidential campaign in the Philippines, which was considered the first "social media election." Then-candidate Rodrigo Duterte used an extensive media campaign to amplify his message and smear opponents on Facebook, the predominant social media platform (Quitzon 2021). As a result of his systematic disinformation campaign, Duterte was the subject of 64 percent of all Philippine election-related conversations on the site the month before the election (Etter 2017). While in power, Duterte created an organized digital army of trolls and bots

---

[7] It's worth noting the IRA did not rely on explicit voter suppression. Cirone and Hobbs (2023) analyzed IRA messaging on Twitter (X) during the 2016 US presidential campaign. They found that direct forms of voter suppression, especially tweets encouraging election boycotts or discouraging users to vote, by IRA accounts was rare.

[8] See https://tinyurl.com/yc7t7r5e.

who used disinformation to manipulate voters, attack his political opponents, undermine national newspapers, and intimidate voters, via a network of real and fake Facebook pages. Fatima Gaw, assistant professor at the University of the Philippines (UP) Diliman, wrote that Duterte aims to "institutionalize disinformation at the state level" (Toquero 2022). The main opposition party copied many of these strategies in response; thus disinformation narratives also helped to distort the 2022 presidential election (Grounds and Goff 2022). This playbook is rapidly spreading – politicians in Brazil and India have adopted similar techniques to target voters with disinformation to win elections (Seo and Faris 2021).

11.2 TRUST IN DEMOCRATIC ELECTIONS

"#Wahlbetrug!"
> – a hashtag meaning election fraud, used almost 5,000 times on
> Twitter (X) within twenty-four hours of the June 6, 2021
> election in Germany[9]

Free and fair elections are a minimum requirement of a functioning democracy, but the health of the regime also requires faith in democratic institutions. Citizens must trust that elections are free and fair, and that the opposition will honor the outcome; this trust should also be nonpartisan. Such democratic norms provide the foundation for citizens' conception of democracy (Davis et al. 2021). Public trust in elections is also vital for regime legitimacy (Norris 2014), and if it erodes the democratic compact can unwind (Anderson et al. 2005). Recently, many argue that the commitment of leaders to democratic norms is also declining Levitsky and Ziblatt (2019) and citizens may become desensitized to democratic norm violations (Arceneaux and Truex 2022).

The media – and now social media – has a direct impact on citizens' perceptions of democratic politics. If social media narratives paint politics as dysfunctional, and enable widespread disinformation about the legitimacy of elections, it erodes trust and confidence in the democratic process (Coleman 2012; Belanger 2017). Social media can also provide a platform for and reinforce norm violations regarding democracy. Here, I focus on a specific tactic of disinformation that undermines faith in democratic elections – narratives about electoral integrity. Narratives that sow doubt in the electoral process can be propagated by coordinated, foreign interference campaigns (who seek to destabilize democracy), but the most recent and salient cases involve domestic actors; in particular, politicians who are losing and want to promote electoral fraud for political gain.

One key example is the #StopTheSteal movement in the US. The Trump presidency (2016–20) embarked on a systematic campaign to undermine US

[9] https://tinyurl.com/ypwwe9ka.

democracy and discredit the electoral process (Lieberman et al. 2019, Donovan et al. 2022), constantly pushing false statements that in-person voting machines and mail-in ballots were subject to fraud. These statements originated with then-President Trump (via statements, interviews, and social media posting) but were amplified across Facebook, Twitter (X), and other social media platforms by the RNC (Republican National Committee), Trump's campaign, party elites, and partisan news outlets (such as Fox and Breitbart) (Benkler et al. 2018). Stop the Steal was a disinformation and conspiracy-based narrative that claimed that the US was plagued by widespread electoral fraud, which laid a "justification" for Trump to refuse to concede the 2020 election; this was, of course, contrary to existing empirical evidence that there is no systematic voter fraud in the US (e.g., Wu et al. 2023).[10] On social media, this false narrative was tagged by supporters using #StopTheSteal, and in the days following the election, its use exploded on Twitter (X) and particularly Facebook; while social media platforms tried to moderate and remove thousands of pages and posts of false content, platforms struggled to contain the viral movement (Bond and Allyn 2021; Donovan et al. 2022). This movement would culminate in the January 6 insurrection.

Why was Stop the Steal so prevalent? The Stop the Steal narrative went viral, for a number of reasons. The Stop the Steal narrative was highly partisan and confirmed preexisting beliefs and identity politics; we know from studies of disinformation that this helps fake news spread (Bail 2016; Mason 2018; Osmundsen et al. 2020). There are a number of psychological reasons why people knowingly share misinformation that isn't related to accuracy – content that is controversial, unexpected, partisan, or provocative is more likely to be shared (Rudat and Buder 2015; Chen et al. 2015; Chadwick et al. 2018; Altay et al. 2022). Notably, this narrative was put in place and reinforced by elites, which bolstered its spread reach and legitimacy. On social media, internet users rely on endorsement cues (such as likes and shares), which are fueled by engagement-based algorithms that boost disinformation (Metzger et al. 2010; Li and Sakamoto 2014). Stop the Steal demonstrates how a false narrative, with no basis in truth, can quickly reach large number of citizens and mobilize antidemocratic actors (Donovan et al. 2022).

Disinformation about electoral integrity is not limited to the United Sates. The global reach of social media can also demonstrate to the world how successful electoral fraud narratives can be taken directly from the US playbook. The Institute for Strategic Dialogue (Craig et al. 2023) examined elections between January 2021 and January 2023 in France, Germany, Australia, and Brazil, and uncovered numerous attempts to spread voter fraud narratives.

We worry such incidences undermine faith in democratic institutions. Prior research has shown that across the world high levels of electoral fraud are

---

[10] Also see https://tinyurl.com/2dvb5z73.

associated with less satisfaction with democracy (Fortin-Rittenberger 2017). Norris (2019) does a comparative study using World Values Survey data to study perceptions of electoral integrity in established and new democracies, and finds that doubts about electoral integrity undermine general satisfaction with how democracy works. Recent work on disinformation in the United Sates has also shown that exposure to unfounded claims of voter fraud undermines confidence in democratic elections, especially among copartisans. Clayton et al. (2021) conducted a survey experiment during the 2020 US election to study the effect of exposure to Trump's claims of voter fraud on attitudes toward democracy. They found that while attacks on election integrity don't affect support for democracy, exposure to such rhetoric decreases trust in elections and increases beliefs that elections are rigged among Trump supporters. In the 2016 presidential election, and the 2018 midterm elections, Albertson and Guiler (2020) and Berlinski et al. (2021) found similar results, in that exposure to claims of manipulation and fraud confidence in electoral integrity but not democracy; however, Berlinski et al. (2021) also found that corrective messages from mainstream sources do *not* measurably reduce the damage these accusations inflict, suggesting electoral fraud narratives can do lasting damage.

But the risk doesn't stop there. Even more dangerously, disinformation creates false narratives that can then be used by antidemocratic actors as justifications for further restrictions on media freedom or the democratic process. For example, in the US the narrative of "election security concerns" has led to the widespread introduction of state-level laws making it harder for individuals to vote (Brennan Center 2022; Voting Rights Lab 2022). The active discussion and passage of these laws then reinforces the concept that the election is broken, further damaging democracy. Now both democratic and nondemocratic leaders globally are executing disinformation campaigns, persecuting journalists, and using disinformation as an excuse to further restrict media access (Gunitsky 2015). Election integrity is a serious issue, as Sinan Aral (2020) writes in his recent book *The Hype Machine*, "If our elections lack integrity, no amount of free speech or inclusion can save our democracies, because voting protects all other rights."

11.3 THE PROBLEM WITH ELITES

> "I'm more troubled by the fact that other Republican officials who clearly know better are going along with this, are humoring him in this fashion. It is one more step in delegitimizing not just the incoming Biden administration, but democracy generally. And that's a dangerous path."
>
> – Former US president Obama, discussing Trump's false claims of widespread voter fraud[11]

---

[11] https://tinyurl.com/4hfubjmz.

Disinformation regarding elections can come from a variety of sources, but election disinformation is increasingly coming from democratic elites and leaders. Autocrats are well known for using social media as information control and to discredit political opposition (Gunitsky 2015). But what's alarming is this is now a problem for democracies, where disinformation on social media can exploit both norms of the free market of ideas and the sheer volume of information made possible by new technologies. Elites can use disinformation to help win reelection, promote their policy agenda, or to avoid accountability for their performance in office (Flynn et al. 2017), and democratically elected politicians, leaders, and partisan media networks with extensive reach are creating and disseminating information effectively designed to undermine trust in democracy. But why should we consider elite disinformation a more dangerous trend? This is concerning because, generally, we know that citizens take cues from elites. Prior research has shown individuals are more likely to trust information that is presented by experts or political leaders (Brulle et al. 2012; LaChapelle et al. 2014). If elites are spreading disinformation, it is much more damaging than disinformation by the average social media user.

Political parties have purposely spread or amplified misinformation during democratic elections in Brazil (Dourado and Salgado 2021), Nigeria (Hassan 2019), and India (Gowen and Gowen 2018). Here, disinformation surrounding elections can spread via messaging apps, like WhatsApp, WeChat, or Telegram; a recent report by the Computational Propaganda Project at Oxford University documents that messaging services hosted disinformation campaigns in India, Brazil, Pakistan, Zimbabwe, China, Iran, Thailand, and Mexico. In particular, India, the world's largest democracy, has witnessed democratic political parties engaging in large-scale disinformation campaigns. Multiple parties, including the governing party the BJP, run large-scale misinformation campaigns via coordinated WhatsApp groups that attack opponents and minorities, and spread fake news; Prime Minister Narendra Modi's own smartphone app was also a source of misinformation (Funke 2019). A series of voter hoaxes went viral, depicting pictures of rigged voting machines and electoral fraud, also coming from democratic elites. Eventually, targeted disinformation in India resulted in violence and deaths by lynching (Poona and Bansal 2019).

Elite rhetoric is already having consequences for citizens' beliefs. The 2020 US presidential election was characterized by a widescale disinformation campaign alleging voter fraud. False and misleading claims were promoted by the president himself (Kessler and Rizzo 2020), and supported by party elites and conservative-funded media empires (Benkler et al. 2018; Darcy 2020). As a result, a number of studies have found that supporters of Trump were much more likely to believe and support lies relating to electoral fraud. Pennycook and Rand (2021) used survey data during the election and found that a majority (>77 percent) of Trump voters in their sample falsely believed that there was election fraud and that Trump won the election (despite no meaningful evidence of voter fraud). Other studies have found similar results, that Trump supporters increased belief in false claims. This narrative is also persistent, and could be an issue for future US presidential elections.

Finally, elite networks can coordinate and manipulate the media like never before. Billionaire elites are now influencing politics, constructing networks of wealthy donors and controlling media empires; the Koch network in the US used disinformation to attack democracy (MacLean 2020). Such actors have an immense amount of reach – Goel et al. (2016) studied a billion diffusion events on Twitter (X), and found that users with large audiences were the primary reason messages went viral, opposed to individual peer-to-peer transmissions. This can also be exploited by foreign actors – a key part of Moscow's strategy was using US media organizations and US officials to "launder" disinformation narratives in the US in 2020. Persily (2017) highlights the US case, and sums it up well in writing:

How does one characterize a campaign, for example, in which the chief strategist is also the chairman of a media website (Breitbart) that is the campaign's chief promoter and whose articles the candidate retweets to tens of millions of his followers, with those tweets then picked up and rebroadcast on cable-television news channels, including one (RT, formerly known as Russia Today) that is funded by a foreign government?

If influential and domestic media personalities coordinate, to push the same disinformation narratives, this is dangerous.

11.4 GOING FORWARD

Social media is here to stay, but that doesn't mean it has to have a negative effect on democratic elections. We know disinformation presents a significant threat to electoral integrity, democratic legitimacy, and public trust (Persily and Tucker 2020). But knowing all the challenges presented in this chapter, we can start to consider solutions. First and foremost, countries need to develop comprehensive plans to address disinformation, particularly during elections. Countries like Canada, Sweden, and Denmark developed comprehensive national security plans to address foreign disinformation; these plans tackled both cybersecurity but also media literacy and public resilience campaigns (Cederberg 2018; Jeangène Vilmer et al. 2018; Tenove 2020). France and Germany have adopted forceful electoral policies to counter misinformation during elections (Tworek and Leerssen 2019; Bayer 2021; Couzighou 2021). Governments should also encourage political parties to follow basic cybersecurity practices, and invest resources in combating disinformation (Brattberg and Maurer 2018; Ohlin 2021), as well as prosecute actors who obstruct people's right to vote.

Thankfully, there are many existing strategies to combat online disinformation, with empirical research to support their use (Wittenberg and Berinsky 2020). Kozyreva et al. (2024) provide a tool box of individual-level interventions, reviewing nine distinct types (accuracy prompts, debunking and rebuttals, friction, inoculation, lateral reading and verification strategies, media-literacy tips, social norms, source-credibility labels, and warning and fact-checking labels). Specifically for elections, one way to combat misperceptions is by the use of "prebunking," a new type of intervention that consists of preemptively warning and exposing individuals to misinformation narratives and strategies. Building on psychological inoculation theory, researchers argue that exposing people to weaker doses of misinformation can help them develop psychological resistance (or "mental antibodies") against such tactics (Roozenbeek and van der Linden 2018). Prebunking initiatives can be simple information campaigns, and executed by governmental or trusted organizations. In the case of democratic elections, government or electoral officials can publish information campaigns with accurate information aimed at preventing election fake news (Brennan Center 2022). Public information campaigns should be multilingual, and make sure to reach underrepresented groups that are often targeted by misinformation. Prebunking, and the use of social media more generally, should also be seen as a vehicle for prodemocratic narratives (Repucci 2019).

Mainstream media provides an important check against disinformation (Watts et al. 2021), and prior research has found an association between secure funding for public media systems and well-informed political cultures with high levels of engagement with democratic processes (Neff and Pickard 2021). It's clear the level of societal "resilience" to disinformation matters – cross-national research indicates countries with high levels of audience fragmentation, weak public service media, and a large digital advertising market will face problems with disinformation undermining democracy (Humprecht et al. 2020). A long-term election protection plan could include providing more public funding support for local mainstream print and digital news outlets. However, public funds can also be redirected by antidemocratic elites in power – the Fidesz government in Hungary is a recent case in point of using government funds to spread disinformation about opponents[12] – and so institutions should be made resilient to co-optation.

Social media platforms will need to play a considerable role in regulating content during democratic elections. It is now clear platforms have played a key role in fostering insurrections, violence, trafficking, and electoral fraud across the globe, and are struggling to define and consistently execute content moderation policies (*Wall Street Journal*: Facebook Files 2022). In the long term, there will need to be more regulation of social media companies; in the short term, however, this is complex, for a number of reasons. Economic incentives rule platform activity – platforms are for-profit entities; algorithms used by these companies maximize engagement (to gain advertising revenue), not accurate information. The economic clout and lobbying capabilities of

---

[12] https://tinyurl.com/yact5jkj.

powerful tech companies also make it difficult to hold platforms to account. Media regulation is also sensitive in liberal democracies because of potential impacts on freedom of expression; this problem is exacerbated if political parties are sources of disinformation.

Large-scale regulation revolves around to what extent to make platforms responsible for content. Debates in the US have been focused on modifying Section 230 of the Communications Decency Act (CDA), but this will be challenging and perhaps have adverse effects; instead, ancillary and independent regulation is more promising (Hwang 2020) and regulation can take many forms (Rochefort 2020). Meanwhile Europe is an example of innovation in social media regulation. Germany was notable for passing legislation that holds platforms accountable for unlawful content, and the EU GDPR establishes a comprehensive framework for consumer privacy and data protection (Fukuyama and Grotto 2020) that applies to all member states. The EU also created the Digital Services Act, which is a very significant step in regulating online platforms and search engines. More generally, any regulation should be independent from both partisan actors and leadership of the dominant social media companies (Epstein 2021)

While regulation is in development, it is important for governments, journalists, and the public to keep pressure on social media firms (Margetts 2019). This should be focused on two dimensions. First, to incentivize platforms to hire more foreign language staff for developing countries, invest in content moderation, and develop strategies to protect democratic elections (Brennan Center 2022; *Wall Street Journal*: Facebook Files 2022). Second, to pressure social media firms for more transparency, including the disclosure of platform data directly to the public or to researchers (MacCarthy 2022; Panditharatne 2022). Content aimed at voter suppression efforts can be moderated and removed by social media platforms. Facebook and Twitter (X) in particular have already removed thousands of fake posts, ads, and accounts that relate to voter suppression and intimidation during US and worldwide elections, but platforms must continue to aggressively police election disinformation.[13]

CONCLUSION

All this is not to say that social media is always bad for democracy or elections. It can be used to improve electoral participation, for example via voter turnout initiatives (Bond and Allyn 2021) and electoral campaigns (Jungherr et al. 2020), give underrepresented groups a voice in politics, and can foster largescale social movements, "hashtag activism," or regime protests (Jackson et al. 2020). But disinformation during elections is here to stay. And it's clear that there are democratic norms that need to be slowly rebuilt, by the very elite actors that are destroying them for political gain. Politicians or parties that

---

[13] https://tinyurl.com/2uaav342; April Glaser, 2018, Twitter Removed 10,000 Bots Pretending to Be Democrats Telling Other Democrats Not to Vote, SLATE (Nov. 2), https://tinyurl.com/zycevxe7.

spread disinformation should be held accountable at the ballot box, and rhetoric that is both partisan and antidemocratic should not be mistaken for polarization. Given the challenges highlighted in this chapter, ultimately there must be consequences for spreading disinformation, particularly for democratic leaders and elites.

But forewarned is forearmed – by understanding the threats disinformation poses for democratic elections, we can better insulate ourselves from the negative effects of social media. Widespread information campaigns and digital literacy, more resources invested during elections to counteract cyber-influence efforts, funding public media and professional journalism, and holding platforms accountable for disinformation are all ultimately achievable policy solutions to help protect democratic elections.

REFERENCES

Albertson, B. and Guiler, K. (2020). "Conspiracy Theories, Election Rigging, and Support for Democratic Norms." *Research & Politics* 7 (3): 2053168020959859. CrossRefGoogle Scholar.

Altay, S., de Araujo, E., and Mercier, H. (2022). "'If This Account Is True, It Is Most Enormously Wonderful': Interestingness-If-True and the Sharing of True and False News." *Digital Journalism*, 10 (3): 373–394. www.tandfonline.com/doi/full/10.1080/21670811.2021.1941163.

Anderson, C. J., Blais, A., Bowler, S., Donovan, T., and Listhaug, A. (2005). *Loser's Consent: Elections and Democratic Legitimacy*. Oxford: Oxford University Press.

Aral, S. (2020). *The Hype Machine*. New York, NY: Penguin Random House.

Arceneaux, K. and Truex, R. (2022). "Donald Trump and the Lie." *Perspectives on Politics* 21 (3): 863–879. doi:10.1017/S1537592722000901.

Ashok D., Luceri, L., Badaway, A., and Ferrara, E. (2019). Perils and Challenges of Social Media and Election Manipulation Analysis: The 2018 US Midterms. In Companion Proceedings of the 2019 World Wide Web Conference (WWW 2019). Association for Computing Machinery, New York, NY, 237–247. https://doi.org/10.1145/3308560.3316486.

Bail, C. A., Guay, B., Maloney, E., Combs, A., Sunshine Hillygus, D., Merhout, F., Freelon, D., and Volfovsky, A. (2019). "Assessing the Russian Internet Research Agency's Impact on the Political Attitudes and Behaviors of American Twitter Users in Late 2017." *Proceedings of the National Academy of Sciences* 117 (1): 243–250. https://doi.org/10.1073/pnas.1906420116.

Bail, C. A. (2016). "Emotional Feedback and the Viral Spread of Social Media Messages about Autism Spectrum Disorders." *American Journal of Public Health* 106 (7):1173–1180. doi: 10.2105/AJPH.2016.303181.

Bayer, J. (2021). Policies and Measures to Counter Disinformation in Germany: The Power of Informational Communities." Heinrich Böll Stiftung, October 13. https://tinyurl.com/mtbejmxw.

Bartels, L., Daxecker, U. E., Hyde, S. D., Lindberg, S. I., and Noorudin, I. (2023). "The Forum: Global Challenges to Democracy? Perspectives on Democratic Backsliding." *International Studies Review*. https://doi.org/10.1093/isr/viad019.

Belanger, E. (2017). "Political Trust and Voting Behavior." In *Handbook on Political Trust*. Eds S. Zmerli and T. W. G. van der Meer. Cheltenham: Edward Elgar Publishing, chapter 15.

Benkler, Y., Faris, R., and Roberts, H. (2018). *Network Propaganda: Manipulation, Disinformation, and Radicalization in American Politics*. New York, NY: Oxford Academic. https://doi.org/10.1093/oso/9780190923624.001.0001.

Berlinski, N., Doyle, M., Guess, A., Levy, G., Lyons, B., Montgomery, J., Nyhan, B., and Reifler, J. (2021). "The Effects of Unsubstantiated Claims of Voter Fraud on Confidence in Elections." *Journal of Experimental Political Science* 10 (1): 34–49. doi:10.1017/XPS.2021.18.

Bond, S. and Allyn, B. (2021). How the 'Stop the Steal' Movement Outwitted Facebook Ahead of the Jan. 6 Insurrection. NPR, October 22. www.npr.org/2021/10/22/1048543513/facebook-groups-jan-6-insurrection.

Bradshaw, S. and Howard, P. N. (2019). The Global Disinformation Order: 2019 Global Inventory of Organised Social Media Manipulation. Copyright, Fair Use, Scholarly Communication, etc. 207. https://digitalcommons.unl.edu/scholcom/207.

Brattberg, E. and Maurer, T. (2018). Russian Election Interference: Europe's Counter to Fake News and Cyber Attacks. Carnegie Endowment for International Peace Brief. May. https://tinyurl.com/yryrv5dr.

Brennan Center. (2022). https://tinyurl.com/y6k6nntz.

Brulle R. J., Carmichael J., and Jenkins J. C. (2012). "Shifting Public Opinion on Climate Change: An Empirical Assessment of Factors Influencing Concern over Climate Change in the US, 2002–2010." *Climatic Change* 114 (2): 169–188.

Cederberg, G. (2018). Catching Swedish Phish: How Sweden Is Protecting Its 2018 Elections. Cambridge: Belfer Center for Science and International Affairs, Harvard Kennedy School. https://tinyurl.com/2abxxkjm.

Chadwick, A., Vaccari C., and O'Loughlin B. (2018). "Do Tabloids Poison the Well of Social Media? Explaining Democratically Dysfunctional News Sharing." *New Media & Society* 20 (11): 4255–4274.

Chen, X., Sin, S. C. J., Theng, Y. L., and Lee, C. S. (2015) Why Do Social Media Users Share Misinformation? In Proceedings of the 15th ACM/IEEE-CS Joint Conference on Digital Libraries,111–114. ACM.

Cheeseman, N., Fisher, J., Hitchen, J., and Hassan, I. (2020). "Social Media Disruption: Nigeria's WhatsApp Politics." *Journal of Democracy* 31 (3): 145–159.

Cirone, A. and Hobbs, W. (2023). "Asymmetric Flooding as a Tool for Foreign Influence on Social Media." *Political Science Research and Methods* 11 (1): 160–171. doi:10.1017/psrm.2022.9.

Clayton, K., Davis, N. T., Nyhan, B., Porter, E., Ryan, T. J., and Wood, T. J. (2021). "Elite Rhetoric Can Undermine Democratic Norms." *Proceedings of the National Academy of Sciences* 118 (23): e2024125118.

Coleman, S. (2012). "Believing the News: From Sinking Trust to Atrophied Efficacy." *European Journal of Communication* 27 (1): 35–45. https://journals.sagepub.com/doi/full/10.1177/0267323112438806 .

Couzigou, I. (2021). "The French Legislation against Digital Information Manipulation in Electoral Campaigns: A Scope Limited by Freedom of Expression." *Election Law Journal: Rules, Politics, and Policy* 20 (1): 98–115.

Craig J., Simmons, C., and Bhatnagar, R. (2023). How January 6 Inspired Election Disinformation around the World. Institute for Strategic Dialogue, January 3. https://tinyurl.com/4vsrrzx9.

Crime and Security Research Institute. (2021). China-Linked Influence Operation on Twitter Detected Engaging with the Presidential Election. https://crimeandsecurity .org/feed/china-linked-io-us-2020.

Darcy, O. (2020). Fox News Hosts Sow Distrust in Legitimacy of Election. CNN Business, November 5. www.cnn.com/2020/11/05/media/fox-news-prime-time-election/index.html.

Davis, N. T., Goidel, K., and Zhao, Y. (2021). "The Meanings of Democracy among Mass Publics." *Social Indicators Research: An International and Interdisciplinary Journal for Quality-of-Life Measurement* 153 (3): 849–921.

DiResta, R., Shaffer, D., Ruppel, B., Sullivan, D., Matney, R., Fox, R., Albright, D., and Johnson, B. (2019). "The Tactics & Tropes of the Internet Research Agency." https://digitalcommons.unl.edu/senatedocs/2/.

Donovan, J., Dreyfuss, E., and Friedberg, B. (2022). *Meme Wars: The Untold Story of the Online Battles Upending Democracy in America.* London: Bloomsbury Publishing.

Dourado, T. and Salgado, S. (2021). "Disinformation in the Brazilian Pre-Election context: Probing the Content, Spread and Implications of Fake News About Lula da Silva." *The Communication Review* 24 (4): 297–319. https://doi.org/10.1080/10714421.2021.1981705.

Eady, G., Paskhalis, T., Zilinsky, J. et al. (2023). "Exposure to the Russian Internet Research Agency Foreign Influence Campaign on Twitter in the 2016 US Election and Its Relationship to Attitudes and Voting Behavior." *Nature Communications* 14 (62). https://doi.org/10.1038/s41467-022-35576-9.

Epstein, B. (2020). "Why It Is So Difficult to Regulate Disinformation Online." In *The Disinformation Age. SSRC Anxieties of Democracy.* Eds W. L. Bennett and S. Livingston. Cambridge: Cambridge University Press, pp. 190–210.

Etter, L. (2017). What Happens When the Government Uses Facebook as a Weapon? Bloomberg, December 7. https://tinyurl.com/55muvd2n.

Flynn, D. J., Nyhan, B., and Reifler, J. (2017). "The Nature and Origins of Misperceptions: Understanding False and Unsupported Beliefs About Politics." *Advances in Political Psychology* 38: 127–150. https://doi.org/10.1111/pops.12394.

Funke, D. (2019). India's Election Ends This Week. And at Least One Political Party Is Spreading Hoaxes about Voter Fraud. Pointer. May 23. https://tinyurl.com/mt54y5p4.

Fortin-Rittberger, J., Harfst, P., and Dingler, S. C. (2017). "The Costs of Electoral Fraud: Establishing the Link between Electoral Integrity, Winning an Election, and Satisfaction with Democracy." *Journal of Elections, Public Opinion and Parties* 27 (3): 350–368. https://pmc.ncbi.nlm.nih.gov/articles/PMC5546066/.

Fukuyama F. and Grotto, A. (2020). "Comparative Media Regulation in the United States and Europe." In *Social Media and Democracy: The State of the Field, Prospects for Reform (SSRC Anxieties of Democracy).* Eds N. Persily and J. Tucker. Cambridge: Cambridge University Press, pp. 199–219.

Goel, S., Anderson, A., Hofman, J., and Watts, D. J. (2016). "The Structural Virality of Online Diffusion." *Management Science* 62 (1): 180–196.

Gowen, A. and E. Dwoskin. (2018). WhatsApp Launches New Controls after Widespread App-Fuelled Mob Violence in India. Washington Post, July 19. https://tinyurl.com/y64kr9zv.

Grounds, K. and Goff, M. (2022). Disinformation, Disruption, and the Shifting Media Ecosystem in the 2022 Philippines Election. Asia Pacific Foundation of Canada, May 5 https://tinyurl.com/jzrvj6rr .

Gunitsky, S. (2015). "Corrupting the Cyber-Commons: Social Media as a Tool of Autocratic Stability." *Perspectives on Politics* 13 (1): 42–54. doi:10.1017/S1537592714003120.

Hassan, I. (2019). How Fake News Spreads, Sowing Distrust Ahead of Nigeria's Elections. *African Arguments*. https://africanarguments.org/2019/01/31/nigeria-fake-news-2019-election/.

Howard, P. N., Ganesh, B., Liotsiou, D., Kelly, J., and Francois, C. (2018). *The IRA, Social Media and Political Polarization in the United States, 2012–2018*. University of Oxford.

Humprecht, E., Esser F., and van Aelst, P. (2020). "Resilience to Online Disinformation: A Framework for Cross-National Comparative Research." *The International Journal of Press/Politics* 25 (3): 493–516.

Hwang, T. "Amendment of Section 230." (2020). In *Social Media and Democracy: The State of the Field, Prospects for Reform (SSRC Anxieties of Democracy)*. Eds N. Persily and J. Tucker. Cambridge: Cambridge University Press, p. 252. doi:10.1017/9781108890960.

Jackson, S. J., Bailey, M., and Foucault Welles, B. (2020). #HashtagActivism: Networks of Race and Gender Justice. Cambridge: MIT Press.

Jeangène Vilmer, J. B., Escorcia, A., Guillaume, M., and Herrera, J. (2018). Information Manipulation: A Challenge for Our Democracies. Report by the Policy Planning Staff (CAPS, Ministry for Europe and Foreign Affairs) and the Institute for Strategic Research (IRSEM, Ministry for the Armed Forces). www.diplomatie.gouv.fr/IMG/pdf/information_manipulation_rvb_cle838736.pdf.

Jungherr, A. (2016). "Twitter Use in Election Campaigns: A Systematic Literature Review." *Journal of Information Technology & Politics* 13 (1): 72–91. doi:10.1080/19331681.2015.1132401.

Jungherr, A., Rivero. G., and Gayo-Avello, D. (2020). "Retooling Politics." In *Retooling Politics: How Digital Media Are Shaping Democracy*. Eds A. Jungherr, G. Rivero, and D. Gayo-Avello. Cambridge: Cambridge University Press, pp. i–ii.

Kessler, G. and Rizzo, S. (2020). President Trump's False Claims of Vote Fraud: A Chronology. *The Washington Post*, November 5. https://tinyurl.com/4357s8pt.

Kim, Y. M., Hsu, J., Neiman, D., Kou, C., Bankston, L., Yun Kim, S., Heinrich, R., Baragwanath, R., and Raskutti, G. (2018). "The Stealth Media? Groups and Targets behind Divisive Issue Campaigns on Facebook." *Political Communication* 35 (4): 515–541. doi:10.1080/10584609.2018.1476425.

Kozyreva, A. et al. (2024). Toolbox of Individual-Level Interventions against Online Misinformation. Nature Human Behavior. https://doi.org/10.1038/s41562-024-01881-0.

Lachapelle, E., Montpetit, É., and Gauvin, J.-P. (2014). "Expert Framing and Political Worldviews." *Policy Studies Journal* 42 (4): 674–697. https://doi.org/10.1111/psj.12073.

Lee Myers, S. and Mozur, P. (2019). China Is Waging a Disinformation War against Hong Kong Protesters. *New York Times*, September 3. www.nytimes.com/2019/08/13/world/asia/hong-kong-protests-china.html.

Levitsky, S. and Ziblatt, D. (2019). *How Democracies Die*. Harlow, England: Penguin Books.

Li, H. and Sakamoto, Y. (2014) "Social Impacts in Social Media: An Examination of Perceived Truthfulness and Sharing of Information." *Computers in Human Behavior* 41: 278–287.

Lieberman, R., Mettler, S., Pepinsky, T., Roberts, K., and Valelly, R. (2019). "The Trump Presidency and American Democracy: A Historical and Comparative Analysis." *Perspectives on Politics* 17 (2): 470–479. doi:10.1017/S1537592718003286.

MacCarthy, M. (2022). Transparency Recommendations for Regulatory Regimes of Digital Platforms. CIGI Report, March 8. https://tinyurl.com/tzep28ur /.

MacLean, N. (2020). "'Since We Are Greatly Outnumbered'": Why and How the Koch Network Uses Disinformation to Thwart Democracy. In *The Disinformation Age (SSRC Anxieties of Democracy)*. Eds W. L. Bennett and S. Livingston. Cambridge: Cambridge University Press, pp. 120–150. doi:10.1017/9781108914628.005.

Manin, B. (1997). *The Principles of Representative Government (Themes in the Social Sciences)*. Cambridge: Cambridge University Press. doi:10.1017/CBO9780511659935.

Margetts, H. (2019). "Rethinking Democracy with Social Media." *The Political Quarterly* 90: 107–123. https://doi.org/10.1111/1467-923X.12574.

Mason, L. (2018). Uncivil Agreement. How Politics Became Our Identity. University of Chicago Press.

McKay, S. and Tenove, C. (2021). "Disinformation as a Threat to Deliberative Democracy." *Political Research Quarterly* 74 (3): 703–717.

Metzger, M. J., Flanagin, A. J., and Medders, R. B. (2010). "Social and Heuristic Approaches to Credibility Evaluation Online." *Journal of Communication* 60 (3): 413–439. doi:10.1111/j.1460-2466.2010.01488.x.

National Intelligence Council. (2021). Intelligence Community Assessment: Foreign Threats to the 2020 US Federal Elections. March 10. www.dni.gov/files/ODNI/documents/assessments/ICA-declass-16MAR21.pdf.

Neff, T. and Pickard, V. (2021). "Funding Democracy: Public Media and Democratic Health in 33 Countries." *The International Journal of Press/Politics* 29 (3). https://doi.org/10.1177/19401612211060255.

Norris, Pi. (2014). Why Electoral Integrity Matters. Cambridge: Cambridge University Press.

Norris, P. (2019). "Do Perceptions of Electoral Malpractice Undermine Democratic Satisfaction? The US in Comparative Perspective." *International Political Science Review* 40 (1): 5–22. https://doi.org/10.1177/0192512118806783.

Ohlin, J. D. (2021). A Roadmap for Fighting Election Interference. AJIL Unbound. AMA. c115: 69–73. doi:10.1017/aju.2020.87.

Osmundsen, M., Bor, A., Vahlstrup, P. B., Bechmann, A., and Petersen, M. (2020). Partisan Polarization Is the Primary Psychological Motivation behind Political Fake News Sharing on Twitter. March 25. https://doi.org/10.1017/S0003055421000290.

Panditharatne, M. (2022). Law Requiring Social Media Transparency Would Break New Ground. Brennan Center Report, April 6. https://tinyurl.com/423vw6x2.

Pennycook, G. and Rand, D. G. (2021). Research Note: Examining False Beliefs about Voter Fraud in the Wake of the 2020 Presidential Election. *Harvard Kennedy School (HKS) Misinformation Review.* https://doi.org/10.37016/mr-2020-51.

Pereira, G., Bueno Bojczuk Camargo, I., and Parks, L. (2022). "WhatsApp Disruptions in Brazil: A Content Analysis of User and News Media Responses, 2015–2018." *Global Media and Communication* 18 (1): 113–148. https://doi.org/10.1177/17427665211038530.

Persily, N. (2017). "Can Democracy Survive the Internet?" *Journal of Democracy* 28 (2), 63–76. https://doi.org/10.1353/jod.2017.0025.

Persily, N. and Tucker J. (2020). *Social Media and Democracy: The State of the Field, Prospects for Reform (SSRC Anxieties of Democracy).* Cambridge: Cambridge University Press.

Pew Research Center. (2022). Social Media Seen as Mostly Good for Democracy across Many Nations, but US, Is a Major Outlier. December. https://tinyurl.com/273wtwmj.

Poona, S. and Bansal, S. (2019). Misinformation Is Endangering India's Election. *The Atlantic*, April 1. https://tinyurl.com/yh4acc2u.

Przeworski, A., Stokes, S., and Manin, B. (Eds.). (1999). *Democracy, Accountability, and Representation (Cambridge Studies in the Theory of Democracy).* Cambridge: Cambridge University Press.

Quirk, D. (2021). "Lawfare in the Disinformation Age: Chinese Interference in Taiwan 2020 Elections." *Harvard International Law Journal* 62 (5): 525–567.

Quitzon, J. (2021). Social Media Misinformation and the 2022 Philippine Elections. Center for Strategic and International Studies, November 22. https://tinyurl.com/bde7d7c4 .

Repucci, S. (2019). Media Freedom: A Downward Spiral. Freedom House Report: Freedom and the Media 2019. https://tinyurl.com/2s3hfbws.

Resende, G., Melo, P., Reis, J. et al. (2019). Analyzing Textual (Mis)Information Shared in WhatsApp Groups. In Proceedings of the 10th ACM Conference on Web Science – WebSci19, Boston, July. https://dl.acm.org/doi/10.1145/3292522.3326029.

Rochefort, A. (2020). "Regulating Social Media Platforms: A Comparative Policy Analysis." *Communication Law and Policy* 25 (2): 225–260. doi:10.1080/10811680.2020.1735194.

Roozenbeek, J. and van der Linden, S. (2018). "The Fake News Game: Actively Inoculating against the Risk of Misinformation." *Journal of Risk Research* 22 (5): 570–580. https://doi.org/10.1080/13669877.2018.1443491.

Roose, K. (2018). "We Asked for Examples of Election Misinformation: You Delivered." *New York Times*, November 4. www.nytimes.com/2018/11/04/us/politics/election-misinformation-facebook.html.

Rudat, A. and Buder, J. (2015). "Making Retweeting Social: The Influence of Content and Context Information on Sharing News in Twitter." *Computers in Human Behavior* 46: 75–84. 10.1016/j.chb.2015.01.005.

Seo, H. and Faris, R. (2021). "Comparative Approaches to Mis/Disinformation: Introduction." *International Journal of Communication* 15: 1165–1172.

Tenove, C. (2020). "Protecting Democracy from Disinformation: Normative Threats and Policy Responses." *The International Journal of Press/Politics* 25 (3): 517–537. https://doi.org/10.1177/1940161220918740.

Theocharis, Y., Roberts, M. Barberá, P., and Tucker, J. (2017). "From Liberation to Turmoil: Social Media and Democracy." *Journal of Democracy* 28 (4): 46–59.

Tucker, J. et al. (2018). "Social Media, Political Polarization, and Political Disinformation: A Review of the Scientific Literature." https://tinyurl.com/52tu62sx. Pp. 1–29.

Toquero, L. (2022). Détente Instituionalized Disinformation, and Paved the Way for a Marcos Victory. rappler.com, June 19. https://tinyurl.com/w8at4cra.

Tworek, H. and Leerssen, P. (2019). An Analysis of Germany's NetzDG Law. Transatlantic. https://dare.uva.nl/search?identifier=3dc07e3e-a988-4f61-bb8c-388d903504a7.

Vandewalker, I. (2020). Digital Disinformation and Vote Suppression. Brennan Center for Justice Report. https://tinyurl.com/5fekzby3.

Voting Rights Lab. (2022). The State of State Election Law: A Review of 2021–22 and a First Look at 2023. December. https://votingrightslab.org/wp-content/uploads/2022/12/.

Wall Street Journal. The Facebook Files Archive. (2022). www.wsj.com/articles/facebook-files-xcheck-zuckerberg-elite-rules-11631541353.

Watts, D. J., Rothschild, D. M., and Mobius, M. (2021). "Measuring the News and Its Impact on Democracy." *Proceedings of the National Academy of Sciences* 118 (15). https://doi.org/10.1073/pnas.1912443118.

Watts, D. J. and Rothschild, D. M. (2017). Don't Blame the Election on Fake News: Blame It on the Media. *Columbia Journalism Review*. www.cjr.org/analysis/fake-news-media-election-trump.php.

Wittenberg, C. and Berinsky, A. (2020). "Misinformation and Its Correction." In *Social Media and Democracy: The State of the Field, Prospects for Reform*. Eds N. Persily and J. Tucker. Cambridge: Cambridge University Press, pp. 163–198.

Woolley, S. (2022). In Many Democracies, Disinformation Targets the Most Vulnerable. Center for International Governance Innovation. July 18. https://tinyurl.com/2evd3s83/.

Wu, J., Yorgason, C., Folsz, H., Handan-Nader, C., Myers, A., Nowacki, T., Thompson, D. M., Yoder, J., and Hall, A. B. (2023). Are Dead People Voting by Mail? Evidence from Washington State Administrative Records. Working Paper. https://tinyurl.com/yhtbk8ke.

12

The Indispensability of Dominance

M. Steven Fish

What does Donald Trump have that Hillary Clinton didn't? What does India's Narendra Modi have that Rahul Gandhi doesn't? Brazil's Jair Bolsonaro, that Fernando Haddad didn't (but that Luiz Inàcio Lula da Silva, aka Lula, does)? Vladimir Putin, that Grigory Yavlinsky didn't (but that Volodymyr Zelensky does)?

The answer lies in an area that liberal political strategists aren't focusing on, pollsters aren't measuring, and political scientists aren't studying: the politics of dominance. While twenty-first-century liberals pore over polls and focus on offering more attractive policies, illiberal leaders have grasped what neuroscientist Steven Stanton and colleagues have found: "Political elections are dominance competitions."[1]

Dominance is a *style* or a *way* of leadership. Unlike economic, cultural, or institutional conditions, political actors can control it themselves.

Many liberals have come to regard dominance as a dirty business, best left to authoritarians. But it is one of the most potentially powerful tools in every political actor's arsenal, and it can be used for good or ill. Liberals can overmatch their opponents on dominance while remaining true to their own principles.

Dominance is a way to win elections, and we now know that ceaseless electoral victories by liberal parties are the only way to ensure democracy's persistence. As attentive institution-builders and diligent rule-followers, liberals have long assumed that when it comes to electoral competition in democracies, norms and laws are sovereign. They often believe that electoral institutions are self-enforcing and that political actors will be punished for breaking them, whether by law enforcement in the case of outright illegality or by voters in the case of norm violations. But when some winners in elections are wont to

---

[1] Steven J. Stanton et al., "Dominance, Politics, and Physiology," *PLOS ONE* 4, 10, e7543, 2009.

resolve the dilemma they face by weaponizing institutions to enable themselves to remain in power even if voters turn against them, the antidotes liberals normally rely on to ensure perpetual free competition are no longer operative.

Voters' normative commitments to democracy may constrain illiberal parties. But if one of the major party's supporters fail to punish their leaders for violating norms of fair play or even the law, the key normative constraint on democracy-wrecking behavior may vanish in a flash. Separation of powers and institutional checks and balances can help check imperious behavior. But if an illiberal party gains control of all branches of government at the national level, as it did in India and Hungary and as it now threatens to do in the United States, democracy's days may be numbered.

In the United States, leveraging office to tilt the playing field to lock in permanent advantages is now the heart of one party's strategy. That means gerrymandering districts, taking control of the electoral machinery away from nonpartisan commissions and vesting it with Republican operatives who are willing to falsify results, loading the courts with extremists who have dubious commitments to the Constitution, depressing voter turnout among young people, Blacks, and the poor, threatening elections officials with violence, and discrediting the legitimacy of the electoral process by claiming that contests they lose are rigged.

Thus, resolving the winner's dilemma in a democracy-menacing manner isn't just an afterthought entertained by a slice of MAGAmen who like Viktor Orbán's style. It may be a necessary condition for the Republicans to hold power while pursuing policies that are out of step with majority opinion. Under such conditions, the only way to ensure the persistence of democracy is to make sure the Republicans consistently lose national elections until they return to behaving like a responsible conservative party. Self-government in America now depends, pure and simple, on the electoral performance of the Democratic Party. Everything else is details.

12.1 THEORY AND ELEMENTS OF DOMINANCE

In a nutshell, high-dominance leadership is *reality-shaping* and *conflict-embracing*, and it *favors the language of the aggressor, the righteous, and the triumphant*. Low-dominance leadership is *reality-taking* and *conflict-averse*, and it inclines to the *language of the aggressed-upon and the endangered*.

Reality-shaping means striving to make opinion. The archetypal high-dominance leader crafts a narrative that casts himself, his allies, and his forebears as intrepid, successful protagonists. Even if the past includes darkness and defeats, he offers a vision of redemption, celebrating past victories as harbingers of still greater glories to come. He treats narratives and beliefs that oppose his own as falsehoods, not valid alternatives. He asks not "What do the people want to hear?" but rather "What do I want the people to believe?" His message does not shift in sync with opinion polls. He does not assume his audience knows the truth – *his* truth – without perpetual reminders. He stays on the case until his listeners get it – and then he keeps reminding them. A reality-shaping leader can earn a reputation for courage, staunchness, and trustworthiness. He may also inspire intense loyalty in followers and bend opinion to suit his aims.

In addition to being reality-shaping, the high-dominance leader is *conflict-embracing*, especially when facing aggressive opponents. She is happiest on the attack and chafes at playing defense. If she says something that causes controversy, she doubles down rather than qualify or apologize. In cases where she errs, she has the courage to correct course and move on. She prefers preemption to reaction. She seeks to win outright and big, not just avoid loss. She is risk-acceptant, not risk-averse. She grasps that membership is rewarding only if one's team is distinctive and morally superior to its opponents, so she knows that forging a strong in-group identity among her supporters *requires* us-versus-them framing.[2] In particularly contentious situations, she treats opponents as foes, not would-be collaborators. A conflict-embracing leader can establish a reputation as an implacable, all-weather fighter, thus arousing allies, intimidating enemies, and impressing neutral parties. She can also enable the formation of strong in-group identity, which deepens bonds among her supporters and potentially attracts leaners and the unaffiliated.

Finally, the high-dominance leader's *language* reflects her reality-shaping and conflict-embracing orientation. She uses the argot of onslaught and conquest. Embracing provocative parlance, she sometimes uses transgressive language. When dealing with extremists, her rhetoric may belittle and ridicule, turning opponents into objects of scorn and contempt. She creates an image of herself as mighty and her opponent as weak; herself as a victor and her opponent as a loser; herself as capable and her opponent as hapless; herself as patriotic and her opponent as disloyal; herself as protector and her opponent as vulnerable; herself as righteous and her opponent as immoral. Above all, everything she says and does conveys *confidence*, *optimism*, and *exuberance*.

What do these concepts and categories have to do with why liberals so often fail to trounce even adversaries who are morally and experientially unqualified for office?

Everyone is familiar with the Republican phrase "owning the libs." It even has its own *Wikipedia* page: "The phrase 'own the libs' comes from slang usage of the word 'own,' meaning 'to dominate,' 'to defeat,' or, 'to humiliate'."[3] Liberals know they don't enjoy being "owned" but aren't sure what to do about it – or even whether anything should be done at all. The notion of turning the tables and *owning their opponents* instead rarely even occurs to them.

---

[2] Gulnaz Sharafutdinova, *Red Mirror: Putin's Leadership and Russia's Insecure Identity* (New York: Oxford University Press, 2020), p. 60.
[3] "Owning the Libs," *Wikipedia*.

But no one longs to be led by those who are dominated by others. This orientation is baked into our DNA. As psychologist Dan McAdams argues, the desire for dominant leaders is "very old, awesomely intuitive, and deeply ingrained." According to him, Trump prevailed in 2016 "because of a primal appeal that has generally gone unspoken. It is an appeal that derives ultimately from our human evolutionary heritage." Once in office, dominance remained Trump's trump card: "No US president in recent memory, and perhaps none ever, has tapped so effectively into the primal psychology of dominance." McAdams suggests that Trump had little *but* dominance going for him.[4]

Political scientist Jeffrey E. Cohen has examined the concept of strength in the context of presidential leadership. While noting the shortage of studies on "strong leadership," Cohen proposed several key traits that the public might see as signs of strength, including being "resolute ... not willing to back down ... tough ... in control of events." After examining public opinion polls between 1971 and 2008, he found: "No matter how the question is worded or the selections offered, strong leadership ranks as one of the most important traits that voters want in their ideal president."[5]

Some psychologists study what is known as "fearless dominance," which roughly means boldness. Psychologist Scott O. Lilienfeld and colleagues found that American presidents who score high on fearless dominance are more successful in elections, managing crises, and dealing with Congress.[6] As of 2012, the twentieth- and twenty-first-century American presidents who scored highest were Theodore Roosevelt, John F. Kennedy, Franklin D. Roosevelt, Ronald Reagan, Bill Clinton, George W. Bush, Dwight Eisenhower, and Lyndon B. Johnson. Other research suggests that the trait is positively associated with competence, ethical decision-making, persuasiveness, and heroism in leaders.[7]

High-dominance orientation isn't all that people seek in leaders. McAdams distinguishes between "dominance" leaders, who rely on shows of strength and mastery over others, and "prestige" leaders, who demonstrate "a degree of

---

[4] Dan P. McAdams, "The Appeal of the Primal Leader: Human Evolution and Donald J. Trump," *Evolutionary Studies in Imaginative Culture* 1, 2 (Fall 2017), pp. 1–13 (quoted pp. 2, 5).

[5] Jeffrey E. Cohen, *Presidential Leadership in Public Opinion* (New York: Cambridge University Press, 2015), pp. 14, 15, 33.

[6] Scott O. Lilienfeld et al., "Fearless Dominance and the U.S. Presidency: Implications of Psychopathic Personality Traits for Successful and Unsuccessful Political Leadership," *Journal of Personality and Social Psychology* 103, 3 (2012), pp. 489–505.

[7] Cameron Anderson and Gavin J. Kilduff, "Why Do Dominant Personalities Attain Influence in Face-to-Face Groups? The Competence-Signaling Effects of Trait Dominance," *Journal of Personality and Social Psychology* 96, 2 (2009), pp. 491–503; Gerben A. van Kleef et al., "No Guts, No Glory? How Risk-Taking Shapes Dominance, Prestige, and Leadership Endorsement," *Journal of Applied Psychology* 106, 11 (2021), pp. 1673–1697; and Hanna Aileen Genau and Gerhard Blickle, "Fearless Dominance: The Upside of Psychopathy?" in Derek Lusk and Theodore L. Hayes, eds., *Overcoming Bad Leadership in Organizations* (New York: Oxford University Press, 2022), pp. 423–441.

magnanimity, generosity, forbearance, and dignity in their leadership roles." Human evolution and growth in the complexity of communities led people to appreciate both qualities in their leaders.

These days, liberals almost always lead in the prestige department. This gives them an invaluable comparative advantage.

But prestige often isn't enough. As McAdams shows, people never quit seeking dominance in leaders. And there is no necessary contradiction between "dominance" and "prestige" qualities, as Presidents Roosevelt, Kennedy, Johnson, and Clinton showed. South Africa's Nelson Mandela, India's Jawaharlal Nehru, and Britain's Winston Churchill and Margaret Thatcher similarly exhibited an abundance of both high-dominance and high-prestige traits. Among contemporary leaders, Ukraine's Volodymyr Zelensky, Estonia's Kaja Kallas, Brazil's Luiz Inácio "Lula" da Silva, and Poland's Donald Tusk are high-prestige, high-dominance leaders.

Low-dominance leaders go into political battle with one hand tied behind their backs, and in recent years liberals have tended toward low dominance while their illiberal opponents have moved in the opposite direction. The trend is palpable in everyday politics, even if it has gone unobserved and undertheorized in political science.

12.2 THE DEMOCRATS' DOMINANCE DEFICIT

Nowhere is the trend more pronounced than in the United States, and nowhere is the partisan difference in dominance styles more glaring. In archetypal, exaggerated form, we may characterize the parties' orientations along each dimension of dominance as follows:

Reality-shaping versus reality-taking: While the Republicans try to make opinion, the Democrats take it. When opinion doesn't move their way, Republicans double down; the Democrats back down. The Republicans pursue even unpopular policies with abandon. The Democrats often refrain from defending even popular policies lest the polls turn against them. The Republicans act as if their policies have more support than they do; the Democrats act as if theirs have less. The Republicans tell voters what they think; the Democrats tell voters what they think they want to hear. The Republicans pound their own truths – whether true or not – into listeners' heads. The Democrats present their case now and then and hope their audience will remember. Republicans connect the dots for voters; the Democrats expect voters will make the inferences on their own. The Republicans treat even petty wins as conquests. The Democrats are loath to trumpet even their transformational feats.

Conflict-embracing versus conflict-averse: The Republicans savor conflict. They don't hesitate to treat the Democrats like enemies. The Democrats dislike conflict and find us-versus-them politics distasteful. The Republicans play offense; the Democrats play defense. When the Republicans say something controversial, they push forward; when Democrats cause a stir, they walk it back. The Republicans attack; the Democrats react. The Republicans accept risk and play to win; the Democrats abhor risk and hope not to lose. The Republicans' messaging tries to stoke their base; the Democrats' messaging aims not to stoke the Republican base.

Language of the aggressor, the righteous, and the triumphant versus that of the aggressed-upon and the endangered: The Republicans use entertaining, aggressive, provocative language; the Democrats bore with bromides. The Republicans cast themselves as imposing, indomitable, menacing, and triumphant; the Democrats present themselves as imposed upon, vulnerable, menaced, and in danger of defeat. The Republicans call their opponents weak, lame, gutless, pathetic, disloyal, unpatriotic, disgraceful, immoral, and disgusting. Democrats cast their adversaries as callous, unfair, ruthless, terrifying, hurtful, heartless, scary, and offensive. The Democrats call the Republicans bullies but leave them in charge of the playground.

This assessment obviously puts the matter starkly, without attention to nuance or exceptions. For the most part, however, twenty-first-century Democrats, including party leaders Joe Biden, Al Gore, John Kerry, and Hillary Clinton, have fallen short on dominance. The high-dominance orientation of many of their twentieth century forebears is conspicuous by its scarcity today.

When taken to extremes, high-dominance orientation can be a political liability. From one perspective, the Republicans' push for unpopular abortion bans showed temerity. Some Republicans may accept electoral losses as an acceptable trade-off for achieving a policy dream. But by all accounts, their radical abortion laws prevented their takeover of the Senate in the 2022 midterm elections, and the issue continues to dog them in 2024.[8] What is more, pressing the lie that Trump beat Biden in 2020, treating vaccines as deadly, and claiming climate change isn't happening go far beyond functional high-dominance reality-shaping and veer off into dysfunctional, delusional reality-rejection.

Authoritarians have fallen into this trap elsewhere as well, as with Vladimir Putin's invasion of Ukraine. Putin's belief that 200,000 Russian troops could easily conquer and annex an independence-minded nation of forty-four million people is what hubris-driven high-dominance irrationality looks like. Reality-shaping, if untempered by a grasp of the reality one seeks to influence, can lead to disaster.

But high-dominance overreach isn't a danger for liberals these days. They have the opposite problem – which helps explain how high-dominance

---

[8] Seth Masket, "Republicans Paid a Price for Overturning Roe. It May Have Been Worth It," *Politico*, November 19, 2022; Ashley Kirzinger, "How the Supreme Court's Dobbs Decision Played in the 2022 Midterm Election," *KKF*, November 11, 2022; and Jennifer Rubin, "Republicans' Abortion Woes Worsen," *Washington Post*, April 2, 2024.

authoritarians like Trump and Putin have forced the world to accommodate their twisted visions.

12.3 THE HIGH COST OF LOW-DOMINANCE LEADERSHIP

To American voters, the current-day Democrats' low-dominance ways may smell like weakness. In a 2022 CBS News survey on parties' traits, the most frequently cited description of the Democratic Party was "weak."[9] In a 2024 Gallup poll, 38 percent regarded Biden as "a strong and decisive leader," compared to 57 percent for Trump.[10]

A reputation for weakness may be a singularly damaging liability. In 2016 exit polls, more than twice as many voters said they wanted a "strong leader" as one who "shares my values" and "cares about people like me" combined, and Trump was regarded as the "stronger leader."[11] Similarly, 2020 exit polls showed that voters valued a "strong leader" over other qualities.[12]

During presidential election years beginning in the 1980s, the American National Election Studies has queried respondents on candidates' traits.[13] One question reads: "Think about the [Democratic/Republican] presidential candidate. In your opinion does the phrase 'provides strong leadership' describe the candidate extremely well, quite well, not too well, or not well at all?" "Strong leadership" is a reasonable proxy for high-dominance leadership.

In all five elections in which one candidate enjoyed an edge on perceptions of "strength," he won the election that November. In the remaining six elections, the candidates scored the same on strong leadership.

The survey also asks respondents whether they think each candidate "is knowledgeable." In five elections, the candidates tied on perceptions of knowledgeability; in three elections, the candidate seen as more knowledgeable prevailed; and in three, he or she lost the election. A reputation for knowledgeability might be a great thing, but it's not clear that it helps much in elections.

What about perceptions of whether the candidate cares? It's hard to think of anything Democratic candidates spend more energy conveying. What's less

[9] Anthony Salvanto et al., "More Americans Label Republican Party as Extreme and Democratic Party as Weak: CBS News Poll," *CBS News*, May 22, 2022.

[10] Jeffrey M. Jones, "Biden Bests Trump on Likability; Trump Seen as Better Leader," *Gallup News*, April 3, 2024.

[11] Steven Shepard, "Early Exit Polls: Voters Say They Want a 'Strong Leader,'" *Politico*, November 8, 2016; and Reena Flores, "Poll: Hillary Clinton, Donald Trump Neck-and-Neck in National Race," *CBS News*, June 29, 2016.

[12] "2020 Elections, National Exit Polls: How Different Groups Voted," *New York Times* (undated).

[13] American National Election Studies. Response categories were altered between the earlier surveys and those conducted since 2008, so the analysts recoded responses on a zero-to-one scale, which is what is used here.

clear is whether voters care about whether their leaders care. The candidate who was seen as more caring won five times and lost four times; one time the candidates were seen as equally caring.

In these studies, "strength" never loses. Knowledgeable and caring lose about half the time.

12.4 WHY DO LIBERALS DISLIKE DOMINANCE?

Trump's takeover of the Republicans helps explain his party's unequivocal embrace of dominance. Trump is all dominance all the time, and his party has become an expression of his personality and style.

The Democrats' current low-dominance ways are in part Trump-related. No liberal wants to be anything like Trump, whom McAdams characterizes as "an alpha chimp" who is ever engaged in a "charging display."[14] Defeat by Trump, moreover, ground down liberals' confidence. The conversion of the Republican Party into a cult of Trump and a democracy-destruction machine only deepened the Democrats' political PTSD.

Biden's 2020 victory boosted the Democrats but wasn't sufficient to remoralize them. The election showed once and for all that almost half the American nation cared less about democracy than about tax breaks, anti-wokeness, whiteness, or whatever else they get from Trump. His enduring suzerainty over his party even after his defeat and the January 6 insurrection, as well as the flabbergasting fact that espousing the Big Lie became a requisite for leadership in the party, made the Republicans seem even more ghastly and indomitable.[15] How does one go on the offensive against people who won't play defense even after defeat?

But Trump-trauma isn't the only reason for the Democrats' defensive, low-dominance orientation. Some requirements of high-dominance behavior may feel like violations of their own ethics and even liberal identities. A reality-shaping and conflict-embracing orientation requires treating opponents' claims as untruthful rather than as legitimate alternatives; giving expression to one's own aggressive impulses; believing in and asserting one's own superiority; regarding some opponents as implacable rather than neglected or misunderstood; and embracing an us-versus-them mentality. Each of these rubs many contemporary liberals the wrong way.

Writing in the wake of Al Gore's and then John Kerry's losses to George W. Bush, political psychologist Drew Westen argued: "Democrats tend to be conflicted about the appropriate use of aggression, and hence to hide their fear of confrontation behind the compassion, empathy, and tolerance that are central features of the morality of the left." According to Westen, Democrats

---

[14] McAdams, "The Appeal of the Primal Leader," p. 5.
[15] Ben Schrekinger, "Democrats Traumatized by 2016 Are Having Pre-midterms Nightmares," *Politico*, November 4, 2018.

have typically come to respond to opponents' attacks with a flurry of factual corrections, accusations of lying, expressions of disappointment, and complaints of unfair play – all of which, Westen says, "reinforces the view of Democrats as weak and woosie" and as "the supplicant to the attacker."[16]

Shortly after Trump beat Hillary Clinton, psychologist John T. Jost and psychoanalyst Orsolya Hunyady argued that the liberal "sees herself as driven by her own compassion and is therefore uncomfortable about her own competitive and aggressive impulses."[17] Embracing one's own superiority can be problematic as well. Since liberals often attach supreme value to equality, "[o]n some abstract level, liberals feel compelled to proclaim that conservative intuitions are equally acceptable, equally valuable, and equally valid to their own intuitions." Liberals therefore go to any lengths to sustain a good people/ bad leaders picture of politics: "They struggle to separate Trump and his actions from the people who elevated him to power, and in doing so, they retain the ability to be empathetic and critical ... Do conservatives engage in similar contortions of a political psychological nature? No, because their philosophy (and their psychology) does not require it."

Who, then, is to blame for the harms liberals see multiplying all around them? According to Jost and Hunyady, liberals' "psychological discomfort with placing blame squarely onto 'the other'" drives them to "introspection or 'self-examination'," a move that rarely happens among most authoritarian conservatives.

The liberals' mentality does not generate the basis for a robust us-versus-them mentality, an important component of high-dominance style. That requires regarding political foes as beyond the pale and responsible for their own actions. It requires "othering" them – and for many liberals, there is no higher crime. If MAGA Republicans are decent folks who are just duped by a bad leader, how can one regard them as enemies?

The felt need to affirm everyone's needs and desires and to engage in introspection are, in proper proportion, virtues, and they provide liberals with a distinct comparative advantage.

But like all virtues, they can become dysfunctional if taken to extremes. A no-enemies mentality is laudable when reality justifies it, but it can prevent actors from defending themselves when there really are barbarians at the gates. Introspection is necessary to making needed adjustments in tactics, but it can also lock one into self-recrimination and lead one to take responsibility for problems that are not of one's own making. Keen empathic inclination can even cause one to exaggerate the suffering of others and offer measures that make little sense to those one seeks to help.

---

[16] Drew Westen, *The Political Brain: The Role of Emotion in Deciding the Fate of the Nation* (New York: Public Affairs, 2007), pp. 160, 339.

[17] John T. Jost and Orsolya Hunyady, "Mass Psychology in the Age of Trump," *Democracy* 48 (Spring 2018), pp. 1–18 (quoted pp. 9–11).

Introspection and shouldering responsibility also offer the liberal an alternative to embracing harsh conflict. After all, the more he can focus on his own shortcomings, the less he must confront opponents aggressively. He can assure himself that if he just makes peoples' lives better, plays by the rules, and offers enough understanding, he can achieve his goals without continual, open confrontation.

12.5 SOME MANIFESTATIONS AND CONSEQUENCES OF LOW-DOMINANCE MESSAGING

These tendencies are manifest across multiple domains in the Democratic Party's messaging. One is found in the largely ineffectual way the party frames and responds to the challenge of working-class voters' defection to the Republicans. In the twenty-first century, the Democrats have largely turned away from the aggressive credit-claiming and optimistic spirit that characterized the party's approach between the time of Franklin D. Roosevelt and Bill Clinton toward a kind of pity party for working-class voters. Doleful condolences for "struggling working families" for whom the American Dream is "fading," "dying," or "slipping further and further away" have become the verbal coin of liberals' appeals on the economy – even while the Democrats are in power.[18] In many Democrats' telling, working-class voters feel neglected, uncared for, scared silly about the prices of their prescription drugs – and above all, in desperate need of a government-provided break. With only a bit of exaggeration, we could say that the Democrats' central message to working-class Americans has become: *The American Dream is dying – especially for people like you. The only way you can revive it is by accepting government aid. And if you're not smart enough to realize how desperately you need it, just wait until you get old and sick and the Republicans won't cover your preexisting conditions!*

There is every indication that working-class voters regard such messaging as more condescending than comforting, and little evidence that it is staunching the flow of this demographic to the Republicans. In 2016, 64 percent of noncollege-educated white voters chose Trump over a Democrat who ran on promises to pump government resources into working people's pockets. In 2020, after enacting a tax cut and other policies that disproportionately benefited the rich, Trump won 65 percent of noncollege whites. After a two-year spending blitz that aimed to boost working-class incomes under Biden,

---

[18] Katie Reilly, "Hillary Clinton Says She Regrets Part of Her 'Deplorables' Comment," *Time*, September 10, 2016; "Biden Campaign Press Release: Texas Congresswoman and Congressional Hispanic Caucus Member Sylvia Garcia Endorses Joe Biden for President," The American Presidency Project, February 19, 2020; Remarks of Pramila Jayapal, "How a Loss in Virginia, Close Race in New Jersey Could Affect Dem Midterm Plan," *PBS Newshour*, November 3, 2021; and Remarks by President Biden on the Authorization of the COVID-19 Vaccine for Children Ages 5 to 11, November 3, 2021.

66 percent of noncollege whites voted Republican in the 2022 midterms. Nor has the Democrats' approach proven effective among voters of color. After swinging to the GOP (Grand Old Party) by 8 percentage points between 2016 and 2020, Hispanic voters swung two more points toward that party in 2022. In a November 2023 CNN/SSRS poll, 46 percent of Hispanics and 23 percent of Blacks said they intended to vote for Trump; men of color overall split 49–46 percent for the Republican. Neither rising African American and Hispanic incomes nor Biden's exemplary record on civil rights is arresting the movement of nonwhites to the Republicans.[19]

Indeed, the Democrats' low-dominance, pathos-soaked messaging is failing across the demographic spectrum. In the 2022 Florida governor's race, Ron DeSantis scored a nineteen-point victory over the conflict-allergic Democratic former governor, Charlie Crist, who ran on listening to voters' kitchen-table concerns and healing partisan divisions. Hispanic voters were key: DeSantis won 58 percent of them, up from the 44 percent in 2018. And despite what liberals characterized as DeSantis's overtly racist policies and messaging, DeSantis even improved his standing among African Americans, from 14 to 17 percent between 2018 and 2022.[20]

In their explanation for their loss, Democrats predictably focused on their own ostensible failure to express their concern for voters' economic pain – neglecting the fact that Crist talked about little else in his campaign.[21] The Republicans offered a different take. Explaining DeSantis's impending landslide on the eve of the election, one Republican strategist remarked: "The key takeaway that I hear from Hispanics over and over again, is some variation of 'he [DeSantis] has cojones'."[22]

The Democrats' billowing spirit of pity and introspection also feeds a swelling current in twenty-first-century-liberal political culture: a well-intentioned but politically maladaptive cult of empathy that regards celebration of progress as tantamount to insensitivity to those who still suffer. They also seem to see celebration as politically hazardous, fearing it would leave still-suffering people feeling unloved and therefore more vulnerable to illiberal

[19] "Exit Polls," *CNN.com*, November 4, 2020; Timothy Noah, "The Democrats Lost Some Working-Class Support in the Mid-terms," *The New Republic*, November 10, 2022; Jennifer Agiesta, "CNN Poll: Trump Narrowly Leads Biden in Hypothetical Rematch," *CNN.com*, November 7, 2023; and "Cross-Tabs: October 2023 Times/Siena Poll of the 2024 Battlegrounds," *New York Times*, November 5, 2023.

[20] Carmen Sesin, "Why Florida Latinos Turned out in Favor of Republicans," *NBC News*, November 15, 2022; Adriana Gomez Licon and Steve Peoples, "GOP Rides Latino Support as Miami-Dade Turns Red," *Associated Press*, November 9, 2022; and "A Lesson in Racial Politics: Blacks Care about Issues More than They Care about Skin Color," *Clarion Ledger*, November 24, 2018.

[21] Margie Menzel, "Democrats Examine Their Mistakes in 2022: With a Focus on Black Voters," *WUSF Public Media*, November 21, 2022.

[22] Carmen Sesin, "Buoyed by Latinos, DeSantis Could Become the First Republican Candidate for Governor to Win Miami-Dade in 20 Years," *NBC News*, October 21, 2022.

demagogues' appeals. Liberals also may fear that salute and sanguinity will breed complacency and risk making them sound like their opponents.

The problem with such a mindset is that reveling in one's accomplishments and weaving them into a story that projects future triumphs is indispensable to bending public consciousness and opinion to one's own advantage. It's central to high-dominance leadership. Messaging shaped by fear of celebration risks leaving the base uninspired, independents unimpressed, opponents contemptuous, and voters in general clueless about the liberals' feats.

The Democrats' (non-)messaging on poverty provides an example. Most Americans have no idea that, thanks to the Democrats, child poverty plummeted by more than two-and-a-half times between 1993 and 2019. When Bill Clinton took office in 1993, 28 percent of American children lived in poverty; in 2019, 11 percent did. Poverty plunged in every state, and children in every group made stunning gains. And as if all that isn't good enough, in 2021 the overall child poverty rate fell to 5 percent, the lowest point on record.[23]

What is more, most of the drop is due to a gaggle of programs that Democrats championed over Republican resistance. Why do liberals fail to tell this extraordinary success story?

A writer at the *New York Times* inadvertently revealed the reason. Shortly after the *Times* reported the data, David Leonhardt wrote: "I am guessing that many readers are surprised to hear about the big drop in child poverty since the 1990s. I'll confess that I was – and I have been covering economics for the past two decades." Leonhardt speculated about the reason: "Journalists and academic experts ... worry that we will come off as blasé or Pollyannaish when we report good news ... I understand why many people are reluctant to focus on the poverty decline. The US has not solved poverty."[24]

Liberals do fear seeming blasé and Pollyannaish. Beyond that, they (perhaps subconsciously) reason, if people knew the good news, they might think we've come far enough. Perhaps worst of all, liberals fear sounding callous to those who are still poor.

But that approach undercuts liberals' messaging and fails to tell the truth.

The Democrats could brandish the news to shape public opinion on poverty and how to conquer it, while bolstering their reputations for efficacy.

Instead, they essentially *hide* the glad tidings – even from themselves.

Failure to celebrate progress and aggressively claim credit may undermine the Democrats with multiple constituencies. The effects may be especially damaging among those who are the most progressive and likely to vote for

---

[23] Dana Thomson et al., "Lessons from a Historic Decline in Child Poverty," *Child Trends*, 2022; Jason DeParle, "Expanded Safety Net Drives Sharp Drop in Child Poverty," *New York Times*, September 11, 2022; and Isaac Shapiro and Danilo Trisi, "Child Poverty Falls to Record Low, Comprehensive Measure Shows Stronger Government Policies Account for Long-Term Improvement," *Center on Budget and Policy Priorities*, October 5, 2017.

[24] David Leonhardt, "Poverty, Plunging," *New York Times*, September 14, 2022.

the Democrats but least likely to turn out at the polls: young Americans. Among voting-age Americans under 35 years of age, an overwhelming 76 percent say that the government is spending too little on poverty alleviation.[25]

Refusal to acclaim progress also risks making liberals look odd and ungrateful to nonprogressive but swayable voters. Acknowledging past strides is surely a better way to soften up nonprogressive independents and non-MAGA Republicans than conveying that nothing these folks have ever done or ever could do – paying higher taxes to fund food stamps, home energy assistance, and children's nutrition programs, contributing to charitable causes – would make a difference anyway. It bears noting that 70 percent of all Americans, including 66 percent of whites and 71 percent of working-class Americans, believe the government spends too little on fighting poverty.[26]

Failure to propagate gains also means declining to honor the sacrifice of those who lived and died for justice, and those who give their all for it today. It is difficult to see how the labors and lives of Jane Addams, Eleanor Roosevelt, Medgar Evers, and Robert F. Kennedy – or for that matter the countless thousands of activists whose names will never be known – are exalted by tacit denials that their work ever amounted to much.

In fact, hiding progress might dampen progressive activism and thereby shape politicians' perceptions in a manner that slants policy to the right. David E. Broockman and Christopher Skovron find that state legislators from both parties grossly overestimate their constituents' support for conservative positions, and the product is legislation that is out of sync with public opinion. The authors note: "[W]hile voter turnout for conservatives and liberals differs only slightly, conservatives have recently been significantly more likely to participate in the public sphere in other ways, such as by contacting their legislators or attending town hall meetings."[27] The authors don't offer an explanation for superior energy of Republican civil society, but one may speculate that the Republicans' habit of ceaselessly publicizing their wins might inspire political engagement more than liberals' bashfulness does. Evidence that spurring activism is best achieved by staying mum on progress for which one's own partisans are responsible is decidedly lacking in the literatures on social movements, civil society, and party competition.

The liberals' low-dominance refusal to take the win was on display in the 2022 midterms. During Biden's first year in office the American economy grew at its fastest rate since 1984. Growth slowed in 2022, but at the time of the election it stood at a respectable 3 percent. And there was more good news on

---

[25] General Social Survey (GSS); John Della Volpe, "Ring the Alarm," *JDV on Gen Z+*, June 15, 2023; and Myah Ward, "Young Voters Are Getting Less Likely to Identify as Dems. It Spells Trouble for Biden," *Politico*, July 13, 2023.

[26] GSS.

[27] David E. Broockman and Christopher Skovron, "Bias in Perceptions of Public Opinion Among Elites," *American Political Science Review* 112, 3 (August 2018), pp. 542–563 (quoted p. 542).

poverty as well, evidence that could powerfully bolster Biden's case for his dearest issue, the child tax credit: Two months before the election, the Census Bureau issued data showing that child poverty had taken another hit, declining from 11 percent in 2019 to 5 percent in 2021, on Biden's and the Democrats' watch. The overall poverty rate for all Americans fell to 8 percent, the lowest ever recorded. Yet, even as manufacturing was booming, labor power was escalating, unions were growing, and strikes were proliferating for the first time in half a century, the Democrats, as if acting on cue from their opponents, focused on the one piece of bad news: inflation.[28]

The Democrats even abandoned their plans to run on their treasured policies. After over a year of fretting that the Republicans would leave them nothing to run on, they managed to enact a raft of popular, high-ticket spending bills. Once the Republicans started calling the programs inflationary, however, the Democrats' strategy changed. As the *New York Times*'s Jim Tankersley noted three weeks before the election,

Democratic candidates in competitive Senate races this fall have spent little time on the trail or the airwaves touting the centerpiece provisions of their party's $1.9 trillion economic rescue package, which party leaders had hoped would help stave off losses in the House and Senate in midterm elections. In part, that is because the rescue plan has become fodder for Republicans to attack Democrats over rapidly rising prices, accusing them of overstimulating the economy with too much cash.

As a result, "Some Democrats worry that voters have been swayed by the persistent Republican argument that the aid was the driving factor behind rapidly rising prices of food, rent and other daily staples."[29]

Inflation was indeed a top concern for voters. But rather than simply assuming that voters would buy Republicans' arguments blaming the Democrats' programs, the Democrats could have told their own story of how Trump's best friends abroad, Putin and Saudi Arabia's Mohammed bin Salman, sent inflation soaring with their wars and production cuts while the Democrats' bold measures – the child tax credit, the American Rescue Plan, the Infrastructure and Jobs Act, the Inflation Reduction Act among them – enabled people to keep their heads above water even as prices rose. They could have fortified their case for the child tax credit by touting its proven effectiveness in lifting kids out of poverty.

Rather than invoke a heroic narrative of their conquest of want and defense of the common person, they recited bromides about their deep concerns for the anguish voters must be feeling over the rising price of a tankful for their Dodge Ram 3500s.

[28] John Creamer et al., "Poverty in the United States: 2021," US Census Bureau, September 13, 2022; and Jim Tankersley et al., "Factory Jobs are Booming Like It's the 1970s," *New York Times*, September 26, 2022.

[29] Jim Tankersley, "The Democrats Spent $2 Trillion to Save the Economy. They Don't Want to Talk about It," *New York Times*, October 16, 2022.

The Supreme Court's serendipitous repeal of Roe v. Wade gave the Democrats something to run on after they abandoned standing on their growth-and-equity-promoting economic policies. Together with the Republicans' nomination of deeply flawed Trump-endorsed candidates, it saved the Democrats from a rout in 2022.[30]

Whether such luck will hold for the Democrats during the 2024 showdown is unclear at the time of this writing. Throughout Biden's time in office, America's economy has grown at a rate that is the envy of other rich countries. By almost every measure, Biden's economy has outperformed Trump's, even once COVID is factored in. Biden's interventionist policies have arguably had the most powerful favorable effect on the economy of any president since Franklin D. Roosevelt.[31]

Yet, as of March 18, 2024, half of Americans said the economy was "getting worse," compared to a quarter who thought it was "getting better."[32]

The situation presents a snapshot of a much larger picture that spells constant trouble for the Democrats: Despite an avalanche of contrary evidence, Americans consistently think that the Republicans are superior at managing the economy.[33]

The enigma unravels when we focus on messaging. While he was in office, Trump picked a single indictor that did generally perform well, the stock market, and treated it as the supreme measure of economic performance. He hammered into voters' heads that they had him to credit for the roaring good times. The Republican messaging machine never fails to reinforce his story of glorious performance on their own party's watch.[34]

Voters often believe what their leaders tell them. In a January 2024 NBC News poll, respondents said they trusted Trump more than Biden on managing the economy. Trump enjoyed a 22-point advantage – the biggest edge of any candidate in the poll's history dating back to 1992.[35] In an April 2024 CNN

[30] Ashley Kirzinger, "How the Supreme Court's Decision Played in the 2022 Midterm Election"; and Nate Cohn, "Trump's Drag on Republicans Quantified: A Five Point Penalty," *New York Times*, November 16, 2022.
[31] Noah Sheidlower, "The US Economy Is Doing Way Better than the Rest of the Rich World," *Business Insider*, July 7, 2023; Bryan Mena, "The US Economy Grew at a Blistering Rate Despite High Interest Rates," *CNN.com*, October 26, 2023; Emily Peck, "Charted: Workers Win as Wage Growth Outpaces Inflation," *Axios*, February 5, 2024; Nicole Goodkind, "Dow Closes Just Points away from 40,000 as US Markets Rally to New Records," *CNN.com*, March 21, 2024; and Jeffrey Sonnenfeld and Steven Tian, "Bidenomics' Critics Are Being Proven Wrong. Happy Days Are Here Again," *Fortune*, July 23, 2023.
[32] "State of the US Economy," *YouGov*, March 18, 2024.
[33] Timothy Noah, "No, the Republicans Aren't Better at Managing the Economy than the Democrats," *The New Republic*, May 3, 2022.
[34] Jonnelle Marte, "Trump Touts Stock Market Run, but Who Benefits?" *Reuters*, February 5, 2020; Gene Marks, "Fellow Republicans, It's Time to Admit that the US Economy Isn't Bad," *The Guardian*, January 21, 2024.
[35] "NBC News Poll: January 2024." See also David Brooks, "The Political Failure of Bidenomics," *New York Times*, February 22, 2024.

poll, 55 percent said they saw Trump's presidency as a success, compared to 39 percent who rated Biden's presidency as a success.[36]

Such conditions are making a hash of Biden's effort to make the election a referendum on Trump rather a celebration of his own accomplishments – itself a signature low-dominance strategy. And even if the Democrats manage to squeak by on the Republicans' abortion bans and Trump's sheer awfulness in 2024, the question remains as to how the Democrats can win – and how democracy will survive in America – if the Republicans eventually ease up on their deeply unpopular policies and replace Trump with a figure like Orbán or Modi, one who combines high-dominance orientation with political astuteness and disciplined party organization.

12.6 WHY LIBERALS NEED NOT RECOIL FROM DOMINANCE

Twenty-first-century liberals look askance at dominance politics. They tend to regard it as bellicose (and even violent), exclusively (and even toxically) masculine, personalist (and antipluralistic), dictatorial (and therefore undemocratic), hubristic (and thus prone to create calamity), selfish (and disdainful of the interests of others), uncivilized (and thereby regressive), and rightist (and ergo antiprogressive).

But high-dominance leadership need be none of the things that liberals detest. Contemporary world history knows no expression of higher dominance orientation than the Freedom Riders.[37] They were the young Black and white activists who electrified the world by riding buses into the Deep South to protest the nonenforcement of Supreme Court decisions banning segregation of public transportation. They encountered violent mobs along their 1961 journey. But even when the police would not protect them and hospitals would not treat their wounds, they pushed on anyway.

John Lewis, Diana Nash, James Farmer, and their fellow Riders were high-dominance archetypes. They sought to refashion reality, not accommodate themselves to it. They disdained public opinion. They forged a spectacular heroic narrative that inspired generations thereafter. Their antiviolent courage altered opinion and propelled legislation that enfranchised African Americans and finally made the United States a full democracy.

They were brazenly conflict-embracing. They barged into areas where they were hated and attended church services surrounded by mobs wielding baseball bats and bicycle chains. They were whipped, clubbed, jeered, and jailed, but they just kept going. Playing defense was not for them.

They spoke the language of winning and redemption. One searches in vain for doubt, complaint, defeatism, or defensiveness in their public statements.

---

[36] Stephen Collinson, "Biden Is up against Nostalgia for Trump," *CNN.com*, April 29, 2024.
[37] Raymond Arsenault, *Freedom Riders: 1961 and the Struggle for Racial Justice* (New York: Oxford University Press, 2006).

Nor did the Freedom Riders fit any of the other negative stereotypes of high-dominance leadership. They were led collectively, in part by women. They were anti-authoritarian, lacking in hubris. They were other-regarding, nonviolent, and militantly progressive.

And they were *stronger* than the racists as well. In the decades after their audacious sojourns, the nation's laws and opinions on intermarriage and integrated schools and housing underwent radical liberalization.

Such high-dominance style was standard practice for Democratic elites during the middle third of the twentieth century as well, and it enabled the enactment of every progressive program their low-dominance successors are staging a rearguard effort to salvage today. On the eve of his first reelection, Franklin D. Roosevelt thundered, in words that a bolder Biden could readily borrow: "I should like to have it said of my first Administration that in it the forces of selfishness and of lust for power met their match. I should like to have it said of my second Administration that in it these forces met their master."[38] Kennedy hammered home that the Republicans' limp social welfare policies and tepid approach to civil rights failed to show the world what America was made of, and he never hesitated to trumpet triumphs.[39] Lyndon B. Johnson's high-dominance – perhaps hyper-dominance would be a more apt term – style mixed bigot-busting rhetoric with ferocious arm-twisting to muscle voting rights, color-blind immigration policy, and Medicare into law.[40] No one was less solicitous of prevailing opinion and more intent on transforming it than Martin Luther King. At the height of his fame and influence, his conscience compelled him to take up the yoke of opposing the Vietnam War.[41] The shift dimmed his popularity, and like his Galilean lord, he was murdered amidst a diminishing band of supporters. Only a half-decade after his assassination – and many thousands of dead Americans and Vietnamese later – would public opinion finally converge with his own.[42]

King's masterful takedowns of civil rights' enemies exemplify his own distinctive high-dominance messaging style. In his "Speech on the Civil Rights

[38] Franklin D. Roosevelt, Speech at Madison Square Garden, October 31, 1936, *YouTube*.

[39] John F. Kennedy, Election Eve Speech, Boston Garden, November 7, 1960, *YouTube*; and John F. Kennedy, "Remarks Intended for Delivery to the Texas State Committee in the Municipal Auditorium in Austin, November 22, 1963 [Undelivered]," John F. Kennedy Presidential Museum and Library.

[40] Lyndon B. Johnson, Speech before Congress on Voting Rights, March 15, 1965, Presidential Speeches, University of Virginia Miller Center; Lyndon B. Johnson, Remarks at the Signing of the Immigration Bill, Liberty Island, New York, October 3, 1965, The American Presidency Project, University of California, Santa Barbara; and Robert A. Caro, *The Years of Lyndon Johnson: Master of the Senate* (New York: Vintage, 2002).

[41] Martin Luther King, Jr., "Beyond Vietnam: A Time to Break Silence," *BlackPast*, January 28, 2007.

[42] Frank Newport, "Martin Luther King Jr.: Revered More after Death than before," *Gallup News*, January 16, 2006; and James C. Cobb, "When Martin Luther King Jr. Was Killed, He Was Less Popular than Donald Trump Is Today," *USA Today*, April 4, 2018.

Movement in the United States and the Anti-Apartheid Movement in South Africa," delivered in London en route to receive the Nobel Peace Prize in 1964, King took on Barry Goldwater, the 1964 American Republican presidential nominee who opposed all manner of civil rights legislation. King said that he could "go halfway with Brother Goldwater" on the idea that legislation couldn't solve racism. With tongue planted firmly in cheek, he then smoothly eviscerated Goldwater's stance: "It may be true that the law can't make a man love me, but it can restrain him from lynching me." King's reference to "Brother Goldwater" bore no hint of sarcasm. But King also knew that he was owning his opponent by wielding what he always called "the weapon of love" to establish moral superiority. With his uncompromising, high-dominance eloquence, King never gave his opponents a chance.[43]

King, like Roosevelt, Kennedy, and Johnson, exerted dominance in liberal ways and to prodemocratic ends. Unlike high-dominance authoritarians such as Trump and Putin, these leaders obeyed the law, told the truth, and honored liberal values. None cultivated adulatory cults to themselves. While Trump conveys "only I can do it," much the way all dictators and would-be dictators do, King argued that no unaided human power – still less a single leader such as himself – could serve as history's agent. Only a whole justice-seeking people, guided by Providence itself, could take on such a role.

Similarly, Mohandas Gandhi's and Jawaharlal Nehru's reality-shaping, conflict-embracing command of India's anticolonial struggle was marked by its pacifism, democratic drive, and other-regarding motivations. Their indomitable high-dominance messaging enabled them to forge a hegemonic political party, the Indian National Congress (INC), as well as a brilliant liberal-national narrative that dominated Indian politics until Modi's ethnonational narrative eclipsed it.

Before 2024, Modi's high-dominance style went unmatched by his liberal opponents. India's economic growth slowed during Modi's first term (2014–2019), creating an opening for an INC comeback. But in 2019, the INC was led by Rahul Gandhi, who never tired of assuring audiences that he genuinely loved the man he sought to unseat as prime minister.[44] Four years later, Nehru's gluten-free great-grandson completed his Bharat Jodo Yatra, a 3,750-kilometer trek through the country to reignite support for his party, by opening up about his eating habits ("Telangana was a bit spicy for me. Chilies were over the top. There I struggled. I don't eat that much chilies").[45] Yet in the 2024 campaign, Rahul adopted harder rhetoric and excoriated Modi for abandoning India's

---

[43] Martin Luther King, "Speech on the Civil Rights Movement in the United States and the Anti-Apartheid Movement in South Africa," December 7, 1964, London, reprinted in *Democracy Now!* January 21, 2019.

[44] "I Genuinely Feel Love for Modi: Raul Gandhi on Why He Hugged the PM," *YouTube*, March 13, 2019.

[45] "Bharat Jodo Yatra," *Indian Express*, January 23, 2023.

tradition of democracy and tolerance. Modi's party lost seats to Rahul's coalition, forcing Modi to rely on coalition partners to form a government.[46]

To be sure, liberal high-dominance leadership is in evidence in many places, and nowhere more than in Brazil. Lula has long called Bolsonaristas what they are without the craven qualifiers – "semi," "pseudo," "quasi" – that most Democratic leaders, and notably Biden, prefer for America's MAGA fascists. During Bolsonaro's term, Lula used language that emasculated, ridiculed, and belittled the then-president and his supporters for their assault on democracy, regressive economics, destruction of the Amazon rainforest, and vax-skepticism. Overmatching Bolsonaro's dominance helped Lula beat Bolsonaro in October 2022 – and save Brazilian democracy in the bargain. When Bolsonaro supporters then ransacked government buildings in Brasília a week after Lula's inauguration, the new president thundered against the "vandals, neo-fascists, and fanatics" and followed up with a promise to vanquish the "new monster" that is the "fanatical far right." Lula's reality-shaping, conflict-embracing, hard-talking messaging might help explain why all of Brazil's parliamentary parties – including Bolsonaro's – condemned the January 8, 2023 attacks.[47]

Nor is liberal high-dominance leadership distinctly male, as the women leading the push against Putin in Europe demonstrate. Chief among them is the indomitable president of the European Commission, Ursula von der Leyen. The Estonian prime minister, Kaja Kallas, has become the go-to person for incisive insights on Putin and Russian imperialism.[48] The former Finnish prime minister, Sanna Marin, helped guide her country's accession to NATO, and her response to a reporter's question on Biden's suggestion that Putin might need a face-saving escape from the fix he created for himself by invading Ukraine provided a glimpse into how she deals with Putin. From her pithy response ("The way out of the conflict is for Russia to leave Ukraine. That's the way out of the conflict") to her derisive chuckle, as she walked away from the reporter, at the ridiculous premise that Putin could be appeased, the glamorous thirty-six year old furnished a twenty-nine-second display of high-dominance messaging. And this is the kind of leadership that delights as well as inspires: Two days after she made her statement it had been viewed online over four million times.[49]

These cases bear out Deborah Jordan Brooks's landmark study, which concluded: "I do not find any evidence that women face a gendered double

---

[46] Samanth Subramanian, "Time Is Running Out for Rahul Gandhi's Vision of India," *New York Times*, April 22, 2024.

[47] "Brazil Protests: Lula Vows to Punish 'Neo-Fascists' after Bolsonaro Supporters Storm Congress," *The Guardian*, January 8, 2023. "Brazil's Lula Vows to Defeat 'Fanatical Far Right' after January 8 Riots," *Agence France-Press*, January 20, 2022.

[48] Steven Erlanger, "Estonia's Tough Voice on Ukraine Urges No Compromise with Putin," *New York Times*, May 16, 2022; and Jeremy Cliffe, "Europe's New Iron Lady: Estonian Prime Minister Kaja Kallas," *The New Statesman*, May 11, 2022.

[49] Nick Mordowanec, "Video of Finnish PM Explaining Putin's 'Way Out' of Ukraine Viewed 4M Times," *Newsweek*, October 7, 2022.

bind. In fact, to the extent that any of the results are related to candidate gender, it is that women *benefit* from toughness more than their male counterparts on a couple of key measures" (emphasis in the original).[50]

12.7 DOMINANCE FOREGONE, DOMINANCE READILY WITHIN REACH

Liberals yearn for dominance as much as anyone else, even if they are uncomfortable admitting it. They show as much when one of their own breaks the liberal low-dominance norm. As Trump delivered his State of the Union Address in 2019, Nancy Pelosi offered a witheringly condescending look and mock applause – and the images went viral. Governor Gavin Newsom picked a fight with his Sunshine State counterpart, whom he (accidentally on purpose) called "Ron DeSantos." Admonishing his copartisans to take on DeSantis's textbook bans and assaults on LGBT rights, he asked: "Where is the Democratic Party? Why aren't we standing up more firmly, more resolutely? ... where's the counteroffensive?" – and Democrats nationwide broke into speculation about him replacing Biden in 2024.[51] Rep. Jasmine Crockett's lawyerly but gleeful assaults on MAGA colleagues in the House of Representatives are portraits of high-dominance messaging. The attention Crockett is getting from elated Democrats, and the MAGA media's jittery efforts to pull her down, demonstrate the payoffs of her departure from the low-dominance norm.[52]

Biden's Republican-owning 2024 State of the Union Address and his staff's decision to leak the briny language he uses to describe Trump in private delighted the Democrats – and won rare kudos from Republican strategists.[53] But these flashes of dominance aren't nearly enough to change the game.

On the global stage, Biden is no stranger to high-dominance leadership. He's got Putin's number and shows no inclination to appease him. He doesn't react to his opponents' moves; he heads them off. He weaponizes intelligence by publicizing Putin's plans in advance, often preempting Russian attacks.

[50] Deborah J. Brooks, *He Runs, She Runs: Why Gender Stereotypes Do Not Harm Women Candidates* (Princeton, NJ: Princeton University Press, 2013), p. 111 (emphasis in the original).

[51] Eric Ting, "Gavin Newsom Goes Scorched Earth on Ron DeSantis, Joe Manchin, Democratic Party, More over Roe v. Wade News," *SFGate*, May 4, 2022.

[52] Walter Einenkel, "Rep. Crockett Has 5 Minutes of Mic-Drop Moments during Impeachment Hearing," *Daily Kos*, September 28, 2023; Grace Yarrow, "Dallas Congresswoman Jasmine Crockett Is Going Viral – Just the Way She Wants It," *The Texas Tribune*, January 15, 2024; and Alexander Hall, "Texas Democrat Roasted for Claiming Biden Only Guilty of Loving Hunter 'Unconditionally,'" *Fox News*, September 29, 2023.

[53] Zeke Miller and Seung Min Kim, "Biden Uses Feisty State of the Union to Contrast with Trump, Sell Voters on a Second Term," *Associated Press*, March 8, 2024; Ashlee Banks, "Congressional Democrats Praise Biden after State of the Union Address," *The Grio*, March 8, 2024; and Kristine Parks, "CNN Finds Biden Relatable after Reportedly Cursing at Trump in Private: 'Connects' with Voters," *Fox News*, February 2, 2024.

Ignoring critics on the left and the right, he leans on allies in a hundred ways to maintain unity in support of Ukraine. He slaps stiff controls on American exports of technology to China at the very moment Xi Jinping declares himself dictator for life. He sticks up for freedom rhetorically as well as militarily, framing the conflict between democracies and autocracies in appropriately black-and-white terms.

The fruits of his high-dominance ways are manifold: an invigorated Western alliance; restoration of American prestige; and despots who thought democracies were dissolute learning the hard way to respect people who govern themselves.[54]

In short, in foreign affairs Biden shows a face that he rarely reveals at home. He shapes reality rather than just taking it. He acts boldly, without being stymied by anticipation of his opponents' reactions. He embraces conflict rather than avoiding it. He embraces risk and prefers playing offense. He doesn't shrink from the language of wickedness and righteousness. If Biden and his party treated democracy's foes at home like they deal with them in the outside world, the possibility of a second Trump term might seem far-fetched.

Biden and his party treat their delivery of the world from Putin's clutches like they treat the delivery of millions of children from poverty: They leave the good news untold and largely ignore it in their messaging. They neglect to hammer at what would have happened had Putin's favorite won in 2020 – a rudderless West, an enslaved Ukraine, a panicked Europe, and an America left to Putin's and Xi's predations. They act as if voters wouldn't care anyway, and make little effort to shape their visions and opinions. Biden's failure ever to make a vigorous prime-time speech on the urgency of aiding Ukraine might have enabled the pro-Putin faction in the Republican Party to halt aid and gravely endanger Ukraine's war effort for months, until an eleventh-hour deal finally reopened the flow in April 2024. Recognizing that high-dominance messaging is as important to defeating Putin's favorite American party and leader as it is to putting down Putin may ultimately determine whether democracy survives in the United States – and whether the American government remains on the side of democracy in the world.

---

[54] Richard Wike et al., "International Public Opinion of the US Remains Positive," Pew Research Center, June 22, 2022; Anne Applebaum, "The Brutal Alternate World in Which the US Abandoned Ukraine," *The Atlantic*, December 22, 2022.

PART III

INTERNATIONAL DIMENSIONS OF THE STRUGGLE
BETWEEN DEMOCRACY AND AUTOCRACY

13

The Security Imperative and Right Nationalist Politics in Contemporary Europe

Mabel Berezin

13.1 TRACKING THE NATIONALIST RIGHT FROM OUTRAGE TO QUIESCENCE

In 2000, the Austrian Freedom Party (FPÖ) under the leadership of Jorg Haider became part of a national governing coalition. The coalition generated outrage in Austria and throughout Europe. Fourteen European Union (EU) member states issued sanctions against the Austrian government. The FPÖ was right wing and had Nazi roots. Including such a party in a democratic governing coalition violated the cordon sanitaire that postwar European governments had established against any party that even suggested right-wing extremism. The sanctions, and the continental outrage, lasted a mere five months. Business went on as usual and the coalition itself lasted a mere two years. But there was outrage – if only temporary (Mueller 2000; Judt 2000).

Fast forward to 2022 where the nationalist right dominated spring and fall national elections. Viktor Orban returned to leadership in Hungary with a greater margin of victory than even he with his electoral rigging thought possible (Scheppele 2022). In the second round of the 2022 French presidential election, Marine Le Pen received 42 percent of the votes. She came closer to Emmanuel Macron than she had in the 2017 election where she received only 34 percent of the votes. To her surprise, Le Pen's party the *Rassemblement National* (RN) won eighty-nine seats in the June elections for the National Assembly.[1] The Sweden Democrats managed to obtain 21 percent of the vote in the September parliamentary election (Elgenius and Rydgren 2024). The Italian general election in mid-September was the *coup de grâce*. Giorgia Meloni leader of the *Fratelli d'Italia* a right-wing nationalist party sailed to victory as prime minister. Hardly noticed in the 2018 Italian

---

[1] French election figures cited in this chapter come from www.archives-resultats-elections.interieur.gouv.fr/.

elections where they polled 4 percent of the vote, the *Fratelli* won in 2022 with a solid 26 percent. Meloni had been a member of the *Aleanza Nazionale* (AN) a party that Gianfranco Fini founded in 1994 from the remains of the *Movimento Sociale Italiano* (MSI, Italian Social Movement) a party that had direct roots back to Mussolini's fascist party (Puleo and Piccolino 2022). Meloni founded *Fratelli* in 2012 after the AN folded. There was some consternation in the international press where headlines such as "fascism returns" appeared. Italian intellectuals (e.g., Galli della Loggia 2022; Urbinati 2022) engaged in intense debates about Meloni's party and its negative potential. In general, Italian reaction to the election was sanguine with the financial press voicing the least concern. European leaders got in line with a wait-and-see attitude. Instead of talking about Meloni as a neofascist, the public conversation shifted to her being Italy's first woman prime minister (Berezin 2023).

13.2   "HIDDEN" AND NOT SO HIDDEN "CURRENTS" THAT CHALLENGE DEMOCRACY

Where did the outrage go in the years between Haider and Meloni? What happened in Europe and beyond between 2000 and 2022 that led to the "normalization" of right nationalist politics in country after country.[2] To explore this question, this chapter analyzes the trajectory of right politics in what was formerly known as Western Europe. The chapter is historical in that it seeks to identify continuities, commonalities, and contingent events that pushed the right forward in the last twenty years. Temporality is the chapter's organizing principle. The attenuation of security is the red thread that runs through it. The chapter proceeds in four stages: the *longue durée* of the European nationalist right; the stabilization period that succeeded the crises of 2015; the effect of the Covid surprise; and, lastly, the need for a reinvention of security. Secondary sources and where appropriate election data and political speech provide the evidence for the argument advanced.

   In a short twenty-year period, right nationalists in election after election have gone from the margins to the center of European politics. In terms of the themes of this book, a question emerges as to whether right nationalist parties represent the unraveling of European postwar democracy or a signal that popular attachment to democracy was not as strong as some had imagined (Conway 2020; Rovny 2023). Democratic reconstruction after fascism, Nazism, and authoritarianism in Western Europe was incomplete until the 1970s. Portugal's Antonio Salazar died in 1970 and Spain's Francesco Franco in 1975. Recent evidence suggests that citizens in some European states are converging toward

---

[2] Berezin's writing uses the term right nationalist rather than populist to describe these groups and will do so in most instances in this chapter.

right wing if not outright antidemocratic values that inform electoral choices (Delage 2021).

Analysts often view the electoral viability of right nationalist parties as constitutive of democratic backsliding. This chapter argues that the diversity of national iterations of right politics suggest that something more complicated than a rejection of democracy is occurring. As chapters in this volume suggest (Beissinger Chapter 10; Bernhard Chapter 9; Bohle and Hozić Chapter 14; Greskovits Chapter 8; Rosenfeld and Cayton Chapter 5), countries in the former Eastern Bloc with relatively new democracies share a greater vulnerability to democratic backsliding than the countries that occupy the old Western Europe. Hungary under Viktor Orban is the poster child case for the slow and steading dismantling of democratic institutions. Nationalist leaders in France, Italy, the Netherlands, Sweden, and others are not aiming to dismantle the democratic institutions of their respective national states. If anything, they are looking to preserve these states in their postwar form. For example, Emmanuel Macron's 2023 pension reform that raised the French legal retirement age from sixty-two to sixty-four set off demonstrations throughout France. Left and right parties opposed it (Caulcutt 2023). The unpopular reform gave Marine Le Pen a boost at the polls (Regan 2023). After the disaster of Brexit, right-wing parties have shifted to working within the EU aiming to rewrite treaties and not to leave it. Jordan Bardella, the president of the RN launched the 2024 European Parliament campaign with the slogan "France is back, Europe lives again."

If European citizens were sanguine about democracy, they were attached to the thick security that the postwar years brought – what the French called the *trente glorieuses*, the thirty glorious years between 1945 and 1975. Berezin (2013; 2019a) argues that "thick security" was lost in the years that ensued since 1975. Thick security incorporates both the feeling and fact of security as embedded in national social, economic, political, and cultural institutions. Nation-states are institutional locations of thick security that lend a collective emotional security to citizens. Citizenship, defense, social welfare systems, and common language are all, from this perspective, aspects of real and felt security. This concept is political and not psychological and tied to the institutions of the modern nation-state.

In the years between 1975 and today, thick security became attenuated if not destroyed in various ways and in various national contexts. A short chapter such as this can only provide a road map to the social and cultural fissures that contribute to the current political moment. This chapter looks at the trajectory of events in Europe between 2000 and today. Events are "templates of possibility" (Berezin 2012) that open ways of collective imagining of the future that may or may not lead to antidemocratic results. Events so conceived bear a kinship relation to what Keynes (2009 [1919]) described as "hidden currents, flowing continually beneath the surface of political history, of which no one can predict the outcome" (p. 165). This is a chapter about hidden and not so hidden currents and often unanticipated outcomes that led to new political moments.

13.3   THE LONGUE DURÉE OF THE NATIONALIST RIGHT: CONTINUITY AND CONTINGENCY

Nationalist right parties did not just appear in contemporary Europe. Their history goes back to at least the beginning of the postwar period (Von Beyme 1988). Allied bombs and peace treaties did not eviscerate the impulses behind fascism and Nazism. Fascist and Nazi parties may have been banned after 1945, but right-wing parties continued albeit with new names. The Italian MSI is the classic example. The relative success of contemporary right parties' results from the intersection between long-standing populist parties and the contingency of crisis events in 2015. The *organizational continuity* of various national iterations of populist or right nationalist parties and the *contingency of unexpected events* acted as accelerants on nationalist and right-wing dispositions that were already in place. The evidence of current history supports this argument. In contrast, drawing on behavioral psychology, Valentin (2024) arrives at the same place. He argues that norms around voting for the nationalist right have shifted. Instead of being an outlier political choice, citizens now think of nationalist right candidates as legitimate political choices.

Trajectory matters. The decade of the 1970s, the time of the first Gulf oil crisis, is the period during which the postwar European social contract began to unravel and where the context that supported the development of the nationalist right began to appear (Eichengreen 2007). Since the millennium, populist parties and voices have expanded their constituencies across Europe. Berezin (2009) covers the years between 1990 and 2007, the period in which the European right began to gain electoral viability. Bohle and Hozić (Chapter 14 this volume) locate the shift toward right politics in the aftermath of the riots of 1968. Focusing on Helmut Kohl, they argue that he redrew the boundaries of the German Christian Democratic Union (CDU) to lock in a nationalist conservative ideology that rippled across Europe. He made sure the party aligned with the European People's Party (EPP) – the conservative party within the European Parliament. Kohl's actions represented an attempt to lock in European conservatism in the post-1968 period. According to Bohle and Hozić, Kohl's actions which targeted politics and culture opened the door toward democratic backsliding particularly in the East. Bohle and Hozić offer a political explanation of the rise of nationalist politics related to reaction to 1968 to lock in conservatism at the expense of socialism. If we look to France and Italy as prominent examples, May 1968 and the Hot Autumn (*Autumno Caldo*) of 1969 were background noise but hardly causal in the development of right-wing politics.

This chapter argues that structural shifts in the economy (global markets) and polity (institutionalization of the EU) drove the nationalist reaction in the West. But these shifts only mattered in the face of destabilizing events. If time had stopped in 2008, right nationalist parties would have continued to occupy their tertiary niche in European politics. The first round of the European sovereign debt crisis in 2008 changed their trajectories. The austerity measures that came with the crisis destabilized what was becoming in the years between 2000 and 2009 an increasingly fragile social, political, and cultural equilibrium (Blyth 2013). The first sign of changes in the valence of these parties appeared in the 2009 European parliamentary elections where populist parties entered the parliament in increased numbers and center left parties suffered significant losses (EurActiv 2009).

The debt crisis opened the door to nationalist mobilization and populist electoral gains across Europe even in places as unlikely as social democratic Sweden and Finland – countries which had significant electoral breakthroughs which took place in 2010 and 2011, respectively. The corresponding weakening of left parties received less attention during this period. Beginning in the 1980s, European left parties became technocratic and cosmopolitan in orientation, increasingly aligned with neoliberal ideas, and less representative of their traditional worker base (Cronin, Ross, and Shoch 2011). The distinction between center right and center left parties eroded (Berman 2016; Berman and Snegovaya 2019).

Figure 13.1 maps patterns of populist and left voting in national parliamentary elections from 1970 to 2014.[3] The data represents aggregations of election results from thirty-seven right parties and thirty-six left parties. The five bars running through the graphs represent historically sensible periods in the political development of Europe in that period. The periods are: 1970–79 Post-war Social Contract Ends; 1980–89 Neoliberal policies begin; 1990–99 European integration accelerates; 2000–08 Monetary union; 2009–14 Crisis begins. The election data is descriptive. It maps the volatility in post-1970s European politics and the evolution of what the late Peter Mair (2013) labelled the "void" – declining voter participation – as well as revealing distinct patterns. First, there is a long-term tendency to vote for right nationalist parties across the European continent. What has changed is right nationalism's valence in political life. Second, as right parties increased their vote share, there is a corresponding decline in left-wing vote share.

The decline, and in some instances evisceration, of the center left in recent years came as no surprise – to those who were following the trends. For

---

[3] Data for these descriptions and Figure 13.1 was gathered from Mackie and Rose (1991) and the national election websites of each represented country http://eed.nsd.uib.no/. Between 1970 and 2014, there were 188 national parliamentary elections. Countries included in the data set are Austria, Belgium, Denmark, Finland, France, Germany, Greece, Italy, Netherlands, Norway, Portugal, Spain, Sweden, Switzerland, and the UK.

Patterns

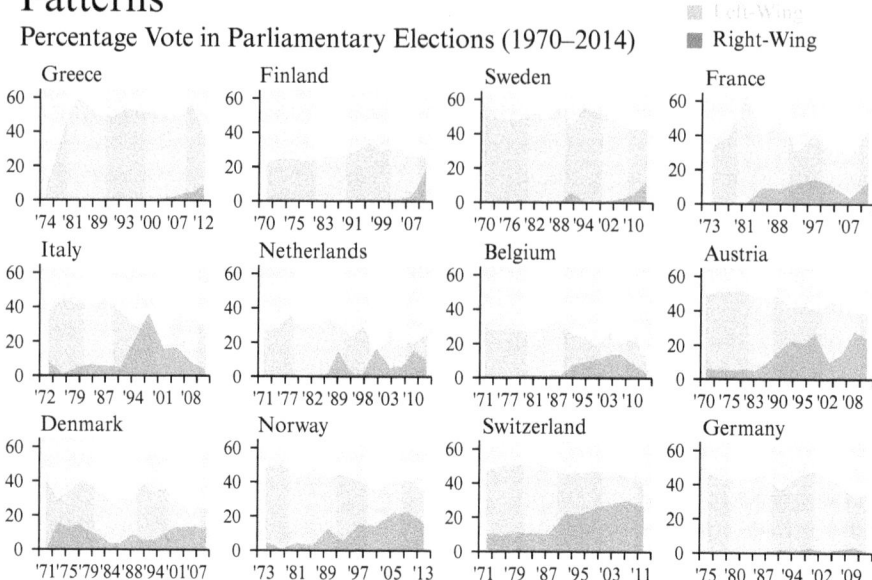

Percentage Vote in Parliamentary Elections (1970–2014)

FIGURE 13.1 Left/right parties percentage of votes in national parliamentary elections 1970–2014.

example, in the first round of the French Presidential election in 2012, the traditional left (Francois Hollande) and traditional right (Nicolas Sarkozy) came in first and second respectively with less than a percentage point spread between them. Marine Le Pen came in third place and Jean-Luc Mélenchon's far left *La France Insoumise* came in fourth. In the first round of the 2022 presidential election, Emmanuel Macron's party *En Marche!* came in first, Marine Le Pen's RN, formerly *Front National*, came in second, Mélenchon came in third and Eric Zemmour's far right party *Reconquête!* came in fourth. Between 2012 and 2022, traditional French parties had dropped out of competition. The parties of Macron, Mélenchon, and Zemmour were less than ten years old. Marine Le Pen's party founded by her father in 1972 was the only established party.

Up to 2014, nationalist right voting patterns reveal distinct geographic variation (Broz, Frieden, and Weymouth 2021). These patterns can be labelled: Nordic (Norway, Sweden, and Denmark); Alpine (Austria and Switzerland); Core (France, Netherlands, and Belgium); and, lastly, the Mediterranean exception (Italy, Spain, Portugal, and Greece). Until recently, right politics manifested itself in the Mediterranean principally as a left or national separatist phenomenon. This changed beginning in 2013 when *Vox* was founded in Spain, in 2018 the *Lega* surged in Italy under Matteo Salvini, and ended recently with the March 2024 surge of Portugal's nationalism *Chega* party.

Between 2014 and 2024, there was the election of Giorgia Meloni and her nationalist *Brothers of Italy* party which had been nowhere on the Italian political landscape as recently as 2020 (Puleo and Piccolino 2022). The almost complete absence of nationalism in Britain and Germany, again until 2017, is notable (Berezin and Davidson 2018).

13.4 CRISIS AS TURNING POINT: BETWEEN 2014 AND 2019

Long-term secular trends alone were not enough to generate the electoral momentum that became visible after the first European sovereign debt crisis in 2010 and has accelerated ever since. Political ruptures are as important as continuities. The patterns revealed in Figure 13.1 were stable until 2015 when a triple crisis hit (Berezin 2019a). First, came the January 7 attack in Paris with the Charlie Hebdo murders. This was followed by the Greek austerity crisis in July and then the fall refugee crisis when a record 1.3 million refugees sought asylum in Europe. The refugee crisis was visually stunning as pictures of boats of refugees circulated on social media. German Prime Minister Angela Merkel's "We can do it" meaning that Europe was capable of taking as many refugees as possible produced backlash instead of support. 2015 rolled toward its end with three coordinated terror attacks in Paris in November that killed more than 130 people who were out enjoying themselves in a theater and cafe on a Friday night.

The three crises of 2015 – terror, austerity, and refugee – produced a perfect storm that rippled across European politics (Berezin 2015a; 2015b; 2019a) widened the opening for right nationalist parties that already existed to mobilize nationalist feelings that were already there. These crises of 2015 remained either unresolved or imperfectly resolved and the main collective vehicle for ameliorating these crises – the EU – proved ineffective at managing them (Bartels 2023; Bhabha 2018; Mody 2018).

In 2016, a series of events – two rounds of the Austrian presidential election and Brexit in the spring, a terrorist event in Nice in July, and the November American presidential election put Europeans on edge. By 2016, populism became the term *du jour* for these disparate phenomena in contemporary European politics (Berezin 2019b) and interest in populism crossed from the media to the academic. A "newness" narrative, as if populism had never been a part of the European landscape before 2016, colored much media and academic discussion. In spring 2017, the election of Emmanuel Macron as president in France, the final defeat of Norbert Hofer in Austria, and the poor showing of Geert Wilders in the Netherlands election generated a premature populism has been "defeated" counternarrative.

In addition to their improving national electoral fortunes, right nationalist parties changed in salient ways between the 2014 and the 2019 European parliamentary election. In late 2017, trans-European right-wing parties started to "talk" to each other about collaborating. The *Lega* in Italy an aggressive right-wing party under the leadership of Matteo Salvini rallied a parliamentary group, the *Europe of Nations and Freedom*, under the banner of a "Europe of Common Sense." By the spring of 2018, populist or Eurosceptic parties learned the lesson of Brexit and they now aimed to "reform" Europe from within rather than withdraw from it.

Approaching the 2019 European parliamentary elections, several fault lines plagued the European project. First, scholars such as Andreas Wimmer (2018) and others (*Foreign Affairs* 2019) have recently argued the nation-state is a stickier attachment than some policymakers and academics would have us believe. Second, with Angela Merkel gone as the leader of her party and Emmanuel Macron distracted by the *gilets jaunes* crisis in France, there was a leadership vacuum in the months leading up to the election. Third, the center left and center right were weakening across Europe – leaving the political space void of parties that could buffer the extremes.

In sum, the history shows that the "newness" and the "defeat" narratives were flawed albeit for varied reasons. The "newness" narrative suggests a lack of attention on the part of media, and public intellectuals both inside and outside of academia. While there is considerable national variation in the form and content of populist parties and movements, there are constants that apply across cases (Halikiopoulou and Vlandas 2022). First, contemporary European populism is not a new political phenomenon nor is it simply a replay of the politics of the 1930s. If we search for historical analogies, the period of the industrial revolution might be a more likely comparison (James 2016). What scholars are labeling as populism has been an increasingly salient part of the European political landscape since the millennium (Berezin 2009). Some populist parties originated in the immediate postwar period, others in the 1970s and 1980s, and yet others are of more recent vintage.

Second, the optimism around populism's defeat in spring 2017 was premature. Populism did not disappear. Electoral events were unstable. In fall 2017, the *Alternative for Germany* (AFD) achieved electoral success in the German elections. A year later, the March 2018 Italian parliamentary elections overturned Italy's entire political landscape and the September 2018 Swedish elections were a breakthrough for the Sweden Democrats. December 2018 saw the emergence of the unclassifiable *gilets jaunes* in France. All these events suggested that populism is nowhere near being defeated.

Third, in contrast to other contributions to this volume, this chapter does not assume a single or stable definition of populism. This essay argues that populism evokes a political mood rather than a single ideology. Bohle and Hozić (Chapter 14 this volume) make an analogous argument when they suggest that what they label (neo)conservative consists of multiple ideologies such as "nationalism, anticommunism, xenophobia, racism ..." This chapter emphasizes the practice dimension of populism. It argues that populism is a historically contingent aggregation of collective preferences with no coherent ideology to unite them (Berezin 2019b). Populism exists in left and right variants, as well as contextually specific national variations. The eclecticism of populism (at least to a political theorist) despite some common features explains why it eludes parsimonious definition. Lastly, the Trump phenomenon and the European instances while they appear to be kinship phenomena are different configurations of cultural, political, and social processes– a distinction with a profound difference.

13.5 POPULISM IS POPULAR: THE 2019 EUROPEAN PARLIAMENT ELECTION

On the morning of May 27, 2019, the outcome of the European parliamentary elections dominated national and global news media. Low participation rates among the EU twenty-seven nation-state members characterize these elections which began in 1979 and which occur every five years (Hobolt and de Vries 2016). In the past, pundits, policymakers, and scholars viewed these elections as largely pro forma – a symbolic bow to trans-European participation and democracy. The 2019 elections were different. Scholars and policymakers anticipated (and feared) that trans-European nationalist right, Eurosceptic, or populist parties would achieve results that would surge, enabling them to block or disrupt the parliament's agenda (Dennison and Zerka 2019). Anxiety about the European nationalist right began to gain in intensity in 2016 when Brexit occurred and accelerated due to a series of high-profile national parliamentary elections such as Italy and Sweden in 2018 and the French presidential election in 2017. Even the usually reserved European Council of Foreign Relations put out a policy brief in January 2019 entitled, "The 2019 European Election: How Anti-Europeans Plan to Wreck Europe and What Can Be Done to Stop It" (Dennison and Zerka 2019).

The anticipated surge did not, in fact, happen. By Sunday evening, the *BBC News Service* put out the following headline "European elections 2019: Euro press sees populist advance 'halted.'" The historian Harold James, a usually prescient commentator on European politics, observed with a hint of surprise in *Project Syndicate* that "The more interesting outcome of the election was the relative weakness of populist right-wing and nationalist parties" (James 2019).

The populist right did not do as well as expected, yet this did not mean that the 2019 election lacked significance. "Surge" and "no surge" narratives obscure the fact that the nationalist right neither underperformed nor overperformed. The 2019 European parliamentary election is a turning point similar to the triple crises of 2015 in the political trajectory of the European nationalist right. In 2019, the traditional European center left and right parties did poorly. The traditional left arguably disappeared across the continent. The morning after the election, Marine Le Pen head of the former French National Front, nowRN, tweeted #OnArrive. The 2019 European parliamentary election signaled the "end of the beginning" of the populist right. Populism was arguably popular.

The last time citizens of EU member states displayed enthusiasm for the European parliamentary elections was in 1979 when turnout was 61.9 percent. That was the year that the elections began. In the five parliamentary elections that have occurred since then, the number of member states has increased from nine to twenty-eight. Voter participation decreased with each passing year to a low of 42.6 percent in 2014. Over the years, pundits, policymakers, and scholars viewed these elections as largely pro forma – a symbolic bow to trans-European participation and democracy or a place to register a protest. The elections are often as much about national issues as European issues.

The 2019 parliamentary election mattered even though the populist "surge" did not materialize. First, the participation rate across the twenty-eight members was 50 percent higher than at any point since 1999. National participation rates jumped in Denmark, Germany, France, Spain, and Austria. All countries where national issues played out. Second, the Greens – the unexpected result – surged in Germany and came in a surprising third place in France. Third, the traditional center left and right parties were wiped out in France and Italy. With some notable exceptions such as Denmark and Austria, center left parties performed poorly across Europe. The success of the Social Democrats in Denmark was widely attributed to its toughening stance on immigration and refugees. Mette Frederiksen notably saying, "The left left the people, the people did not leave us."

13.6   #ON ARRIVE: CEMENTING THE TENSION BETWEEN THE LOCAL AND THE GLOBAL

The 2019 European parliamentary elections were as much about stability as about rupture. Many of the outcomes stood for the culmination of long-term trends. As polls predicted, the nationalist right came in first in Italy and France – with 34 percent and 23 percent of the vote, respectively. Even though Matteo Salvini and his *Lega* were the more flamboyant of the two, Marine Le Pen and the French results were the more interesting. Commentators made much of the fact that Marine Le Pen's 23.3 percent versus Macron's 22.4 percent was not significant because her 23 percent was lower than her 24 percent in 2014 where she also came in first. But that assessment did not consider the political differences in France between 2014 and 2019. In 2014, the traditional center right (UMP – Union for a Popular Movement) and Socialist Party were still in the game and only nine parties ran with a 42 percent participation rate. In 2019, the traditional parties of the French left and right had collapsed, thirteen parties fielded candidates and the participation rate was 50 percent. The two parties that came in after Le Pen's RN, Macron's coalition and the Greens, were all new to the top slot positions. Given the changes in the voting landscape, Le Pen faced tougher competition than she had in 2014, where she arguably represented a protest vote rather than a nationwide change of direction.

In Marine Le Pen's concession speech delivered after losing the 2017 French presidential election, she identified the conflict between "globalists and patriots" as defining the future of France and of Europe. She might have substituted the word "nationalists" for "patriots." Le Pen points to a division between those who could take advantage of the mobility, freedoms, and opportunities that the EU afforded and those who were metaphorically and physically stuck in place. This antagonism between the local and the global, the nation and Europe was a central theme of the 2019 European parliamentary election. See, for example, French President Emmanuel Macron's "Dear Europe" letter (March 4, 2019) that he sent to major European newspapers in advance of the elections in which he called for a "European renaissance" to confront encroaching nationalism. In the days after the election, Macron was already meeting with Angela Merkel with the intention of still leading this renaissance.

The antagonism between the local and the global emerged long before 2017 and 2019. Theresa May in her 2016 speech to the Conservative Party Conference put the Brexit vote in the global/local context when she said: "But if you believe you're a citizen of the world, you're a citizen of nowhere. You don't understand what the very word 'citizenship' means." Emmanuel Macron in his November 11, 2018 Armistice Day Speech described the local, really meaning national, through another lens:

Let us remember let's take away none of the purity, the idealism, the higher principles that existed in the patriotism of our elders. In those dark hours, that vision of France as a generous nation, of France as a project, of France promoting universal values, was the exact opposite of the egotism of a people who look after only their interests, because patriotism is the exact opposite of nationalism: nationalism is a betrayal of it. In saying "our interests first and who cares about the rest!" you wipe out what's most valuable about a nation, what brings it alive, what leads it to greatness and what is most important: its moral values.

In Macron's view, global consciousness is the essence of national morality – a clever formulation that, like many of Macron's formulations, has not captured the French public's or any other European public's imagination.

The 2019 European parliamentary election confirmed that the nationalist right is a *constitutive* element of European politics – firmly embedded in the political landscape. The ongoing failure to resolve the contradiction between national requirements and global or transnational aspirations drove the entrenchment of the nationalist right. On the day after the 2019 parliamentary election, Marine Le Pen declared a "people's victory." The hashtag from the Le Pen's campaign #*on arrive* (we arrive) captures the outcome in France and across Europe. The nationalist or populist right was no longer marginal to European politics.

13.7 FROM COVID TO UKRAINE: THE POLITICAL POWER OF UNEXPECTED EVENTS

The outcomes of the 2019 European parliamentary elections were flat in contrast to the anxiety that proceeded them. Contingent or unexpected events push in new directions or produce new insights (Berezin 2012). Less than a year after the election in February 2020 Covid, a global and unexpected event, struck Europe. Unlike the triple crises of 2015, Covid's impact was universal, and the contagion required immediate remedies. The virus was global, but policy solutions were national. The first trans-European response was that states closed their national borders and restricted movement (Herszenhorn 2020; Gerbaudo 2021). Baldwin (2021) documents that Covid policy followed divergent national paths based on past national practices in the face of infectious disease and epidemics. National solutions fed into long-standing policy preferences of the populist right, so Covid policy had little immediate effect upon their standing (Stavrakakis and Katsambekis 2020). Controversies arose over whether vaccine development and dispersal would occur at the national or EU level (Weintraub, Bitton, and Rosenberg 2020). Covid policy was in tune with long-held right beliefs around national sovereignty and against one-size-fits-all EU decisions. Once developed, the Covid vaccine gave rise to antivax movements that were outside the mainstream of left and right politics (Della Porta and Lavizzari 2023).

Two years after Covid emerged as a threat on February 23, 2022, Russia invaded Ukraine and shook the European continent and the globe. In contrast to Covid, this unexpected event pushed against individual national responses. The invasion of Ukraine forced the EU and its members to take a united stand against Putin. Even those right-wingers such as Marine Le Pen and Matteo Salvini who had flirted with if not outright supported Putin in the past stood firmly against him and supported the EU's use of sanctions. In contrast to the weak sanctions that the EU imposed on Austria in 2000, the sanctions against Putin were meant to go for the Russian jugular and were global and far-reaching in scope (Session 20 of the Congressional Study Group 2022). With respect to Europe, some countries are more dependent than others for Russian fuel. The rising cost of home heating oil in a frigid winter and petrol for cars is a challenge to the moral unity of Europe around the defense of Ukraine. The *gilets jaunes* in 2018 in France started over the price of fuel. Fuel costs are already emerging as a fault line in German reaction to Russia and Ukraine. The combination of sanctions and fighting on the part of the Ukrainians has still not deterred Russia. It is too soon to see how Ukraine will play itself out – particularly with respect to right nationalist European politics.

13.8 THE END OF THICK SECURITY AND THE LEGITIMIZATION OF THE NATIONALIST RIGHT

In the years between 2000 and today, *thick security* weakened and left European nation-states vulnerable to political, economic, and cultural ruptures with no organizational fallback in sight. *Illiberal Politics in Neoliberal Times* (Berezin 2009, pp. 5–8; pp. 243–258) argued that the rise of the nationalist right was primarily a response to changes in the nature and structure of the European nation-state and its security regimes. Expanded Europeanization and globalization were the twin catalysts that changed and weakened those security regimes. In the ten years between 2009 and 2019, a "post-security" polity (Berezin 2013; 2019a) emerged that lacked the institutions that guarded security in the past. Postsecurity implies the absence of security mechanisms not the absence of a need for security. In contrast to postwar Europe that guaranteed security, solidarity, and identity, the *postsecurity polity* privileges markets and peoples that cross borders, fosters austerity that threatens solidarity, and supports multicultural inclusion at the expense of nationalist exclusion. The triple crises of 2015 – terror, refugee, and debt – became unsolvable in European terms and remain partially solved today. Covid and the Ukraine invasion threatened security in new and different ways. In this context, the nationalist right become legitimate political actors who claim to offer solutions to multiple insecurities that traditional political actors were failing to provide.

Security encapsulates what others have analyzed in terms of trust and risk. The concept of *thick security* (Berezin 2009) incorporates both the feeling and fact of security as embedded in national social, economic, political, and cultural institutions. In this formulation, nation-states are institutional locations of *thick security* that lend a collective emotional security to citizens. Citizenship, defense, social welfare systems, and common language are all, from this perspective, aspects of real and felt security. This concept of security differs from Giddens (1990) concept of *ontological security* because *thick security* is political and not psychological and is still tied, as responses to Covid have demonstrated, to the institutions of the modern nation-state. As such, it follows, although its original iterations predate them, recent work on the value of nations and nationalism (e.g., Wimmer 2018; Tamir 2019; *Foreign Affairs* 2019).

Explaining the ascendance and appeal of the populist nationalist right in terms of a security crisis is a more robust way of thinking of current events than explanations that focus on conceptions of cultural identity (Fukuyama 2018; Norris and Inglehart 2019) or purely economistic explanations (Eichengreen 2018). *Thick security* incorporates the economic, the cultural, and the political. Futurity is constitutive of security. Security stabilizes collective meanings around institutional locations – it provides a sense of what happened today will happen tomorrow. Theorizing security in this broad way weds institutions to culture, emotion, and historical legacy as well as the more standard ideas of security contained in concepts of social welfare and solidarity.

If a nation-state tampers with a security regime and does not provide an alternative that replicates the collective benefits of the old security regime, citizens, particularly those who do not benefit from new institutional forms, might perceive the nation-state's actions in terms of social betrayal (Margalit 2017). In short, an institutionalized party that acts like the old European left used to act on behalf of its citizens is absent in Europe and arguably the United States. Left parties in Europe, or what remains of them, are as identified with austerity politics and EU policies in general as center right parties are. This lack of differentiation is behind the corresponding failure, and in some instances collapse, of the left in recent elections. It also makes the right nationalist parties easily assume the role of the party that does care about the people.

For example, in the spring of 2024, farmers took to the streets of virtually all major cities in Europe to protest various aspects of European environmental policy that would cut into their livelihoods (Mathiesen, Camut, Weise, Cooper, and Guillot 2024). Riding through the streets on their yellow tractors, farmers were colorful if disruptive protestors. Marine Le Pen visited angry farmers in the north of France in January 2024. She made the point that she, in contrast to Macron, cared about them. She said: "We need to put a stop to free trade agreements, which obviously put them [farmers] in competition with products that are not subject to the same constraints. I am waiting to see them [the government] do what is necessary. They have been in power for seven years. How many years are we supposed to play dumb?" (Priore 2024).

How do nation-states reestablish *thick security* in a postsecurity polity? Economic historian Emma Rothschild (1995) argued that the character of security had altered fundamentally in the post-Communist era. In contrast to the past where security issues were national, contemporary security issues such as climate change, disease, migration, terrorism, and finance (although the last three were not on Rothschild's list) are transnational in scope. The globalization of security and its opposites – insecurity, threats, and fears – raise questions of responsibility and render contemporary security crises less tractable of solutions. Populists have stepped into a void with simple solutions to difficult problems that require complex and transnational solutions.

The triple crises – terror, austerity, and refugees, coupled with war and Covid – discussed in this chapter represent contemporary security crises of the type that Rothschild imagined. These crises exacerbated economic fissures and cultural fault lines in the EU project and brought into focus institutional problems that nations formerly resolved. Nation-states, the bedrock of pre-EU Europe, institutionalized a form of *practical security* that lent collective *emotional security* to citizens.

Political security was in citizenship laws and internal and external defense ministries. National social welfare systems produced *economic security* and social solidarity as a byproduct. Linguistic, educational, and even religious policies created *cultural security* because they enforced assumptions, if not realities, of similarity and identity. The triple crises now exacerbated by Covid and Ukraine force Europe to recalibrate itself and to produce a new form of *thick security* that makes sense in the twenty-first century.

13.9 KEEPING THE JACK-IN-THE BOX AND THE SECURITY IMPERATIVE

Thick security is a moral imperative. Anthropologist Clifford Geertz (1996, p. 262) inadvertently captured a core component of the security imperative when he observed:

For it is still the case that no one lives in the world in general. Everybody, even the exiled, the drifting, the diasporic, or the perpetually moving, lives in some confine and limited stretch of it ... The banalities and distractions of the way we live now lead us, often enough, to lose sight of how much it matters just where we are and what it is like to be there.

This tension between the place-ness of the national and the placeless-ness of the global encapsulates the policy dilemma and security crises before Europe as well as other nation-states confronting populist politics.

Interviewed in the *Financial Times* (Milne 2020), Timo Soini, former leader of the *True Finns* the Finnish nationalist right party, sums up the dangers inherent in ignoring the national. Emphasizing the dilemma of the global versus national, he quipped "Globalism is God for godless people." While religiosity is not particularly high in Europe even among its nationalist champions, Soini's bons mots get to the point of why commitment to globalism and all that it entails is not leaving the scene anytime soon. When the *Times* reporter asked Soini if he thought that Covid would finally attenuate the political weight of the right, he pointed to the economic bill that would come due to the EU after the impact of Covid had diminished. He argued: "When there is a time that you must pay it all back [*EU subsidies*], that is when the backlash will come. I will not say it is a knockout for populism currently. They will go down temporarily and then come back, like a jack-in-the-box."

To keep the jack-in-the box, European political parties today need to develop a new voice that is not so nationalist that it encourages xenophobia and not so cosmopolitan that it ignores the struggles of ordinary people. More importantly, politicians and policymakers need to reinvent security and recognize it as a collective moral imperative. It is time to end World War II metaphors in thinking about populism. Policymakers, academics, and activists need to think about new sources of collective social solidarity and resilience in a world that is radically altered, technologically, demographically, and geo-politically not only from 1933 but also from 1968 and 1989. The elections of 2022 in Sweden, France, and Italy make it clear that the populist right is embedded in European politics. But even if they do not win elections, the right poses a challenge to democratic ideals and practices. Until politicians, social scientists, and policymakers confront these generalized security issues, the populist right will only need to show up, if not to win elections, then at least to define the boundaries of policy and public discourse. As of this writing, the

European Council on Foreign Relations forecasts a "sharp right turn" in the 2024 European Parliament elections (Cunningham, Hix, Dennison, and Learmouth 2024). This time the box is wide open and right-wing parties are unlikely to reenter it.

REFERENCES

"The New Nationalism." 2019. *Foreign Affairs* 98 (2).

Baldwin, Peter. 2021. *Fighting the First Wave: Why the Coronavirus Was Tackled So Differently across the Globe.* Cambridge: Cambridge University Press.

Bartels, Larry M. 2023. *Democracy Erodes from the Top.* Princeton, NJ: Princeton University Press.

Berezin, Mabel. 2009. *Illiberal Politics in Neoliberal Times: Culture, Security, and Populism in the New Europe.* Cambridge: Cambridge University Press.

Berezin, Mabel. 2012. "Events as Templates of Possibility: An Analytic Typology of Political Facts." In *The Oxford Handbook of Cultural Sociology*, Jeffrey C. Alexander, Ronald Jacobs and Philip Smith, eds. New York: Oxford University Press: 613–635.

Berezin, Mabel. 2013. "The Normalization of the Right in Post-Security Europe." In *Politics in the Age of Austerity*, Armin Schaefer and Wolfgang Streeck, eds. Cambridge: Polity Press: 239–261.

Berezin, Mabel. 2015a. "Globalization Backlash." In *Emerging Trends in the Social and Berezin, Mabel Behavioral Sciences*, Robert Scott and Stephen Kosslyn, eds. Hoboken, NJ: John Wiley and Sons. http://onlinelibrary.wiley.com/doi/10.1002/9781118900772.etrds0151/abstract.

Berezin, Mabel. 2015b. "Extremist Politics before and after Charlie Hebdo." *Global Dialogue* 5 (1). https://tinyurl.com/muzcd5pr.

Berezin, Mabel. 2018. (Co-authored with Thomas Davidson). "Britain First and the UK Independence Party: Social Media and the Movement Party Dynamic." "Special Issue: *Contesting Trump*." *Mobilization* 23 (4): 485–511.

Berezin, Mabel. 2019a "Past Is Prologue: Electoral Events of Spring 2012 and the Old 'New' Nationalism in Post-Security Europe." In *Populism and the Crisis of Democracy*, Gregor Fitzi, Jurgen Mackert and Bryan S. Turner, eds. Vol. 1. Concepts and Theories. London: Routledge: 109–129.

Berezin, Mabel. 2019b. "Populism and Fascism: Are They Useful Categories for Comparative Sociological Analysis?" *Annual Review of Sociology* 45: 345–361.

Berezin, Mabel. 2023. "Georgia Meloni and the Fascist Past: How Does It Matter?" *Logos*. https://tinyurl.com/4f2ebdup.

Berman, Sheri. 2016. "The Specter Haunting Europe: The Lost Left." *Journal of Democracy* 27 (4): 69–76.

Berman, Sheri, and Maria Snegovaya. 2019. "Populism and the Decline of Social Democracy." *Journal of Democracy* 30 (3): 5–19.

Bhabha, Jacqueline. 2018. *Can We Solve the Migration Crisis?* Cambridge: Polity.

Blyth, Mark. 2013. *Austerity: The History of a Dangerous Idea.* First Ed. Oxford; New York: Oxford University Press.

Broz, J. Lawrence, Jeffry Frieden, and Stephen Weymouth. 2021. "Populism in Place: The Economic Geography of the Globalization Backlash." *International Organization* 75 (2): 464–94.

Caulcutt, Clea. 2023. "Macron Signs Pensions Reform into Law after Top Court Clears Measure." *Politico*. www.politico.eu/article/france-court-macron-pension-reform-bill-64/.

Conway, Martin. 2020. *Western Europe's Democratic Age: 1945–1968*. Princeton, NJ: Princeton University Press.

Cronin, James, George Ross, and James Shoch. 2011. *What's Left of the Left: Democrats and Social Democrats in Challenging Times*. Durham, NC: Duke.

Cunningham, Kevin, Susi Dennison, Simon Hix, and Imogen Learmonth. 2024. "A Sharp Right Turn: A Forecast for the 2024 European Parliament Elections." *ECFR*. https://tinyurl.com/4wuw428s.

Delage, Victor. 2021. "The Conversion of Europeans to Right-Wing Values: France, Germany, Italy and the United Kingdom." Fondation pour L'innovation Politique. Fondapol.org. www.fondapol.org/en/study/the-conversion-of-europeans-to-right-wing-values/.

Della Porta, Donatella, and Anna Lavizzari. 2023. "Waves in Cycle: The Protests against Anti-Contagion Measures and Vaccination in Covid-19 Times in Italy." *Partecipazione e Conflitto* 15 (3): 720–740.

Dennison, Susi, and Powet Zerka. 2019. "The 2019 European Election: How Anti-Europeans Plan to Wreck Europe and What Can Be Done to Stop It." European Council on Foreign Relations (https://ecfr.eu/special/the_2019_european_election/), February.

Eichengreen, Barry. 2007. *The European Economy Since 1945: Coordinated Capitalism and Beyond*. Princeton, NJ: Princeton University Press.

Eichengreen, Barry. 2018. *The Populist Temptation*. New York: Oxford University Press.

Elgenius, Gabriella, and Jens Rydgren. 2024. "The Politics of Ethnic Nationalism, Nostalgia and Anti-Immigrant Framing: The Trajectory of the Sweden Democrats 1989–2022." In *Migration and Nationalism*, Michael Samers and Jens Rydgren, eds. Cheltenham: Edward Elgar Publishing, 114–135.

EurActiv 2009. Centre-Right Wins European Elections. https://tinyurl.com/28k2vpv3.

Fukuyama, Francis. 2018. *Identity: The Demand for Dignity and the Politics of Resentment*. New York: Farrar, Straus and Giroux.

Galli della Loggia, Ernesto. 2022. "La storia d'Italia e le ombre del passato." *Corriere della Sera* August 18.

Geertz, Clifford. 1996. "Afterward." In *Senses of Place* Steven Feld and Keith H. Basso, eds. Santa Fe, NM: School of American Research Press, 261–262.

Gerbaudo, Paolo. 2021. *The Great Recoil: Politics after Populism and Pandemic*. First Ed. Brooklyn, NY: Verso.

Giddens, Anthony. 1990. *The Consequences of Modernity*. Stanford, CA: Stanford.

Halikiopoulou, Daphne, and Tim Vlandas. 2022. "Understanding Right-Wing Populism and What to Do about It." Report by Friedrich Ebert Stiftung. Available at SSRN. https://ssrn.com/abstract=4122538 or http://dx.doi.org/10.2139/ssrn.4122538.

Herszenhorn, David M. 2020. "Coronavirus Border Controls Imperil EU Freedoms." *Politico Europe*. www.politico.eu/article/coronavirus-border-controls-imperil-eu-freedoms/.

Hobolt, Sara and de Vries, Catherine E. 2016. "Public Support for European Integration." *Annual Review of Political Science* 19: 413–432.

James, Harold. 2016. "Déclassé: Nothing New Under the Sun." *The American Interest.* www.the-american-interest.com/2016/09/23/declasse-nothing-new-under-the-sun/.

James, Harold. 2019. "Game of EU Thrones." *Project Syndicate* May 27. https://tinyurl.com/2eka86un.

Judt, Tony. 2000. "Tale from the Vienna Woods." *The New York Review of Books* March 23.

Keynes, John Maynard. (1919) 2009. *The Economic Consequences of the Peace.* Rockville, MD: Serenity.

Mackie, Thomas T., and Richard Rose, eds. 1991. *The International Almanac of Electoral History.* Washington, DC: Congressional Quarterly Inc.

Macron, Emmanuel. 2018. "Discours du Président de la République, Emmanuel Macron à la cérémonie internationale du Centenaire de l'Armistice du 11 Novembre 1918 à l'Arc de Triomphe Élysée." https://tinyurl.com/bdzkva3v.

Macron, Emmanuel. 2019. "Dear Europe, Brexit Is a Lesson for All of Us: It's Time for Renewal." *The Guardian* March 4. https://www.theguardian.com/commentisfree/2019/mar/04/europe-brexit-uk.

Mair, Peter. 2013. *Ruling the Void: The Hollowing of Western Democracy.* London: Verso.

Margalit, Avishai. 2017. *On Betrayal.* Cambridge, MA: Harvard University Press.

Mathiesen, Karl, Nicolas Camut, Zia Weise, Charlie Cooper, and Louise Guillot. 2024. "Bears, Cars and Angry Farmers Fuel Green Backlash." *Politico.* https://tinyurl.com/3vj6rd4z.

Milne. Richard. 2020. "Timo Soini: Globalism Is God for Godless People." *Financial Times* May 5. www.ft.com/content/f4b70ce6-9395-11ea-abcd-371e24b679ed.

Mody, Ashoka. 2018. *EuroTragedy.* New York: Oxford.

Mueller, Wolfgang C. 2000. "The Austrian Election of October 1999: A Shift to the Right." *West European Politics.* doi: 10.1080/01402380008425391.

Norris, Pippa, and Ronald Inglehart. 2019. *Cultural Backlash: Trump, Brexit and Authoritarian Populism.* New York: Cambridge University Press.

Priore, Thibault. 2024. "Colère des agriculteurs: Marine Le Pen dénonce leur situation 'catastrophique.'" *lejdd.fr.* https://tinyurl.com/47k26z86.

Puleo, Leonardo, and Gianluca Piccolino. 2022. "Back to the Post-Fascist Past or Landing in the Populist Radical Right? The Brothers of Italy between Continuity and Change." *South European Society and Politics.* doi: 10.1080/13608746.2022.2126247.

Regan, James. 2023. "Macron Loses Voters to Far Right over Pensions, Poll Shows." *Bloomberg.Com* March 25.

Rothschild, Emma. 1995. "What Is Security." *Daedalus* 124 (3): 53–98.

Rovny, Jan. 2023. "Antidote to Backsliding: Ethnic Politics and Democratic Resilience." *American Political Science Review.* doi:10.1017/S000305542200140X.

Scheppele, Kim. 2022. "How Viktor Orbán Wins." *Journal of Democracy* 33 (3): 45–61.

Session 20 of the Congressional Study Group. 2022. "Sanctions on Russia over Ukraine." *Brookings.* www.brookings.edu/research/sanctions-on-russia-over-ukraine/.

Stavrakakis, Yannis, and Giorgos Katsambekis. 2020. "Populism and the Pandemic: A Collaborative Report." Loughborough University. https://tinyurl.com/tnhf345s.

Tamir, Yael. 2019. *Why Nationalism?* Princeton, NJ: Princeton University Press.

Urbinati, Nadia. 2022. "Invece di fare gli esami di democrazia agli ex fascisti si legittima il partito della fiamma." *Domani* August 22.

Valentim, Vicente. 2024. *The Normalization of the Radical Right: A Norms Theory of Political Supply and Demand*. Oxford: Oxford University Press.

Von Beyme, Klaus. 1988. "Right-Wing Extremism in Post-War Europe." *West European Politics* 11 (2): 1–18.

Weintraub, Rebecca, Asaf Bitton, and Mark L. Rosenberg. 2020. "The Danger of Vaccine Nationalism." *Harvard Business Review* May 22.

Wimmer, Andreas. 2018. *Nation Building*. Princeton, NJ: Princeton University Press.

14

The Long Shadow of 1968: Christian Democracy's Struggle for Dominance and Democratic Backsliding in Europe

Dorothee Bohle and Aida A. Hozić

14.1 INTRODUCTION

The global retreat of democracy is often seen as a relatively recent phenomenon, closely connected to the fallout of the Great Financial Crisis, and affecting mostly "third wave" democracies, although Brexit and the rise of Donald Trump might have arguably brought home the message that even old – first wave – democracies are not immune to the trend. It is also often associated with strongmen taking over mainstream conservative parties, winning elections, and then taking advantage of existing democratic institutions to "concentrate powers, marginalize opponents, and neutralize or dismantle essential checks and balances" (Roberts et al. Chapter 1 this volume). Much like the literature on third wave democratization, the backsliding literature is preoccupied with democracies' supposedly "bare essentials": competitive elections which produce winners and losers, games that elites engage in to cope with "losers or winners dilemma," and the institutional conditions that might make some democracies more resilient to malevolent elite games than others (ibid.).

The debate on democratic backsliding in Eastern Europe is no exception to this. Most of it is concerned with the concrete strategies that the likes of Viktor Orbán, Prime Minister of Hungary since 2010, and Jarosław Kaczyński, president of the ultraconservative PiS (Law and Justice) party in Poland, pursued to win elections, and, once successful, the "playbook" they followed to dismantle liberal institutions and constitutional checks and balances (e.g., Vachudova 2020; Scheppele 2018). In the European context, hope is placed on

Acknowledgements: We presented a first version of the chapter at a workshop at the Department of Government at Cornell University on Global Challenges to Democracy: Cross Regional Challenges, on May 13–14, 2022. We thank all conference participants for comments on our draft. Special thanks go to the three editors of this volume and two anonymous reviewers. Very special thanks go to Fabio Wolkenstein who provided an extensive critique of our draft. The remaining lack of clarity, omissions, and mistakes are ours and ours only.

the Western half of the continent and especially the EU to reign in democratic backsliding.

Our chapter intervenes in this debate with three modifications to existing literature. First, we challenge the *timing* of the retreat of global democracy. Rather than seeing it as recent phenomenon, we argue that the seeds of democratic backsliding on the European continent were planted long ago. Much in line with Roberts et al. (Chapter 1 this volume), we see the timing embedded in "democracy's dialectic," that is the countermobilization of authoritarian currents as a reaction to democracy's advances in and since 1968. While this dialectical process has been widely documented for the US (Cooper 2017; Tarrow 2017; Skocpol and Williamson 2016), it is often overlooked that on the European continent conservative forces as well as forces of the new right also sought to reposition themselves in order to wrestle back the supposed hegemony from the left.

This struggle for dominance, second, was fought in the *ideological* realm as much as in the institutional and electoral arena. In stressing the role of ideology, we differ from Berezin (Chapter 13 this volume) who views the current politics on the right as a "mood rather than a single ideology." We also differ from those authors who see in mainstream conservative parties' recurrent tacit or open support of authoritarian political forces purely strategic electoral motives (e.g., Kelemen 2020). While we certainly do not deny that strategic electoral moves are important for office-seeking political parties, we think that the ideological openness to and production of illiberal ideas underpin such tactical moves and the wilful ignorance of authoritarian tendencies.

In making our argument we build on the literature that has shown that – consciously or unconsciously – conservative and new right forces during the 1970s and 1980s have followed a Gramscian script when trying to rebuild their power (e.g., Leggewie 1987b; Biebricher 2018: 87; Hall 1988; Abrahamsen et al. 2024). As conservative and new right forces saw a power base of the left in cultural institutions – primarily education and the media – they often fought hard to win back "cultural hegemony." As the famous report of the Trilateral Commission on the "governability of democracies" put it, the development of "adversary culture" by left-wing intellectuals ("terrorists") was a threat "as serious as those posed in the past by the aristocratic cliques, fascist movements, and communist parties." (Crozier et al. 1975: 7). Hence, ideology – with a considerable material base in public institutions and defining influence on access to power – was an essential part of democracy's dialectics, and one that is often overlooked in current debates. Typical tropes of (neo)conservative ideology such as nationalism, anticommunism, xenophobia, racism, masculinity, and law and order thus have been very much a staple of conservative thinking and politics long before Europe's Eastern European strongmen rallied against multiculturalism and embraced illiberalism as their ideological platform.

Third, for Europeans conservative and new right forces, ideological reorientation on the domestic level was only one of the strategies for wrestling back power from the left. Equally important was their *internationalization* strategy (Wolkenstein 2023). As European integration picked up, and Social Democrats were perceived as particularly powerful on the European level, Europe's conservatives sought to strengthen international cooperation with a broad range of like-minded political parties. Out of this cooperation, ultimately the EU's powerful European People's Party (EPP) grouping emerged, which is widely seen as one of the international enablers of democratic backsliding in the East (e.g., Kelemen 2020).

Ultimately, the argument that we seek to develop here is that democratic backsliding in Eastern Europe is enabled by a long-term struggle over political dominance in which mainstream conservative political parties seek to cement their power on domestic and European levels. This struggle is multidimensional, encompassing the articulation of a conservative ideology and a tactical strategy not shying away from embracing political allies with clear autocratic leanings. This struggle has its roots in the challenge posed by 1968 to conservativism, and thus far precedes the end of the cold war.

In order to make our case, we will look at how German Christian Democracy has reinvented itself in reaction to 1968 and its aftermath. German Christian Democracy is a crucial case. As the biggest member state of the EU, where Christian Democracy has remained an important political player and has shaped the Eastern enlargement, it is key to understanding the international context which has enabled the likes of Viktor Orbán to come to power and dismantle democracy.

The chapter is structured as follows. In the next section we discuss the ideological reinvention of German Christian Democracy as a reaction to the perceived challenges of 1968 and its aftermath. The third section looks at the strategic moves of said party, paying particular attention to its internationalization strategy which culminated in the EPP as a "broad tent" of conservative forces on the European level. Sections four and five illustrate how this particular context has shaped the ascent of authoritarian governments in Eastern Europe. Section four focuses on the – quite well-known – Hungarian case, whereas section five on the less known role of German and European conservatives in supporting authoritarianism in the Western Balkans. The final section concludes with implications for the study and practice of democracy.

14.2 REINVENTING GERMAN CHRISTIAN DEMOCRACY AFTER 1968

Cold War and post-Cold War Europe was shaped profoundly by Christian Democratic parties in power (Invernizzi Accetti 2019). Nowhere was this more pronounced than in (West) Germany, where Christian Democrats were the dominant government party from 1949 to 1969, and then again from 1981. German Christian Democrats strengthened during the upheavals of the end of the Cold War by becoming the party of unification and were ousted only in 1997. After a brief stint in opposition, they made a comeback to power in 2005.

In the first, immediate post-World War II period, the rule of Christian Democracy coincided with what Wolkenstein (2022) calls a "20 years anomaly in the history of Christian Democracy" namely that "in contrast to their immediate predecessors, the postwar Christian Democrats were largely convinced democrats who worked for peace, reconstruction and stability in Europe – at least when it came to a certain setting of representative democratic institutions." However, Wolkenstein cautions, the democratic commitment of Christian Democracy even in this historic phase was limited: a strong leadership style prevailed, there was open admiration for dictators Franco and Salazar, democracy was narrowly conceived as elitist with limited mass involvement in politics, and as nonliberal, rooted in a conservative understanding of the social order (Wolkenstein 2022: 8, 86–95). As he sees it, the main democratic achievement of postwar Christian Democracy was that it did not topple the democratic postwar order, but rather pursued its conservative, paternalistic, and hierarchical brand of policy largely within its framework.

This brand came under increasing pressure from the 1960s onward. As elsewhere in Europe, in Germany it was the cultural revolution of the 1960s, a more self-confident Social Democracy, and new – feminist, civil rights, pacifist, green – social movements which pushed for more liberal and participatory forms of democratic governance. Social Democracy's policy of détente also took the sting out of the "communist danger," challenging Christian Democracy's fervent anticommunism. Having narrowly lost power in 1969, German Christian Democrats were presented "with a real challenge: How could it 'update' its electoral offer without alienating some of its most committed voters, who held on to more conservative values – not to mention older party members?" (Wolkenstein 2023: 3).

The 1970s and 1980s ushered in a renewal of Christian Democracy – a long and partly contradictory process to address that challenge. Programmatically, Germany's Christian Democracy became more liberal, also gradually losing its Christian identity. At the same time, however, it also opened to political forces and ideas further to the right. This was particularly true for the Bavarian Christian Social Union (CSU) under its chairman Franz Josef Strauß.[1] When Strauß paid a visit to Chile's dictator Augusto Pinochet in 1977, he commented on the military dictatorship, "In view of the chaos that prevailed in Chile, the word order suddenly has a sweet sound again for the Chileans" (Bayernkurier, September 22, 1973; quoted in Bösch 2024: 275, translation ours). For our

---

[1] Helmut Kohl was leader of the Christian Democratic Union (CDU) from 1973 to 1998, and Chancellor of Germany from 1982 to 1998. CDU has been in alliance with the Bavarian Christian Socialist Union (CSU). During the period of interest, its leader Franz Josef Strauß (chairman of the CSU 1961–1988; Prime Minister of Bavaria 1979–1988) shaped the party's strategy. Later CSU leaders continued his opening to the radical right.

purpose, one specific characteristic is notable. The reinvention of German Christian Democracy was not only electoral-strategic, although this element of course often prevailed, but the Christian Democratic alliance under its leader Helmut Kohl also sought to assume moral and cultural leadership. The hopes for a *geistig moralische* Wende (spiritual-moral change), that Kohl's ascent to power epitomized, emerged out of a conservative reaction to the cultural achievements of 1968. During the 1970s and 1980s, conservative intellectuals, think tanks, and politicians formulated a trenchant critique of the spirit of 1968, which consciously or unconsciously followed a Gramscian script (Leggewie 1987b; Biebricher 2018: 87). That is, conservative forces saw a major danger in that 1968ers had taken over cultural positions – such as schools, universities, and idea production – and were prepared to fight the left on this very cultural terrain. As education was carried out in a sizeable public sector, the fight over culture also had material underpinnings.

At the same time, modernizers within the Christian Democratic Union (CDU) picked up some of the agenda of newly emerging social movements, while simultaneously putting a wedge between old and new social movements. This endeavor was so successful that a leading Social Democrat acknowledged in 1986 that "the intellectuals of the right have destroyed the argumentative ability of our functionaries and supporters" (Peter Glotz, quoted in Leggewie 1987b: 298).[2]

It is true that many of the conservative intellectuals were disappointed with the actual implementation of their ideas once Kohl took power in 1982 (e.g., Wirsching 2012). Even so, however, moral-political questions were important for Kohl, even if his cabinets fell short of implementing many of them. For Kohl, 1968 had ushered in a spiritual – moral – crisis. Much like Margaret Thatcher in the United Kingdom, Kohl saw Germany as a country confronted with "a deep sense of insecurity, fed by fear and helplessness, fear of economic decline, worry about jobs, fear of environmental destruction, fear of arms race, fear of many young people about their future." To overcome this crisis, spiritual leadership was needed, something he saw lacking in the governing Social Democrats (Kohl quoted in Biebricher 2018: 49, translation ours). In retrospect, four tenets of the "real existing" spiritual-moral renewal stand out: the rejection of the "socialist way," the re-evaluation of the family, the renaissance of classic bourgeois virtues, and the normalization of nationalism (Hoeres 2013: 106, 117).

In terms of fighting socialism, Kohl "sought to generate fear of a decline of 'freedom' in the FRG due to constant intimidation by the dogmatic ideologies that he ascribed to the communist regimes in the East, the '68 generation and sometimes even the Social Democrats" (Wicke 2015: 211). His party was the

---

[2] Space prevents us from going into detail. Hoeres (2013), Leggewie (1987, 1988), and Biebricher (2018) provide good summaries of the intellectuals, idea production, and conservative networks of the renewal period.

only one that could guarantee freedom. In 1976, the CDU campaigned with the slogan "For the love of Germany: freedom instead of socialism." While coined and launched by the conservative Alfred Dregger, the slogan also responded to the more radical formulation by CSU leader Franz Josef Strauß, who was the first to put the notion of freedom as the alternative to socialism in the center of his party' programmatic renewal. The slogan was directed against the new Ostpolitik, the GDR, but also the Social Democrats. In Strauß' reading, freedom already had strong neoliberal connotations, including "a withdrawal of the state, the downsizing of the welfare state, limiting the power of ... trade unions" and fostering competition (Wolkenstein 2023: 13/14).

The reevaluation of the family manifested itself mostly in conservative family policies, and repeated – albeit ultimately unsuccessful – pushes to limit women's reproductive rights. While in Northern European countries public infrastructure for childcare had been expanded since the 1960s, and the dual earner model of employment became the norm, under the Kohl government tax incentives encouraged married women to withdraw from the labor market, and newly introduced childcare allowances, parental leave policies, and the recognition of a baby year as part of women's' pension contribution all conspired to reward stay-at-home mothers (Gottfried and O'Reilly 2002; Wirsching 2012). Interestingly, these family policies were conceived by one of the modernizers, Heiner Geißler, who explicitly targeted trade unions and the Social Democratic Party (SPD). He accused them of only defending their privileged role, while the "new social question" concerned women with children and the elderly (Ostner 2010: 55).

The renaissance of bourgeois virtues is mostly reflected in a rejection of the "entitlement bubble" supposedly unleashed by welfare state expansion. For Kohl, instead, behavioral orientations such as a willingness to make sacrifices and to work hard and perform are seen as civic duties. Importantly, Kohl ties these virtues back to the founding myth of West Germany: economic reconstruction and the ensuing economic miracle. According to Kohl, "What succeeded in 1949 under heavy psychological wounds and material burdens is possible again today" (Kohl, quoted in Biebricher 2018: 51, translation ours). Thus, the spirit of 1948 was to be mobilized against the spirit of 1968 (Biebricher 2018: 51).

Kohl's major spiritual project however was that of normalizing German nationalism (Wicke 2015). Aiming "to dampen the postnational aberrations of 1968" (Wicke 2015: 5), he promoted nationalism as the foundation of Western liberal societies and of European integration, and sought to "reconcile the categorial principle of Westbindung with the promotion and revival of national identity" (ibid. 210). He did so by combining and rehabilitating a romantic and partly even *völkisch* nationalism. He downplayed the responsibility of conservative forces for Hitler's rise to power and the continuities between Nazi Germany and West Germany, and sought to relativize Germany's historical responsibility for the holocaust and World War

II.[3] He also expressed a commitment to the restoration of Germany's territorial unity long before this was a distinct possibility. Territorial unity – including the challenge of existing borders – was also meant as a signal to one of the right-nationalist constituencies of the CDU/CSU, namely Germans expelled from Eastern Europe after World War II. The initial opposition of the CDU/CSU against the Social Democratic Ostpolitik brought the Federation of German expellees (*Bund der Vertriebenen*) again close to the CDU/CSU. The latter, especially, saw the expellees as an important clientele for wrestling back power from the Social Democrats.

Importantly, both the relativization of Nazi Germany and the aim of restoring Germany's national territorial unit were always embedded in a firm commitment to the EU and West-integration. West-integration and nationalism were thus not contradictory. Rather, the normalization of nationalism was only possible within the framework of the EU, which was to be deepened and strengthened at the same time. According to Betz (1988: 144), Kohl promoted a form of historical consciousness and nationalism with which Germans could identify and regain confidence, while also fending off tendencies toward anti-Western neonationalism that had appeared on the far right. Kohl's determination to achieve Germany's unification once the opportunity arose, while combining it with strong commitment to the deepening of European integration, epitomizes this nationalist-Western strategy.

To be sure, for most committed conservatives, the CDU's attempt at seizing moral-political leadership was more than disappointing. Kohl's unwavering commitment to European integration, the inconsistencies when it came to concrete policies, the presence of very different streams and networks within the CDU all left their marks on policymaking. Along with many other factors, they pointed to a healthy dose of pragmatism rather than ideological commitment to nationalist and conservative ideas. The latter was more pronounced by the CSU, whose chairman Strauß famously declared that there must be no viable party to the right of the CSU, a political strategy that was picked up also by his successors.[4] However, even in its meagre record, there is no denying that the CDU/CSU response to the cultural revolution of 1968 and the SPD decade pushed right-wing ideas, such as staunch anticommunism,

---

[3] The dispute that broke out in 1986 between West German historians (the famous *Historikerstreit*) epitomizes the revision of German history and identity. The debate evolved around three questions: Was the holocaust a singular event? Was Germany alone responsible for unleashing World War II? Was Nazism only suicidal, or did it have a modernization impulse too? Taken together, the debate sought to relativize German "guilt," allow for a "normal" German identity, and restore Germany's place as a reliable Western ally that was first to fight the communist danger. The relativization of Germany's history has been part of Kohl's governmental agenda, as witnessed in his project of a national history museum, and the visits with French President Mitterrand in Verdun and with American President Ronald Reagan in Bitburg (e.g., Ely 1995, Biebricher 2018).

[4] E.g. https://tinyurl.com/3eymw4vp.

restauration of the family value and civic virtues, and the normalization of German nationalism onto the agenda. While Kohl embodied the more liberal and moderate version of this thinking, Strauß catered to more radical political forces on the right. Pursuing right-wing ideas was however only one of the strategies with which Christian Democrats tried to establish their dominance in the new context. The other was to build up an international network of more or less like-minded parties to counter the socialist and Eurocommunist international networks through a "black international."[5]

14.3 BUILDING A "BLACK INTERNATIONAL" AND ENLARGING IT EASTWARDS

The internationalization of European Christian Democracy started in the mid 1970s. In 1976, the EPP was founded. Initially, there were two different visions about its purpose. German Christian Democrats, especially the CSU, aimed at creating a broad antisocialist alliance of conservative and right-wing liberal parties of EU and non-EU countries alike.[6] The second vision of the EPP was that of the Italian, Dutch, and Belgian Christian Democracy, who preferred an ideologically coherent grouping. The EPP was initially built on the preferences of the latter group, but ultimately the vision of German Christian Democrats prevailed. In fact, the CSU never gave up its idea of a more radically conservative and antisocialist transnational alliance. In 1977, at the CSU headquarters in Munich, twelve parties from ten countries decided to set up a "European Democratic Union" (EDU) – according to the will of its initiator, Strauß, a kind of Socialist International with the opposite political platform. For Strauß, the issue was not "the flawless stamp of Christian-democratic provenance," but "the question facing Europe is: will the future of Europe be liberal or socialist?" (Der Spiegel 1977). The EDU was to unite a broad spectrum of conservative and right-wing parties inside and outside of the EU, such as the British conservatives, or the Austrian People's Party. According to Wolkenstein (2023:14/15), the EDU was used by Strauß "as a lever to promote [his] more conservative political commitments ... and ... as an opportunity to battle the left *within* and *without* the Christian Democratic Family" (emphasis in the original).

The EDU was also to become the template for the EPP. From the 1980s onward, the EPP increasingly gave up its Christian Democratic coherence in a quest for more members. A most influential decision was to admit Spain's newly founded *Partido Popular* (PP). The PP emerged from a merger of *Alianza Popular* with several conservative right-wing parties. Under its President Aznar who also led the PP into the EPP, the PP was reorganized into a "cohesive and

---

[5] The term "black international" was – to our best knowledge – first used in the newspaper *Die Furche* (1977).

[6] For reasons of simplicity, we use EU also for its precursor, the European Economic Community.

highly specialized and hierarchical organization," whose leader had an "extraordinary range of powers" (Balfour 2004: 149). Although the PP aimed to recast itself as a centrist political party, the values of Opus Dei, and not even well-hidden remnants of Francoism, kept it firmly on the right under Aznar's leadership. Aznar himself did not shy away from political polarization. He "believed that those who were not with him were against him and came close to saying that those who were against him could not be democrats" (Woodworth 2004: 8).

The PPs influence in the EPP became especially important once the Italian Christian Democrats disappeared as a consequence of the *Mani pulite* investigations of the 1990s. It became the most important party next to the German CDU/CSU, and from 1999 on Aznar's personal secretary became the EPPs Secretary General (Martens 2008: 117). The PP, like its German counterpart, thought enlargement of the EPP essential in order for it to keep its power. Consequently, in the 1990s, the EPP "embraced Berlusconi's Forza Italia, French Gaullists and Nordic conservatives while reaching a working pact with Britain's Tory MEPs. Two loose criteria for membership prevailed: a distaste for socialism, and allegiance to the EU project" (Barker 2019).

This "merger and acquisition spree" (Barker 2019) of political parties on the right was primarily driven by strategic considerations, as Berlusconi, together with the French neo-Gaullists, threatened to form a new European Party. EPP leaders feared that such a group would attract members of the EPP, and that the EPP would be split into a left and right wing, and thus lose its crucial position of power. At a meeting with central EPP figures convened by Kohl in 1998 in his cottage, the EPP developed a seven-point blueprint for the right-wing takeover of Brussels, which included renouncing the "exclusive Christian Democratic values," taking in as many conservative parties as possible, as well as the merger between the EPP and the "looser, nationally oriented EDU" (Martens 2008: 142–43, Barker 2019). The cottage memo also spelled out a more efficient organization of the party group. As a consequence, "by 1999, this political M&A spree had helped create the biggest party in the European Parliament, knocking the Socialists off the top spot for the first time. Within a decade, its representation around the EU summit table grew from two of 15 leaders to 16 of 27 in 2012, precooking positions on treaties, bailouts and assorted EU disputes" (Barker 2019). The M&A (mergers and acquisitions) spree also translated into positions in the Brussels machinery, with the EPP dominating the European Commission and its presidency, as well as the Council.

A particularly important opportunity for consolidating the EPP's power was its enlargement to Eastern Europe. The cottage memo also set the foundation for this process. Point three of the memo reads:

The EPP must remain a key player. If we limit ourselves effectively to the present formation, we will never achieve a majority position. We should think of new members. Among other things, a European party cannot limit itself solely to European Union parties. For this reason, we should accept within our ranks parties from candidate Member States from Central and Eastern Europe. (Martens 2008: 143)

The concerns about new East European members of the EPP political family varied. Potential affiliates might have lacked Christian Democratic credentials, their ideological orientation was uncertain, their organizational and infrastructural capacity was weak. Party systems were fluid and the political scene on the center right "often proved confused and certainly overpopulated" (Delsoldato 2002: 278). The neocommunists, it was feared, could "show their face in many ways" (van Laarhoven 2008). The selection process was influenced by member parties – "there were constantly real and pressing reasons for this or that (western European) party as to why certain (central or eastern European) parties should immediately be admitted" (Jansen 1998: 152). To facilitate the process and ensure its "pedagogical responsibility," EPP changed its statutes – in Madrid in 1995, and in Toulouse in 1997 – and created new categories of membership – observer status for parties from noncandidate countries and associate membership for parties from candidate countries. Established criteria required that prospective members adhere to Christian Democratic principles and operate in countries which have "a system based on liberty, democracy, and a rule of law." In reality, however, politics

tended to prevail over ideological orientation and the larger parties happened to be more easily recognized as sister parties, external competition (that is, between the EPP and the PES[7] and on a minor scale, the ELDR[8]), over internal cohesion ... superficial affinity turned out to be more important than in-depth knowledge, which was partly due to the difficulty of understanding postcommunist political systems. (Delsoldato 2022: 282)

The result of this pragmatic outreach to new members became obvious after the first two waves of enlargement. While the number of political parties in the EPP increased from eleven to just fourteen between 1976 and 1989, there were seventy-four parties under its umbrella in 2010 (Zotti 2010). To socialize these parties into their new family the Eastern enlargement of the EPP was preceded and accompanied by a "soft foreign policy" through a network of political foundations and institutes, which "arranged chances for like-minded people from both parts of Europe to meet and debate in the course of seminars they organized" (Jansen 1998: 150). The key player in political education of new members was the Robert Schuman Institute (RSI), a 1995 successor to the Academy for Central and Eastern Europe, founded in 1991 by the European Union of Christian Democrats (EUCD)[9] in Budapest. In 2002, Robert Schuman

[7] PES – The Party of European Socialists.
[8] ELDR – The Group of the European Liberal Democrat and Reform Party was a liberal political group of the European Parliament between 1976 and 2004.
[9] The European Union of Christian Democrats was a predecessor, competitor, and partner of the EPP. Founded in 1965, it brought together Christian Democratic values to common European political platforms. After the creation of the EPP in 1976, the EUCD and EPP were divided over the openness to non-Christian Democratic parties (the EPP was in favor). After the end of the

was also joined by the Center for Political Parliamentary Education and Training (CET), funded by the EPP and also located in Budapest. Their work was often complemented by the work of German political foundations, particularly Konrad Adenauer Stiftung (KAS) (affiliated with CDU) and Hanns Seidel Stiftung (affiliated with CSU). The institutes and foundations, along with the EPP's Working Group ("Central and Eastern Europe," renamed "Enlargement" and then "EPP Membership") trained, educated, and vetted membership applications from prospective political parties in Eastern Europe and the Balkans. Their work was frequently synchronized with activities of the US International Republican Institute. In the words of Gabor Berczeli, the RSI Director, the Institute and its affiliates "trained the full spectrum of people in politics, from the figurehead politicians to the advisers and also regular party workers" (Crumpton 2021: 8).

The reliance on political foundations and institutes was the continuation of West Germany's Cold War foreign policy, constrained by the legacy of World War II. Concerned about open interference in other countries' affairs, yet also very much involved in the Cold War struggle against communism, Germany had long relied on the work of its foundations to project its civilian power (Harnisch and Maull 2001; Wolff 2013). Thus, even after 1989, when democracy promotion became the norm, Germany "has been prioritising a rather 'soft conditionality' while preferring dialogue, incentives and long-term strategies of taking influence; coercive measures have been (and are) the exception" (Wolff 2013).

To recap, thus far we have argued that German Christian Democracy has countered its decline in the aftermath of 1968 by a double strategy: the proclamation of an updated reservoir of conservative ideas domestically, and an internationalization strategy out of which the powerful EPP has emerged. While the internationalization strategy has come at the expense of ideological cohesion, members of the EPP are united in a fusion of nationalism, commitment to European integration, and anticommunism. Importantly, internationalization has extended to the EU's new East European members and candidate countries. It is to this process that we now turn. The following two sections will illustrate how the internationalization strategy of German Christian Democracy in the East has enabled rather than tamed democratic backsliding in the East, with its customary "soft conditionality" as a charitable explanation for complacency vis-à-vis budding and established autocrats.

14.4 THE DISCRETE CHARM OF VIKTOR ORBÁN'S ULTRACONSERVATIVE PROJECT

As widely documented, the EPP, and within it first and foremost members of the German CDU/CSU, has systematically backed Hungarian Prime Minister

Cold War, as the EPP grew exponentially, the EUCD lost its purpose and eventually disbanded in 1999 (Tensen et al. 2014).

Viktor Orbán despite the fact that from his second term of office in 2010, he started to systematically dismantle democratic checks and balances. Existing literature mostly attributes this to a pure power strategy, as coddling Eastern Europe's autocrats allows to maximize seats in the European Parliament (Kelemen 2020). While this argument is not wrong, it is incomplete. Below, we argue that CDU/CSU support also reflects shared values and beliefs among right-wing conservatives who were disenchanted with Angela Merkel's pragmatic and centrist leadership.

In 2014, a letter by former German Chancellor Helmut Kohl to Viktor Orbán made headlines. In this letter, Kohl addressed his "dear friend Viktor" in light of the upcoming parliamentary elections and assured him of his support. He stressed the need for stability in Europe and continued, "I know we agree that in order to achieve stability, value-based politics that is reliable, shows leadership, and thus offers people a clear perspective is needed" (Letter by Kohl reproduced in Balogh 2014, translation ours). There has been some debate whether this letter indeed came from Kohl, who had been in bad health since 2008, and was widely seen as not any longer being able to clearly articulate himself. The point we want to stress here, however, is that even if the letter most likely did not stem from Kohl, it could have. This is because both politicians stressed the need for a moral-value-based leadership.

Indeed, in his infamous "illiberal democracy" speech at the twenty-fifth Băile Tuşnad Summer Open University and Student Camp, 2014, Orbán stressed such conservative virtues as families, hard work, aversion against debt, and the significance of Christianity and nationalism for community building. In 2018, in his address to the twenty-ninth Băile Tuşnad University, he became more offensive, contrasting his brand of Christian Democracy to that of liberal democracy. As he formulates it:

Let us confidently declare that Christian democracy is not liberal. ... And we can specifically say this in connection with a few important issues ... Liberal democracy is in favour of multiculturalism, while Christian democracy gives priority to Christian culture; this is an illiberal concept. Liberal democracy is pro-immigration, while Christian democracy is anti-immigration; this is again a genuinely illiberal concept. And liberal democracy sides with adaptable family models, while Christian democracy rests on the foundations of the Christian family model; once more, this is an illiberal concept. (Orbán 2018)

Importantly, Orbán's concept of Christian democracy is conceived within the framework of his project of building an illiberal and authoritarian state, and it is increasingly embedded in an attempt to conquer Christian democracy on the European level (Bohle et al. 2023). Thus, Orbán reclaims a political project that is compatible with some of the values that informed Kohl's attempt at spiritual-moral leadership, but he radicalizes these values and puts them in the service of his authoritarian state building and European ambitions. This project appealed in particular to those forces in the CDU/CSU who were convinced that Kohl's successor, Angela Merkel, turned the party too much to the center. This became particularly visible during the so-called refugee crisis, where Merkel's policy of opening borders came under strong criticism from the CSU, and Orbán's hard-liner approach – building fences, denying the right to asylum, inhuman treatment of refugees – was seen as Merkel's antipode. At the height of the crisis, Horst Seehofer, then chairman of the CSU and Prime Minister of Bavaria invited Orbán to a party meeting and also paid a visit to Budapest. Still, in 2019, Seehofer defended Orbán's democratic credentials (Fischer 2015; Die Welt 2019).

This value-based backing of Orbán also shows in the close ties that KAS kept to Fidesz even during the 2010s and early 2020s. Thus, in 2011, then president of KAS, and former president of the European Parliament and EPP member, Hans-Gert Pöttering paid a visit to Hungary just on the day when the new constitution that is widely perceived as ushering in Hungary's democratic backsliding was adopted (KAS 2011). Already in 2004, Pöttering – together with Ursula Braun-Moser, then president of the awarding foundation – presented Viktor Orbán the Mérite Européen, an award that is given to people who do a lot for Europe (Magyar Nemzet 2004). Ursula Braun-Moser was an economist and right-wing member of the CDU who took a special interest in Eastern Europe. She was also an EPP member between 1984 and 1994. In 2014, she became a member of the far-right *Alternative für Deutschland* (AFD).

The Hungarian KAS has remained a close ally to Orbán. In an interview with *Budapester Zeitung* in 2021, Frank Spengler, who was at the helm of the foundation from 2014 to 2021, accords most of the criticism toward Orbán to a lack of knowledge. He defined his task in a balanced reporting from Hungary, in which "both sides" would get space to express themselves. While he does acknowledge disagreements between German Christian Democracy and Fidesz, he however argues that there is a common ideological ground in the commitment to fundamental values of Christianity, subsidiarity, and human dignity (Urbán 2021; Mainka 2021).

Another former KAS employee, Bence Bauer, who worked for the foundation for more than ten years, became director of the German-Hungarian Institute for European Cooperation at the Matthias Corvinus Collegium (MCC). MCC, founded in 1996 by a businessman close to Fidesz, has since 2020 become a major educational enterprise and think tank that aims to spread ultraconservative values domestically and abroad. In 2020, the foundation behind it received about 1.7 billion euros in the forms of shares, public money, and real estate – an endowment more sizeable than that of all Hungarian universities taken together. MCC has erected or plans to erect branches in thirty-five European cities. One of its most recent additions is a think tank in Brussels (Lau 2022; Enyedi 2023). The stated goal of the MCC is to "prepare the next patriotic generation," and to this aim it engages

in a number of educational activities (Becker et al. 2022; Lau 2022). According to Lau (2022), former KAS employee Bauer,

who grew up in Ludwigsburg in a German-Hungarian family, was always a convinced anti-communist. In his office at the MCC is a small altar with a piece of Iron Curtain barbed wire with a crown of thorns inside. A gold-framed portrait of Helmut Kohl stands in a glass case underneath, at the bottom one of Konrad Adenauer. Bauer believes that Hungary is consistently misunderstood in Germany, to Germany's detriment. Hungary, he hints, lives the values that Germany lost in its multiculturalism." (Lau 2022, translation ours)

KAS frequently co-organizes events with MCC, and serves as a door opener for the foundation to Germany (Becker et al. 2022). Thus, for instance, Merkel's successor as chairman of the CDU, Friedrich Merz, an outspoken conservative, had his book *Neue Zeit. Neue Verantwortung* (New Times, New Responsibility) translated and published by MCC – the only translation of the book so far. Werner Patzelt, professor emeritus and well-known conservative member of the Saxonian CDU who had repeatedly warned that the party had moved too much to the center and advocated a coalition between CDU and AFD for the Saxonian state, served as guest professor at MCC.

14.5 CONSERVATIVE EMBRACE BEYOND HUNGARY

Even though the former Yugoslav states have been excluded from discussions about democratic backsliding (primarily because it is assumed that most states in the Balkans were not – unlike Hungary and Poland – *consolidated* democracies to begin with), they merit attention in this context as important sites of German and CDU/CSU political interventions, dating back many decades. In addition, and again unlike in Hungary and Poland, CDU/CSU support for sister – Christian or people's – political parties from Slovenia to Macedonia cannot be fully explained by strategic calculations of EPP expansion in the European parliament as it has never been limited to EU members or candidates only. The checkered nature of European integration in the Western Balkans has only amplified the importance of Germany in this corner of Europe as its politicians act as the principal brokers of access to the EU. And while the Balkans strategic and economic significance is not immediately obvious (for instance, Bosnia and Herzegovina, once a major VW producer, these days only exports labor to Germany), the region is a polygon where right-wing politicians and great powers test their limits and expand boundaries of permissible politics. Not even the violence and destructive power of nationalism in the former Yugoslavia could challenge CDU/CSU ideological commitments to the region's conservative leaders, who were early champions of historical revisionism, Christian family values, and anticommunism (despite – or sometimes perhaps – because of their own communist backgrounds). Instead, local nationalism(s) mask the significance of transnational embeddedness and networks, and the degree to which extreme positions (anti-Semitism, Islamophobia, homophobia, misogyny) travel across borders while their proponents politically support and legitimize each other.

The backing of Croatian and Slovenian Christian/nationalist parties and leaders pre-dates the Yugoslav wars. German unilateral recognition of Croatian and Slovenian independence in 1991 was controversial for years (Crawford 1996), as was its role in the illegal arming of Croats throughout the Bosnian war. Both were prompted by the CSU, due in part to the large presence of a Croatian diaspora in Bavaria but also the important role that the Vatican and the Catholic Church have played in the region. Kohl's embrace of Croatian President Franjo Tudjman remained steadfast until his death in 1999, despite the latter's anti-Semitism, Euroscepticism, and suspected involvement in war crimes. Demonization of communists and rehabilitation of the Croatian Nazi collaborators – Croatian Ustashe – remain the cornerstones of HDZ (Hrvatska Demokratska Zajednica) ideology. And while the EPP did not accept Tudjman's party (HDZ) even as an observer until 2002, its lobbying was crucial for Croatia's accession and eventual admission into the EU in 2008.

In Slovenia, where the political party landscape continued to change throughout the 1990s and early 2000s, the CDU/CSU – and the EPP – backed several political parties and a handful of politicians – most notably Alojz Peterle, a founder of the Christian Democrats in 1990, and Janez Janša, a former communist whose political trajectory over the last three decades has covered the entire political spectrum from left to right. In 2008, during Slovenian presidency of the European Council, Janša initiated hearings on "Crimes Committed by Totalitarian Regimes," pushing for a common platform on European memory and conscience (Hozić 2014). Meanwhile, his continued involvement in arms trade and procurement (including illegal arms trafficking in the 1990s) led to Janša's sentencing on corruption charges in 2013. His return to power in 2020 was marked by a sharp turn toward authoritarianism in Slovenian politics, primarily manifest – as in Hungary – in attacks on the courts, media, and cultural institutions. Nonetheless, Janša continued to enjoy the EPP's backing even in his 2022 electoral loss.

The Macedonian nationalist VMRO-DPMNE party (Internal Macedonian Revolutionary Organization – Democratic Party for Macedonian National Unity), especially under the leadership of Nikola Gruevski (2004–2017), was also a beneficiary of CDU/CSU support. The VMRO-DPNE cadre was trained by the RSI, KAS, and other foundations in the EPP orbit. During his term as prime minister (2006–2016), Gruevski consolidated his power by taking control of the media through massive pro-government advertising campaigns, large infrastructure projects such as "Skopje 2014," highlighting historical continuities between contemporary Macedonia and Alexander the Great, and through escalation of tensions with the Albanian minority and with Greece over the country's name (Crowther 2017). By 2014, even Angela Merkel's government had cooled off its financial support for Gruevski's infrastructure loans and played a crucial role in managing the country's 2015–2017 political crisis (Weber 2019). And yet, in 2015, at the celebration of the fifteenth anniversary of KAS' work in FYR (Former Yugoslav Republic) Macedonia, appearing side by side with Prime Minster Gruevski, Stiftung's Secretary General Michael Thielen reaffirmed its support for VMRO-DPMNE and proudly stated that they were able "to organize more than 500 events with 20.000 participants and to publish over 100 publications" (Government of the Republic of North Macedonia 2015). At the height of the opposition protests against Gruevski's government in September 2016, he was still able to visit Berlin with his VMRO-DPMNE delegation (Deutsche Welle 2016). The visit was arranged by a CSU legislator Tobias Zach, who resigned from the Bundestag in 2021 over VMRO-DPMNE payments for his consultancy services (Marusic 2021). After losing the elections in 2016, Gruevski would eventually find asylum in Hungary with the help of its intelligence services and at the behest of his long-term supporter Viktor Orbán. The CDU/CSU and KAS support for VMRO-DPMNE has remained steadfast in the last presidential elections of 2024.

And in Bosnia and Herzegovina, which has been in the protectorate status since the end of the war in 1995, CDU/CSU was able to install one of its own – a CSU politician Christian Schmidt, a former Minister of Agriculture (2014–2018) – into the position of the High Representative, just a month before Angela Merkel's departure from office in September of 2021. Schmidt has since openly used the extraordinary powers vested in his office (the so-called "Bonn powers") to promote the political interests of the Bosnian HDZ party – an affiliate of the Croatian HDZ. Right after the elections in October 2022, Schmidt introduced controversial changes in the Bosnian electoral law guaranteeing a disproportionate number of seats – and thus a role in the government – to HDZ. Croatia, with implicit support of EPP and right-wing politicians in the EU – such as Jancz Janša and Viktor Orbán – has long lobbied for the "third entity" in Bosnia and Herzegovina, which would be controlled by the Croat minority and solidify ethnic partition of the country. Schmidt's intervention in the electoral law is seen as a step in that direction, greatly influenced by his own role in CSU and in the Hanns Seidel Stiftung, long-term supporters of both the Croat and Bosnian HDZ.

14.6 CONCLUSION

In this chapter, we aimed to establish that the current wave of democratic backsliding in Europe was also enabled by conservative Christian Democratic parties, particularly by the German CDU/CSU, whose adaptation to crises, socioeconomic change, and mobilizations on the left have always entailed ideological and strategic expansions to the right. While much has been written about the collapse of the left in Europe, the vacuum that was created by the "Third Way" politics, and the coziness of the German SPD leadership with

Vladimir Putin, European and especially German center right parties have never been examined with similar scrutiny. Rather, they have been portrayed as the victims of the electoral move to the right or of the predatory parties on the extreme right. Our account, instead, draws attention to the steady and stealth work of the German Christian Democrats and German foundations on the normalization of far-right ideas and politics. The EPP's Ursula van der Leyen's embrace of the Italian neofascist Prime Minister Giorgia Meloni in the 2024 EU parliamentary election is a case in point. This is not to say that German Christian Democrats were or are the only epicenter of European right-wing politics in the last decades. The Vatican has always played an important background role in anticommunist and antigender politics globally (Graff and Korolczuk 2022) and, by the beginning of the twenty-first century, Putin's Russia and the US Christian right coalition had also transnationalized their operations (Cooley and Nexon 2021). This, however, does not change the key implication of our argument: Democratic backsliding in Europe is not a momentary blip caused by exogenous shocks and located in a handful of East European countries. Identity politics and culture wars are not emotional triggers in the otherwise liberal environment but issues with profound political and material consequences – from franchise to employment to the composition of families. We tried to show that right-wing politics has deep ideological roots, and its proponents are well networked within and beyond Europe. While space prevented us from elaborating on this aspect, we also submit that their endgame is socioeconomic transformation rather than cosmetic political regime change. Democracy has never been the only game in town. In order to survive, in Europe and elsewhere, democracy must mean more than just winning elections.

REFERENCES

Abrahamsen, Rita, Jean-François Drolet, Michael C. Williams, Srdjan Vucetic, Karin Narita, and Alexandra Gheciu. *World of the Right: Radical Conservatism and Global Order*. Cambridge: Cambridge University Press, 2024.

Balfour, Sebastian. "The Reinvention of Spanish Conservatism: The Popular Party Since 1989" in Sebastian Balfour (ed.) *The Politics of Contemporary Spain*. London: Routledge, 2004, pp.146–68. https://doi.org/10.4324/9780203002759.

Balogh, Eva S. "Helmut Kohl's Letter to Viktor Orbán." *Hungarian Spectrum* (blog), March 25, 2014. https://hungarianspectrum.org/2014/03/25/helmut-kohls-letter-to-viktor-orban/.

Barker, Alex. "European Elections: Is the Party Over for the Centre-Right?" *Financial Times*, May 15, 2019. www.ft.com/content/dbebc290-7589-11e9-be7d-6d846537acab.

Becker, Andrea, Silvio Duwe, and Daniel Laufer. "Orban, die Konrad-Adenauer-Stiftung und rechte Netzwerke," May 19, 2022. https://tinyurl.com/yc8c7rxs.

Betz, Hans-Georg. "Deutschlandpolitik on the Margins: On the Evolution of Contemporary New Right Nationalism in the Federal Republic." *New German Critique* 44: 127–57, 1988.

Biebricher, Thomas. *Geistig-moralische Wende. Die Erschöpfung des deutschen Konservatismus*. Berlin: Matthes & Seitz Berlin, 2018.

Bohle, Dorothee, Béla Greskovits, and Marek Naczyk. "The Gramscian Politics of Europe's Rule of Law Crisis." *Journal of European Public Policy*, 1–24, online first. 2023. https://doi.org/10.1080/13501763.2023.2182342.

Bösch, Frank. *Deals mit Diktaturen: Eine andere Geschichte der Bundesrepublik*. Munich: C. H. Beck, 2024.

Cooley, Alexander, and Daniel Nexon. *Exit from Hegemony: The Unraveling of the American Global Order*. New York: Oxford University Press, 2021.

Cooper, Melinda. *Family Values: Between Neoliberalism and the New Social Conservatism*. Reprint Edition. New York: Zone Books, 2017.

Crawford, Beverly. "Explaining Defection from International Cooperation: Germany's Unilateral Recognition of Croatia." *World Politics* 48 (4): 482–521, 1996. doi:10.1353/wp.1996.0015.

Crowther, William. "Ethnic Condominium and Illiberalism in Macedonia." *East European Politics and Societies* 31 (4): 739–61, 2017.

Crozier, Michel, Samuel P. Huntington, and Joji Watanuki. *The Crisis of Democracy*. Vol. 70. New York: New York University Press, 1975.

Crumpton, Charlie. "Gabor Berczeli, Director of the Robert Schuman Institute, on the History and Future Plans for Supporting the Centre-Right through Training, Development and Youth Engagement." *BullsEye Magazine*, March 14, 8–9, 2021. https://issuu.com/eurdemstu/docs/bulls_eye_no80_b__2_.

Delsoldato, Giorgia. "Eastward Enlargement by the European Union and Transnational Parties." *International Political Science Review* 23 (3): 269–89, 2002. https://doi.org/10.1177/0192512102023003004.

Der Spiegel. "Kreuth international." March 20, 1977. https://tinyurl.com/7ce2cfs2.

Deutsche Welle. Што бара Груевски во Берлин? September 6, 2016. www.dw.com/mk/што-бара-груевски-во-берлин/a-19529726.

Die Furche. "Christdemokraten aller Länder." August 5, 1977. www.furche.at/meinung/die-schwarze-internationale-organisiert-sich-6862683.

Die Welt. "Horst Seehofer nimmt 'Demokraten' Viktor Orbán gegen Kritik in Schutz." – April 20, 2019. https://tinyurl.com/39f79r9r.

Ely, John. "The 'Frankfurter Allgemeine Zeitung' and Contemporary National-Conservatism." *German Politics & Society* 13 (2) (35): 81–121, 1995.

Enyedi, Zsolt. Illiberal Conservatism, Civilizationist Ethnocentrism, and Paternalistic Populism in Orbán's Hungary. Budapest: Central European University, Democracy Institute, 2023.

Fischer, Sebastian. "Flüchtlinge: Viktor Orban auf CSU-Klausur in Banz." *Der Spiegel*, September 23, 2015, sec. Politik. https://tinyurl.com/yc6xaxyw.

Gottfried, Heidi, and Jacqueline O'Reilly. "Reregulating Breadwinner Models in Socially Conservative Welfare Systems: Comparing Germany and Japan." *Social Politics: International Studies in Gender, State & Society* 9 (1): 29–59, 2002.

Government of the Republic of North Macedonia. "Konrad Adenauer Foundation Marks 15 Years of Its Activity in Macedonia." March 12, 2015. https://vlada.mk/node/11527?ln=en-gb.

Graff, Agnieszka, and Elżbieta Korolczuk. *Anti-Gender Politics in the Populist Moment*. London: Taylor & Francis, 2022. https://library.oapen.org/handle/20.500.12657/50542.

Hall, Stuart. *The Hard Road to Renewal: Thatcherism and the Crisis of the Left.* London: Verso, 1988.

Harnisch, Sebastian, and Hanns W. Maull (eds.). *Germany As a Civilian Power? The Foreign Policy of the Berlin Republic.* Manchester: Manchester University Press, 2001.

Hoeres, Peter. "Von Der 'Tendenzwende' zur 'geistig-Moralischen Wende': Konstruktion Und Kritik Konservativer Signaturen in Den 1970er Und 1980er Jahren." *Vierteljahrshefte Für Zeitgeschichte* 61 (1): 93–119, 2013.

Hozić, Aida A. "It Happened Elsewhere: Remembering 1989 in the Former Yugoslavia" in Michael Bernhard and Jan Kubik (eds.) *Twenty Years After: 1989 and the Politics of Memory.* New York: Oxford University Press, 2014, pp. 233–260.

Invernizzi Accetti, Carlo. *What Is Christian Democracy? Politics, Religion and Ideology.* Cambridge: Cambridge University Press, 2019. https://doi.org/10.1017/9781108 368162.

Jansen, Thomas. *The European Peoples' Party: Origins and Development.* New York: Palgrave Macmillan, 1998.

Jansen, Thomas, und Steven Van Hecke. *At Europe's Service: The Origins and Evolution of the European People's Party.* Dordrecht: Springer Science & Business Media, 2011.

KAS. "Hans-Gert Pöttering trifft Präsident Schmitt und Ministerpräsident Orbán." Auslandsbüro Ungarn, April 20, 2011. https://tinyurl.com/mussfrb5.

Kelemen, R. Daniel. "The European Union's Authoritarian Equilibrium." *Journal of European Public Policy* 27 (3): 481–99 (2020).

Lau, Mariam. "Viktor Orbáns Politik: Die Orbanologie." *Die Zeit*, December 21, 2022, sec. Politik. www.zeit.de/2022/53/viktor-orban-politik-ungarn-budapest/ seite-2.

Leggewie, Claus. *Der Geist steht rechts. Ausflüge in die Denkfabrik der Wende.* Berlin: Rotbuch Verlag, 1987a.

    "Kulturelle Hegemonie: Gramsci und die Folgen." *Leviathan* 15 (2): 285–304, 1987b.

Magyar Nemzet. "Mérite Européen-Díj Orbán Viktornak." *Magyar Nemzet*, March 16, 2004. https://tinyurl.com/4f5977vu.

Mainka, Jan. "Es gibt genug Verbindendes." *Budapest Zeitung*, February 28, 2021. https://tinyurl.com/5n99msv4.

Martens, Wilfried. *Europe: I Struggle, I Overcome: Memoirs.* Dordrecht: Springer, 2008. https://epdf.pub/europe-i-struggle-i-overcome.html.

Marusic, Sinisa Jakov. "German MP who Lobbied for North Macedonia's Ousted Regime Resigns." *Balkan Insight*, March 19, 2021. https://tinyurl.com/2u2x4hs2.

Orbán, Viktor. "Prime Minister Viktor Orbán's Speech at the 29th Bálványos Summer Open University and Student Camp – Miniszterelnok.Hu." July 2018. https:// tinyurl.com/4dwd5x9e.

Ostner, Ilona. "Farewell to the Family As We Know It: Family Policy Change in Germany." *German Policy Studies/Politikfeldanalyse* 6 (1): 211–44, 2010.

Scheppele, Kim Lane "Autocratic Legalism." *The University of Chicago Law Review* 85 (2): 545–84, 2018.

Skocpol, Theda, and Vanessa Williamson. *The Tea Party and the Remaking of Republican Conservatism.* New York: Oxford University Press, 2016.

Tarrow, Sidney. "Trump, Social Movements, and the Rhythms of Resistance." In Presentation at the Presidential Roundtable. Montreal, 2017.

Tensen, Barend, Vít Novotný, Federico Ottavio Reho, and Steven Van Hecke "The Christian Democratic Origins of the European People's Party: Values and Relevance for Policies." Wilfried Martens Center, November 2014. https://tinyurl.com/86ucyhxy.

Urbán, Zsuzsa. "Konrad-Adenauer-Stiftung: 'Genug Verbindendes.'" *Budapester Zeitung*, February 28, 2021. https://tinyurl.com/4b2z26an.

Vachudova, Milada. "Ethnopopulism and Democratic Backsliding in Central Europe." *East European Politics* 36 (3): 318–40, 2020.

van Laarhoven, Jan. "Political party building in Eastern Europe." *European View* 7: 75–80, 2008. doi: 10.1007/s12290-008-0041-y.

Weber, Bodo. "Contested, yet Indispensable Leadership: Germany's Role in Macedonia's Euro-Atlantic Integration." Foundation Open Society – Macedonia, February 2019. https://fosm.mk/wp-content/up-loads/publications/Germany_Role_in_Macedonia.pdf.

Wicke, Christian. *Helmut Kohl's Quest for Normality: His Representation of the German Nation and Himself*. 1st ed. New York: Berghahn Books, 2015.

Wirsching, Andreas. "Eine Ära Kohl? Die Widersprüchliche Signatur Deutscher Regierungspolitik 1982–1998." *Archiv Für Sozialgeschichte* 52: 667–86, 2012.

Wolff, Jonas. "Democracy Promotion and Civilian Power: The Example of Germany's 'Value-Oriented' Foreign Policy." *German Politics* 22 (4): 477–93, 2013. doi: 10.1080/09644008.2013.853043.

Wolkenstein, Fabio. "Between 'Progressive Realism' and Conservative Internationalism: The Transformation of Austrian and German Christian Democracy in the 1970s." unpublished manuscript, Vienna, 2023.

Wolkenstein, Fabio. *Die Dunkle Seite Der Christdemokratie. Geschichte Einer Autoritären Versuchung*. Munich: C. H. Beck Verlag, 2022.

Woodworth, Paddy. "Spain Changes Course: Aznar's Legacy, Zapatero's Prospects." *World Policy Journal* 21 (2): 7–26, 2004.

Zotti, Stefan. "The European People's Party: Identity and Integration" in Werner Fasslabend and Josef Pröll (eds.) *The European People's Party: Successes and Future Challenges*. Vienna: Edition Noir, 2010, p.13–33.

15

Foro Madrid and the Transnationalization of the Far-Right

Stefano Palestini and Cristóbal Rovira Kaltwasser

15.1 INTRODUCTION

While the roots of the contemporary surge in far-right parties trace back to Western Europe (Mudde, 2007), notably exemplified by the Austrian Freedom Party (FPÖ) and the French National Front (FN), it has undeniably evolved into a global phenomenon. Far-right forces have permeated diverse regions, including Australia (One Nation Party), Brazil (Jair Bolsonaro), Chile (José Antonio Kast's Republican Party), India (Modi's Indian People's Party, BJP), Turkey (Recep Tayyip Erdoğan's Justice and Development Party, AKP), and the United States (Donald Trump). The emergence of analogous far-right actors worldwide is not coincidental but reflects a reactionary response to the growing prominence of liberal norms and policies in recent decades. This trend is intricately linked to the rising political clout of various historically marginalized groups. As the latter gain influence and push for accommodation policies, there is an increased likelihood of a backlash from segments of society harboring far-right sentiments, as noted by Bustikova (2020).

Despite the escalating political influence and electoral weight of the far-right, there remains a significant dearth of studies investigating the potential diffusion of far-right ideas and strategies. Addressing this critical research gap, this chapter aims to scrutinize the Foro Madrid, a nascent transnational advocacy network (TAN) predominantly comprising far-right political entities. Originating from VOX, a far-right party in Spain, the Foro Madrid seeks to forge an alliance between Europe and Latin America to counterbalance leftist influence. Through an in-depth analysis of the Foro Madrid, our objectives are threefold. First, we aim to illustrate the far-right's willingness to engage in

Cristóbal Rovira Kaltwasser would like to acknowledge support from Fondo Nacional de Desarrollo Científico y Tecnológico (FONDECYT Project 1220053) and the Centre for Social Conflict and Cohesion Studies (COES; CONICYT/FONDAP/15130009).

international collaboration, forming transnational networks to champion ideas and interests across national boundaries. Contrary to conventional assumptions, we demonstrate, in line with a burgeoning literature in international relations (IR), that such networks not solely coalesce around progressive or liberal norms but can also propagate retrogressive and illiberal agendas. Second, we endeavor to provide an extensive overview of the Foro Madrid, delving into its articulated discourse and the strategies employed to garner support from different actors within the network. This examination draws upon a diverse array of evidence, including official tweets, declarations, and articles authored by participants of the Foro Madrid since its inception in 2020. Lastly, we aim to unravel the paradoxical nature of the Foro Madrid's ideology, ostensibly championing liberalism while resorting to the articulation of illiberal tropes in practice. By discussing the prospects of this transnational network in light of its recent achievements, we discuss the complexities and contradictions inherent within contemporary far-right forces.

Our empirical investigation relies on a qualitative content analysis of the discourse disseminated by the Foro Madrid across various mediums. We systematized and codified all tweets emanating from the Foro Madrid's official account, established in October 2021. Our dataset encompasses 1,369 tweets and retweets generated by the account, which boasts an approximate audience of 20,000 followers. Additionally, we scrutinized three pivotal manifestos: the Carta de Madrid issued in October 2020, the Declaración of Bogotá issued in February 2022, and the Declaración of Lima issued in April 2023. Moreover, our analysis extends to fifty-five articles published in the VOX online newspaper, *La Gaceta de la Iberósfera*. This approach allows us to comprehensively examine the ideas propagated by the Foro Madrid, shedding light on its objectives, strategies, and broader implications.

The rest of this contribution is divided into three parts. We first introduce the concept of TANs as a tool to analyze contemporary far-right movements such as Foro Madrid. Then we describe the origins of the network, the construction of its discourse, and the main political strategies. We conclude with some thoughts about the threat that the Foro Madrid posits to liberal democracy and propose some ideas about how to push forward a research agenda on illiberal TANs.

15.2 TRANSNATIONAL ADVOCACY NETWORKS AND THE FAR-RIGHT

Since its inception by Margaret E. Keck and Katheryn Sikkink in 1998, the concept of TANs has evolved significantly within the international landscape. Initially conceived to spotlight a category of actors largely overlooked by the field of IR, Keck and Sikkink aimed to illuminate the influence wielded by activists, social movements, and nongovernmental organizations in shaping international politics. These networks operated by networking and exerting pressure on intergovernmental organizations (IGOs) and states. The TANs scrutinized by Keck and Sikkink predominantly championed causes such as human rights, environmental protection, and women's rights, aligning themselves with the liberal order or, at the very least, not challenging its fundamental norms and institutions. In fact, these networks often played a pivotal role in upholding liberal norms infringed upon by rogue states and illiberal regimes. From a liberal perspective, TANs were regarded favorably as agents promoting progressive values and ideals.

However, researchers engaging with the concept of TANs must strive to disentangle it from any inherent liberal bias, as noted by scholars such as Bob (2012), Deitelhoff (2020), and Wojczewski (2024). Consequently, the concept should be viewed as "ideologically neutral," capable of elucidating real-world networks that either uphold and reinforce liberal norms or challenge them, advocating for alternative illiberal normative orders. For instance, Encarnación (2020) offers a comparative analysis of networks opposing gay rights movements in the United States and Latin America. Similarly, Sanders (2018) and Cupać and Ebetürk (2020) explore the frames and strategies employed by TANs comprising antifeminist NGOs (nongovernmental organizations) with the aim of curtailing women's rights. Additionally, Bob (2013) illustrates how proponents of gun rights in the United States, Australia, Canada, and Britain, spearheaded by the National Rifle Association, mobilized and networked to counteract a TAN advocating for gun control at the UN level. This dynamic interplay between movements and countermovements, as elucidated by Bob, has recently been conceptualized as "backlash politics." This phenomenon represents a distinctive form of political contestation characterized by retrogressive objectives, employing extraordinary tactics, and attaining a level of visibility in mainstream public discourse, as outlined by Alter and Zürn (2020).

The concept of TANs proves to be analytically relevant in understanding the essence of the Foro Madrid and its aspirations. First, the Foro Madrid embodies a network rather than a formalized organization, with no intention of morphing into one. It functions as a loose conglomerate of entities, predominantly national political parties, within the far-right spectrum, yet harboring significant ideological and organizational divergences among them. Participants engage with the network driven by the expectation of gains that outweigh potential costs. Key among these gains is the anticipation of support and assistance in their respective electoral competitions for national power, alongside the opportunity to cultivate an international presence. Unlike formal organizations, where membership entails binding commitments, participation in a network such as the Foro Madrid is marked by flexibility – entities can choose to engage or disengage based on their interests. Indeed, the parties and organizations comprising the Foro Madrid have exhibited selective participation in certain gatherings and workshops while abstaining from others, illustrating the fluid nature of their involvement.

Second, the Foro Madrid embodies a transnational character, distinguishing itself with its unique trans-American and trans-Atlantic framework. It serves as a nexus for political parties and organizations spanning the Americas, from the United States to Chile, as well as several European nations. Unlike other networks confined to a single nation, the Foro Madrid endeavors to exert influence and shape political landscapes across the entire spectrum of countries comprising its imagined community of reference: the so-called Iberosphere. The transnational essence of the Foro Madrid has caused discord among certain far-right forces espousing strong nationalist ideologies. For instance, the Uruguayan Cabildo Abierto party has opted out of participation in the Foro Madrid, citing concerns over its perceived neocolonialist leanings, allegedly controlled by VOX, and its pronounced internationalist stance (Tanscheit, 2023). Similarly, Nayib Bukele and his party "Nuevas Ideas" have refrained from publicly engaging with either VOX or the Foro Madrid (Meléndez, 2023), underscoring the complexities and tensions inherent within transnational far-right networks.

Third, the Foro Madrid operates as an advocacy network, a designation indicating its commitment to promoting and championing specific causes aligned with particular international norms or normative frameworks. The concept of "advocacy" within TANs underscores their active engagement in promoting these causes. For instance, Sikkink's examination of TANs in Latin America revealed their orientation toward promoting transitional justice in countries transitioning from military dictatorships to democratic regimes (Keck and Sikkink, 1998). Their cause was intricately linked to the safeguarding of human rights, justice, and the rule of law. Crucially, due to their advocacy-oriented nature, the actions of TANs are inherently public. This distinguishes them significantly from other types of transnational networks that operate clandestinely or purposefully seek to evade public scrutiny, such as illicit transnational networks, terrorist organizations, or intelligence and secret services networks. In contrast, TANs actively strive to enter the public discourse, recognizing that the publicity of their actions is integral to their strategy for mobilization and exerting pressure (Alter and Zürn, 2020).

The Foro Madrid aligns closely with this concept of advocacy as well. It ardently pursues a cause: the liberation of the Iberosphere from the influence of leftist forces. Within the discourse of the Foro Madrid, this cause is intricately tied to international norms, particularly the safeguarding of liberal democracy, which the organization contends is under threat from leftist parties and leaders. Moreover, the Foro Madrid invokes anticommunism, a notion that held significant prominence during the Cold War era and has been reinvigorated through a variety of rhetorical strategies, as we will elucidate below. At the same time, the Foro Madrid actively seeks publicity, a notable departure from previous transnational networks of extreme-right organizations, which typically operated clandestinely

(Albanese and Del Hierro, 2016). To grasp the essence of the Foro Madrid and its activities, one need only peruse their social media posts and online manifestos. These sources provide invaluable insights into the organization's objectives, strategies, and ideological orientation.

In summary, the Foro Madrid aligns with the definition of a TAN, albeit with an illiberal orientation. Unlike mainstream right-wing parties, the far-right forces networking within the Foro Madrid distinguish themselves through the adoption of extreme policy stances and a direct assault on the liberal democratic model (Bale and Rovira Kaltwasser, 2021). By exploiting cultural anxieties in a radical manner and denouncing actors and institutions – such as the judiciary and the media – allegedly imposing measures against the wishes of the majority, the far-right endeavors to carve out a political niche to the right of the mainstream right. Indeed, existing research suggests that the ideological content of the far-right constitutes a reactionary response to the spread of liberal ideals associated with the "silent revolution" delineated by Inglehart (1990). This theory posits that advanced capitalist societies underwent an unprecedented process of economic modernization during the 1960s and 1970s, precipitating a gradual shift toward more progressive societal values. However, not all segments of society embraced this value transformation, laying the groundwork for a cultural backlash articulated by various far-right actors. As Rydgren (2005) contends, the initial far-right parties formulated a distinct ideological framework that was later adopted, modified, and adapted to diverse national contexts across Western Europe and beyond. This illustrates the evolutionary trajectory of far-right forces and their resonance in contemporary political landscapes.

Nevertheless, significant variations exist between countries in terms of which progressive values the far-right primarily challenges, as not every society experiences the same cultural anxieties with equal intensity. Depending on the political landscape in which it operates, the far-right strategically politicizes specific issues that resonate with segments of the voting public in conflict with progressive ideals. In broader terms, one could argue that the far-right opposes the adaptation toward historically marginalized groups, which have been gaining increasing material and symbolic recognition (Bustikova, 2020). Here, the far-right's focus lies not necessarily in the eradication of minorities, but rather in quelling their aspirations for greater political empowerment, influence over public policies, access to government resources, and attainment of relevant positions. The central issue revolves around which historically marginalized groups have advanced and are perceived as challengers, a variable contingent upon national and regional contexts. For instance, in Latin America, existing research suggest that shifts in the status quo of minority–majority relations are directly linked to issues such as gender and sexual identity, whereas in Europe, migration takes precedence (Mayka and Smith, 2021; Rovira Kaltwasser, 2023, 2024).

15.3 THE ORIGINS AND EVOLUTION OF THE FORO MADRID

In March 2020, Santiago Abascal, the leader of the Spanish party VOX, embarked on a diplomatic mission to Washington and several Latin American capitals. His objective was clear: to unveil a visionary project aimed at uniting like-minded parties and movements sharing the conviction that the left poses a grave threat to democracy and must be staunchly opposed. During his visit to Washington, Abascal articulated the concept that would later evolve into the Foro Madrid to a receptive audience. This audience comprised individuals and entities who concurred with the notion that political and economic instability in the Iberosphere was intrinsically linked to the ascendance of leftist forces. Acting as a normative entrepreneur, Abascal presented his idea to key figures within the Trump administration, including members of the US Congress such as Marco Rubio (Representative for Florida, and later State Secretary under the second Trump administration), as well as the Secretary General of the Organization of American States (OAS), Luis Almagro. These individuals had played pivotal roles in orchestrating the international response to the democracy crises in Venezuela and Nicaragua (Palestini and Martinelli, 2023).

Abascal envisioned the establishment of a network comprising "defenders of liberal democracy and the rule of law" (Carta de Madrid, 2020) and planned to convene an inaugural gathering in Madrid in June 2020. However, this event was ultimately postponed due to the COVID-19 pandemic. Despite the setback, Abascal proceeded with the launch of the Fundación Disenso in September 2020. This think tank aimed at forging connections with right-wing forces in the Western Hemisphere, thus entering into direct competition with the Spanish mainstream right party, the Popular Party, which already maintained well-established ties with mainstream right parties in Latin America.

Just one month after the establishment of the Fundación Disenso, Abascal publicly unveiled the Carta de Madrid in October 2020. This concise manifesto outlined the core principles and strategic concepts underpinning the Foro Madrid. Concurrently, VOX acquired an online newspaper, renaming it *La Gaceta de la Iberósfera*, which subsequently became the official newspaper of both VOX and the Foro Madrid. The *Gazeta*'s director, Hermann Tertsch, an active member of VOX and member of the European Parliament, has forged extensive connections with the Latin American right. Following his election to the European Parliament within the European Conservatives and Reformists group (ECR group), Tertsch assumed roles on the Commission of Foreign Affairs and the Mixed Commission EU-Mexico, in addition to serving as vice president of the Euro-Latin American Parliamentary Assembly. Tertsch also assumed the directorship of the Foro Madrid, a position he shares with Rocío Monasterio, a Cuban-Spanish parliamentarian from VOX.

As depicted in Figure 15.1, the Foro Madrid exhibits an average of 60 tweets per month, punctuated by two notable peaks corresponding to the regional

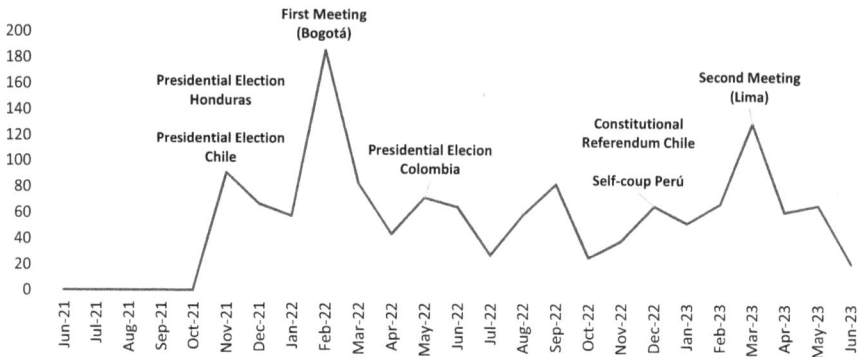

FIGURE 15.1 Tweets per month and crucial events.

meetings held in Bogotá in February 2022 and Lima in March 2023, both titled "In Defense of Freedom, Democracy, and the Rule of Law." The Bogotá gathering boasted active participation from twenty-five speakers, including representatives of right-wing parties from Argentina, Brazil, Bolivia, Colombia, Mexico, Peru, and Venezuela. European parties were also well represented, with members from VOX and Poland's Law and Justice Party in attendance. Notable speakers included former Colombian president Álvaro Uribe, current Argentinean president Javier Milei, Eduardo Bolsonaro (son of Jair Bolsonaro), Venezuelan opposition leader María Corina Machado, and Anna Fotyga, a member of the European Parliament affiliated with the ECR group.

The second regional meeting convened in Lima witnessed the active participation of thirty-eight speakers, including representatives from political parties and civil society members, who delivered presentations or brief interventions. In addition to the parties and countries previously represented in Bogotá, the Lima gathering welcomed party representatives from Chile, Cuba, El Salvador, Honduras, Guatemala, Nicaragua, and Paraguay. Notably, Rob Roos from the Dutch populist radical right party J21 represented the European contingent. Both the Bogotá and Lima meetings were open to the public, free of charge, and broadcasted via online streaming platforms.

The Twitter account associated with Foro Madrid has demonstrated sustained engagement during pivotal events throughout Latin America, including significant presidential elections in Colombia, Brazil, Chile, and Honduras. Throughout these electoral periods, members of Foro Madrid effectively utilized various social media platforms to critique and condemn left-wing candidates. In anticipation of the 2022 vote on a new Constitution in Chile, Foro Madrid actively voiced apprehensions regarding the potential risks associated with its approval. Moreover, following the controversial rise to power of left-wing president Pedro Castillo in Peru, Foro Madrid remained

TABLE 15.1 *Parties that participated in the regional meetings of the Foro Madrid*

Country	Party
Americas	
Argentina	La Libertad Avanza
Bolivia	Comité Cívico Pro-Santa Cruz; Movimiento Nacionalista Revolucionario
Brazil	Partido Social Liberal
Chile	Partido Republicano
Colombia	Centro Democrático
Cuba	Asamblea de la Resistencia Cubana
Honduras	Partido Nacional
Nicaragua	Cambio, Justicia y Democracia
Peru	Alianza por el Progreso; Avanza País; Fuerza Popular; Movimiento Vamos Vecino; Peruanos por el Cambio; Renovación Popular
Venezuela	Vente Venezuela
Europe	
Netherlands	J21
Poland	Law and Justice
Spain	VOX

vocal in denouncing the perceived implications of his administration. Table 15.1 presents a comprehensive summary of all participating parties in the two regional gatherings organized by Foro Madrid.

It is important to highlight that not all the political parties listed have a clearly defined far-right agenda, such as "Peruanos por el Cambio" in Peru. Consequently, one could argue that the observed trend of increasing alignment between mainstream and far-right ideologies, as noted by scholars (Brown, Mondon, and Winter, 2021; Mudde, 2019), may be further reinforced by the activities of TANs like Foro Madrid. An intriguing observation from Table 15.1 is that the majority of participants hail from Latin American parties. This suggests a notable inclination among Latin American far-right political actors to draw inspiration from their European counterparts rather than vice versa. This tendency might be partially attributed to the relatively entrenched presence of far-right parties within European societies, contrasting with the novelty of far-right forces in Latin America. Consequently, Latin American entities exhibit a keen interest in understanding the strategies that have propelled the success of their European counterparts. Furthermore, it's noteworthy that the narrative put forth by VOX resonates particularly well with certain segments of the Latin American electorate. This resonance is especially apparent among those who harbor concerns about the perceived dominance of radical leftist ideologies and feminist agendas. While these themes are prominent in VOX's discourse, they may not necessarily feature as prominently in other far-right forces in Europe (Rama, Zanotti, Turnbull-Dugarte, and Santana, 2021).

Clifford Bob (2012: 5) has argued that many transnational networks – especially illiberal ones – emerge to counterbalance other extant transnational networks: "Contention between networks – not just between a single network and target states or corporations – is therefore endemic." This is also evident for the Foro Madrid, which was conceived by Abascal, Tertsch, and other leaders of VOX as a way to counterbalance the well-established Foro de São Paulo, a network of left-wing parties and organizations in Latin America. In many ways – not only by name – Foro Madrid mimicries the Foro de São Paulo: It is a network of political parties and organizations, it provides a forum for sharing information and discussing political strategies, it assists their participants in their domestic electoral competitions. By doing basically the same, Foro Madrid aims at counterbalancing Foro de São Paulo's influence in the region.

While Foro Madrid represents a recent development, the Foro de São Paulo is as a long-standing TAN composed of Latin American left-wing parties and organizations. Its origins trace back to 1990, emerging from an initiative spearheaded by Luiz Inácio Lula da Silva and Fidel Castro. Their aim was to unite traditional leftist parties (including communist and socialist factions) with newer parties and left-wing movements. This initiative arose in response to the fall of the Berlin Wall and the subsequent wave of democratization across Latin America. During its initial years, the Foro de São Paulo – denoting regular meetings rather than a singular entity – advocated for an alternative development model to neoliberalism. However, by the mid 2000s, a shift in ideological dominance occurred within the Latin American left. Hugo Chávez's vision of *Socialismo del Siglo XXI* took center stage within the network, leading to the marginalization of various social-democratic parties in the process (De la Torre, 2017).

As we delve into the dynamics of Foro Madrid, it becomes evident that both the Foro de São Paulo and the Grupo de Puebla – formed in 2019 as a collective of left-wing leaders, including numerous former heads of state – serve as pivotal elements in shaping the discourse of Foro Madrid. They are not merely perceived as adversaries to be overcome; rather, as networks comprising various leftist parties and leaders, they afford Foro Madrid's members the opportunity to assert that the entire leftist spectrum is interconnected in activities deemed antidemocratic.

An examination of Foro Madrid through the lens of TANs necessitates a keen focus on both discourse and actions. Symbolic politics, as articulated by Keck and Sikkink, constitutes a fundamental aspect of TAN operations. Through a range of rhetorical devices identifiable via discourse analysis, TAN members construct a narrative characterized by causes, values, adversaries, and allies. These devices serve to simplify complexity, making nuanced messages more accessible and appealing to broader audiences. From a constructivist standpoint, frames emerge as discursive tools fashioned from ideologies and other cultural elements. Over time, frames have the capacity to reshape ideologies themselves. Crucially, frames play a pivotal role in bridging ideologies and discourses with tangible action. As Froio (2022: 3) succinctly states, "if ideologies encapsulate a group's collective beliefs and unified responses to social issues …, frames serve as strategic tools that articulate, amplify, and reconfigure these beliefs to achieve specific political objectives."

However, discourses and frames alone are insufficient. TANs must also take action. They devise strategies to achieve specific goals and advance their cause. Similar to social movements, from which Keck and Sikkink draw significant inspiration, TANs face the risk of disintegration if they fail to demonstrate tangible results. We will delve now into both the rhetorical devices utilized by Foro Madrid and its principal political strategies, examining their limitations and accomplishments.

15.3.1 Rhetoric Devices

The narrative propagated by VOX through Foro Madrid is strikingly straightforward: the encroachment of leftist ideologies poses a significant threat to liberal democracy and prosperity within the Iberosphere (Carta de Madrid, 2020). Central to this narrative is the Carta de Madrid, the primary manifesto, which defines the Iberosphere as a collective of free and sovereign nations, comprising over 700 million individuals who share a deep-seated cultural heritage. However, this envisioned community, akin to Benedict Anderson's notion of an imagined community, finds itself besieged "by totalitarian regimes inspired by communism, bolstered by drug trafficking organizations, and aided by third countries, all under the auspices of Cuba" (Carta de Madrid, 2020). Although the Carta de Madrid does not explicitly mention third countries, other declarations and tweets from Foro Madrid highlight China, Russia, and Iran (Declaración de Lima, 2023) as notable antagonists.

The delineation of challenges and adversaries extends beyond the overarching "imagined community" to individual nations, as illustrated in the subsequent table showcasing select diagnostic frames propagated through Foro Madrid's Twitter account.

The narrative of Foro Madrid is deeply rooted in a prevalent ideology across Latin America: anticommunism. This ideology is constructed using four rhetorical devices. First, empty signifiers are extensively employed. Terms such as "democracy," "freedom," and "the rule of law" feature prominently in nearly every tweet, adorn the titles of regional meetings in Bogotá and Lima, are reiterated in declarations, and serve as the three ideological pillars of the

TABLE 15.2 *Example of diagnostic frames developed for the Iberosphere and for different countries*

Iberosphere	The Iberosphere is under threat once again. https://twitter.com/user/status/1455933996488085508.
Bolivia	The tyranny advances in #Bolivia, freedom, the respect to the judicial order, and any attempt at opposition are smashed. https://twitter.com/user/status/1560546036921552897.
Brazil	The elections in #Brazil can put in danger the existence of the three fundamental pillars of the Carta de Madrid in the entire region: democracy, freedom, and the rule of law. https://twitter.com/user/status/1488917397851590665.
Chile	Inspired by his allies in Cuba, Venezuela, and Nicaragua, [president] Boric and his partners of the Communist Party want to destroy the current order to implement a new model of society which, as we have seen in other countries of the Iberosphere, will ruin Chile. https://twitter.com/user/status/1461753781025185794.
Colombia	The background of Petro's ministers demonstrates that his intention is to promote drug trafficking, to destroy the armed forces, to empower the terrorists of FARC and ELN, and provide impunity for corruption. https://twitter.com/user/status/1555144598305079298.
El Salvador	Because of the absence of rule of law, all democratic sectors on both sides of the Atlantic must condemn Bukele's intentions of reelection and do away with what is left of the Republic. https://twitter.com/user/status/1570761922055925761.
Guatemala	The superficiality of the campaign, the popular disaffection, and the irregularities in the inscription of the candidates open conditions for the Foro de São Pualo and the Grupo de Puebla to take advantage of the electoral process and to continue expanding their model of misery. https://twitter.com/user/status/1669005209270472704.
Honduras	This Sunday, tyranny comes back to Honduras. https://twitter.com/user/status/1463520609925623813.
Mexico	AMLO's new decisions can only be interpreted in one way: he wants to do away with democracy, pushing forward a reform that destroys the National Electoral Institute and that subordinates all the electoral bodies to himself and his party. https://twitter.com/user/status/1592217651748933633.
Nicaragua	Mirroring Castro's dictatorship, the Ortega-Murillo see how their family dictatorship can survive without major consequences. https://twitter.com/user/status/1456308512888401925.
Peru	Foro Madrid warns the democratic institutions of Peru that this mission is part of Foro de São Paulo's and Grupo de Puebla's strategies led by Evo Morales to break the government down and bring Pedro Castillo back into power. https://twitter.com/user/status/1623623417000783877.

Own compilation and translation

network. Members of Foro Madrid present themselves as champions of democracy, freedom, and the rule of law in the Iberosphere, yet, remarkably, none of these concepts are ever explicitly defined. They are strategically left devoid of substantive content. Similarly, "communism" functions as an empty signifier, infused with emotional weight: danger, fear, threat. Leaders and parties with even remote connections to communism are derogatorily associated with this concept. As empty signifiers, these terms are wielded to evoke emotions and unite individuals around the defense of democracy, freedom, and the rule of law – regardless of the specific interpretations attached to these ideals – in the face of perceived communist threats.

A second rhetorical device employed by Foro Madrid involves the deliberate conflation of the authoritarian and democratic left. According to Foro Madrid's narrative, the ideological foundation of the entire "left" is encapsulated in the term "Castro-communism," referencing the late Cuban revolutionary leader, Fidel Castro. This narrative suggests that this ideology is shared across the spectrum of leftist regimes, spanning from the authoritarian Maduro's regime in Venezuela and Ortega's regime in Nicaragua to recently elected leftist governments that lean toward social democracy in their programmatic agendas. In practice, however, a significant portion of Foro Madrid's criticisms and condemnations are directed toward democratically elected leaders, such as Gustavo Petro in Colombia, Gabriel Boric in Chile, Lula in Brazil, and Xiomara Castro in Honduras. Figure 15.2 illustrates that Gustavo Petro features most prominently in Foro Madrid's discursive output, receiving far more frequent attacks than authoritarian leaders like Maduro, Ortega, or Cuba's president Miguel Díaz-Canel, who is effectively ignored altogether.

A third rhetorical device is hyperbole. This is specifically the case with the antagonism with Foro de São Paulo and Grupo de Puebla whose influence and power is blown out of proportion. Foro Madrid frames these networks as shadowy and almost clandestine organizations, financed by the narcotraffic, and aimed at destabilizing liberal democratic governments and bringing Castro-communist governments into power. During the first regional meeting in Bogotá, Fundación Disenso presented a twenty-four-minute documentary entitled *Desenmascarando el Foro de São Paulo, una amenaza para la Libertad en la Iberosfera* (Unmasking the Foro de São Paulo, a threat against freedom in the Iberosphere). The video, accessible in YouTube, consists of interviews with prominent figures of the far-right in Latin America and Europe, who present a fearful image of the Foro de São Paulo and the type of societies that it tries to bring about. Among the interviewees who appear in the video are Santiago Abascal, Italian prime minister Giorgia Meloni, and Eduardo Bolsonaro. The documentary portrays Foro de São Paulo as a very powerful organization attributing to it strong leverage on Latin American politics. It picks up a narrative that was first put forward by OAS Secretary General Luis Almagro, according to which the Foro de São Paulo was the force

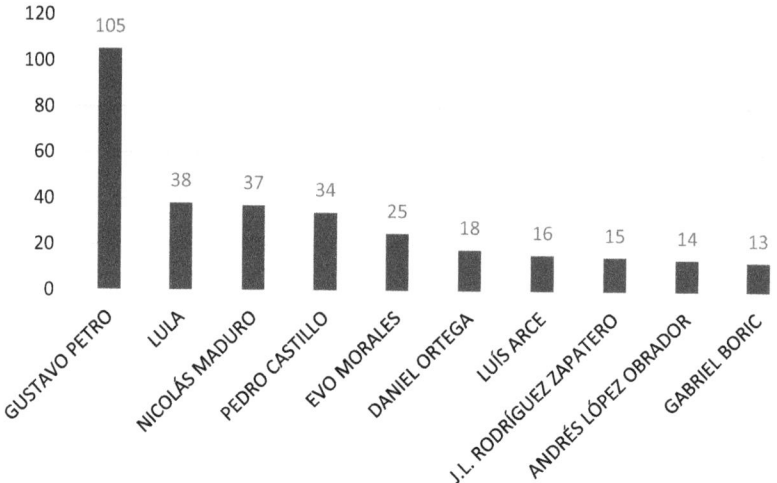

FIGURE 15.2 Most mentioned opponents (number of tweets).
Source: Foro Madrid's Twitter account

behind the social revolts that affected center-right governments in Ecuador, Chile, and Colombia in 2019.

The recent currents of destabilization of the political systems of the hemisphere have their origins in the strategy of the Bolivarian and Cuban dictatorships, which seek to reposition themselves once again, not through a process of re-institutionalization and re-democratization, but through their old methodology of exporting polarization and bad practices, to essentially finance, support and promote political and social conflict. (OAS, 2019)

Almagro's statement was disseminated through official OAS channels, despite the lack of evidence regarding the orchestration of revolts in Ecuador, Chile, and Colombia by foreign actors in general, and Foro de São Paulo in particular.[1] Nonetheless, Almagro's argument became ingrained in the primary narrative of Foro Madrid members, lending credibility to the notion that Foro de São Paulo is a formidable insurgent network capable of toppling governments. In the documentary *Desenmascarando el Foro de São Paulo*, Santiago Abascal asserts that "[Foro de São Paulo's] actions have contributed to destabilizing a large number of nations, as is currently happening in Chile and Colombia." This assertion echoes Almagro's claim and is reiterated in numerous articles of *La Gaceta de la Iberósfera* (Ríos García, 2021).

---

[1] To be sure the only piece of evidence was the fact that Nicolás Maduro called the revolts the "Bolivarian breeze." Almagro makes reference to the "Bolivarian breeze" in his statement; later, VOX will also make wide use of Maduro's figure of speech.

Finally, Foro Madrid constructs its discourse through issue-linkage, intertwining four perceived threats: the left, drug trafficking and organized crime, terrorism, and corruption. This tactic aims to expand the targeted audience and enhance the persuasiveness of the diagnosis. The underlying message suggests that by opposing the left, one is not only safeguarding liberal democracy but also combating the security challenges afflicting Latin American societies and economies. However, this narrative relies on partial evidence and generalization. While specific members of Foro de São Paulo may indeed have connections to drug trafficking (for instance, the connection between drug trafficking and Maduro's regime, as documented by Corrales, 2020), portraying the organization as structurally linked and financed by the drug trafficking industry and terrorism constitutes a misrepresentation.

This is further underscored by the prominent role that Gustavo Petro, a former guerrilla member, plays in Foro Madrid's naming and shaming campaigns. Despite Petro's democratic election, he is depicted as a former terrorist with ties to guerrilla groups and drug trafficking. For instance, one source asserts, "The Foro Madrid has shown during the last months that Petro's project for Colombia is the project of narcotrafficking, the FARC, the Foro de São Paulo, and the Grupo de Puebla. A project to impose communism in Colombia and lay the ground for Colombia to become another satellite of the dictatorships in Venezuela and Cuba" (Panorama País, 2022).

Issue-linkage is visually apparent in the satirical caricatures utilized by *La Gaceta de la Iberósfera*. In one illustration, various left-wing leaders are depicted standing behind Venezuela's autocrat, Nicolás Maduro, symbolizing Foro de São Paulo and Grupo de Puebla. Adjacent to Maduro stands Colombian President Gustavo Petro, while in the foreground there is a pot bearing the image of an ETA militant (from the Basque separatist organization), a symbol employed by La Gazeta and VOX to represent terrorists. Additionally, lying on the floor is a character adorned with an anticommunism symbol, representing Ecuadorian politician Fernando Villavicencio, who was killed in August 2023 (*La Gaceta de la Iberósfera*, 2023a). The picture syntheses the Foro Madrid discourse: the democratic and autocratic left are equally associated to communism and violence and equally connected with terrorism.

15.3.2 Main Strategies

In addition to articulating a narrative, Foro Madrid has implemented three primary political strategies during its brief existence. The first strategy involves networking far-right political parties. While this might seem straightforward, it's crucial to note that prior to Foro Madrid, connections between these parties were at best weak, if not entirely absent. Many members of Foro Madrid are relatively young parties, such as the "Republican Party" of Chile (founded in 2019) or "Freedom Advances" in Argentina (founded in 2021). Before the inception of Foro Madrid by VOX, these parties were primarily focused on their nationally bound electoral competitions, with limited electoral victories to show. Through regional gatherings and workshops, VOX has successfully brought these parties together and forged connections with well-established European far-right parties, such as Law and Justice. While the involvement of European partners is still in its early stages, it's evident that VOX is leveraging lessons learned from the ECR group to export them to their Latin American counterparts. Under the leadership of Hermann Tertsch, VOX has organized two encounters between the ECR and Foro Madrid (Europa Press, 2023). These encounters serve two interconnected goals: First, they aid VOX in projecting an image of a party with international influence; second, they assist Latin American far-right parties in establishing ties with successful European far-right counterparts. It's likely that much of the learning and knowledge transfer from North to South occurs through these informal ties.

Foro Madrid has also undertaken Electoral Observation Missions (EOMs) in several Latin American countries. EOMs gained prominence as instruments of democracy promotion, particularly following the end of the Cold War. For two decades, they were exclusively implemented by liberal democratic international NGOs (such as the Carter Center and Human Rights Watch) and international organizations (such as the European Union and the OAS) (Carothers, 2015). Foro Madrid's EOMs aim to project an image of a liberal actor committed to upholding fair and transparent elections. On its website, Foro Madrid asserts that through the observation of seven elections, it has solidified itself as a robust international alliance for electoral observation, capable of identifying, exposing, and thwarting fraudulent intentions attributed to the radical left in Ibero-America (Foro Madrid, 2023a).

However, Foro Madrid's EOMs fall short of meeting the standards of well-established electoral monitoring, as their reports appear to lack impartiality and instead align with the organization's narrative of portraying the left as a threat to democracy. In the case of Colombia's general elections, which were widely regarded as fair and open by the OAS, Foro Madrid stated, for example, "The sum of irregularities and crimes during the presidential elections in Colombia 2022 are reason enough to declare the results invalid ... Colombian institutions must take the necessary constitutional measures to invalidate Gustavo Petro's mandate and promptly remove him from office" (Foro Madrid, 2023b). This approach by Foro Madrid's EOMs appears consistent with a trend observed in illiberal organizations over the past decade, wherein they systematically implement what has been termed "zombie" electoral monitoring. Such monitoring serves as a tool to advance foreign policy interests and support preferred – typically nondemocratic – political forces during electoral competitions (Debre and Morgenbesser, 2017; Cooley, 2015).

Moreover, Foro Madrid has sought to expand its network by cultivating international partnerships. One of the primary methods through which TANs engage in activism is by exerting pressure not only on governments but also, and particularly, on international organizations, either through lobbying or by shaping ideas (Keck and Sikkink, 1998; Sanders, 2018; Bob, 2012). While Foro Madrid's actions in this regard are still in their early stages, one of the initial actors that Abascal sought to align with was OAS Secretary General Luis Almagro. Before assuming his role as the executive head of the OAS, Almagro had served as the foreign minister of the left-wing government of President José Mujica in Uruguay. Initially supported by left-wing governments, he faced resistance from right-wing governments. However, upon assuming office, he quickly emerged as a key figure in international efforts to bring about regime change in Maduro's Venezuela. His tenure at the OAS has been characterized by unprecedented activism compared to his predecessors, making him a central international partner not only for Maduro's opposition but also for the Latin American right in general (Palestini and Martinelli, 2023).

In the Declaración of Bogotá, members of Foro Madrid expressed their belief in the necessity to support the OAS, particularly its Secretary General Luis Almagro, in light of Grupo de Puebla's intentions to dissolve the OAS and replace it with the Community of Latin American and Caribbean States (Declaración of Bogotá, 2022). This unusual endorsement of an international political figure in one of Foro Madrid's manifestos serves as evidence of VOX's interest in garnering OAS support. Furthermore, in March 2023, a delegation from Foro Madrid met with Luis Almagro at the OAS headquarters in Washington to present him with an open letter, cautioning against international attempts to destabilize Peru and offering him their support (*La Gaceta de la Iberósfera*, 2023b). The open letter was signed by 118 political figures from various countries, including Javier Milei, Ryszard Antoni Legutko (Law and Justice, Poland), Eniko Gyiori (Fidesz, Hungary), and Carlo Fidanza (Fratelli d'Italia).

Under the leadership of Tertsch, VOX has also secured the support of the Heritage Foundation, a conservative think tank based in Washington DC. In September 2022, Tertsch orchestrated a workshop titled "Terrorism and Freedom," which was hosted by the Heritage Foundation. The workshop brought together victims and relatives of victims of terrorist acts, alongside members of right-wing parties. Its objective was to explore the connections between terrorism and the left, while neglecting any potential links between terrorism and the right.

These strategies – networking, organizing workshops and EOMs, and cultivating support from international organizations – are in line with the activities typically undertaken by TANs. VOX, particularly Abascal and Tertsch, can be viewed as normative entrepreneurs who bring together diverse parties and construct the network to advance their ideological agenda.

15.4 CONCLUSIONS

As the editors of this volume aptly emphasize (Valerie J. Bunce, Thomas B. Pepinsky, Rachel Beatty Reid, and Kenneth M. Roberts), the world is currently witnessing a resurgence of autocratization, impacting both institutionally fragile cases of third-wave democracies as well as regional exemplars of democracy. This process of democratic erosion typically arises internally, spurred by the growing influence of new political actors who engage in electoral competition while advocating for illiberal agendas. One of the primary actors in this phenomenon is the far-right, representing a diverse array of political forces united in their opposition to the further advancement of historically marginalized sectors. Given the varying contexts, the far-right identifies different internal adversaries to be confronted. For instance, while the European far-right focuses on immigrants, particularly from the Muslim world, the Latin American far-right is particularly concerned about accommodating women in politics (Rovira Kaltwasser, 2023). Nevertheless, significant ideological commonalities exist among far-right forces globally, particularly in their opposition to liberal norms and progressive values.

In historical terms, the rise of the far-right began as early as the start of the 1990s in Europe, while in many other countries it remains a relatively recent phenomenon. This trend is particularly noticeable in Latin America, where the region has only recently begun to witness the ascent of far-right forces. In this contribution, we delve into how the emergence of TANs – such as Foro Madrid – can facilitate the diffusion of a far-right script from North to South, encompassing both discursive and strategic aspects. Just as the spread of liberal democracy in the 1980s and 1990s was influenced by progressive TANs, the success of figures like Jair Bolsonaro in Brazil and Javier Milei in Argentina cannot be fully understood without examining the influence of illiberal TANs. This contribution posits that Foro Madrid should be viewed as a network of far-right actors dedicated to promoting various forms of illiberal ideas. At the heart of this network lies the Spanish populist radical right party VOX, which serves as a driving force aiming to translate the ideological framework of the European far-right into the Latin American context. Thus, this discussion underscores the importance of recognizing far-right TANs that support national entities seeking to transform democracy from within, particularly amid the ongoing process of democratic erosion worldwide.

The assertion that Foro Madrid poses a threat to liberal democracy may appear paradoxical for a TAN that outwardly portrays itself on social media and online platforms as a defender of liberal democracy against communism and the radical left. However, Foro Madrid poses a significant challenge to liberal democracy in two crucial ways: first, by espousing an antipluralist discourse, and second, by providing support to national parties with illiberal political agendas. Throughout the political history of the Americas, spanning both the United States and Latin American countries, the anticommunist narrative has frequently been wielded in an antipluralist manner, aiming to exclude certain political forces from the democratic process and the political sphere. Foro Madrid follows this trend. In the discourse of Foro Madrid, the left is not merely viewed as a political opponent to be opposed ideologically and

contested electorally, but rather as an existential threat that must be eradicated from democratic competition altogether. Through various rhetorical devices – including the manipulation of liberal democracy and communism as empty signifiers, the conflation of the authoritarian and democratic left, and the association of the left with security threats such as terrorism – Foro Madrid constructs a comprehensive narrative in which the viability of liberal democracy is contingent upon the absence of "the left." By framing the situation as "liberal democracy under attack," Foro Madrid effectively securitizes democracy, shifting the political contestation with "the left" beyond the realm of politics and into the domain of security and survival.

As the study of far-right TANs is still in its nascent stage, we aim to conclude this contribution by proposing three research avenues that future studies could explore in greater depth. First, it is worthwhile to investigate the identification of additional TANs centered around the advancement of illiberal values, which directly or indirectly provide support to the agendas of far-right political forces at the national level.[2] For instance, a recent report by the European Parliamentary Forum for Sexual and Reproductive Rights (Datta, 2021) unveils the existence of 707.2 million US dollars in antigender funding over the period from 2009 to 2018. This funding originates from a restricted group of fifty-four organizations, spanning NGOs, foundations, religious entities, and political parties. The report vividly illustrates how the concept of TANs can elucidate this network of actors focused on challenging sexual and reproductive health and rights, thereby dedicating time and resources to the promotion of illiberal ideas that can significantly impact marginalized groups or communities.

Second, future studies can aim to better understand the processes of diffusion of far-right ideas, particularly in terms of translation and adaptation. While an analysis of Foro Madrid suggests that the far-right script originated in Europe and is now being enacted in Latin America, detailed case studies may reveal a more nuanced process of translation and adaptation. It would be erroneous to assume that Latin American far-right actors are simply replicating ideas formulated by their European counterparts (Rovira Kaltwasser and Sandoval, 2024). For instance, Milei's discourse emphasizes libertarian positions (Vommaro, 2023), which are relatively uncommon in the European context. Additionally, Bolsonaro consistently advocates for the military (Rennó, 2023), a stance that is nearly absent within the European far-right.

Third and finally, the presence of illiberal TANs such as Foro Madrid underscores the argument put forth by various scholars (as highlighted in the Introduction to this volume) who contend that the process of democratic backsliding is intricately linked to the actions of elites rather than solely the electorate. While it is undeniable that the voting public may eventually lend

---

[2] In this regard, the recent book on *The Right against Rights* (Payne, Zulver, and Escoffier, 2023) is particularly illuminating.

support to far-right actors, it is the elites who consciously promote narratives that are antithetical to the liberal conception of democracy. This suggests that we are witnessing the rise of political forces that actively seek to dismantle fundamental aspects of liberal democracy from within. Consequently, scholars and policymakers should not only endeavor to identify these actors but also their collaborators. Without the backing of these facilitators (such as mainstream right-wing parties, media outlets, and segments of the business community), far-right forces would struggle to gain access to power and govern effectively.

REFERENCES

Albanese, M., & del Hierro, P. (2016). *Transnational Fascism in the Twentieth Century: Spain, Italy and the Global Neo-Fascist Network*. London: Bloomsbury.

Alter, K. J., & Zürn, M. (2020). Theorising backlash politics: conclusion to a special issue on backlash politics in comparison. *British Journal of Politics & International Relations*, 22(4), 739–752. https://doi.org/10.1177/1369148120947956.

Bale, T., & Rovira Kaltwasser, C. (eds.) (2021). Riding The Populist Wave: Europe's Mainstream Right in Crisis. Cambridge: Cambridge University Press.

Bob, C. (2013). The global right wing and theories of transnational advocacy. *International Spectator*, 48(4), 71–85. https://doi.org/10.1080/03932729.2013.847685.

Bob. C. (2012). *The Global Right and the Clash of World Politics*. Cambridge: Cambridge University Press.

Brown, K., Mondon A., & Winter, A. (2023). The far right, the mainstream and mainstreaming: towards a heuristic framework. *Journal of Political Ideologies*, 28(2), 162–179, DOI: 10.1080/13569317.2021.1949829.

Bustikova, L. (2020). *Extreme Reactions: Radical Right Mobilization in Eastern Europe*. Cambridge: Cambridge University Press.

Carothers, T. (2015). Democracy aid at 25: time to choose. *Journal of Democracy*, 26(1), 77–97.

Carta de Madrid (2020). https://foromadrid.org/carta-de-madrid/.

Cooley, A. (2015). Authoritarianism goes global: countering democratic norms. *Journal of Democracy*, 26(3), 49–63.

Corrales, J. (2020). Why Maduro has not fallen. *Journal of Democracy*, 31(3), 39–53.

Cupać, J., & Ebetürk, I. (2020). The personal is global political: the antifeminist backlash in the United Nations. *British Journal of Politics & International Relations*, 22(4), 702–714. https://doi.org/10.1177/1369148120948733.

Datta, N. (2021). Tip of the Iceberg: Religious Extremist Funders against Humans Right for Sexuality and Reproductive Health in Europe 2009–2018. European Parliamentary Forum for Sexual & Reproductive Rights.

De la Torre, C. (2017). Hugo Chávez and the diffusion of Bolivarianism. *Democratization*, 24(7), 1271–1288. https://doi.org/10.1080/13510347.2017.1307825.

Debre, M. J., & Morgenbesser, L. (2017). Out of the shadows: autocratic regimes, election observation and legitimation. *Contemporary Politics*, 23(3), 328–347. https://doi.org/10.1080/13569775.2017.1304318.

Declaración de Bogotá (2022). https://tinyurl.com/zvud2778.

Declaración de Lima (2023). https://tinyurl.com/bdftejwy.

Deitelhoff, N. (2020). What's in a name? Contestation and backlash against international norms and institutions. *British Journal of Politics & International Relations*, 22(4), 715–727. https://doi.org/10.1177/1369148120945906.

Encarnación, O. G. (2020). The gay rights backlash: contrasting views from the United States and Latin America. *British Journal of Politics & International Relations*, 22(4), 654–665. https://doi.org/10.1177/1369148120946671.

Europa Press (2023). Abascal reunirá en Madrid a líderes conservadores iberoamericanos coincidiendo con la celebración del 12 de octubre. https://tinyurl.com/dc9mde7b.

Foro Madrid (2023a). Foro Madrid desplegó dos misiones de observación electoral simultáneas en Ecuador y en Guatemala. https://tinyurl.com/2s33z44k.

Foro Madrid (2023b). La Elección de Gustavo Petro como Presidente de Colombia debe anularse. https://tinyurl.com/4y2ds46p.

Froio, C. (2024). The Rassemblement National and COVID-19: how nativism, authoritarianism and expert populism did not pay off during the pandemic. *Government and Opposition*, 59(4): 1071–1091.

Inglehart, R. (1990). Culture Shift in Advanced Industrial Society. Princeton: Princeton University Press. https://doi.org/10.2307/j.ctv346rbz.

Keck, M. E., & Sikkink, K. (1998). Activists beyond Borders. Ithaca: Cornell University Press. https://doi.org/10.7591/9780801471292.

La Gaceta de la Iberósfera (2023a). Alarma para la oposición al Foro de Sao Paulo y al Grupo de Puebla tras el asesinato de Villavicencio. https://tinyurl.com/bdd26k89.

La Gaceta de la Iberósfera (2023b). Foro Madrid se reúne en Washington con Luis Almagro, secretario general de la OEA. https://tinyurl.com/3aw9s9hv/.

Mayka, L., & Smith, A. (2021). Introduction: the Grassroots Right in Latin America: Patterns, Causes, and Consequences. *Latin American Politics and Society*, 65(4), 1–20. https://doi.org/10.1017/lap.2021.20.

Meléndez, C. (2023). La ultraderecha en el Perú: la irrupción electoral de Renovación Popular a nivel nacional y subnacional. Fundación Friedrich Ebert. www.fes.de/cgi-bin/gbv.cgi?id=20677&ty=pdf.

Mudde, C. (2007). *Populist Radical Right Parties in Europe*. Cambridge: Cambridge University Press. https://doi.org/10.1017/CBO9780511492037.

Mudde, C. (2019). *The Far Right Today*. Cambridge: Polity.

OAS (2019). Statement of the OAS General Secretariat, October 16th, 2019.

Palestini, S., & Martinelli, E. (2023). Enforcing peoples' right to democracy: transnational activism and regional powers in contemporary Inter-American relations. *European Journal of International Relations*, 29(3), 780–805.

Panorama País (2022). Elecciones legislativas en Colombia 2022: escenarios y amenazas a la democracia. https://tinyurl.com/mr469jww.

Payne, L. A., Zulver, J., & Escoffier, S. (eds.) (2023). *The Right against Rights in Latin America*. Oxford: Oxford University Press.

Rama, J., Zanotti, L., Turnbull-Dugarte, S., & Santana, A. (2021). *VOX: The Rise of the Spanish Populist Radical Right*. London: Routledge.

Ríos García, M. (2021). Bolivia, Chile, Colombia … así avanza la "brisa bolivariana" en Iberoamérica. *La Gaceta de la Iberósfera*. https://tinyurl.com/mrbptzpa.

Rennó, Lucio (2023). La Ultraderecha en Brasil: de Bolsonaro al Bolsonarismo. Fundación Friedrich Ebert. https://library.fes.de/pdf-files/bueros/chile/20672.pdf.

Rovira Kaltwasser, C. (2024). El ascenso de la ultraderecha en América Latina: inesperado, rápido y duradero. *LASA Forum*, 54(4), 9–15. https://forum.lasaweb .org/files/vol54-issue4/dossier-2.pdf.

Rovira Kaltwasser, C. (2023). La Ultraderecha en América Latina: Definiciones y explicaciones. Fundación Friedrich Ebert. https://library.fes.de/pdf-files/bueros/ chile/20670.pdf.

Rovira Kaltwasser, C., & Sandoval, C. (2024). Diffusion and global circulation of populist discourse, in Stravakakis, Y., & Katsambekis, G. (eds.). *Elgar Research Handbook on Populism*. Cheltenham: Edward Elgar Publishing, 540–550.

Rydgren, J. (2005). Is extreme right-wing populism contagious? Explaining the emergence of a new party family. *European Journal of Political Research*, 44(3), 413–437. https://doi.org/10.1111/j.1475-6765.2005.00233.x.

Sanders, R. (2018). Norm spoiling: undermining the international women's rights agenda. *International Affairs*, 94(2), 271–291. https://doi.org/10.1093/ia/iiy023.

Tanscheit, T. (2023). Jair Bolsonaro and the defining attributes of the populist radical right in Brazil. *Journal of Language and Politics*, 22(3), 324–341. https://doi.org/ 10.1075/jlp.22133.tan.

Vommaro, G. (2023). La ultraderecha en Argentina: Entre el oportunismo y la innovación de Milei. Fundación Friedrich Ebert. www.fes.de/cgi-bin/gbv.cgi? id=20671&ty=pdf.

Wojczewski, T. (2024). The international cooperation of the populist radical right: building counter-hegemony in international relations. *International Relations*, online first. https://doi.org/10.1177/00471178231222888.

16

Conclusion

Valerie J. Bunce

16.1 INTRODUCTION

Until recently, most studies of democracy and democratization proceeded from two premises. The first was that new democracies were considerably more fragile than older ones. While young democracies were still immersed in a pitched battle between authoritarian and democratic forces, their well-established counterparts had succeeded in bringing that struggle to a close. Democracy had emerged hegemonic. While the future of long-lived democracies was easy to predict – essentially, more of the same – the future of new democracies was not. Distinctive to the latter group was the burden of two types of uncertainty. The uncertain outcomes that define all democracies (as a result of competitive elections) were joined with the uncertain future of the democratic project itself.

The second premise was that some new democracies were better positioned than others to survive and prosper. For example, the more successful transitions to democracy benefited from certain historical assets, such as a tradition of civilian control over the military, a moderate level of economic development, and a democratic past. Also helpful to sustaining the democratic experiment were founding elections that were won by political leaders who were committed to democracy; a vibrant civil society; and the selection of political institutions, including parliaments, parties, and electoral systems, that struck a balance among representation of interests, political accountability, and effective policymaking.

Over the past decade or so, however, both premises, so foundational for so long to our thinking about democracy and democratization, have been called into serious question. Thus, many of the "settled" older democracies, such as the United States, Venezuela, and India, now appear to be "unsettled." The radical right in Europe, moreover, has moved from the fringes of political life in many countries to its center, winning power in Italy and making a strong, but thus far unsuccessful, bid to do the same in France.

At the same time, while many new democracies have shown themselves to be every bit as short-lived as many analysts expected (Russia and Burma are cases in point), some of the most promising transitions to democracy of the 1980s and 1990s are facing powerful authoritarian challenges. Indeed, Viktor Orban, in power since 2010, has engineered a transition from democracy to authoritarianism (or what he calls "illiberal democracy") in Hungary. Perhaps even more surprising, he has done so while Hungary has remained a member of the European Union.

Poland, the other front-runner in the race to democracy in postcommunist Eastern and Central Europe in the 1990s, is not that far behind Hungary in transitioning to authoritarian rule. What stands in the way of regime change in Poland, in contrast to Hungary, is more effective pushback from civil society, opposition parties, and the courts. Law and Justice, the ruling party in Poland, is also hampered by being less corrupt and having much less parliamentary support than its counterpart in Hungary.

There has been, therefore, a good deal more democratic backsliding around the world – and in unexpected places – than our understanding of democracy had led us to anticipate. These developments leave us with three questions. How and why has democratic backsliding taken place in the United States, Europe, Southeast Asia, and sub-Saharan Africa? Why have these autocratic challenges to democracy succeeded or failed? Finally, what do our answers to these questions tell us about the practice of democracy and the process of democratization?

The purpose of this volume has been to bring together a group of regional experts to grapple with precisely these issues. Not surprisingly, many of the details about de-democratization differ, depending on democratic endowments and the country and/or the region being analyzed. Far more surprising is that our chapters also converge around three sets of arguments regarding democratic backsliding. It is to these arguments that we now turn.

16.2 DEMOCRACY'S DIALECTIC

No democracy, irrespective of its age or its political and economic assets, appears to be immune to authoritarian threats. As we discussed in the Introduction to this volume, authoritarian forces are present in every democracy. Sometimes they are well hidden and of less political consequence, and sometimes they are quite visible and, at the least, undermine the quality of democracy and, at the most, bring the democratic experiment to an end.

How this continuing battle between democratic and authoritarian forces plays out varies among countries. Sometimes the ongoing struggle between democratic and authoritarian forces fuels a repeating dynamic wherein countries go back and forth between the two types of regimes, without either type able to establish deep roots (as argued by Meredith L. Weiss and Allen Hicken in their Chapter 3 on Southeast Asia). In sub-Saharan Africa, we find another variant, wherein limited state capacity produces a low-level equilibrium in which democratic forces play a circumscribed political role, but not as limited a one as their authoritarian counterparts (see Chapter 4 by Jaimie Bleck and Nicolas van de Walle on sub-Saharan Africa).

A final variant on the dialectical dance between authoritarian and democratic forces is what we find in the cases of India and the United States. In both countries, a long-lived democratic story is periodically "interrupted" by bursts of illiberal politics. These bursts can be short-lived or sustained, and they are usually in reaction to movements and policies that have succeeded in deepening democracy. In the case of India, we are referring, for example, to Indira Gandhi's Emergency of the mid 1970s and, since the 2014 election, the authoritarian politics of Narendra Modi and his party, the BJP (Bharatiya Janata Party) (see Chapter 2 by Milan Vaishnav).

Over the course of its democratic experiment, the United States features even more instances where authoritarian forces have gained the upper hand.[1] Thus, as David A. Bateman, Robert C. Lieberman, and Aaron Childree note in their Chapter 6 in this volume, the postpandemic rush by many US states to curtail popular access to voting is a far from original move on the part of authoritarian forces to narrow the definition of citizenship and thereby exert more control over policy and politics in the (once) United States. One could counter, of course, that the US experiment with democracy is much longer than India's and thus more likely to feature authoritarian "exceptions" to the democratic rule. The problem with this argument is that, by any reasonable standard, the United States was not in fact fully democratic until 1965, when the Voting Rights Act was passed by a coalition of Democrats and Republicans in the US Congress. In this sense, India has been a democracy longer than the United States.

There are four related implications that we can draw from this discussion of democracy as a dialectical process. If democracy is always contested, then the struggle for democracy never ends. This point is reinforced by a familiar, but often forgotten, argument that figures prominently in the literature on democratization; that is, that democracy is a process, not an outcome. Democracy does not get "finished." It is not an end state. The contestation over the form and extent of democracy, and whom it benefits, is itself a perpetual process that drives such reactionary struggles between authoritarian forces and democratic ones.

---

[1] See Suzanne Mettler and Robert Lieberman, *Four Threats: The Recurring Crises of American Democracy*. New York: St. Martin's Press, 2020 and Robert C. Lieberman, Suzanne Mettler, and Kenneth Roberts, eds., *Democratic Resilience: Can the United States Withstand Rising Polarization?* Cambridge: Cambridge University Press, 2022.

Second, in light of the dialectical perspective, the distinctions we have repeatedly drawn between new and old democracies and between new democracies that have a strong case for survival versus those that do not begin to blur. The differences between these categories, as this book demonstrates, are at most matters of degree, not kind.

Third, democratic consolidation, a key concept in the literature on the third wave, is at best misleading and at worst dead wrong. Democracies are consolidated – until they aren't. Democracy is the only game in town – until it isn't. Both observations are true, because authoritarian forces – whether within or outside the establishment and whether consisting primarily of individuals or rooted in parties or movements – are never permanently eliminated from the democratic game. Authoritarian challenges to democracy are always a possibility.

The final implication builds on the previous ones. Much of the literature on democracy and democratization rested on an imperial understanding of what democracy was and what it needed to be sustainable. The usually unstated assumption was that the West invented and certainly perfected democracy, and that the West knew best, as a result, how to build and defend it at home and abroad. When joined with the presumption of progress, the Western-centric understanding of the development of democracy– like its cousin, modernization theory – encouraged analysts to draw clear distinctions between old and new democracies; to give credence to democratic consolidation; and to envision democratization as a process that proceeded through stages. The attention to actors and institutions in this volume demonstrates that threats to democracy and resilience emerge from two sides of the same coin: they can come from nominally democratic institutions like the courts, the legislature, the bureaucracy, civil society, and political parties, and certainly the elected executive. In the West, as in the rest of the world, the dialectical process of democracy plays out in contestations across and within these institutions and actors.

16.3 SUBVERTING DEMOCRACY

Authoritarian challenges to democracy, therefore, are always a possibility. As analysts and as citizens, we cannot take democracy for granted.

But how and when do challenges to democracy move from the periphery of political life to its center? Contributors to this volume concur that the answer to this question necessarily takes us back to the building blocks of democratic life. Each of these building blocks provides insights into not just the rise and flourishing of democracy, but also its decline. They are, at once, the core of democracy and the drivers of democratic backsliding.

As Dankwart Rustow argued more than 50 years ago, democracy is not even a political possibility until a consensus has formed about the borders of the state and the meaning, composition, and boundaries of the nation.[2] For Rustow, once this issue was settled, it was precisely that – settled. He did not imagine that long-established agreements about the nation and the state could unravel. If he had entertained that possibility, however, he would have envisioned the world in which we find ourselves. Democracies are in serious trouble when conflicts about the state and the nation erupt among citizens, political leaders, and political parties.

As we now know from many examples of democratic backsliding that have been analyzed in this volume, however, the rise and empowerment of politicians and parties on the extreme right were fed in part by a return to precisely those issues – in particular, growing anger about immigration, expanding societal diversity, a decline in traditional values, and the increasing political and economic influence of minority groups (see the chapters by Béla Greskovits (Chapter 8), Milan Vaishnav (Chapter 2), Michael Bernhard (Chapter 9), Lindsay Mayka (Chapter 7), David A. Bateman, Robert C. Lieberman, and Aaron Childree (Chapter 6), and Mabel Berezin (Chapter 13)). It was no accident that these concerns arose in a time when many citizens began to feel, for good reasons, that the pie was no longer expanding. The gains of "the others," so to speak, accounted for their losses – in social status above all, but also in money and political influence. One politician who understood these feelings and had a style of political rhetoric that was unusually good at tapping into them was Donald Trump (see Chapter 12 by M. Steven Fish on domination). Three quotations from his January 6, 2021 speech to his followers (many of whom thereafter stormed the US Capitol) capture this populist dynamic: "Our country has had enough. We will not take it anymore." "We will not let them silence your voices." "You're the real people. You are the people that built this nation."

Donald Trump also benefited from and contributed to the cross-national diffusion of extreme right ideologies (see Stefano Palestini and Cristóbal Rovira Kaltwasser's Chapter 15). However, we can also point to an intrastate process of diffusion that stoked heated concerns about the national question. The rise of majority-based nationalism – for example, white nationalism in the United States and Hindu nationalism in India – was a reaction to the politics and policies of minority-based nationalisms. First, as the right-wing attack on "critical race theory" in the United States indicates, to include the experiences of minorities in the history of the United States is to exclude and downgrade the experiences of the majority. At the same time, majority-based nationalist movements borrowed some of the innovative repertoires that minority-based movements had used so effectively to expand their rights.

As a result, the idea of the nation became a source of conflict, rather than consensus. Rather than putting parameters on political conflict, these issues fanned the flames. A precondition for democracy was no longer in place, and democracy paid a price.

---

[2] Dankwart Rustow, "Transitions to Democracy: Toward a Dynamic Model." *Comparative Politics*, 2 (April 1970), pp. 337–363.

Contributors to this volume have also analyzed the contradictory effects of democratic institutions. In contrast to earlier debates about the optimal design of democratic institutions, we now recognize that all democracies feature institutional flaws that can be exploited by clever autocrats in their quest for power. Moreover, just as institutions can erode over time, thereby making them less effective precisely when challenges to democracy are more likely to present themselves (as Milan Vaishnav argues in the case of India and its "referee" institutions in Chapter 2), so institutional reforms, even those that are supposed to improve the quality of elections, often have unexpected consequences (see Chapter 4 by Jaimie Bleck and Nicolas van de Walle and Chapter 9 by Michael Bernhard).

Indeed, we can scale up this argument to the international level. As Dorothee Bohle and Aida A. Hozić have argued in Chapter 14, the European Union has not just been a promoter of democratic change, primarily by providing resources to new democracies on the continent and requiring them to meet a long list of preconditions before they can become full members. It has also tolerated and even supported authoritarian politics and policies among some of its member states. For example, the Christian Right served as the key player in the founding and expansion of the European Union; the European Parliament has served as a haven for right wing extremist parties; and voting procedures have made it very hard for the European Union to punish member states that have strayed from the democratic path.

The sustainability of democracy also depends on a vibrant civil society. Civil society's role is especially important, as Michael Bernhard (Chapter 9) and Mark R. Beissinger (Chapter 10) remind us, when democracy is under threat and two most important defenders of democracy – that is, democratic institutions and democratic elections – are unable and/or unwilling to protect democracy. In her contribution to this volume (Chapter 7), however, Lindsay Mayka reminds us that civil society can also be a major reason why democracy is in trouble in the first place. Rather than saving democracy, it can subvert it. This is particularly the case when extreme right movements champion violence and seek to marginalize certain groups within the population.

Another core component of democratic life is political parties, which serve, at least ideally, the key functions of recruiting leaders, structuring the electorate, anchoring political competition, and generating policy debates and alternatives. Many of the authors in this volume argue that the weakening of the party systems, which has meant in effect that parties are underperforming with respect to all of these tasks, has had one of two costs. It has provided space for fringe parties to expand their political support, or it has generated pressures on major parties to succumb to the extremists within their ranks. While France and Italy are examples of the former, the United States – specifically the Republican Party – is an example of the latter. As these examples indicate, moreover, no party system, however it is designed, is immune to these problems.

Finally, free, fair, and regular elections are a hallmark of democracy. For the contributors to this volume, however, elections have often served as a site for democratic backsliding. This is more likely to happen when politicians, parties, and publics are polarized. Polarization is a problem for democracy for many reasons. It weakens the influence of moderates and strengthens the impact of extremists – within parties and, more generally, within the citizenry. It discourages the cooperation among politicians that is necessary to offset the costs of political competition and to make public policy. Polarization also makes party members and identifiers stay put, no matter what their party and its leaders do. This is because, while your party might be disappointing, the other party is dangerous. As a result, in a polarized political environment, the costs of party defections are extremely high. This also means that deviant behavior and extremist priorities are more likely to be tolerated.

Perhaps the biggest problem of polarization, however, is that it inflates the gains of winning and the costs of losing. Too much is riding on elections, which makes them destabilizing and dangerous processes. This issue leads us back, in turn, to the introductory essay in this volume, where we argued that democracy depends upon meeting two conditions associated with elections: winners accepting that their hold on power is limited in both time and degree, and losers complying with the results of the election. In high-stakes elections, however, winners are much more likely to take a trend in the direction of majoritarian governance many steps further. They grab whatever power they can get hold of in the hopes of implementing their policies, staying in power, and/or preventing the opposition from winning future contests. Ambition, greed, fears, and even ideology (as Béla Greskovits reminds us with respect to the Hungarian circles in Chapter 8) push them to govern like – or be – autocrats. By contrast, losers are far more likely to challenge the election results. This is because polarization leads them to fear their opponent's "extremist" policy agenda; doubt whether the election was free and fair (because after all they are not dangerous, and they are supported by everyone they know); and question whether the victor will hold subsequent elections or conduct them in ways that will be free and fair. Events in the United States from 2016 to 2022 – the election of Donald Trump in November, 2016, his four years in office, his loss to Joe Biden in the 2020 election, and the "stop the steal" campaign Trump headed thereafter, culminating in the January 6, 2021 assault on the US Capitol – are a remarkably "efficient" example of virtually all of these dynamics.

A key theme of this volume, therefore, is that what defines and supports democracy can also undermine it. Civil society, political parties, elections, and the like are, in this sense, empty vessels. The same holds true for political leaders in democracies and their rhetorical styles, as M. Steve Fish (Chapter 12) reminds us.

The idea of seeing democracy's core components as empty vessels helps us understand, in turn, the dialectics of democracy. Both authoritarian and democratic forces can make use of the building blocks of democracy. They are more likely to do so, moreover, under two conditions – as we have seen in our discussion. One is when the other side makes progress and thereby threatens the values and interests of the other side (see, especially, the Introductory essay and the chapters by Weiss and Hicken (Chapter 3), especially the Malaysian case, and Bateman, Lieberman, and Childree (Chapter 6)). The other is when ideas and repertoires of one side diffuse to the other. This volume provides two examples: the influences of minority nationalism on the development and strategies of majority nationalism and the influences of liberal civil society on the organization and practices of illiberal civil society.

To these cases of cross-national diffusion we can add a third. The "stop the steal" movements that alleged voter fraud in the 2020 US presidential election and the 2022 Brazilian presidential election that led in both countries to violent attacks on governmental institutions bear a remarkable resemblance to the "color revolutions" that took place in postcommunist Europe and Eurasia from 1998 to 2005.[3] In these cases, charges of electoral fraud were mounted by the democratic opposition and leveled at competitive authoritarian regimes. These were attractive precedents for right-wing populist movements in democratic countries, because they often resulted in winners fleeing office and losers taking power. What authoritarian players in democratic societies did not notice, however, was that there were numerous dress rehearsals for these challenges, and a lot of preparation went into these successful challenges of electoral results, including careful documentation of actual electoral fraud.

16.4 DEFENDING DEMOCRACY

The final issue that the contributors to this volume have addressed is how challenges to democracy have been and can be countered. One of the most obvious ways is for democratic leaders and their supporters to defeat authoritarian politicians and parties at the polls. Unfortunately, this is much easier said than done. Mounting a successful campaign against an authoritarian is a very difficult task. Part of the problem is that authoritarian incumbents, as in Poland, Hungary, India, Venezuela, and the United States, have placed a priority on taming the media, packing the courts, and changing the electoral system, all in ways that reduce the ability of the opposition to win power. Authoritarian leaders are also far more adept than their democratic counterparts at playing a dominance game. As M. Steven Fish argues in Chapter 12 in this volume, they make opinion, rather than follow it, and they embrace conflict, rather than devise ways to dampen it. They revel in polarization.

Another part of the problem is that challenges to democracy in recent years take very different forms than they once did. Would-be dictators typically do not announce an end to the democratic game. Instead, they proceed slowly and often undercover. Thus, they build on longer-term trends of expanding

---

[3] Valerie J. Bunce and Sharon Wolchik, *Defeating Authoritarian Leaders in Postcommunist Countries*. Cambridge: Cambridge University Press, 2011.

executive power (and weakening of the legislature); they nibble away at civil liberties and political rights; they exploit opportunities provided by flawed political institutions; they flood the bureaucracy with their supporters; and they claim all the while that they are committed to democracy, but committed to denationalizing it; that is, tailoring it to local circumstances. Thus, autocratic-minded leaders like to add adjectives to democracy – leaders in Thailand, for example, speak of Thai-style democracy; Orban in Hungary speaks of illiberal democracy; and Putin in Russia prefers "managed democracy." For that matter, the Bolsheviks used to boast about Soviet democracy. Such strategies mean that democratic opponents are shooting at a moving target that, from the public's vantage point, is not necessarily waging a war on democracy.

An alternative to using elections to restore democracy is the mobilization of prodemocratic civil society forces, as Michael Bernhard and Mark R. Beissinger argue in their chapters (Chapters 9 and 10). Civil society is particularly effective in countering authoritarian challenges when it is cohesive; mobilizes earlier rather than later in the face of threats to democracy; and has ties to major prodemocratic political parties. A final factor that makes civil society groups more effective in countering authoritarian forces is whether they establish a working relationship with political institutions before they have been compromised, if not gutted, by authoritarian rulers.

Finally, while we are uncomfortable as social scientists with such arguments, we must admit that there is a certain amount of luck involved when democracies survive the test of authoritarian challenges. In the US case, a handful of individuals in key states and in key institutions in Washington resisted strong pressures by Trump and his close allies to take actions that would sabotage democracy. At the same time, while most Republicans either agreed with Trump's agenda or decided to look the other way, thereby enabling and extending his assault on democracy, some Republicans eventually decided to defect – in response to the attack on the Capitol on January 6, 2021 or, later, when they complied with the January 6 Committee's request for testimony. It was only a few, but that few were well placed.

The case of the United States reminds us, however, that, even when elections, civil society, and luck converge to produce the removal of an authoritarian leader from power, this "victory" does not signal the end of the authoritarian threat to democracy. The dialectics of democracy are still in play. Moreover, the authoritarian interlude casts a long shadow. A lot of damage has been done. Finally, while the leader is gone, his followers and the factors that gave rise to both are still in place and play.

In this way, we return to an overarching theme of this book. Democracy cannot be taken for granted. Oddly enough, that is even, maybe especially, the case when democracy is on a roll.

Index

For EU product safety concerns, contact us at Calle de José Abascal, 56–1°,
28003 Madrid, Spain or eugpsr@cambridge.org.

www.ingramcontent.com/pod-product-compliance
Ingram Content Group UK Ltd.
Pitfield, Milton Keynes, MK11 3LW, UK
UKHW020432240426
470322UK00017B/474